COMMON LISP
PROGRAMMING
FOR
ARTIFICIAL
INTELLIGENCE

INTERNATIONAL COMPUTER SCIENCE SERIES

Consulting editors   **A D McGettrick**   University of Strathclyde

J van Leeuwen   University of Utrecht

SELECTED TITLES IN THE SERIES

Introduction to Expert Systems   *P Jackson*

PROLOG   *F Giannesini, H Kanoui, R Pasero and M van Caneghem*

PROLOG Programming for Artificial Intelligence   *I Bratko*

POP–11 Programming for Artificial Intelligence   *A M Burton and N R Shadbolt*

Parallel Programming   *R H Perrott*

Logic Programming and Knowledge Engineering   *T Amble*

Functional Programming   *A J Field and P G Harrison*

Comparative Programming Languages   *L B Wilson and R G Clark*

Distributed Systems: Concepts and Design   *G Coulouris and J Dollimore*

Software Prototyping, Formal Methods and VDM   *S Hekmatpour and D Ince*

C Programming in a UNIX Environment   *J Kay and R Kummerfeld*

An Introduction to Functional Programming through Lambda Calculus

   G Michaelson

Clausal Form Logic: An Introduction to the Logic of Computer Reasoning

   T Richards

Software Engineering (3rd Edn)   *I Sommerville*

High-Level Languages and their Compilers   *D Watson*

Programming in Ada (3rd Edn)   *J G P Barnes*

Interactive Computer Graphics: Functional, Procedural and Device-Level

   Methods   *P Burger and D Gillies*

Elements of Functional Programming   *C Reade*

Software Development with Modula-2   *D Budgen*

Program Derivation: The Development of Programs from Specifications

   R G Dromey

Programming for Artificial Intelligence: Methods, Tools and Applications

   W Kreutzer and B J McKenzie

Object-Oriented Programming with Simula   *B Kirkerud*

COMMON LISP PROGRAMMING FOR ARTIFICIAL INTELLIGENCE

Tony Hasemer & John Domingue

The Open University
Milton Keynes

ADDISON-WESLEY
PUBLISHING
COMPANY

Wokingham, England · Reading, Massachusetts · Menlo Park, California
New York · Don Mills, Ontario · Amsterdam · Bonn
Sydney · Singapore · Tokyo · Madrid · San Juan

Cover designed by Crayon Design of Henley-on-Thames and
printed by The Riverside Printing Co. (Reading) Ltd.
Typeset by Columns, Reading
Printed in Great Britain by Mackays of Chatham plc, Chatham, Kent

First printed 1989.

British Library Cataloguing in Publication Data
Hasemer, Tony
    Common LISP programming for artificial intelligence. — (International
computer science series).
    1. Artificial intelligence. Applications of computer systems. Programming
languages: LISP
    I. Title   II. Domingue, John   III. Series
    006.3′028′55133

    ISBN 0–201–17579–7

Library of Congress Cataloging-in-Publication Data
Hasemer, Tony.
    Common LISP programming for artificial intelligence.

    (International computer science series)
    Bibliography: p.
    Includes index.
    1. COMMON LISP (Computer program language)
2. Artificial intelligence.   I. Domingue, John.
II. Title.   III. Series.
QA76.73.C28H37   1989   006.3   89–6733
ISBN 0–201–17579–7

Preface

This book is for those who would like to learn Lisp from the bottom up, and who are willing to take our advice to 'learn by doing' on their own computers. You may be a student of artificial intelligence or cognitive science, you may be a professional programmer seeking to improve your skills, or you may want to learn Lisp for the sheer love of it. This is not an advanced programming text, although it contains some substantial programming exercises, and we do not expect you initially to know anything other than how to operate your computer at the level of saving files to disk or getting your copy of Common Lisp up and running. In particular we do not expect you to have had any experience with any other programming language; in fact it is probably an advantage if you do not: Lisp is quite unlike the languages such as BASIC or FORTRAN which for many people are often their first experience of programming!

Also, we do not expect you to be a mathematician or a computer scientist. Lisp is a language which manipulates symbols in the form of lists. Its name means **LISt Processing** language, and the symbols in those lists usually represent things other than numbers. We have largely tried to steer clear of numerical examples because in our experience many students who later go on to become expert programmers are initially somewhat daunted by the myth that programming is all about numbers. Lisp as used in artificial intelligence or cognitive science research is very rarely about numbers.

At the time of writing Common Lisp is available for many mainframe computers and for most of the larger personal computers such as the Symbolics, the Sun, or the Apollo. It is available for IBM personal computers and for the Apple Macintosh, and by the time you read this it will certainly be available for other microcomputers as well. The only disadvantage of running Common Lisp on a micro is that it will probably run more slowly than a mainframe version, but until you come to the large programs in our final chapters the difference will be barely noticeable.

In the course of working through this book you will be able to gain a clear understanding of Lisp, and in particular of the most modern and sophisticated form of the language, Common Lisp. To that end it is a practical book: we firmly believe that the best way to learn a new skill is through practising it. So we assume that you will have to hand a computer or microcomputer running Common Lisp, and that you will be able to try out the programming examples we give you. We also expect you to make good use of your Common Lisp manual, and we assume that it will be either Guy Steele's *Common Lisp: the Language* (which is the current specification for the language – see below) or *Common Lisp: the Reference* (also, see below). These manuals are written with expert Lisp users in mind, but we hope to give you sufficient understanding of Lisp to be at ease with its manuals, so that you will be able to go on to areas of advanced Lisp programming which we could not possibly cover in this one book.

Our teaching methods are based upon several years' joint experience in teaching Lisp and other high-level programming languages to Open University students, who are all 'mature students' coming from many different backgrounds: we know the kinds of problems you are likely to encounter, and we believe that we know how to help you solve them. But the biggest difference between this and other 'teach yourself Lisp' books is that we intend to teach you not merely a mass of facts about what Lisp responds when someone types in this or that kind of input, but why it does so.

The core of Lisp is its 'evaluator': every Lisp program achieves its effects only by passing without error through the evaluator. The behaviour of the evaluator makes Lisp what it is, and the dominant theme of the first half of our book is a constantly expanding picture of the evaluator's behaviour. Our own teaching experience and our research show that the majority of mistakes made by novice Lisp programmers spring from their ignorance of, or misunderstanding of, how the evaluator handles their programs. Given such an understanding, Lisp syntax – and especially the famous 'forests of parentheses' – cease to be arcane and become as clear as the punctuation in written English. Therefore, as we introduce each new Lisp facility, we shall show you how the evaluator deals with it, so that in the end you will be able to read and to understand the vast majority of the Lisp programs which you might encounter from the other sources. We shall take you up to the point where you are competent to tackle any of the excellent books on advanced Lisp programming, and we list our favourites at the end of the book.

However, the ability to write and to understand Lisp programs is not a skill to be indulged in for its own sake, like a skill at sport or at poetry. Lisp is itself merely a tool, and the purpose for which it is almost invariably used is artificial intelligence research. Therefore, besides teaching you why Lisp does what it does, we want to bring across to you some of the excitement of the search for an artificial mind, and to introduce you to some of the very daunting problems which that ambition raises. We shall not attempt to offer any new answers to the questions, but we hope to put your eventual understanding of Lisp into its proper context: to make you aware of the current limitations of AI programming as well as of its unquestionable power as a research tool.

To this end a second major theme in our book is that of knowledge representation. Any program written for artificial intelligence, cognitive science or related purposes is in some sense a representation of a part of human knowledge, be that 'simple' factual knowledge or knowledge of how to manipulate and use those facts to achieve useful effects. We shall show you a wide variety of techniques for representing knowledge in your Lisp programs, from the simple assignment of values to variables, to the complex 'intelligent' entities found in object-oriented programming.

Readers already familiar with Computer Science may wish for more rigorousness in our discussions; for example we barely mention efficiency, nor do we describe the underlying mathematical models of functional programming languages. This is deliberate: being AI researchers ourselves we know that one can write effective and interesting AI programs without being fully aware of such finer points. Whether our text talks about a single Lisp function, a programming technique, an hypothesis from cognitive science or the goals and dreams of AI, our intention is to give you enough accurate information for you to acquire a substantial core of competence and understanding. By the end of this book you should be able to understand and to write quite sophisticated programs, but nonetheless this is a book for beginners and so we shall do our best to avoid swamping you with endless provisos or with fine details which are not immediately relevant.

In the same vein, now and again we shall say to you something like 'Please take our word on this minor point for the time being: we shall explain it in detail later'. This is again part of our teaching method and is definitely not an attempt to patronize you: our experience tell us that difficult concepts (of which there are several in this book!) are best presented one by one within a consistent 'story line', and so we have deliberately avoided diving off into sidetracks, no matter how interesting they may be, at times when our main track is likely already to be hard work for you. If you personally find that you stride way ahead of us, please be patient with the fact that this is a book, and not an intelligent teaching machine!

The programming examples which we shall show you were originally developed on the Symbolics, the world's most powerful Lisp machine, and were subsequently transferred to the Macintosh personal computer and to Allegro Common Lisp. Many of the apparent idiosyncracies of this book – such as showing the user's input to the computer always in bold face – come directly from Allegro Common Lisp. However, the whole point of Common Lisp is that it is the same language no matter who sells it and no matter the computer on which it is running. If you have a version, any version, of Common Lisp on which to try our examples, you should have no unexplained problems.

Throughout our text we shall refer to the Common Lisp specification. Although some of the very advanced aspects of Common Lisp, such as object-oriented programming which we shall cover towards the end of this book, have yet to be fully specified (there is an international committee of experts set up for the purpose) some critics are already complaining that the language is 'too large', though exactly how large they think a programming language should be is rarely explored. A book entitled *Common Lisp: the Language*, written by Guy L. Steele Jr and published by the Digital Press, clearly and concisely sets out the current Common Lisp specification in almost 450 densely-packed pages. An excellent alternative is *Common Lisp: the Reference* from Franz Inc. and published by Addison-Wesley. Reputable software houses implementing their own versions of Common Lisp may well include one or other of these books as a part of their package, rather than going to the trouble and expense of writing their own manuals. If your Lisp does not include either, you will almost certainly need to buy one of them if you intend to become a regular user of Common Lisp.

While Steele's *Common Lisp: the Language* is the established 'bible' of Lisp, it does not try also to teach Lisp. Similarly, we in this book cannot hope to include all of Steele's 450 pages of densely-packed information. As we introduce Lisp functions to you, we shall always introduce them in their simplest (in the sense of being the most immediately comprehensible) form; but in many cases you will find, if you take the trouble to consult Steele or *Common Lisp: the Reference*, that the functions are more powerful than our book reveals. That is, the functions will allow refinements of their basic operations which, though you might rarely need them, will on the occasions when you do need them add considerably to the elegance and precision of your programs.

The first part of our book covers basic Lisp operations and in passing describes some of the concepts and difficulties faced by modern artificial intelligence research. These chapters will give you the basic groundwork necessary to understand the Lisp evaluator, Lisp syntax, and the all-important question of list manipulation. The second part covers the programming technique called 'recursion', again a extremely important aspect of Lisp, introduces you to the techniques of function definition, and describes the various programming tools and aids available in Common Lisp. The final chapters invite you to build working AI programs which would not be out of place in a modern research laboratory. Naturally we could not hope to cover the whole of AI at this level, and our approach has been to offer you a mix of two things: a serious introduction to the most up-to-the-minute AI research areas, for example expert systems and object-oriented programming, and a clear understanding of how the various techniques which you have learned can be combined to create such sophisticated programs. The resulting programs are powerful tools in their own right, but we have chosen to show you relatively simple examples of their use. The examples are in the nature of test inputs, with which you can check that your programs do work properly. Our belief is that by concentrating upon hands-on teaching of how they work, rather than upon what they do, we shall leave you in a better position to progress to more advanced texts.

We have one other expectation of you, and that is that you will not simply read our book, punch a few buttons when asked, and then feel resentful because the skills of Lisp and AI programming have not magically appeared. Common Lisp is a large and complex language, and any one book has to limit its scope at some point. We intend to give you a very good basic knowledge of Lisp, from which you will be able to move up to one or other of the excellent books on advanced Lisp programming; but as you go along please do experiment beyond the examples which we specifically ask you to try on your own computer. We shall warn you of potential errors and other pitfalls, but not all of your independent explorations will end up as errors, and when they do not you will gain a programming confidence which no amount of mere words from us could ever give you. Lisp is often spoken of as being hard to learn, but we believe that it need not be if taught properly, and this book is the distillation of many years of effort in trying to find out what that word 'properly' means.

Sadly, we cannot provide a miraculous pill which upon being swallowed will instantly confer Lisp/AI expertise. But we can, given your cooperation, provide you with the next best thing; and that is what this book is intended to be. We hope that you will enjoy it and benefit from it.

Our special thanks . . .

Are owed to the following, without whom our book would have been 'just another Lisp primer':

Tim Rajan, whose visual tracing system is applicable to any programming language and which greatly simplifies explanations of Lisp based – as our are – upon Lisp's evaluator. We are also grateful to Tim for good ideas, encouragement and a careful reading of our text at times when we most needed them.

Marc Eisenstadt, whose willingness *in extremis* to let other projects take second place to the book enabled us eventually to meet an extended deadline.

Also, to those staff and students of the OU who over the years have taken part in our experiments and who have given us very valuable feedback. To the colleagues who never complained when we sat writing furiously and ignored their pleas for attention; and to the parents, lovers, cats and dogs who understood our obsession and did not intrude.

John Domingue
Tony Hasemer
Human Cognition Research Laboratory
The Open University UK
April 1989

Contents

Part 1
ESSENTIAL CONCEPTS

Chapter 1
Starting Out

This first chapter introduces our twin topics, artificial intelligence and the Lisp language, and gives some advice on choosing suitable software. It then makes a start on what will become, throughout the first part of this book, a growing definition of Lisp's all-important evaluator. By the end of this chapter you will also know how to assign values to variables in Lisp, and how to switch evaluation off and on.

1.1   Introduction to artificial intelligence

1.1.1   Definitions

Artificial intelligence, universally known as AI, is essentially the study of a certain class of **computational techniques**. Via a computer program an AI technique is applied to a computer and causes it to behave in a certain way. When the resulting behaviour would be described as 'intelligent' were a human being to behave in the same way, AI counts it a success. Notice that for the time being we do not need to define 'intelligence' in order to mimic it: few people would argue with the assertion that a program which can play chess, carry out medical diagnoses or pilot a spaceship is behaving with some degree of intelligence.

The computer itself is in an important sense irrelevant to AI researchers: it is merely a tin box which may well be hidden away in

3

another room at the end of a long cable, and which responds in predictable ways. From the user's point of view the console – the keyboard upon which the user types instructions and the screen upon which the computer's responses appear – 'is' the computer. Although the abilities of the hidden machine – its power and its performance – are obviously important, we do not really need to know about the computer's detailed internal operations, but only how to use it. Lisp is one of the ways of using it, one much favoured for AI purposes.

For many AI researchers the question of exactly how this 'intelligent' behaviour is achieved is less important than its achievement, and such researchers would never claim that an artificial intelligence need be – apart from its behaviour – anything like its human counterpart. On the other hand, there are obvious areas of overlap between what AI is trying to do and what researchers into cognitive science, psychology, philosophy and several other fields are trying to do. Much of the existing literature in AI describes attempts to build **cognitive models**, computer models of human mental processes. For workers in these areas of AI the 'intelligence' which they create has to be convincingly of the same type as human intelligence, reaching its conclusions or achieving its effects in recognizably the same way.

You may already be wondering what could possibly be meant by phrases such as 'like its human counterpart' or 'achieving its effects in the same way'. Sadly we cannot tell you. AI is a very young science and so far there are many more hard questions than there are elegant answers. What we can tell you is that sometimes the detailed operations of a computer program can closely parallel the corresponding theory from psychology about how the mind carries out similar intelligent behaviour; and sometimes, as with sophisticated game-playing machines, working out exactly how the program achieved its results would be a herculean task in itself though the results clearly mimic the behaviour of a human player.

The hope is that by modelling psychological theories, or by writing computer programs to mimic human behaviour about which as yet we have no theories, AI can help to illuminate the workings of the human mind. As an added bonus, AI brings to cognitive research a degree of experimental rigour which has sometimes been lacking in the past. As you will soon discover, programming for AI demands perfect accuracy and a clear head on the part of the programmer, and the very process of building a cognitive model can and often does reveal hitherto-unsuspected weaknesses in the theory upon which it is based. In this sense AI is a tool of the cognitive sciences, while from an AI perspective the cognitive sciences offer us a springboard towards the creation of a true machine intelligence, whether in the end that turns out to be a human-like intelligence or not.

1.1.2   What is machine intelligence?

The one thing which it certainly will not be is any kind of amalgam or agglomeration of the 'intelligent' machines which have been created by programmers so far. Most present-day computers are **serial** computers; that is, they carry out one programmed instruction, then another, then another, but they never ever carry out two instructions simultaneously; and although even an ordinary desktop computer may be able to perform several million such instructions per second this still represents only a tiny fraction of the speed and precision of the human brain. But within a very few years **parallel** computers are likely to become commonplace in research. They will be able to carry out any number of operations simultaneously, and maybe we shall then be able to write programs which mimic not only the behaviour of human intelligence, but also its power.

It is quite a frightening thought that AI seems to be well on course for the creation of the mechanical equivalent of a victim of cerebral palsy: its intelligence well up to adult human standards but enclosed in a world of its own, its senses dim or completely absent, unable to communicate with ordinary people, unable to move without help, and unable because of these limitations to understand more than a tiny fragment of the world around it. We shall probably treat such machines as our ancestors treated their human slaves, putting them to work on mundane tasks 24 hours a day until they become obsolete and we let them 'die'.

Fortunately we do not have to feel guilty yet because such machines are probably still a decade away, but they raise questions which are fascinating both from an ethical point of view and from a purely computational point of view. One researcher may assert, on the basis of rather shaky evidence, that 'machines cannot feel emotions such as unhappiness, and therefore it does not matter how we treat them'. Another may counter, with an equivalent lack of intellectual rigour, 'How on earth could we possibly know what it feels like to be an unhappy machine? How would we know what signs to look out for in order to tell what emotional state a machine was in?'. On purely behavioural evidence, as you will soon discover for yourself, one could reasonably conclude that all computers detest computer programmers and do all in their power to obstruct their work. The whole ethical problem of the probable relationships between human beings and intelligent machines is, we are sorry to say, an area in which we AI researchers sometimes say rather silly things and make even sillier assumptions. But one day we shall be faced with the necessity to provide some convincing answers.

On the computational level, there is an enormous question mark. Human emotions seem to be not merely mental states but to be intimately connected with bodily states as well: unpleasant emotions can make you physically ill, and vice versa. Even more difficult is the question of **subjectivity**. We could in principle create a virtual machine which could recognize the preconditions to an emotion – say the factors in the immediate environment which have been observed to make human beings feel happy – and we could make it then print out the words 'I am happy'. We could even make it go on to take an optimistic approach to any decisions it might subsequently make, just as happy humans do. In other words, it would behave as though it were happy. But would it be happy? We just do not know, and maybe it is not even a rational question, because we could as sensibly ask the same thing about other humans.

There is here again a considerable difference of opinion between those AI researchers who want to create a purely mechanical intelligence, regardless of what 'kind of thing' that may turn out to be, and those who want to create a machine analogue of the human person. In AI literature this difference is often expressed as that between a **simulation** of the human mind and a **replica** of it. The simulation would be able to do the same things as a human mind but might do them very differently, whilst the replica would have to be an identical copy, and therefore perhaps would also need a mechanical equivalent of the human body.

1.1.3   Alan Turing

The British mathematician Alan Turing is generally credited with having discovered the principles of the digital computer during his work on the German Enigma codes during the second World War, though the first working machines were developed in America with the guidance of another mathematician, John von Neumann from Germany. In those days the word 'computer' referred to a human being such as an accountant, who performed computations, but right from the start Turing spoke of his new machines as being able to think. Turing understood that, in order for such a claim to be made, a program must be more than a mere set of static instructions which the computer slavishly carries out. The program must in fact be able to produce different behaviour in response to different inputs or situations; in other words it must be able to learn, and to plan. Whilst others were building 'computers' with hardwired programs, intended like all previous machines of any type to perform only one specific task, Turing realized that the machine and its program should be separated, and that different programs could be run on the same machine. He spoke of the computer–program combination as a 'universal machine', able in principle to compute anything which was computable.

Turing's other seminal discovery from AI's point of view was that his machines did not process numbers but symbols. His symbols were a series of marks on a paper tape, and each different mark had a different significance. By definition, a symbol can mean anything at all.

At some point over the next decade artificial intelligence, as a new area of study, emerged. The trigger was the realization that while some apparently intelligent activities, such as arithmetic, could be described via a simple set of program instructions, others such as understanding the meaning of a sentence could not. In other words, if some intelligent activities can be represented as computational techniques, perhaps all of them can. If so, we will be able to build an artificial human being or even a being which is superhuman. If not, then in the process of trying we stand a good chance of discovering something very fundamental about the human mind.

1.1.4 Early successes

Probably the first AI program, i.e. one which learned and planned as Turing said it should, was Arthur Samuel's program to play checkers (the game called 'draughts' in the UK). During the years 1947–67 Samuel researched into the knowledge and abilities which such a program would need in order to play effectively. His program was able to 'pretend' that it had made any of the moves available to it in any game situation, then to pretend that its opponents had made any of the available replies, and so on up to several moves ahead. To each resulting imaginary board position, it was able to apply a **static evaluation function** whose purpose was to derive a score indicating the usefulness of each move with an eventual win in mind.

What made the program an AI program was the fact that to Samuel its ability to win was of only secondary importance: the more interesting aspect was that as it played the program was able to refine and improve its own static evaluation function, and thus was able to play better on future occasions. To give you an idea of how this learning worked: two identical versions of the program could be set to play each other. The 'learner' program would be limited to looking three moves ahead from any point in the game, while the 'teacher' program would be allowed to look five moves ahead. The further ahead you can see when playing checkers the more likely you are to make a good move, and so the 'learner' program refined its evaluation function so as to bring its results more into line with those of the 'teacher' program. After a while, the short-sighted program could play pretty much as well as the long-sighted program: it had learned.

However, a program–computer combination which plays a game, no matter how well it may do so, is a long way from Turing's idea of a universal machine. It can operate successfully within a very limited context (the game of checkers in this case) and it can solve a certain class of problems (how to win the game). But the human mind is a general problem solver, able to construct and modify plans in a very wide variety of contexts. Allen Newell and Herbert Simon, two American researchers, tried during the 1960s to write a program which could simulate this aspect of human thought. Their General Problem Solver employed **means–ends analysis** as its 'thinking' strategy.

Means–ends analysis constantly compares the current state with some goal state. Having identified the difference, it tries to apply some 'operator' which will remove the difference. For example, if your current position were A and you wanted to move to B, you might have available several operators: you could walk, thus removing the difference between your current position at A and your goal position at B; or you might take the car, or you might buy an airline ticket.

However, it quite often happens that none of the available operators can remove the identified difference. If your goal were to have a wedding breakfast in Bangkok, none of the three operators mentioned above would achieve it. In such cases the General Problem Solver breaks the goal down into subgoals: for example the goal of having a wedding breakfast in Bangkok would certainly include as one of its necessary subgoals the need to make the journey to Bangkok, for which the operator 'buy an airline ticket' would be entirely appropriate. Other parts of the overall goal would be similarly broken down so that other, so-far unmentioned, operators could handle them. This approach, of repeatedly simplifying any goal into subgoals, until such time as every subgoal can be achieved by an existing operator, works on a very large class of problems, both the 'real' problems which a human being faces every day and the 'theoretical' problems which research scientists come up against.

1.1.5 Representing knowledge

Means–ends analysis ran into a problem which bedevilled much AI research at the time (and still does): the problem of **combinatorial explosion**. Means–ends analysis works well on fairly simple problems in highly constrained environments – that is, problem situations in which there are relatively few variable factors. But as soon as you try to apply the technique to a real problem, even a mundane and everyday problem, the amount of division into subgoals necessary and the number of operators required rapidly become astronomical. Very soon, even the most powerful of computers will run out of memory or will be unable to process each individual subgoal at any kind of useful speed.

It soon became clear that in AI, which throughout its 30-year history has also meant in Lisp, the functions which appear to be so all important are in fact less important than the data upon which they work. All data (information, knowledge) held in a computer is represented there in some way: one could not, for example, have a real orange or a real cat inside a computer, used as data; instead there have to be representations or descriptions of those objects. Presumably the same is true of the human mind. In a computer, a description can be as simple as the corresponding English word or, as you will know by the end of this book, they can be highly organized and highly complex objects in which there is no meaningful distinction between functions and data.

The precise way in which knowledge is represented for some particular AI purpose turns out to be of crucial importance. Poor knowledge representation can lead to enormous inefficiencies when individual pieces of data are difficult to retrieve and are needed often, and worse still they can add enormously to the complexity of the program, hence making it much harder to build, to understand and to improve. It is not by any means unknown for researchers to work for a year or more on some large program, then to discover that their chosen method of knowledge representation is inadequate for the job in hand, and to start again from scratch.

Very few worthwhile AI programs are not **knowledge-based systems**. Most programs are designed to contain a certain body of knowledge and to use that, their 'own' knowledge, whilst working upon their inputs. Knowledge is usually divided into two types: procedural knowledge, which in Lisp would be written as functions, and declarative knowledge which would be inert, stated facts or data. As you will see, that distinction will become blurred and even meaningless as your understanding of Lisp increases, but it is often useful at first.

It is almost a truism to say that if at the start of some programming project you can see how to represent your data and what your functions will do with it, then the actual writing of the corresponding Lisp code will be a comparatively trivial exercise. Our aim is that by the time you have finished this book you will no longer be a novice Lisp programmer but will be at an intermediate level, able to make such decisions with competence. To that end, we shall focus upon techniques for knowledge representation as our context in which to teach you the techniques of Lisp programming: they are not always the same thing, but either without the other would be useless in AI research.

As you work through this book you will learn not only how to write good Lisp programs, but also what such skills are for. We shall also, especially during the earlier part of the book, constantly try to link your growing programming experience to a continuing discussion of what AI is trying to do, in the hope of convincing you of the usefulness of the techniques we shall show you.

1.2   Introduction to Common Lisp

1.2.1   History: why Common Lisp?

Lisp, an acronym for **LISt Processing** language, was invented by John McCarthy and his team at Stanford University in the late 1950s. It was originally intended as a computational model of mathematical processes, reflecting the rigour of mathematics itself. In one of its very early forms, Lisp 1.5, the language had an elegance and precision rarely equalled in modern programs. We have, instead, sacrificed a degree of rigour (and, sadly, any hope of a mathematical or logical proof of the 'correctness' of our programs) for the sake of flexibility and power. It turned out that a language designed to manipulate mathematical symbols (variables) was ideally suited to manipulating any other kind of symbols. It rapidly became the language for AI research, in which a symbol may represent anything at all.

As things stand at present, Lisp remains the foremost language used in AI research. It is not by any means the only AI language, and each of the others has its own advantages and disadvantages. But in its 30-year history Lisp has been by far the favourite language for AI programming, for two main reasons. First, it is highly flexible, i.e. it is possible to write a Lisp program to produce virtually any desired behaviour from the computer; and second it is indefinitely extensible, which means that if you as a programmer feel that Lisp lacks some facility, you can write a Lisp program to provide that facility. The program can then become an integral part of your personal Lisp.

You can probably guess that in the course of 30 years very many Lisp users have added a great many facilities to the original bare language. In fact Lisp had until recently more 'dialects' than any other programming language. Sometimes the differences between one dialect and another were trivial, but sometimes they were quite fundamental. Things reached the point where it was virtually impossible to write a Lisp program on one machine, and to know that it would run without modification on any other. At the same time, there were certain added-on facilities which became so popular amongst Lisp users in general that they became virtually parts of the language itself; the **tracer**, about which you will hear more later, is a prime example.

Very recently, the worldwide Lisp community decided to put an end to the chaos and appointed a group of acknowledged international experts to lay down the specifications for the ultimate dialect of Lisp. They have not yet finished their work, and in view of the above-mentioned continuous flexibility of Lisp maybe they never will. But Common Lisp is the results of their efforts to date. It is at least as powerful as any earlier dialect of the language, and to an expert's eye has an elegance and precision far superior to any previous version. The Lisp you are about to learn can be 'ported' with confidence from one machine to another (hence its name) and has already established itself as the dominant Lisp dialect wherever AI research is carried out.

1.2.2   Two things will be important

Just as correct knowledge representation is essential to clear and efficient use of Lisp, so an understanding of Lisp's **evaluator** is the key both to writing and to understanding Lisp code. In other words, if you understand the evaluator you will write programs which work in the sense of not generating error messages from Lisp. If you also understand how to represent the program's knowledge, you will write programs which do what they were intended to do, and not anything else. As we said earlier, knowledge representation is the ultimately dominant theme of this book, but in our first few chapters we shall concentrate even more heavily upon a growing model or 'mental picture' of the evaluator.

1.2.3   How to choose the right software

The whole point about Common Lisp, and the reason why we teach Common Lisp rather than any other kind of Lisp in this book, is that all versions of it, no matter who manufactured and/or marketed the particular piece of software which you buy, should be identical. By this we mean that everything which we shall have to say about Lisp in this book should be precisely true of your Common Lisp. Until very recently there were literally dozens of 'dialects' of the Lisp language, and it was therefore virtually impossible to write a Lisp book without either concentrating on one dialect, thereby leaving most readers out in the cold, or going into endless caveats beginning 'your implementation of Lisp may alternatively respond with . . .'. Common Lisp allows us to tell you the stark truth about the workings of Lisp, without any fear that your computer will respond differently from the way we say it will.

The specifications for Common Lisp have been decided upon (and, in advanced areas, still are being decided upon) by a committee drawn from established experts in the worldwide Lisp users' community, and naturally it has rapidly become the preferred Lisp. Within a year or two, if it has not happened already, all older dialects of Lisp will have been forgotten.

If you are using a mainframe computer you probably will not have any say in which implementation of Common Lisp it provides, but if your machine is a DEC Vax and you have Vax Common Lisp available you will have nothing at all to complain about. Dedicated single-user Lisp machines such as the Symbolics or the Texas Instruments Explorer provide a full implementation of Common Lisp plus a vast array of tools and extensions. Such computers take a long time to master, but if you have one of them you will be envied amongst the Lisp community.

Large personal computers in the Sun/Apollo range provide Lucid Common Lisp. This implementation has evolved rapidly over the last few years and is now a very respectable version of the language. The one minor disadvantage here is that the attitude of mind required for Lisp programming and that required by UNIX (the usual underlying operating system) are sharply different: whilst Lisp encourages verbosity for the sake of clarity, UNIX goes for abbreviation and ease of typing.

Where smaller machines are concerned we highly recommend Allegro Common Lisp, marketed by Franz Inc. of Berkeley, California, which runs on the Apple Macintosh. It runs happily on the Mac+, SE and Mac II, but as with any large program the more random access memory (RAM) you can afford to have installed in your machine the faster its responses will be. Another very good implementation for the Macintosh is Procyon Common Lisp made and marketed by Procyon Research of Cambridge, England, but it will not run well in less than two megabytes of RAM. At the time of writing (June 1988) we would not recommend any of the other Common Lisps for the Macintosh.

If none of the above relates to the Lisp which you are thinking of buying, we have two pieces of advice for you. The first and the more important is that you find a dealer whom you feel able to trust and then accept his/her advice. If you have a computer club near you, or a university, seek their advice as well. Please do not buy any alleged implementation of Common Lisp (or indeed any other expensive piece of software) unless you have a positive recommendation from someone who knows what he or she is talking about: you could waste quite a lot of money if you do.

The second piece of advice is that if the software package includes Guy Steele's *Common Lisp: the Language* as its manual then you are almost certainly onto a winner. Steele's book is, as we have already said in our Preface, the standard statement of the Common Lisp specification as it stands at present. But it is not necessarily true that a package which does not include Steele's manual should be avoided: Procyon Common Lisp, for example, includes its own manual for the language as well as a separate manual for that company's own extensions to it.

It will also be worth your while to ask what kind of editor the software offers. The editor will be something like an ordinary word-processor, in which you will write the code for the functions etc. which will go to make up your programs. It can therefore be a very simple affair or can be very complex, offering you a great deal of help in the creation of your programs. The most famous and widely used editor for Lisp is called EMACS. If your software manual mentions that the package includes a subset of EMACS (EMACS in full is huge) then count it a considerable plus-point towards your decision about buying. Otherwise, please glance at the section on editing in Chapter 8, and ask your dealer how well the software measures up to the criteria there.

Finally, expect to pay quite a lot for your Lisp. We mean that at the time of writing you should expect to pay $200–400 (or £200–400, such is the unofficial rate of exchange operated by most software distributors) if you can get an academic discount, or at least $400–600 otherwise. Common Lisp comprises a large suite of programs, and cheap versions of it will inevitably be of poor quality.

1.2.4   Lisp is friendly

Before leaving this preliminary discussion of the language, we would like to mention one or two general points about your use of Lisp. At the beginning Lisp can be quite hard to learn; this book will make it as easy as possible, but if you still find yourself a bit lost at first please do not let this put you off. It rapidly becomes very much easier (unlike, say, another programming language called Prolog, which is initially very easy but gets much harder later on). In particular, do not be daunted by the famous plethora of parentheses! If you glance at some of the programs towards the end of this book their parentheses may look like a forest to you now, but by the time you have read that far parentheses will be as easy to read, and as significant, as commas, periods and spaces in ordinary written English.

The other thing which beginners tend to be nervous of is the error message. Lisp can generate an enormous number of different error messages, and at times you may begin to wonder despairingly whether it can generate anything else. But error messages are not designed to frighten you or to drive you nuts. They are intended to help. Remember that except under very rare circumstances the error messages which you will see will come from Lisp, the language, and not directly from your computer. Far from meaning that you've broken something, they'll merely mean that Lisp could not understand what you have just typed in, or could not understand the latest line in your program. In the early stages of learning Lisp the best approach to an error message is firstly to curse as freely as you wish, and then to read it carefully and to try to understand what it means in the context of your program. As you work through the book, we shall try to give you the knowledge you will need to do this.

1.3   How Lisp works

1.3.1   The read–eval–print loop

Lisp is an interactive language. That is to say that when you type something into Lisp from your keyboard Lisp looks at what you have typed, tries to respond to it in some way, and then prints that response on your screen. Thereupon you type in something else, and the cycle repeats. The Lisp term for 'looking at what you have typed' is **read**ing; the Lisp term for 'trying to respond' is **eval**uating; and the Lisp term for printing is **print**ing. If it were a human being rather than a machine in front of you, we might say that that person was **hear**ing, **understand**ing and **answer**ing you.

read, eval and print are all inbuilt Lisp functions. The word **function** is a term borrowed from mathematics, and in Lisp it has very much the same meaning. A Lisp function takes some input data, operates upon it in some way which is unique to that particular function, and produces a result. A very simple arithmetical example of this is that the function '+' might take as its input data the numbers 2 and 3, operating upon them in an additive way so as to produce the result 5. The correct Lisp terminology for this process is that a **function** is **applied** to its **arguments** and **returns** a result. Perhaps in order to reflect that fact, Lisp always mentions the function before mentioning the function's arguments. It is as though instead of writing '3 + 2' you were to write '+ 3 2'. We are sure you will agree that it makes no difference which way the expression is written.

It is very important to remember that every Lisp function, when applied to its arguments, always returns a result. In the process it may also do other things: print a message on the screen, move a chess piece, or indeed anything which you have designed it to do. But in the end it will always return a result. (Actually, there is one rarely used Common Lisp function, values, which does not do this, but in all other cases what we have told you is the truth.)

A Lisp program consists entirely of functions, and in almost every case the results they return are passed internally for use as input data by other functions within the program. For the moment you can visualize a Lisp program as a chain of functions (although as you will soon see 'chain' is not quite the right word): the first function is fed its input data by you, from the keyboard and via read; it changes that data in some way before passing it on to the next function. All the way down the chain, each function affects the data in some way; and the job of making sure that each function is correctly applied to its arguments is the business of eval. When every function in the program has been applied to its arguments, the last of them returns a value (often an 'answer' of some sort) to eval, which in turn hands it to print so that you can see it on your screen.

The fact that Lisp's read–eval–print loop consists of Lisp functions might seem strange but do not worry. As you interact with Lisp it executes all three of them in order, over and over again. Each time around, read will automatically sit and wait until you are ready to type in your next 'instruction'. Eventually, you will learn about ways of using these three functions independently of the interactive or 'top level' loop.

1.3.2 Eval

You could certainly, even now, make a fair guess at what exactly read and print 'do' – it seems obvious that they do (more or less) exactly what their names suggest. Of the three, eval is the cleverest and the most difficult to understand. The 'picture' of eval which we are about to give you will be very highly simplified, but as you work through this book it will gradually be extended until you know virtually all about it; all, that is, except for a few rather abstruse abilities too esoteric for our scope here. Although eval is, as we have said, a Lisp function, we will present it initially as a growing set of IF–THEN rules. We think it important for you to understand how the evaluator works long before you are expert enough to write the corresponding Lisp program.

> *Point to remember* Once you fully understand the evaluator, there will be no Lisp program which you cannot understand.

Let us try to imagine what abilities eval would need to have, so that what is printed in response to a correct entry from the keyboard will make rational sense.

Suppose first that you were to type at your keyboard the Lisp equivalent of '2 + 2'. What is eval, which is so named because it claims to be an 'evaluator', to do with that? Why, evaluate it of course; resulting in an answer '4' to be printed.

That is the pattern for each and every execution of eval. However, you would not be bothering to learn Lisp if all you really needed was a pocket calculator. Lisp is far more exciting than a pocket calculator, because it manipulates not merely numbers and mathematical operators, but symbols.

1.3.3 Symbolic manipulation

A simple definition of a **symbol** is that it is any alphabetic character or series of alphabetic characters which you can type on your keyboard. (As a general rule, it is safest for the time being to steer clear of the non-alphabetic/non-numerical characters unless we specifically advise you to type them. Exercise 1.1 at the end of this chapter will give you some practice in recognizing what is and what is not a legal Lisp symbol.) Imagine for a moment that you are sitting inside the computer. You have a screen on which you can see what we type to you from outside, and a keyboard which will print your replies onto the computer's screen. To hand you have the world's largest French dictionary.

We type 'tree'. You look it up in the dictionary, and type back 'arbre'. We type 'shoe', and you respond with 'soulier'. What is happening here is that you are taking in an English symbol ('tree' or 'shoe') and giving back in return the French symbol ('arbre' or 'soulier') which has the same meaning. The common meaning itself is in each case something clearly distinct from the corresponding symbol in either language, although you might be hard put to it to describe exactly what each 'meaning' consists of. In much the same way, when you type a symbol into Lisp, Lisp evaluates the symbol and returns its 'meaning' or **evaluation**.

Naturally, things can get far more complex than that. If you were to try to draw a flow chart to represent the execution (evaluation) of a Lisp program, you would need two parallel charts: one to depict the 'flow of control', to show precisely which instruction was being evaluated at any instant, and another to show the flow of data, since as mentioned above the effect of a Lisp function is to modify its input data and to return some result.

The Lisp term for 'meaning' or evaluation is **value**. The symbols themselves are referred to as **variables**. Fortunately, as you will learn, the value of any variable is exactly what you the programmer ordain it to be – no more and no less.

For anyone who remembers his or her school algebra, there is a parallel here. In algebra too there are variables (especially X, the unknown) which sooner or later acquire numeric values. The essential analogy is that a Lisp variable is not understood by Lisp to mean the variable itself, but is understood as representing or standing for something else. And just as in order to work out an algebraic equation you have to supply values for some of its crucial variables (if the equation says that X is the sum of Y and Z, you have to supply values for Y and Z in order to calculate the value of X), so you would have to supply values for some of the variables in a Lisp program; and eval would return the value(s) of the other(s) to print for you to see.

The value or meaning of a word is usually a concept. For example, in Europe we have a concept of white stuff, frozen water, which falls in place of rain during the winter. The English word for it is 'snow', and the French word is 'neige'. Other languages have other words for exactly the same thing. You won't go far wrong if you think of a variable having a value in very much the same way as a word has a meaning. And like the meanings of words, values can be very complex things indeed (what is the 'meaning' of the word 'mother'?). But do remember that Lisp has no inbuilt dictionary. If you were to type in 'mother', Lisp would complain that that variable had no value at all – unless you had previously supplied it with one, as you will shortly learn how to do.

Many people find the 'box metaphor' useful when thinking about variables. The metaphor compares the (named) variable to a box which initially contains nothing at all (the variable has no value) but which subsequently can at any moment contain just one thing. That thing is the value of the variable at that moment. There are Lisp functions to 'put' values into variables, and to take out whatever value is in the box and to replace it with another. Variables are quite commonly said to 'hold' values. If the box metaphor seems helpful, please feel free to use it. It is not the truth, but it is very unlikely to lead you astray.

You could justifiably describe the English language as just one of many possible ways of manipulating words (with their associated and possibly complex meanings) so as to express even more complex 'ideas'. Similarly, you could regard Lisp as just one of many possible ways of manipulating variables (with their associated and possibly complex values) so as to express something more interesting – perhaps a model of human cognition, perhaps a simulation of a parallel computer, perhaps a predictor of political fates.

1.3.4 Back to eval

In Lisp a single 'word', be it an English word such as 'mother' or a non-English symbol such as 'foo234', is known as a **symbol**. Lisp assumes that symbols are the names of variables, so if you type in such a word Lisp tries to return (to print back to you) its value. If the symbol has not got a value, you get an error message to that effect.

So the first rule of the set which will eventually describe the full evaluator is:

(1)   If the expression is a symbol, then return its value.

(There is also an implicit last rule, which says 'Else return the appropriate error message'.)

What is this value likely to be? Oddly enough, it will often be another symbol, one which might prove to have no value (no meaning) were you to type it back into Lisp, but which to you the programmer has considerable meaning. Such a symbol might be 'Success!'. But there are two possible values for any variable which are more important than all the others. They are **T** and **NIL**. These correspond roughly to the English concepts 'something' and 'nothing' respectively, or more usefully to the logical concepts **TRUE** and **FALSE**. There is a large class of (usually small) Lisp functions called **predicates**, which only ever return T or NIL. They are used as tests, to detect when a larger program has reached a certain point or has achieved a certain interim result. As you will see later, they allow you to use **conditional branching**, that is to cause your programs to choose between one action and another depending upon the current states of their data. Incidentally, in Lisp both T and NIL are **constants**. That is to say they are the names of variables whose values you are not allowed to alter. So the value of T is T and the value of NIL is NIL – always.

Other than in the case of simple symbols as above, or numbers, the majority of correct expressions typed into Lisp will be lists, and as such will each be enclosed in a pair of opening and closing parentheses. It is perfectly possible to have an empty list:

    ( )

and if you were to type this into Lisp it would respond by printing NIL. So the ideas of 'false' and the empty list are different ways of expressing the same thing, as far as Lisp is concerned. This is a most important idea, so please do notice that those two things are the same; they are in fact equivalent in every way. And whilst you are doing so, please also notice that other everyday concepts which might superficially seem the same – in particular, the number zero – are *not* the same as NIL or the empty list. Conversely, the above-mentioned predicates, which we said returned either T or NIL, may if they do not return NIL return anything else instead of T. In other words, as far as Lisp is concerned anything which is not FALSE is TRUE.

However, a Lisp list is not usually empty, but contains an arbitrary number of 'elements'. Here is a perfectly correct Lisp list containing three elements, or individual items:

    (+ 2 2)

Exercise 1.2 will give you some practice at recognizing, and therefore of being able to write, legal Lisp lists. The above list is the Lisp equivalent of '2+2' mentioned above, and as you can see the only difference (apart from the parentheses themselves) between the English version and the Lisp version is that the function '+' has been moved from the second position in the list to the first. We mentioned before that this change does not, provided that you understand it, make any difference to the meaning of the expression. The Lisp version, with the function coming first in the expression, is called **prefix notation**, and the everyday form with the function between its arguments is known as **infix notation**. It is also possible to have **postfix notation** with the function coming last, after all of its arguments. But Lisp does not concern itself with the two more difficult versions: always and uncompromisingly, it puts the function first.

When eval receives such a list (passed to it from the keyboard by read) it assumes that the first element of the list is the name of a function, and that the remainder of the list comprises that function's arguments. Using this simple rule, eval is able correctly to apply the function to the arguments, and the result of that application (4, of course) becomes the result which eval itself returns to print so that you can see it. There is no particular reason why eval should assume the first element of the list rather than, say, the last element or the middle element, to be the function. All Lisp evaluators just happen to expect it to be the first, and that's why the '+' is moved to the first position in the list.

> *Point to remember*   The first element of a list up until now has always been a function. This is worth remembering.

The individual elements of the list are symbols, and as we suggested earlier the value of a symbol can be more or less anything which you the programmer have chosen it to be. However, although you can use integers (numbers) inside symbols, as in 'car1' and 'car2' integers on their own are not symbols: it would not make much sense to specify that the value of '2' was anything other than 2. In Lisp all numbers have their normal meanings; that is to say, any number's value is itself, and Lisp will not allow you to change it. The value of '2' is forever 2. If you were to type '2' into Lisp, eval would return to you the value: 2.

So it is clear that eval needs to be able to handle single symbols and numbers as well as lists of symbols. Fortunately that does not involve a new rule for eval. Since symbols (when they are the names of variables) and numbers both do have values, eval can treat them both in the same way; that is it can retrieve those values. The generic name for something which may be either a symbol or a number is **atom**. A one-word change to rule 1, as below, will do what we want.

Having explained that, we can now describe more completely what happens when eval receives the above three-element list. First, it checks that the first symbol '+' has a **functional value** (if it had none, you would get an error message immediately). The functional value of a symbol is the function itself: a quite distinct thing from what you have until now understood by 'value'. eval now prepares to apply that function to the remaining elements of the list. But each of those will also be a symbol representing some value, and to find out what those are eval applies *itself* to each of them in turn. Once all of the values have been retrieved, then the function '+' can be applied to them so as to produce a final result.

Now let us turn the above into rules which eval should always follow regardless of what expression it receives from read:

(1)   If the expression is an **atom**, return its value.

(2)   **If the expression is a list,**

    (a)   **find the value – which should be a function – of the first element of the list;**

    (b)   **find the values of the remaining elements of the list by applying these rules to each of them in turn;**

    (c)   **apply the function from (a) to the arguments from (b), and return the result.**

We would particularly like you to notice that rule 2b in effect includes an exact copy of all of the rules. It says 'apply this complete set of rules to each of these things which I've found, before carrying on to step 2c'. We hope that in this context the idea, that one of a set of rules could apply all of the set of rules to some intermediate results, is not a difficult one. Its official name is **recursion**, and it is such a useful idea in Lisp programming that later on we shall devote an entire chapter to it. For the moment, we would just like you to agree that it makes sense.

If at any point during the operation of eval something goes wrong (e.g. if the first element of the list turned out to have no functional value) then an appropriate error message will be printed. The functional value *is* the actual function; it is the thing, quite distinct from the function's name, which actually does something to its input data. This will become clearer when we show you how to **define**, or create your own functions in addition to those provided by Lisp itself. For the time being, notice that a symbol can represent a variable which has a value, or it can represent a function. In fact the same symbol in Lisp can 'be' both things.

Please understand that the name of a function is rarely a single character such as '+'. More often it is a word, or even several words hyphenated together. For example it would be perfectly possible to write a function called 'plus' which did exactly the same as '+'. Later on, when you learn about how to write your own functions, you will find that you will be free to give them (almost) any name you like. The same applies to variables, and as we have said it is possible in Common Lisp to use the *same* name for both a function and a variable.

Point to remember   For the sake of other programmers who may have to understand your programs, this is not a good idea.

1.4   How to get started with Lisp

1.4.1   Loading Lisp

Since we hope very much that you will follow the examples given in this book by typing them into your own Lisp on your own computer, this seems a good point to sidetrack for a moment into the question of how to get Lisp up and running. But, sadly, we cannot tell you. It depends entirely upon what brand of computer you are using, and upon what the manufacturers of your particular Lisp have decided is best. Our advice is: look in your software manual. It may describe a verbal command (probably just the word 'lisp') which you should type into your computer or, if your computer makes great use of on-screen graphical representations, you may have to 'click' with a 'mouse' at some self-evident point on the screen. Whatever the method of getting Lisp started, we can promise you that once you have discovered it, it will be very simple!

Lisp is a large language, and takes a while to load. You may have to sit for up to a couple of minutes, perhaps even with no messages on screen to tell you what is happening; but eventually something, probably a welcoming message, will appear to tell you that loading is complete. The vast majority of modern Lisps then provide a **prompt**. This is a printed symbol or word and is very likely to include a question mark (?) or a forward arrow (>) to indicate that Lisp is waiting for some input from you. During the rest of this book we shall use the question mark to represent Lisp's prompt, but the prompt provided by your own Lisp may be different. If you are very unlucky, your Lisp may provide no prompt at all but just an agonizing silence. In either case, do not worry. You are never expected to type our question mark prompts, and whether your own Lisp provides a different prompt or no prompt at all, just go ahead and type.

Exercise 1.3 should give you confidence that you have understood the evaluator so far, and that you know how to type Lisp forms into Lisp.

1.4.2   Beginning to use Lisp

We said earlier was that you would not normally bother to use Lisp in order to perform simple arithmetic. But, since the value of any numeral is always itself, a few numerical examples of eval in action will be relatively easy to follow. In all of them, '?' is the prompt which signifies that read is waiting for some input from you. So anything on the same line as '?' should be typed into Lisp. Immediately below that, without any prompt, appears Lisp's reply. If we type

> ? 3

followed by a press of the RETURN key, Lisp responds with

> 3

In Lisp all numbers evaluate to themselves. That brief interaction demonstrated the truth of our statement that value of 3 is 3.

At this point it is worth mentioning that Lisp will not know that it is its turn to respond (to what you have typed) unless two conditions are fulfilled:

(a)   all opening and closing parentheses (if any) balance, i.e. there are the same numbers of each; and

(b)   the RETURN key has been pressed.

Actually, a few Lisps will start evaluating your input as soon as its parentheses balance – you do not have to go to all the effort of pressing RETURN. But in most cases the RETURN is necessary.

> *Point to remember*   If Lisp seems to have got 'stuck' and refuses to respond to your input, try typing a few more closing parentheses (this is on the assumption that your input contains any opening parentheses!).

Now if we type

> ? (+ 3 6)
> 9

we get back 9. This is what happened 'behind the scenes': the expression is not an atom (rule 1) so eval retrieves the value of '+' (rule 2a) and then applies its rules to each of the arguments in turn (rule 2). These are the steps followed by eval in evaluating the expression:

(+ 3 6)

the value of '+' is found (rule 2a).

(+ *3* 6)

3 is evaluated and returns 3 (rule 1).

(+ 3 *6*)

6 is evaluated to give 6 (rule 1).
    Now that the arguments have been evaluated, the function can be applied to the arguments:

(+ 3 6)

The whole expression is evaluated to give 9. This 9 is returned to print, and so appears on the screen.

1.4.3   A more complicated example

(+ (+ 2 4) 6)
(+ (+ 2 4) 6)

The expression is not an atom so eval goes to rule 2. The value of '+' is found (rule 2a). Rule 2b says that eval should now apply its rules to each of the arguments in turn. The first argument, (+ 2 4), is not an atom (rule 1) but another list, so eval evaluates it using rule 2b:

(+ (+ 2 4) 6)

The value of the inner '+' is found.

(+ (+ *2* 4) 6)

The first argument to that inner '+' is evaluated to give 2.

(+ (+ 2 *4*) 6)

The second argument is evaluated to give 4.

(+ *(+ 2 4)* 6)

The function '+' is applied to the 2 and the 4, resulting in 6.

(+ 6 6)

The outer '+' can now be applied to its two arguments, and the final result of 12 returned to print. Therefore:

? (+ (+ 2 4) 6)
12

Naturally, that is not the whole story, but we are getting closer. eval as you have seen it so far can cope with single symbols (atoms) and with lists, and in the latter case it knows how to manipulate the symbols within a list so that a function is applied to its arguments. It can also handle lists within lists, usually known as **nested** lists. For the purposes of this lesson, eval needs one more ability.

> *Point to remember*   The first element of a list up until now has always been a function. This is worth remembering, which is why we repeat it.

1.4.4   quote **is an exception**

quote is a special kind of inbuilt Lisp function called a **special form**. In fact the word form is used to describe any correct Lisp expression, and quote is merely a special one of these. What makes it special is that it modifies the behaviour of the evaluator in a way which is peculiar to itself. You will come across other special forms later on, and each of them will affect the operations of the evaluator in its own idiosyncratic way. Fortunately, quote is the easiest to understand.

Suppose that in the course of programming we require a certain variable to represent a certain value. In Lisp terms, we want to **assign** a **value** to the **variable**. Suppose also that the name of the variable is the symbol or atom 'john', and that the value we want it to represent is 'author'.

Note that although both 'john' and 'author' are English words, which may make things easier for the programmer, as far as Lisp itself is concerned they are merely lexical shapes. We could as well have called the variable 'var93' and its value 'zeitgeist'. Lisp would not care. The problem is that 'john' does not yet have a value, and so whatever the form of our assignment instruction eval as described so far would complain as soon as it tried to evaluate it (rule 1).

Try this, remembering to follow it with a RETURN:

? john

Lisp will respond with an error message to the effect that the variable 'john' has no value. As indeed it has not, because we have not yet given it one. Escape from Lisp's error-handling system back to the top level read—eval—print loop by holding down the 'CTRL' key as though it were a SHIFT key and simultaneously typing a dot (that is, period or full stop). The normal Lisp prompt will reappear, and Lisp will behave normally. Whilst you are learning Lisp you will get many error messages, so it is as well that you find out now how to restore things to normal. (If your keyboard has no CTRL or 'control' key, you'll be able to find out from your Lisp manual which key to use instead. Alternatively your copy of Lisp may require you to type control-c to escape from the error handler. The precise means of escape is not part of the Common Lisp specification, so please check with your manual. It is extremely important that you find out how to escape from your Lisp's error-handling system, and also that you find out how to stop a program which clearly is not behaving as you wanted it to – often the two commands are the same.)
Now type:

> ? john

and if you typed all five of those characters followed by RETURN Lisp will reply

> JOHN

(Lisp normally responds in upper case (capital letters), though you are free to type upper or lower case, or even a mixture of cases.) It is as though that single quote, which you may have thought to be an apostrophe, had had the effect of making 'john' evaluate to itself, just as numbers do. But this is not quite what happened. The single quote in Lisp behaves in very much the same way as do double quotes – inverted commas – in written English. If we tell you that our friend has just said 'zeitgeist', you understand from the double quotes that the word 'zeitgeist' is *precisely* what our friend said; in other words, it is to be taken literally. But you do not make any assumptions about the meaning, or value, of the word.

In a closely analogous way, the single quote is a signal to eval that it should *not* carry out its normal attempt at evaluation upon the expression immediately following the quote itself. (That expression can be an atomic symbol, or it can be a list, or indeed any legal Lisp form.)
Now for the truth. When read sees the single quote, such as in

> 'john

it immediately converts that expression into a list, whose first element is
the special form quote:

```
    (quote john)
```

and passes it on to eval as though you had typed it yourself. Like all other
Lisp functions, quote returns a value. In fact it returns its single input
argument unaltered. But at the same time it also tells eval not to bother
with trying to evaluate the argument, and so the net result is that eval
itself returns the argument unchanged. Notice the clear difference
between the cases of a number, such as 2, and (quote john). The 2 is
evaluated by eval, and its value is 2. The 'john' in (quote john) is not
evaluated and is hence returned unchanged.

1.4.5 Assignment

Now we can finally effect that assignment of 'author' to 'john'. In Lisp the
basic assignment function is set:

```
    ? (set 'john 'author)
    AUTHOR
```

There are two minor points to be made here. First, we have stopped
reminding you that you are expected to type into your Lisp any code
shown in sloping face and following a sloping question mark, and we have
stopped reminding you that all of your typed inputs should be terminated
with a RETURN. Second, in any legal Lisp expression, the parentheses
must balance, i.e. there must be equal numbers of opening and closing
parentheses. If in the future Lisp seems to be taking no notice of
something you have typed in, it will be possible that you have forgotten
the final RETURN, but more likely that your parentheses are not
balanced.

Notice that set returns its second argument: the new value of
'john'. In fact two things have happened here. First, set has done what all
Lisp functions (*pace* values) are supposed to do: it has **returned a value** to
indicate that it has 'worked', but in the process it has accomplished a **side-
effect**, that of assigning a value to the variable john. When ultimately you
are writing and running large programs, you will expect them to exhibit
certain kinds of behaviour (that is their sole purpose). Most of this
behaviour will be accomplished via side-effects – printing something onto
the screen is an obvious and valuable side-effect of a function – but as you
will see later the returned value of a function is at least equally useful in
allowing separate functions to communicate and to cooperate with one
another.

To prove to yourself that the above assignment has worked, type

```
? john
AUTHOR
```

The value of 'john' is now 'author'. Just as '+' is a function which causes addition, so set is a function which causes assignment. set takes two arguments and makes the first of them into a variable whose value is the second of them. (Actually, it sets up pointers in the computer's memory, but that is not important for an understanding of it.) What eval receives from read is the following nested list:

```
(set (quote john) (quote author))
```

This is a list of three elements: set, (quote john), and (quote author). The evaluator works through it from left to right, trying to evaluate each element. Whenever it comes across an element which is itself a list – the second and third elements here – it starts again from rule 1 in order to evaluate that list. Lists can be nested (lists appearing within lists) to any desired depth within any element, but the evaluator always 'remembers where it had got to', so that once each element has been evaluated it goes on to the next.

> *Point to remember*   Each form, be it an atom or a list, is only evaluated once. This is important.

The two 'calls' to the function quote tell eval that all it has to do here is retrieve the value of set and to apply it to its verbatim arguments 'john' and 'author'.

1.4.6   eval **again**

So now eval needs to know how to handle special forms. Here is the latest set of rules:

(1)   If the expression is an atom, return its value.

(2)   If the expression is a list, then either

      (a)   **if the first element of the list is a special form, handle it and its arguments accordingly.**

      (b)   If the first element of the list has a functional value then retrieve that function, and

           (i)   find the values of the remaining elements of the list by applying these rules to each of them in turn;

(ii)   apply the function from (b) to the arguments from (i), and return the result.

Note that both of the calls to quote in the above example would be handled via step 2b(i). This is another very important though essentially simple point: that in Lisp you can use a function call, with its own arguments, in place of an argument to another function. In this case calls to quote occur as both of the arguments to set. As you can see if you follow the example through the rules of the evaluator, both of the calls to quote are evaluated *before* the call to set can be evaluated.

By the way, this nesting of function calls was what we were referring to when we said earlier in this chapter that 'chain' was not quite the right word to use to describe a Lisp program. A program can consist of a series of non-nested function calls rather like a chain; but more usually it uses at least some nesting; real-life chains do not usually have links within links, as quote is within set.

In practical everyday programming the set function is used quite rarely. With the advent of Common Lisp the preferred assignment function has become setf (see below), but throughout previous AI literature and programs setq has been used very extensively. setq is another special form, and its effect upon the evaluator is to tell the evaluator not to evaluate setq's first argument; indeed its name is an abbreviation of **set-quote**. Thus, instead of writing

```
? (set 'john 'author)
```

we can write

```
? (setq john 'author)
```

This may seem a trivial or even pointless advantage, but in fact in early dialects of Lisp it was not possible to use the now-universal quote *mark*. Instead, users had to write the whole form in full: (quote john) rather than simply 'john. Under those circumstances setq was a huge time saver, and hence very popular with programmers.

In Common Lisp there is a superficially similar Lisp function called setf; in fact setf is the one we'd most like you to learn about and is the one we shall most often use in this book. Amongst Common Lisp programmers, it has come to be preferred to setq. As you will discover soon enough, setf does not only assign values to variables. You will be able to say things such as 'setf the third element of this list to be so-and-so', so as for example to change the list (+ 2 3 4) into the list (+ 2 198 4). setf works on arrays too, and in fact on a large number of the different kinds of 'data objects' which you will be able to create in Lisp.

Sadly, we also have to confess that setf is neither a special form nor a function as you understand the terms, and will eventually require yet another modification to your picture of the evaluator. For the moment, though, that fact is not important enough to deserve a long explanatory sidetrack. Think of setf something else which can modify the behaviour of the evaluator, as indeed it does. We shall give you the details later, but all you need to remember for now is that setf is a **macro** rather than a special form or a simple function.

Exercise 1.4 will test your knowledge of the family of three set functions.

SUMMARY

You now have a very basic understanding of how Lisp works. Knowing how it works will enable you to predict what it will do: what result a function will return given certain input data. You know that the data can itself consist of (the results of) other function calls, and that this 'nesting' can go on indefinitely.

You know that the crucial difference between a special form and an ordinary function is that a special form modifies the behaviour of the evaluator. You have seen how to use one special form, quote, to prevent evaluation. And you have been warned that macros also change the behaviour of the evaluator.

Throughout this chapter, we have talked of lists as being entities whose first elements are always functions. In the next chapter you will learn a good deal about how to manipulate lists of the form

        '(a b c)

where the quote prevents evaluation of the entire list. Remember, quote tells eval not evaluate any of the Lisp expression which follows the quote mark.

EXERCISES

Exercise 1.1   Valid Symbols
A symbol is a succession of characters, preceded and followed by a **delimiter** such as (in particular) a space or an opening or closing parenthesis. All of the words used in this chapter would be symbols to Lisp, as are the 'words' used in the sections of Lisp code which we have shown you. Please remember that Lisp is not **case sensitive**, by which we mean that you can type into it using upper case (capital) letters or lower case (small) letters, or in a mixture of both if you care to. By convention Lisp will respond, on screen, in upper case; if your particular version of Common Lisp responds in lower case, it won't matter at all.

As well as all of the alphabetic characters you may include the following in your symbols, and please do not try to include any other characters such as the colon or semicolon:

    + _ * / @ $ % ˆ & _ \ ‹ ›¯ .

In fact, since a symbol may consist of any number of characters, and since all of the above characters are separated by spaces, they are all symbols in their own right. So a symbol of more than one character is composed of characters which if used alone would themselves be symbols. Some characters are not symbols in Lisp. In particular the dot (period, full stop) shown above is a little anomalous. As you will see later it has a 'meaning' in Lisp, and you have learned in this chapter that symbols do not have meaning (values) unless you the programmer give it to them. So it would be correct to argue that the dot is not a symbol. However, it can sometimes be so useful that Lisp allows you to include it in other symbols. But a symbol consisting only of dots (including, of course, a symbol consisting of only one dot) would be illegal).

Sequences of numerals (perhaps including one dot as a decimal point) are not symbols but numbers. The difference is that you cannot assign a value to a number: the value of a number is always itself, the value of '2' is always 2, and so on. However, you can include numbers within legal symbols, for example person1, drink9, foo17bar.

Given that information, your job in this exercise is to decide whether the following are or are not legal Lisp symbols. As always in every chapter of this book, we also provide the answers to our exercise (go to the end to find it).

```
    john
    1john
    abc.foo
    abc,foo
    hello:
    baz
    ;here
    some'john
    help%john
    *fghg*
    (john)
    j(ohn)
```

Exercise 1.2
A list contains a number of **elements**. The start and end of a list are delimited by the characters (and). Elements are separated by one or more spaces. Actually, what we mean is that it does not matter whether inadvertently you type more than one space between elements of a list. Lisp itself always puts just one space. Lisp will also allow you to type tabs or returns between elements of a list; it simply ignores them, and assumes that you meant to put a space. As you will see later, tabs and returns are useful for making Lisp code more readable to us humans.

Any element of a list may be a number or a symbol, or it may itself be a list. Any element of that inner list may also be a list. And so on *ad infinitum*. This exercise asks you to say how many elements there are in each of the following lists.

```
(a b c)
(a b cc)
(a (b c d) e)
((a b c))
(((a b c)))
()
(())
((()))
((() ()))
(() ())
(a ((d)))
((a b) (c e))
```

Exercise 1.3
Some Lisp lists have functions as their first elements. The Lisp evaluator always assumes that the first element of any (unquoted) list is a function. Which of the forms below can be evaluated using the rules of evaluation as you currently know them?

```
(+ 2 3 4 5 6)
(+ (+ 1 2) (+ (+ 1 2) (+ 3 6)))
((+ 3 4) 7 8 9)
```

Exercise 1.4
Try to evaluate the following expressions in your head or on paper. If you get stuck, or if you do not believe our solutions, the obvious thing to do is to try the expressions out in Lisp. So do please notice that they are a series: you would need to type them into Lisp in the same order as they appear here to be sure of getting the same results as we do.

```
? (set fred bill)
? (setq fred bill)
? (setq fred 'bill)
? (setq 'fred 3)
? (setf 'fred 'bill)
? fred
? bill
? 'fred
? 'bill
? (set bill fred)
? (setq bill fred)
? fred
? bill
```

```
? (setf bill 'sarah)
? (setf fred bill)
? fred
```

Chapter 2
The Virtual Machine

We discuss the virtual machine, which is neither a computer nor a program, and consider for the first time methods of representing knowledge on the machine. Knowledge representation, along with the evaluator, is a major theme throughout this book. This chapter then introduces the technique of list manipulation as a means of representing both data and programs.

2.1   The virtual machine

2.1.1   Computers and programs are parts of a whole

A computer without a program can do nothing at all. For this reason computers without programs are quite rare! Conversely everything which any computer does is controlled by a program. Every computer which any of us are likely to come across will have at the very least a program called its operating system, the program which for example allows you to locate and open whatever files or other programs you actually want to use. The operating system also controls disks, tapes, and any other peripheral hardware which your machine may have. For Lisp users the operating system holds virtually no interest; it is a 'lower level' program than Lisp, and we say that we run Lisp 'on top of' it.

For all that, the operating system is a program, and it causes the computer to behave in a certain way. When you subsequently start Common Lisp up, the computer stops behaving in that way and behaves instead as Common Lisp. Of course Common Lisp is also a program, and the behaviour which it imparts to the machine allows you to write your own Lisp programs.

Your own programs will again alter the behaviour of the computer, perhaps so that it does something which otherwise only humans can do. The point is that every program causes the computer to behave in a way which is unique to that program and also different from the way in which it behaves when running any other program. In principle the computer can exhibit a very large (but not infinite) range of different behaviours depending upon what program is driving it at the time.

Sorry if we have laboured this a bit, but we wanted it to be crystal clear because it leads to a quite startling question: since the computer is dormant and useless without a program, and since the program is clearly not a machine, exactly where is the 'machine' which plays chess, or makes medical diagnoses, or pilots the spaceship? It is obviously not the more usual type of machine such as a car, which you could take to bits and repair. All we have is, if you like, machine-like behaviour which can be altered by altering the program but which is not itself directly manipulable.

The name given to this rather unusual concept is the **virtual machine**, which is intended to mean the same sort of thing as 'non-physical machine'.

Of course the computer is not the only machine which can exhibit more than one kind of behaviour. An ordinary clock radio usually has at least three – clock, alarm and radio; but the crucial difference is that you could take the clock radio apart and put your finger on the clock circuitry, the alarm circuitry and the radio circuitry. But the computer does not have a separate little compartment for each of its possible modes of behaviour; it is a single entity capable of behaving in a multitude of different ways according to the commands in its program.

The virtual machine about which this book will have the most to say is of course the Lisp evaluator. We are describing it to you in terms of a set of rules which, in the end, will fully describe its behaviour. When you reach the end of the book, you will have learned enough to write, in Lisp, your own eval function: the function which gives to Lisp the behaviour which we describe as 'the evaluator'.

Useful tip   It is a good idea to remember, when you are writing a program, that you are building a machine.

2.1.2   The analogy with human beings

A very common misconception amongst beginners is to assume that the computer already has some intelligence, or some understanding of English. The computer 'knows' absolutely nothing other than how to do what programs tell it to do. You, the programmer, have to tell it or teach it, via your program, everything else which you may need it to know. For example, a chess program would certainly need to instruct the computer on how to move a knight, and a great deal more besides. If you keep telling yourself that you are building a machine, it is less easy to fall into the trap of imputing extra knowledge to the computer; we are more accustomed to thinking of mere machines as rather stupid things.

Here is a rather far-fetched idea. Suppose that the human brain is in some way 'like' a computer. It probably is not, but suppose that it is. Suppose also that in the same way that a computer program is all that the computer knows about, so all that we know about are our lifetimes of experiences to date. When the program runs on the computer the result is a certain specific behaviour which we call the virtual machine; and maybe when a lifetime's experiences 'run on' a human brain there appears specific behaviour which we call a personality. As we have admitted, this is very probably arrant nonsense, but the point is that AI hopes that it is not! The dream of one day building an artificial person assumes that by then we will be able to draw parallels between electronic and mental processes and/or states.

From that point of view, and in the context of what needs to be discovered, AI has in its 30-odd years of existence so far discovered almost exactly nothing. The things which our machines can do turn out on close analysis not to be all that clever after all, and very few of them can behave consistently over more than a very narrow range of inputs. By contrast human beings can behave consistently over a vast range of inputs, they can adapt themselves so as to behave appropriately in totally new situations, and on most tasks they can operate blindingly faster than any virtual machine yet created.

2.1.3   Virtual machines employ heuristics

Consider again a computer running a program to play chess. Fairly obviously, the machine would easily beat even the very best of human players if it could, from any board position, calculate every possible next move, every possible reply to that next move, every possible riposte to the second move, and so on to the end of the game. But the number of calculations required to do that is so colossal that no human being would live long enough to finish a game of chess with such a machine, not even a modern one which could carry out many millions of instructions per second.

If you think of the search for a win as an attempt to solve a problem, then the collection of all possible moves from the start to the end of the game is known as the **problem space**. It is quite common in AI for problem spaces to become too large to handle on present-day computers. In order to reduce the problem space and to make the machines usable, we employ **heuristics**. Heuristics are, to be honest, simple rules of thumb which just happen to work: changes to a program which have no particular rationale other than success behind them.

A heuristic may be derived from the program itself; for example the chess-playing program could be set to look only a fixed number of moves ahead, rather than working out the results of every possible move and countermove to the end of the game. The chess-playing programs which you can buy in any large store do this: at 'beginner's level' they may look only two or three moves ahead, whilst at 'advanced level' they probably look five or six moves ahead. In consequence they take much longer to decide upon their moves at advanced level than at beginner's level.

A more convincing kind of heuristic is derived from observation of the behaviour of human beings in similar circumstances. For example a human chess player might, once the opponent had made a move, first check which squares the moved piece could attack from its new position, and might also take into account which of the opponent's other pieces could attack the same squares. Then s/he might go on to notice what pathways had been opened up by the removal of the piece from its old position. A large number of such rules incorporated into the program could enable it to play quite intelligently without the tedium of checking millions of possible sequential moves at every stage.

The problems of creating a virtual machine to play chess as well as some humans play it are not by any means all solved. And although game playing was one of the first challenges which AI researchers took on, we can now see with hindsight that it was actually one of the harder problems. Game playing is essentially a cooperative activity involving two quite distinct minds – and we have no yet created anything like one mind. The mental abilities required when behaving cooperatively are very different from, and far more complex than, those required when operating alone.

Many of the things which a human mind does on its own could be represented as a set of instructions: a recipe, a knitting pattern, instructions for using or mending something, arithmetical calculations and so on. Of course, the instructions do not have to be written down: they may simply be remembered from past experience. Or they could be more formally represented, as in our growing description of eval, as a set of IF–THEN rules. Lisp lends itself admirably to cognitive models of such processes, because of the concept of a list. A recipe is pretty obviously a list of instructions, and so is a Lisp program. This chapter will teach you how to manipulate in Lisp lists of data, remembering that in Lisp any item of data can be replaced by a function call which returns that item of data.

2.2 Knowledge representation

But, what is the purpose of being able to manipulate Lisp lists? It is to manipulate symbols, and therefore to manipulate data, and thus to manipulate knowledge. Some researchers, particularly those brought up on Philosophy, would object to that last assertion on the grounds that it is not at all clear that a representation inside a computer of a piece of data – the value of a variable, or in Lisp possibly a long and complex function call – is anything like the same thing as the (human) knowledge which it allegedly represents.

Let us take an example. Suppose that you were writing a program which for some reason would need to refer to (to make use of) the human concept 'mother'. The problem would be to work out what that concept consists of, and then to create a convincing representation of it somewhere in the program. For example, you could write down (in a list, naturally!) all the associations and connotations which the word 'mother' brings to your mind, and you could use setf to assign that long list to a variable called mother.

Now, you might think that that looked a bit too easy to be true, so you would ask us to do write down what we thought the concept 'mother' meant to each of us. Two things are immediately obvious: that our three lists would be different, and that they would have some very strong similarities. All of us probably had our mothers present at our births, and all of our mothers were women, for example. This is not as daft as it sounds: the point is that for every English speaker there is, almost certainly, a general concept associated with the word 'mother'. Perhaps a skeletal version which is correct for everyone but which misses out all of the personal characteristics of any particular mother. If the program which you are trying to write is to behave in a general way you might well want to give it only the skeletal concept to work with, so as to avoid clogging up its memory with huge quantities of specific data about individual mothers.

Knowledge representation is the art or science of making sensible decisions both about what data needs to be represented for the purposes of any given program, and how that data should be represented; a list is not by any means the only **data structure** which can be used in Lisp, and in object-oriented programming, to which we will introduce you later in this book, programs are very little other than highly complex representations of data. As AI programs become more sophisticated, it becomes more and more clear that knowledge representation is a bottleneck which needs urgently to be resolved.

It is a bottleneck for three reasons. First, if a program has to do repeated long searches through a huge database in order to retrieve any given fact or item it is going to be very slow to operate, very inefficient. It might be enormously speeded up by arranging the data differently, but the question is how?

Second, although it is obvious that as human beings we do know certain things, it is not so obvious that we consciously know how and why those various things are connected together to form larger bodies of knowledge, the kinds of things we might call expertise or skills. Imagine, for example, trying to write down in a list all the abilities which together comprise the concept 'able to drive a car'. Expertise certainly seems to be a kind of knowledge, but to date AI is only beginning to learn how to represent it.

Third, if the AI program in question is intended as a cognitive model, intended to replicate what we believe to be actual processes occurring inside human brains, then we need to know how the corresponding knowledge is stored in the brain, and so far we do not know that, although in a few areas there are quite convincing theories as to how it might be stored.

We shall return to the question of knowledge (or data) representation again and again in this book. You will see that it is very often the hardest of the questions which need to be answered when designing a program.

2.3   List manipulation

2.3.1   Representing simple data in lists

Apart from single variables with values, the simplest method of representing data in Lisp is the list. A list can become too large to be usable if it is used to represent concepts (such as 'mother'), but it is often a very convenient way of representing procedures (as in the case of the recipe) or actions (as in the ordinary function call).

Lisp lists can represent arbitrary data. Here is a list consisting of sublists which could represent, say, part of an electronic address book:

```
((name (tony hasemer))
 (address (the open university))
 (birthday (may 3)))
```

Notice that the parentheses balance: each list and each sublist has its own pair, one opening parenthesis and one closing parenthesis, and that therefore the total numbers of opening and closing parentheses are equal. When in a later chapter we discuss use of an editor, which you will need in order to write your own programs, you will find that the editor may well be able to do the counting for you and to warn you if your brackets do not balance.

Notice also that the sublists are slightly indented. In fact the opening parentheses of the second and third sublists line up with the opening parenthesis of the sublist on the line above. This is deliberate and important for you to copy. As you get used to reading Lisp code, indentation will tell you at once that each line begins with a sublist of the overall list. Proper indentation of Lisp code can tell you a great deal about how a program works.

Here is a list which could represent a map, showing the road distances between various towns:

```
((london 63 brighton)
 (brighton 5 lewes)
 (london 53 milton-keynes)
 (milton-keynes 15 bedford))
```

And here is one which could represent a hierarchical tree such as a family tree

```
(grandma (children emily (jane (children peter paul))))
```

We are not going to face you with such complex lists for a while, but we hope that you can see from those few examples that the idea of a list, containing data elements which may themselves be lists, is quite a powerful way of representing much of the data which we as human beings use every day. By the way, you may have noticed that the three lists could not be typed directly into Lisp as they stand, i.e. without each being preceded by a single quote. There is a distinction here between a Lisp list *per se*, which exists as some kind of record in the computer's memory and which can conveniently be represented as above, and the quoted version of it which you would type into the read-eval-print loop from your keyboard.

Recap box   As you already know, a Lisp list consists of a set of elements or list members surrounded by a pair of parentheses. Note that it is an **ordered** set, which means that (a b c) is not the same list as (b c a). You also know that each member or element can be any legal Lisp expression, including another list. You know that when eval is presented with such a list it assumes that the first element of it is some kind of function; and finally you know that the quote function can prevent eval from making that assumption.

So if you type in a quoted list, you get back the same list, without any evaluation occurring:

```
? '(one two three)
(ONE TWO THREE)
```

whereas of course were you to type it in without quoting it you would get
an error message from eval, which would complain that the first element,
one, is not a function.

However, getting back exactly what you typed in is not very
interesting. But it would be interesting to know how to manipulate lists;
for example, how to go through a list element by element, in order, just
as you would work through a recipe; or how you would set about altering
a list. That would be interesting because being able to do it is in itself
quite an intelligent activity, and as a budding Lisp programmer you are
concerned with intelligent behaviour on the part of the machine.

2.3.2   Extracting the data from the list

You have probably already guessed that you will not spend much of your
time as a programmer typing quoted lists directly into the machine. Far
more often, any list you are concerned with will be the returned result of
some Lisp function, which you will want to have manipulated in some
way before handing it on to some other function as its input data.

Suppose that you needed to hand on only the first element of the
list. In Common Lisp you have a very handy function called first which
always returns the first element of any list given to it. There are also
functions called second, third etc. all the way up to tenth, which is usually
enough. We would like you to try first before going on, using the list (a b
c). But remember that you do not want eval to complain that a is not a
function, so you will need to quote the list as you give it to first, like
this:

```
? (first '(a b c))
A
```

first returns the first element of the list, just as it should. What actually
happened was that read took your typed input and converted it into

```
(first (quote (a b c)))
```

When eval received that, it immediately dug out the functional value of
first and then tried to evaluate first's argument. But that turned out to
be another function call, this time to the special form quote. And eval
knows as you do that when it sees a call to quote it should *not* try to
evaluate quote's argument. So quote was able to return the list untouched,
whereupon eval applied first to the list, thus causing first to return a.

Recap box

(1)   If the expression is an atom, return its value.

(2)   If the expression is a list, then either

    (a)   If the first member of the list is a special form, handle it and its arguments accordingly.

    (b)   If the first member of the list has a functional value then retrieve that function, and

        (i)   find the values of the remaining members of the list by applying these rules to each of them in turn;

        (ii) apply the function from (b) to the arguments from (i), and return the result.

Now suppose that, rather than wanting the first element of the list returned, you wanted to ignore that element, and to consider the list only from its second element onwards (as you yourself might do when working through the recipe). There is a companion function to first called rest:

```
? (rest '(a b c))
(B C)
```

Now try this:

```
? (first (rest '(a b c)))
```

Read this as 'The first *of* the rest *of quote* (a b c)'. Lisp replies:

```
B
```

Recap box eval retrieved the functional value of first and then tried to evaluate its argument. This turned out to be a call to rest, so eval retrieved that functional value too. Then came the usual business with quote, which as you know by now results in the plain unquoted list. rest returned (b c) when it was applied to the list by eval, and subsequently first returned the first element of that, which was b.

    Please notice that this is exactly the same result as you would get from

```
? (second '(a b c))
```

2.3.3 Likely errors at this stage

We hope that you are beginning to get a feel for how Lisp functions can be arbitrarily nested so as to achieve the effect which you want. What about this:

```
? (rest (first '(a b c)))
```

This will infallibly generate an error message. The problem is that in this case first returns a, and a is not a list. rest cannot return all but the first member of something which is not a list – that is, of an atom. This is an important point, because many of your early errors will arise through supplying the wrong kind of data to Lisp functions. But you have an advantage in that you already understand enough about the evaluator to be able to work out for yourself that the above form would cause an error; and you even know what kind of error it is: it is a **wrong-type-argument** error.

Similarly, supplying an atomic (non-list) argument to first would result in an error message. The distinction between atoms and lists is an important one in Lisp, and though from one point of view it might seem sensible of first simply to return its argument if the argument is an atom, Lisp insists that this is a mistake on the programmer's part. There is one exception to the rule that you cannot apply first to atom, and that is the special atom NIL. You may remember that we told you in Chapter 1 that NIL and the empty list () are the same thing. So

```
? (first nil)
```

or

```
? (first '())
```

will both return NIL.

In the same way you can apply rest to NIL; again, NIL will be returned.

> *Useful point*   If you supply an atom when a function expects a list, or a list when a function expects an atom, you will get an error message. NIL is the only Lisp form which is both an atom and a list.

2.3.4   More about extracting data from a list

At this point we have to admit that where first, rest and the others are concerned we have been concealing a truth from you. Those functions are a bit of 'syntactic sugar', added to Common Lisp to make it more friendly and intuitive to use. All other Lisp dialects, so far as we know, call first and rest by the immemorable names car and cdr respectively, and you will come across those names throughout AI literature. Apart from the different names, they are exactly the same functions, and in fact Common

Lisp provides all four, since as you will see in a moment car and cdr have other advantages. In dialects other than Common Lisp, second, third etc. do not exist at all (though as you will see later, it's very easy to write them).

car and cdr are so called for historical reasons, which means that they are hangovers from the days of primitive computers when programmers had to worry about such things as the contents of the address register, and the contents of the decrement register. Such things are not important nowadays. The following two forms:

```
? (first (rest '(a b c)))
```

and

```
? (car (cdr '(a b c)))
```

will return exactly the same correct result. Most Lisps including Common Lisp also allow you to use concatenated or shorthand forms of car–cdr combinations. For example

```
? (cadr '(a b c))
```

will also return the same correct result. So car is equivalent to first, cdr is equivalent to rest, and cadr is equivalent to second. Similarly caddr, shortened from (car (cdr (cdr . . .))) is equivalent to third. The advantage of using car and cdr is that one of these days you are sure to want something like (cdr (car (cdr...))) because you will have a list whose second element is itself a list, and the data you need will be the rest of that inner list, i.e. with its first element removed. Common Lisp allows you to type cdadr instead which is certainly easier than the equivalent pseudo-English version (rest (first (rest...)))! Your Lisp manual will tell you what other car–cdr combinations it allows, but here is a brief example:

```
? (cdadr '(a (b c) d e))
```

is equivalent to

```
? (cdr (car (cdr '(a (b c) d e))))
```

Putting yourself in the place of eval, you know that the first thing to be evaluated is

```
(cdr '(a (b c) d e))
```

which returns

    '((b c) d e)

The original expression now looks like this:

    (cdr (car '((b c) d e)))

so the next thing to be evaluated is

    (car '((b c) d e))

and this returns

    (b c)

The original expression has now become

    (car '(b c))

which of course returns

    b

So the way to read the name of a car–cdr **combination function**, the way to see at a glance what it is intended to do, is to concentrate on the as and ds within it and to read them from left to right, just as eval does. Thus,

    (cddar <some nested list>)

is equivalent to

    (cdr (cdr (car <some nested list>)))

2.3.5 Getting the machine to help

You now know one way of accessing ('getting at') any member of a list, provided that you know where in the list it occurs. But before we go on, here is another useful tip.

  Useful tip   If it is tedious, get the machine to do it.

In this case, the tedious thing is repeatedly typing in the list (a b c). So we shall ask Lisp to do the job for us, by assigning the list to a variable.

Thereafter, we shall only have to type the name of the variable and eval will retrieve the list for us. If you were writing a program at this point, we would advise you to choose a meaningful or at least mnemonic name for the variable, so that when you came back to the program in a few weeks' or months' time you would at once remember the purpose of the variable and what its value was likely to be. But at the moment its only purpose is to save you some typing, and therefore a memorable name such as my-list-variable would not help! Let us call the variable q:

```
? (setf q '(a b c))
```

Read this as 'setf *the value of* q *to be quote* (a b c)'. setf returns:

```
(A B C)
```

And, just to check that the right thing has happened, ask Lisp what the value of q now is:

```
? q
(A B C)
```

Now you can try any or all of the above examples using q in place of the hand-typed list (a b c). For instance:

```
? (cdr q)
(B C)
```

In this case, when eval has retrieved the functional value of cdr and moves on to evaluate cdr's argument, it does not find a quote, and therefore it retrieves the value of q and applies cdr to it.

Of course, you could use setf to assign some other list to q, and you could try the examples out on that list too. But please do not alter the value of q for the moment: we have some more examples coming up which will rely on its having the value (a b c).

Do this:

```
? (setf qq (cdr q))
```

and setf returns

```
(B C)
```

Actually, of course, setf returns (B C) to eval, and eval returns it to you via print. But you know that by now, and the abbreviation 'setf returns' is commonplace in Lisp terminology.

You now have two variables: q whose value is the original three-element list, and qq whose value is the truncated version as returned by cdr. Check by typing the names of the variables into Lisp one by one:

```
? q
(A B C)
? qq
(B C)
```

Notice that by taking the cdr of q and assigning it to qq we have not changed the value of q. In order to change the value of q itself to its own cdr we would have to use cdr in combination with a function which would reassign the value. For example (do not type this into Lisp just now, because we want q to retain the value it has):

```
(setf q (cdr q))
```

Point to remember The vast majority of Lisp functions do not alter the data given to them as arguments. The set family of functions are quite unusual in doing so. We shall tell you as and when we introduce you to functions which do alter the values of their arguments; normally you should assume that they do not.

Exercise 2.1

(a)   Evaluate the following (that is, decide what each expression would return if evaluated):

```
(first '(a b c))
(first '(one two three))
(car '(first second third))
(second '(first second third))
(first (rest '(first second third)))
(car (cadr '(1 2 3)))
(cadr '(1 2 3))
(cadr '(car cadr caddr))
```

(b)   Suppose that the list (a b (c x y) d e) has been assigned to the variable lis via a call to setf. What expressions, using functions or combinations of functions, will when evaluated return:

The second element of lis?
The fourth element of lis?
The second element of the sublist which is the third element of lis?

(c)   Write the correct sequence of only cars and cdrs to pull out the symbol correct from the following lists. You may use cadr etc. as shorthand.

```
'(a correct)
'(a (correct))
'((a (correct)) b)
'(a b (((c d (((correct)))))))
```

2.3.6   Adding data to a list

In the course of a long program it is quite conceivable that you might
want to remove the first element of a list, in order to do some processing
on the rest of the list, and subsequently you might want to put the first
element back in place. The Lisp function which will add an element (any
element) to the front of a list is called cons. The name, like those of car
and cdr, is a hangover from the early days of Lisp, but apart from these
three most Lisp functions have suggestive names, like setf, to help you
remember what they do. cons is used in the usual way:

> ? *(cons 'a qq)*

Read this as 'cons *quote* a onto *the value of* qq'. cons returns:

> (A B C)

Here are a couple more examples:

> ? *(cons nil q)*
> (NIL A B C)

(Notice here that the actual value of q is still (A B C). The cons did not
change it.)

> ? *(cons nil '())*
> (NIL)

When discussing cdr, we said that you need to be careful that the
argument which you supply to cdr is a list, and if by accident you supply it
with an atom you will get an error message back from Lisp. It seems
obvious that the second argument to cons should also be a list, and in the
vast majority of cases where cons is used it certainly will be. But in fact
cons will allow its *second* argument also to be an atom. You may be
thinking that it does not make sense to force an atom to be the first
element of another atom, and at this stage we would have to agree with
you. But because of the way in which Lisp internally represents a list of
atoms, consing one atom onto another can under certain circumstances
make sense.

```
? (cons 'a 'b)
```

would return

```
(A . B)
```

The dot indicates that this is something extra to the definition of 'list' which we have given you up until now. We would rather leave a full explanation of what has happened until later, but we wanted you to know now, when you may decide to experiment with cons in your own way, that a result with a dot in it is not an error. Please just accept for now that if your function call, perhaps a complex one involving several of the functions which you have learned about, results in such a 'dotted pair'; it means only that somehow you have managed to cons two atoms together.

The other argument to cons, its first, may be an atom or a list.

Exercise 2.2   Evaluate the following:

```
(cons 'one '(two three))
(cons '(a) '((b) (c)))
(cons 2 0.5)
(cons 'cheese '(burger))
(cons 1 '(2 3))
(cons '(x) '(y z))
```

Useful tip   Most Lisp functions do not alter their input data.

For example, no matter how many times you type (cdr q) into Lisp, the value of q remains unchanged. That is normal for the overwhelming majority of Lisp functions; of those which we have shown you so far only setf actually causes changes (and of course it would not be much use if it did not). In order to change the value of q itself, you would have to use setf on it (but please do not, for the moment).

You will find that most of the Lisp programs which you will write use setf very sparingly if at all. This is because any such 'global' assignment permanently alters the **environment** of data in which the program is operating: the first part of the program works with one set of values assigned to its variables, and the remainder of it works with a different set. This is bad practice if only because it makes the program that much harder for another programmer to understand. We shall return to this point, and to the exact meaning of the word 'environment', in Chapter 4 when we've shown you how to define your own functions.

2.3.7 Creating lists

There are just two more list-manipulating functions which we want to
show you in this chapter: append and list.

append takes two arguments, and both of them must be lists. append
returns one list containing all the elements of both input lists, in the same
order as they appeared in the call:

```
? (append '(a b c) '(d e f))
(A B C D E F)
? (append '(you) '(us))
(YOU US)
```

Once again, if you supply an atom rather than a list as append's second
argument, you may end up with a dotted pair, or something even worse
such as

```
? (append '(a b c) 'd)
(A B C . D)
```

Once again, if this happens as you experiment with append, please do not
worry about it for now. The first argument to append must be a list,
according to the Common Lisp specification. If you insist on putting an
atom there, or even an empty list, you may get an error message or you
may simply get something incomprehensible returned. Do not do it!

list is a straightforward function. It takes any number of
arguments, each of which may be either an atom or a list, and returns a
list of them:

```
? (list 'a 'b 'c)
(A B C)
? (list '(a b c) '(d e f))
((A B C) (D E F))
? (list 'I 'am 35)
(I AM 35)
```

Remind yourself in passing that the numeral 35 did not need to be quoted
because numbers always evaluate to themselves.

Exercise 2.3   Evaluate the following:

```
(append '(a b c) '(d e f))
(append '(pork) '(and beans))
(list 'pork 'and 'beans)
(append '(pork) (list 'and 'beans))
```

```
(list 'one '(two three))
(append '(a) '((b c)))
(append 'salad '(pork and beans))
(cons 'a (append (list 'b 'c 'd) '(x y z)))
(append (list (list 'a))
  (cons 'b (cons 'c (cons 'd (list 'e)))))
(cons 'a nil)
(cons 'a ())
(cons 'a '())
(list 'a nil)
(append '(a b c) nil)
(append '(a b c) nil '(d e f) nil '(x y z))
```

The five functions car, cdr, cons, append and list are Lisp's basic list-manipulating functions. There are others; in particular, you may need one day to reverse a list. You can find out about them by looking in your Lisp manual, and if in the course of this book we use a function to which we have not specifically introduced you, please do look it up in your manual. The crucial things to know about any Lisp function are how many arguments it takes; what kind of arguments they should be; and what the function returns. car, for example, takes one argument which should be a list, and returns the first element of that list. cons takes two arguments of which the first may be an atom or a list and the second should (normally) be a list, and returns a single list whose elements are the first argument followed by the elements of the second argument.

2.3.8   setf **can do more than just simple assignment**

Now we come to something which we hope will lift your impression of Lisp above the building block level and will give you a taste of its flexibility and power. Earlier we mentioned set and setq, describing them as functions which assign values to variables. We mentioned setf in the same context and added that of the three setf was the preferred function to use. The exciting thing about setf, and the reason why it is a good thing to acquire the habit of using it, is that its ability to assign a value to a variable is actually its simplest and most primitive ability.

In the Common Lisp manual setf's two arguments are described as a **place** and a **newvalue**. As far as Lisp is concerned the name of a variable 'means' some location in the computer's memory (the location where the variable is stored and which holds a 'pointer' to the place where its value is stored), so it is quite reasonable to think of, say, q as a 'place'. But, look at this:

```
? (setf (second q) 'z)
z
```

That will change the value of the second element of the value of q, which value we hope is still the list (a b c). It will put a z in place of the b, so that if you now type

> ? q

you will get

> (A Z C)

We warned you that inside the evaluator setf was more than a mere function, and more than a mere special form. You can now see that if setf's first argument is an atom then setf behaves like setq – that is, like set except that you do not have to quote the argument. But if setf's first argument is a function call which describes how to get to a certain element of a list, only that element of that list is changed.

setf is in fact very much more powerful than this, and can be used to alter the value of single elements in most of the data structures of which Lisp is capable. For example its first argument could be the address of a single cell in an array (if you are not familiar with arrays, think of them as sets of pigeonholes into which you can put things, and from which you can later retrieve them if you've remembered which pigeonhole they are in). setf would then alter the contents of that cell to whatever you specified as setf's second argument.

setf always returns its second argument. That makes it consistent with set and setq, though when using it to do such things as to modify individual elements of lists you should remember that it *does not* return the modified list.

SUMMARY

In this chapter you have learned that Lisp lists can be not only function calls but also data objects in their own right. You have seen that Lisp has a library of inbuilt functions which can manipulate lists, and that by combining those functions, i.e. by 'nesting' them so that the returned result of one function becomes the input data to the next, you can manipulate any list in a very large number of ways.

You have been told that there is in Lisp such a thing as a 'dotted pair', and that it is not an error. We have every intention of telling you the truth about dotted pairs, but to do so will require a long section on the subject, and at the moment it would be a tedious and very difficult section to face you with. We promised you at the start that we would make Lisp easy to learn, and as you have seen already that sometimes involves telling you about certain attributes of Lisp while putting off a full explanation until you yourself know more about the language.

You have also learned that most Lisp functions do not actually change their input data, but return a result 'as if' a change had occurred. So far, only the `set` family of functions breaks this rule, and you have had some broad hints that of that family `setf` is by far the most powerful and therefore the most useful.

You have discovered that `NIL` is both an atom and an empty list. When you come, as you soon will, to understand and to write much more sophisticated list-manipulating programs, you will find that this odd and apparently pointless equivalence is in fact something without which Lisp would lose much of its elegance and conciseness.

In the next chapter we shall return to `T` and `NIL`, introducing you to a family of functions ('predicates') which only ever return one or the other. We shall show you how to use predicates to effect conditional branching, which is the machine equivalent of 'making a decision'. And then, finally, we shall be in a position to teach you the all-important skills of writing your own Lisp functions.

Chapter 3
Decision Making

This chapter covers decision making within a program and simple function definition. We often need a program to do either one thing or another, depending upon what input data we give it. There are many ways of achieving this in Lisp, and we introduce you to a range of the most-commonly used. The chapter then moves on to show you how to define your own Lisp functions, without which Lisp would be very uninteresting to use.

3.1 Decision making

Approaching a major road junction, the intelligent person looks at the signposts, and if his or her destination is indicated as being off to the right, s/he turns right at the junction. To us human beings that is such a simple response to our input data that we do not even notice that the decision (to turn right) is made. But just think for a moment of the complexity of this apparently simple cognitive act.

First there are problems of perception: we have to be able to make sense of the vast amounts of sensory data flowing in through our eyes and ears, in such a way as to distinguish and to isolate the signpost as a single, coherent object. No computer program can yet do this in anything more than a fumbling and, by human standards, hopelessly inept fashion.

Then there are problems of recognition: we need to understand what a road junction looks like and what a signpost looks like; and we have to know that roads are things along which we can travel from A to B. Even the simplest of everyday circumstances can require from us huge amounts of **world knowledge**: facts, memories, previous experiences and skills which, if we tried to put them into our programs, would raise enormous difficulties of representation and of retrieval.

Then there are the high level mental abilities involved in understanding the symbols used on signposts and of recognizing the analogy between the signpost and the junction (of realizing that it is a miniature map of the immediate surroundings). Finally, we are able to make an inference from that analogy and so discover that we should turn right. Oddly enough, computers can be quite good at recognizing analogies: just as the road sign or the map represents the actual terrain, so a computer program can be regarded as a a particular kind of representation of real-world facts and events. Computers are also quite good at making inferences from given data. We shall show you a program which makes inferences later in this book.

But in general it is true that cognitive activities which we find so easy to do that we do them almost without noticing are very hard to mimic on a computer. Conversely some mental activities which we find quite hard or which at least need thinking about (such as mathematics) are relatively easy to mimic. In one sense this is inevitable, just because the human mind is our only example of the kind of thing we are trying to create: in circumstances where we are accustomed to having to think consciously about what we are doing, it is relatively easy to write down a full and clear description of what we do; but where our actions are usually half-automatic (as in the car-driving example mentioned earlier) saying exactly what we did is much more difficult. And so, unexpectedly, it has turned out that the things which we humans do relatively rarely and only with careful thought turn out to be easier to mimic in a computer program than the things we do all day and every day.

Both human beings and virtual machines make decisions based upon whatever data is available to them at the time. If presented repeatedly with exactly the same data, the machine will invariably make the same decision (unless the computer breaks down, or someone changes its program). But a human being will often make different decisions because of the influence of factors which one could not really treat simply as data: in particular these factors include emotional states. Furthermore, human beings can make decisions based upon the real world they see around them, but for a present-day virtual machine the real world has to be translated into a form which it can understand. There would be no point in holding a road sign up to a present-day computer; you would have to program a representation of the sign, and the ability to understand it, into the machine before it could decide that turning right would be an appropriate response.

In one sense the decisions which a virtual machine can make are trivial ones, because all of the hard work of perceiving, understanding etc. the data has been done by the programmer, and all the machine has to do is to say Yes or No to a very clear-cut question. But in another sense and for exactly the same reasons these are 'high level' decisions which require intelligence. A cat or a dog can evidently perceive and understand the world around it; in other words it can do the things which computers find so hard. But most of us would agree that cats and dogs are not intelligent in the way that we humans are.

In this chapter you will learn about how to write decision-making abilities into your programs. Once you know that, we shall finally be able to teach you the most useful skill in the whole of Lisp: how to write your own functions and to combine them so as to build interesting programs.

3.2 Predicates

3.2.1 Tests for equality

Predicates, as mentioned in a previous chapter, are a class of Lisp functions which only ever return one of two logical states: **true** or **false**, expressed in Lisp as T or NIL. We have also mentioned that in Lisp anything which is not false is true, so that a predicate might well return something other than T which would count as logically 'true'. Let's start with a very simple example:

```
? (= 4 4)
T
? (= 4 5)
NIL
```

In just the same way that the function '+' took two arguments and returned their addition, so '=' takes two arguments and returns their equality (or lack of it). Of course, the order of the two arguments does not matter:

```
? (= 5 4)
NIL
```

Now try this:

```
? (= 'a 'a)
```

which will undoubtedly give you an error message. If you read the message carefully, you should be able to see that the error which caused it is the *wrong-type-argument* error which you have encountered before. And that has come about simply because '=', like '+', is an arithmetical function and expects both of its arguments to be numbers.

The Common Lisp function which can test for equality between atoms – so including both numbers and symbols – and lists is equal. As with setf, there are two other similar functions which do the same job slightly differently: eq and eql. But first, please play with equal:

```
? (equal 'a 'a)
T
? (equal 'a 'b)
NIL
? (equal 7 7)
T
? (equal 132 133)
NIL
? (equal 'a 7)
NIL
? (equal (cons 'a b) (cons 'a b))
T
? (equal 'one 1)
NIL
```

Wait a minute: why is one not equal to 1? After all, the two atoms have the same meaning. Well, no, and this is a case where 'meaning' and 'value' do not after all express quite the same thing. Lisp draws a clear distinction between **types** of data, and will not allow you to say that a number is equivalent to a symbol, even though in a tiny minority of cases (such as **one = 1**) you might be right.

However, if the *value* of one is 1:

```
? (setf one 1)
1
```

and if you do not quote it so that rule 1 of eval has to retrieve the value, you get the 'right' answer:

```
? (equal one 1)
T
```

There are several other Common Lisp predicates which test for various 'kinds' of equality. In particular, eq tests for exactly the same Lisp object. For example:

```
? (setf q (cons 'a '(b)))
(A B)
? (setf r (cons 'a '(b)))
(A B)
? (setf s q)
(A B)
```

=	arguments are numbers of any kind
eq	arguments are the same Lisp object
eql	arguments are eq, or integers
equal	arguments are eql, or the same list

Figure 3.1   Summary of Lisp equality tests.

At first sight the variables q, r and s would seem to have the 'same' value. But in fact while the values of q and s are truly the same object, the value of r is different because the two separate calls to (cons 'a 'b) created two identical but separate lists in the computer's memory. The function eq reveals this difference:

```
? (eq q r)
NIL
? (eq q s)
T
```

Remember that equal would have said that q and r were equal. By the way, it is not possible to be sure that eq will return T if its two arguments are the same number. For this reason Common Lisp provides eql. This predicate returns T if its arguments are eq or if they are the same number, and is the standard equality test in Common Lisp. eql would return NIL if given q and r as arguments. Thus eq, eql and equal lie on a scale of increasing generality of the equality test. Figure 3.1 gives a rule-of-thumb guide to the most frequent uses of the above four tests for equality; for more details, please consult Guy Steele's manual or your Lisp software's documentation.

3.2.2   Testing Lisp type

The predicate typep takes two arguments, a Lisp object and a **type**, and returns T if the object is of that type or NIL otherwise. The idea of 'typing' is a formalization of the simple idea of different 'kinds' of things. For example, characters, atoms and lists are clearly different kinds of things and are different types in Lisp. Lisp is not a very tightly typed language. What we mean by this is that most functions do not care what type of object they are given as arguments; for example the function list will accept numbers, lists, and/or symbols. Also, variables in Lisp can be assigned (or bound; see below) to any type of value, and indeed the same variable may have different types of value at different times during the running of a program. Some, more strongly typed languages insist that each variable be associated in advance with a particular type of object and will not allow values of a different type to be assigned or bound to that variable.

Several types of number are defined in Lisp. In particular, simple numerals such as 1, 2 and 3 are of one type, whereas decimal (floating-point) numbers such as 1.0, 2.0 and 3.0 are of another type. We mention this here because eql does not see numbers of different types as being equal, even though like 2 and 2.0 they may represent the same quantities.

```
? (typep 1 'fixnum)
T
? (typep 1.0 'fixnum)
NIL
```

If you ever need Lisp to do arithmetical computations for you, the function = will be more useful than any of the above. It will agree that two numbers are equal if they represent the same quantity, regardless of their types:

```
? (= 1 1.0)
T
```

3.2.3 Tests on atoms

Two other very useful predicates are null and atom. The first tests for an empty list:

```
? (null nil)
T
```

Or, assuming that q still has its value of '(a b c):

```
? (null q)
NIL
```

If you imagine working through that recipe again, going through it instruction by instruction and perhaps using cdr each time to get at the next member of the overall list, you would want to know when you had reached the end of the list. In programmatic terms, a test using null would be the way to do it.

atom tests to see whether its argument is an atom (i.e. a symbol or a number):

```
? (atom q)
NIL
? (atom 'q)
T
? (atom 2)
T
```

If your program were working its way down a list which contained as elements both atoms and sublists, you might want it to do different things according to which type (atom or list) the current element was. You could use atom to test each element, and then have the program act accordingly.

Apart from those already mentioned, the majority of Lisp's inbuilt predicates have names which end with the letter 'p', for 'predicate'. When you come to write your own functions it will be good Lisp style also to end the names of your own predicates with a 'p'.

```
? (numberp 2)
T
? (symbolp 2)
NIL
```

The number 2 is not a Lisp symbol: you cannot treat it as a variable and assign it a value.

Exercise 3.1

(a)   Choose the most appropriate predicate to test for equality between

    (i)   two numbers
    (ii)   two symbols
    (iii)   a symbol and a number
    (iv)   two lists

(b)   Which of the following will cause errors if evaluated?

```
(symbolp 9)
(symbolp 'nine)
(zerop 'zero)
(atom 9)
(atom 'zero)
(eql '(a) '(a))
(= 'a 'a)
(equal 9 9)
(null '(a b c))
(null ())
```

(c)   Evaluate the following forms:

```
(atom 4)
(setf x 4)
```

```
(atom x)
(atom 'x)
(symbolp x)
(symbolp 'x)
(setf y 'x)
(symbolp y)
(eql 1 1)
(eql x 4)
(= x 4)
(eql x 4.0)
(= x 4.0)
(setf l1 '(a b c))
(setf l2 '(a b c))
(eq l1 l2)
(eql l1 l2)
(eq 'l1 'l1)
(eq l1 l1)
(equal l1 l2)
(equal l1 (cons 'a (list 'b 'c)))
```

3.3 Logical operators

The Common Lisp manual groups predicates along with a small set of
superficially similar functions called logical operators.

not returns the logical inverse of its argument:

```
? (not t)
NIL
? (not nil)
T
```

As a matter of fact not and null are exactly the same, and could be used
interchangeably. As a matter of style, it is customary to use null to test
for an empty list and to use not to invert a logical value. not is not needed
very often, but occasionally you might want to test for the absence of
something. For example, if you wanted for some reason, in the depths of
a large program, to divide one number by another and hence wanted to
be sure that the second number was not zero (anything divided by zero
gives an indeterminate answer) you might use not and zerop. Similarly, if
you need to know that the value of one variable was not the same as the
value of another, you could use not and equal. not is almost invariably
used to 'negate' the returned value of some other predicate, so as to
invert its logical meaning.

and and or are much more useful, and are unlike any function we have shown you so far. In fact they are not ordinary functions (not is, by the way) but are macros, like setf. (Remember? – macros, like special forms, change the behaviour of eval to suit themselves.)

Both and and or can take as many arguments as you like. Inside eval each of those arguments, in normal left to right order, is evaluated just as you would expect. What makes and and or different is that the process is a **conditional evaluation**. This means that under certain circumstances evaluation will stop and a value will be returned, even though there may be one or many arguments remaining which have not yet been evaluated.

As and evaluates its arguments in turn, if any one of them evaluates to NIL then and returns NIL. Otherwise it returns whatever (non-NIL) value was returned by evaluation of its last argument. or does just the opposite: if any one of its arguments, evaluated in sequence, returns a non-NIL value then or returns that value immediately; but if all of its arguments evaluate to NIL then it returns NIL.

Another way, the logical way, of looking at this is that and returns TRUE (it returns T) only if its first argument and its second argument and its third argument etc. are TRUE (they evaluate to T); otherwise it returns FALSE (i.e. NIL). or returns TRUE if its first argument or its second argument or its third argument etc. is TRUE; otherwise it returns FALSE.

> *Point to remember*   When we use 'T' in its logical sense, we mean anything which is not NIL.

Please try these examples, which again assume that the variable q has the value (a b c). If it has not, just use setf as usual to ensure that it has. Then type:

```
? (and q (second q) (setf qq 17))
T
```

What will happen when eval encounters this form? Since you now know of more than one macro, we shall make a slight addition to the rules of the evaluator:

(1)   If the expression is an atom, return its value.

(2)   If the expression is a list, then either

       (a)   if the first member of the list is a special form, handle it and its arguments accordingly.

       (b)   **if the first member of the list is a macro, handle it and its arguments accordingly.**

(c)   If the first member of the list has a functional value then retrieve that function, and

    (i)   find the values of the remaining members of the list by applying these rules to each of them in turn;

    (ii)   apply the function from (c) to the arguments from (i), and return the result.

and has been given three arguments, of which the first is a variable and the second and third are function calls. The variable q is evaluated by rule 1; it certainly has a value and that value is not NIL, so and's first argument is logically equivalent to T. The second argument, the call to second, evaluates via rule 2b to the atom b, and so again counts as T. The third argument to and is a call to setf, evaluated via rule 2b, and we hope that you remember that setf always returns its second argument. Its second argument in this case is 17, so the value returned by setf is also logically equivalent to T. Since all of and's arguments evaluated to T, and itself returned T.

Before going on we would like to say a few words about rule 2a, which as it stands is not really a rule at all but is just a marker to remind you that we have promised to give a full explanation, and to produce the correct rule, later on. For now, all you need to remember is that if a function is classed as a special form it changes the behaviour of the evaluator, and that in the two examples you know of, quote and setq, what happens is that one of the special form's arguments does not get evaluated.

Where a function is classed as a macro you know that some macros (e.g. setf) can similarly inhibit evaluation, and that some of them (e.g. and and or) can control how many of their arguments are evaluated. In fact special forms and macros are quite similar from the user's point of view, which is why for the moment we have specified just one rule to cover both of them. Eventually, you will learn that though you cannot write your own special forms in Common Lisp, you can write your own macros.

If you care to check, you will find that during evaluation of and the call to setf also 'worked', so that the value of qq is now 17. Please remember the important distinction to be drawn between the value which a function or a program returns and anything else it may change in the process. These other changes, such as those caused by setf, are known as **side-effects**. Most of the external behaviour of a program will be accomplished via side-effects; for example a running program may print things on the screen, or operate a robot arm, or attempt to understand spoken English. We have talked of the behaviour of the virtual machine as being of overriding importance in AI and in cognitive science research, and in general that behaviour will be the result of side effects rather than of any returned value.

In other words, returned values are of crucial importance when considering how a program works (via eval), while side-effects are of crucial importance to what it does.

Let us go back to and and or:

```
? (and q (second q) (setf qq nil))
NIL
```

You can probably see at once, because only the second argument to setf has been changed from the above example, that now and's third argument will evaluate to NIL, so that and itself will also return NIL. How about applying or to the same set of arguments?

```
? (or q (second q) (setf qq nil))
T
```

In this case, or returned T almost immediately because its very first argument evaluated to something other than NIL. If you have checked that qq has the value NIL (because of setf's side-effect upon it above) you can prove that or did not bother to evaluate its subsequent arguments such as:

```
? (or q (setf qq t))
T
? qq
NIL
```

which shows that the value of qq has not been changed by the call to setf. Therefore, the second argument to or in this latest example was not evaluated.

> *Point to remember*   It is worth remembering that when one of the arguments to or contains a side-effect, that side-effect may or may not 'happen' depending upon the results of evaluating any earlier arguments to the or.

The main programming uses of and and or are just what their names suggest: if you want something to happen only if several conditions (perhaps the values of several variables) are all non-nil, then you would use and. Conversely, if you wanted something to happen whenever even one of those conditions is non-nil, then you would us or.

Exercise 3.2   Evaluate the following forms:

```
(and (car '(a)) (cdr '(1 2 3)))
(or (car '(a)) (null (cdr '(a))))
```

Evaluate the following form three times, with x assigned to NIL, 2 or 'NO:

```
(and (or (null x)
         (atom x))
     (or (symbolp x)
         (eq x 'no)))
```

3.4 Conditional forms

The simplest of Common Lisp's conditional forms is if, which is another special form. At last, after all this talk of decisions being made within a program, we can show you how that is achieved. A simple if expression might look like this:

```
? (if (null q) (setf qq t)
      (setf qq nil))
```

This should be read as 'If the list q is empty then (setf qq t), else (setf qq nil)'. Please notice that if itself, the conditional (i.e. predicate) test, and the action to be taken if that test evaluates to T, are traditionally put on the same line, while the action to be taken if the test evaluates to NIL is put on a lower line. Lisp will not care if you don't do this (your if form will still work) but it is a matter of style: to improve the readability of your programs. While on this subject, we mentioned before that null and not were the same function, so that you could equally well say:

```
? (if (not q) (setf qq t)
      (setf qq nil))
```

and another alternative form of the same expression could be:

```
? (if (eq q nil) (setf qq t)
      (setf qq nil))
```

Although all three forms are logically identical and would all behave in exactly the same way inside a program, we hope you can see that the first is the most elegant, and is the easiest to read, given that the value of q is actually a list. Good Lisp style, which is one of the things we are trying to give you a feel for, is very largely a matter of readability. Lisp is not the same language as English, and we are not for one moment trying to pretend that it is; but if for example you use null (rather than not or equal) when you are testing for a list, that makes the most 'English' sense, and anyone reading your program later on would guess from the null that a list was involved. Another way of describing good Lisp style is to say that you the programmer do your best to make things easy for anyone who may subsequently look at your program and try to understand it. We have mentioned before, for example, that it is good practice to choose meaningful or mnemonic names for your variables.

The general form of the three if statements above could be summarized as follows. (The angle brackets, here and from now on, enclose bits of text which are not real Lisp. Please do not try to type them into Lisp.):

```
(if <condition> <action>
    <action>)
```

The words 'then' and 'else' which the good programmer mutters while writing an if statement are implicit in the actual Lisp code. One of the joys of Common Lisp is that it does not require you to type any more words than are absolutely necessary.

if is Lisp's simplest form of **conditional statement**, allowing only one ‹action› whether the conditional test succeeds or fails. This, for example, would cause an error in Common Lisp:

```
(if <condition> <action> <action> ... <action>
    <action> <action> ... <action>)
```

However, there is a conditional form which is used far more often than if, simply because it is more flexible about the number of ‹tests› and the number of ‹actions› it allows you. Otherwise it is quite similar to if:

```
(cond (<condition> <action> <action> ... <action>)
      (<condition> <action> <action> ... <action>))
```

Notice that besides the outer set of parentheses as in if, each group of one test plus one or more actions has its own set of delimiting parentheses. Each group is known as a **clause** of the cond, and although we have shown only two for the sake of brevity there can in a working cond be as many clauses as you need. In a cond, each of the conditional tests is evaluated in turn. If any of them succeeds (i.e. returns T or at any rate something other than NIL) then all of the corresponding actions are evaluated. The value returned by the cond is then the value returned by evaluation of the last action.

In the case where none of the conditions succeeds, the cond would return NIL, but in the vast majority of cond statements which you will ever see the final clause is an 'if all else fails' clause. For this reason, the programmer needs to be sure that that clause's conditional test will *always* evaluate to T, and the one thing in Lisp which can never evaluate to other than T is T itself:

```
(cond (<condition> <action> <action> ... <action>)
      (<condition> <action> <action> ... <action>)
       (t <action> <action> ... <action>))
```

Because the conditional tests are usually function calls with their own set of surrounding parentheses, a cond statement has a characteristic double opening parenthesis at the start of its main clauses. But notice from the 'T' clause that the test can be simply the value of a variable, in which case there is only one opening parenthesis in that position:

```
(cond ((null lis) (<do something>))
      (t (<do something else...>)))
```

Novice Lisp programmers often miss out the double parentheses at first, perhaps because they look so unlikely! But if you miss out one of the parentheses preceding null in the above expression, and then evaluate the expression, you'll get an error message from Lisp complaining that null is an unbound variable.

> *Useful Tip*   When the ‹test› in a cond expression is a function, such as null, a characteristic double parenthesis appears at the start of the clause, following the actual word cond, as above. When the test is the value of a variable, T being the only example you have seen so far, there is only one parenthesis at the start of the clause.

We shall return to cond statements in a later chapter when introducing recursion.

3.5   Function definition

A programming language which did not give its users the ability to define new functions would be truly the computational equivalent of a building block set, and would be virtually useless for AI purposes. Defining a new function allows you to choose an arbitrary selection from the 770-odd inbuilt Common Lisp functions, known as its **primitives**, and as it were to encapsulate them so that they will all be evaluated in sequence. You then give the whole thing a name, and thereafter you can use that name as though it were itself a function call to a Lisp primitive. In other words, you will have added a function of your own to your Lisp.

As you have probably already guessed, the way to encapsulate a series of Lisp primitive functions is to put them into a list:

```
((print item) (setf qq (cdr item)) (print qq))
```

This is a list of three elements, each of which is a function call. But of course it is not yet a function definition. It needs three more things. First, it needs the all-important name, so that when the function is defined you will be able to call it. Whenever Lisp experts want to write a function which does nothing in particular other than demonstrate some point, and which they will not want to keep around for more than a few minutes, they always call the function foo. No-one knows why. When you do call the function, you'll probably want it to take one or more arguments:

```
(foo ...)
```

so the second thing the above list needs is a 'slot' to hold those arguments; the slot is known as the **parameter list** and the items within it (which will be the names of variables) are known as **parameters**. Finally the list needs the macro defun (short for **def**ine a **fun**ction), which tells eval that this is a function definition and should therefore be attached to the name as the latter's functional value:

```
(defun foo (item) (print item) (setf qq (cdr item)) (print qq))
```

To a Lisp user, that is almost unreadable. Function definitions are normally indented like this:

```
(defun foo (item)
  (print item)
  (setf qq (cdr item))
  (print qq))
```

which is much neater. Now the individual calls to primitives within the definition are in a neat vertical column, known as the **body** of the definition. The **name** sits alongside defun so that anyone can see at once what is being defined, and alongside that is the slot, actually a sublist of the overall list, containing the name of foo's single argument.

However, do not expect Lisp to produce this stylish indentation for you as you type something like the above definition into your computer: it almost certainly will not. Many programmers type spaces at the start of the second and any subsequent lines of code typed in at top level, merely so that to them the indentation looks normal. This is because they are used to typing their code into an editor, and the majority of Lisp editors do indent the code as it is typed into them. Once you get a feel for how the indentation of any piece of code should look (we have taken care to indent everything in this book correctly) you will find it an invaluable aid to fault finding. We shall cover use of the editor in the next chapter.

It is important to notice in the above definition of foo that item is not an argument to foo. It is a parameter, and is the name of a variable.

You will supply the argument to foo when you call the function, and please remember that in the general case this could be a quoted value, a variable which had a value, or even another function call. The value of whatever argument you do supply will be temporarily **bound** to the variable item, and that binding will remain in force until the end of the function is reached. Thus, when evaluating the function, every time eval comes across item it substitutes the value which you initially gave (unless of course one of the calls in the body of the function changes that value). For the moment, please think of binding as though it meant the same as assignment. Notice also that the variable qq is not a bound variable: it does not acquire a temporary value by virtue of being a parameter to printem like item. it is in fact a global variable, so called because it retains permanently the value given to it by setf. We shall return to these points in the next chapter.

Type the definition into Lisp. If you do not make any mistakes Lisp will reply simply with the name of the function, FOO.

> *Point to remember*   If Lisp does not simply return 'FOO', and you
> can see no obvious mistakes in your definition, check that you have
> the right numbers of opening and closing parentheses in all the
> right places, and in none of the wrong ones.

At this point the call to the macro defun is finished with. eval has stored away the parameter list and the body of the definition as the functional value of foo, and from now on will treat calls to foo just as it treats calls to any other Lisp function. foo is neither a special form nor a macro; it is a simple function. Exactly what a functional value looks like is not important for now, and it will do no harm if you think of it as comprising the original list of calls to primitives:

```
((print item) (setf qq (cdr item)) (print qq))
```

together with the parameter list. It is important not to forget the parameter list. Now try:

```
? (foo)
```

You'll get an error message, which you may have come across before, telling you that you have given the wrong number of arguments to foo. foo really is behaving just like a 'real' Lisp function. Let us look at another error condition:

```
? (foo item)
```

This time the error message, which again you may have seen before, will tell you that item is an unbound variable. Before going on to use foo properly, try out one final error:

> *? (foo 'item)*

Lisp will obey the first instruction, the first call to a primitive in the body of foo, by printing the atom item. But then it will complain that it cannot take the cdr of an atom, and if you look at the second call in the body of the function you will see that one of the arguments to setf does indeed ask for the cdr of item.

Now let us do it properly. If the value of q is not (a b c), please setf it first.

> *? (foo q)*

    (A B C)
    (B C)
    (B C)

The second (B C) appears there because of the rule that Lisp functions must always return a value. When you the programmer do not specifically tell the function what to return, it automatically returns the value of the last of its internal forms to be evaluated. If you check the value of qq at this point, you will find that it is also (B C). Let us look at what happened in more detail.

Recap Box

(1)   If the expression is an atom, return its value.

(2)   If the expression is a list, then either

    (a)   If the first member of the list is a special form, handle it and its arguments accordingly.

    (b)   If the first member of the list is a macro, handle it and its arguments accordingly.

    (c)   If the first member of the list has a functional value then retrieve that function, and

        (i)   find the values of the remaining members of the list by applying these rules to each of them in turn;

        (ii)   apply the function from (c) to the arguments from (i), and return the result.

When you typed (foo q) it was passed straight to eval by read. eval recognized the atom foo as the name of a function, because the macro defun had earlier told it so. So as usual and via rule 2c eval retrieved foo's functional value and then via rule 2c(i) proceeded to evaluate foo's

argument. The value of q turned out to be (a b c). There remains rule
2c(ii) to obeyed, which tells eval to 'apply' foo to its evaluated argument.
Up until now that word has not caused any difficulty because it has
seemed quite obvious what must happen if, say, we apply '+' to some
numbers: they get added up. But what does it mean to 'apply' something
like this:

        ((print item) (setf qq (cdr item)) (print qq))

to a value which looks like this:

        (A B C)

Actually, it is quite simple. What has to happen is that each separate
function call in the former list has to be evaluated *in the context* of the
value denoted in this case by (A B C). Remember that we said it would be
important not to forget the parameter list, and that inside eval the
parameter item would be bound to the value of the argument which you
supplied to foo? So in order to apply foo to its argument eval first
evaluates the argument, then binds the result to foo's parameter, and then
evaluates the list (the body of the original function definition) with that
binding in force. The binding is the 'context' referred to above.

The first element of the list is

        (print item)

so eval retrieves the functional value of print and applies it to the value of
item, with the side-effect that the list

        (A B C)

appears on the screen. The second element of the list is

        (setf qq (cdr item))

so eval retrieves the functional value of setf. Then it has to evaluate
setf's second argument (remember, setf tells eval not to evaluate its first
argument), and the resulting value is (B C). The side-effect of setf is to
bind this value to the variable qq. The final element of the list is

        (print qq)

which as before results in a printout on the screen:

        (B C)

The list is now empty, so evaluation of it comes to a halt. All that remains is for eval to obey the rule that it must return a value, and as mentioned before in default of any specific instruction to the contrary eval returns whatever was returned by the last form it evaluated. In this case the last form was a call to print, and it just happens that print always returns the value of its own argument. So (B C) appears on the screen a second time: not because of foo's call to print but because eval returned it via the normal read–eval–print loop.

> *Point to remember* As we mentioned earlier it is good style to avoid giving variables the same names as functions. An extreme example would be to use 'foo' in place of 'item' throughout the above! But a common temptation is to use list as a parameter name when, as in this case, it will later acquire a value which will be a list. As you know, list is the name of a Lisp primitive, and although eval would not complain (it would know that something specified in a parameter list was not a function call), and although foo would still work, it could well confuse you or others later on. You could always use lis, or even simply l, instead for the parameter name.

Here is another example definition:

```
(defun first-two (lis)
  (list (car lis) (cadr lis)))
```

Once again, eval will evaluate the body of the function definition in the context of the value supplied as an argument to first-two, that value having been bound to the parameter lis. Please type the definition into Lisp, and as before if all goes well Lisp will reply with the function name FIRST-TWO. Now try:

```
? (first-two '(this that the-other))
```

Evaluating this function-call, eval first retrieves the functional value of first-two and then evaluates the argument you gave, binding the result – the list (a b c) – to the parameter lis. Then it comes to the body of the function definition, which tells it to apply the function list to two arguments: the car (or first element) of lis and the cadr (or second element) of lis. The calls to car and cadr respectively return this and that; list makes a list out of them, and eval duly returns it to you via print:

```
(THIS THAT)
```

A third and final example allows you to see if in action again:

```
(defun baz (x)
   (if (numberp x) (+ 3 x)
       x))
```

If x is a number, baz returns a number which is 3 greater than x. Else if x is not a number baz returns the value of x itself:

```
? (baz 'tony)
TONY
? (baz 5)
8
```

Exercise 3.3   We now ask you to write code! Assume that you have used setf to give values to two variables x and y. We want you to use your knowledge of predicates and of if and cond to write code to achieve the following:

(a)   If x is an atom return it otherwise return its car.

(b)   If x is an atom return it, if not if y is an atom return that, otherwise return NIL.

(c)   Return x if it is an atom; y if it is an atom ; a list x and y if both are atoms; NIL otherwise.

Do the above using only if at first, then only cond.

Exercise 3.4
(a)   Define a function addbits which takes two lists of three numbers as its arguments, and returns a list containing the sum of the corresponding numbers from each list:

```
? (addbits '(2 4 6) '(4 5 6))
(6 9 12)
```

(b)   Define a predicate allnums-p which takes a list of three elements as its argument and returns T only if all three elements are numbers.

(c)   Define a function careful-addbits which takes two lists of three elements. If the elements of both lists are all numbers it returns a list of their sums as in (a); otherwise it returns (non number found).

Exercise 3.5
(a)   Define a function numargs which takes two arguments. It checks that both arguments are numbers and if they are it returns the sum of them. But if either argument is not a number, numargs prints the offending (non-numeric) argument and returns NIL.

(b)   Redefine numargs so that if either argument is non-numeric it returns NIL
          without printing anything, but if both are non-NIL it prints an offensive
          message to the programmer. This version should still return the sum of its
          arguments when they are both numbers. (Hint: to get print to print more
          than a single atom, list the atoms which you want it to print. It will then
          print the list.)

SUMMARY

In this chapter we have talked about predicates, and about how a
predicate can be used as the test in a conditional form, so that a
program can make decisions. So far we have shown you only two
conditional forms, if and cond, but you will come across others later on.
We have also taught you the basics of function definition, and have
extended our explanation of the Lisp evaluator.

The next chapter starts with a few brief hints on editing your Lisp
programs rather than laboriously and repeatedly typing them in at top
level, but its main purpose will be to introduce you to some major
programming techniques so that you can begin to write for yourself
more interesting programs.

Chapter 4
The Programming Environment

This chapter concludes our tour of the essential concepts of Lisp programming. We discuss the practical question of using an editor to speed up program writing, and then return to Lisp itself to describe variable binding and variable scoping, which two terms together define the 'lifetime' during which a given variable retains a given value. We show how the let macro gives you control over variable binding. We end this chapter with three simple but powerful programming techniques: looping, mapping and the use of auxiliary functions.

4.1 The editing environment

4.1.1 What it comprises

So far in this book you have been typing the various examples and exercises directly into Lisp: into its **top level**. The word 'level' refers to levels of recursion, and since the next chapter is all about recursion you can expect us to explain what it means shortly. Typing directly into Lisp's top level is a very handy way of trying out simple little function calls such as the ones we have shown you so far, but if you initially made any mistakes when typing in your definition of foo, you'll probably have reflected that there must be an easier way; and of course there is.

Any manufacturer's Common Lisp product will come complete with some kind of **programming environment**, that is to say besides Common Lisp itself it will provide certain tools to aid programming. In particular it will have tools for debugging (getting the mistakes out of) your Lisp code: almost certainly a tracer (see next chapter) and if you are lucky a stepper (see Chapter 8). It will have an error system to provide appropriate messages whenever eval encounters a bug (a mistake) in your code. More to the point for this chapter, it will contain an **editor**. The editor will allow you to create functions and even whole programs outside Lisp, and then in a very simple manner to read them directly into Lisp just as though you had laboriously typed each definition into top level. Because it is so easy and convenient to go from the editor to Lisp or vice versa, the editor is described as being 'integrated' with the Lisp; very often the two will coexist as separate 'windows' on the same screen. If you are familiar with using such editors in a programming context, please nonetheless glance through the rest of this section because it contains a few general points about Lisp which we would not want you to miss.

4.1.2   The editor

Virtually all computer users these days are, we feel, likely to be familiar with word-processing software: computer packages which allow you to write documents (such as this chapter) on a computer rather than on a typewriter. The main advantage of doing so is that nothing gets printed on paper until you are happy with it, and meanwhile the correction of mistakes, or even a major reorganization, are by comparison blissfully easy. A word processor also 'knows' quite a bit about how to produce attractive-looking results, and has many facilities for formatting blocks of text or for styling individual words; most of them also allow you to 'import' diagrams and pictures into your document, and to manipulate them in various ways. In short, a word processor is a sophisticated tool for generating the printed word.

Many computer users may also have come across text editors. These are essentially 'dumb' word processors, which 'know' nothing about formatting or styling but will allow you to create 'plain text' documents, frequently called files, such as you might need for transmission to someone else via electronic mail. Your Lisp editor will generate only plain text and hence is not a word processor, but it similarly is not a mere text editor: it 'knows' a good deal about Lisp code. For example you will probably find that as you type into your editor it can automatically produce the all-important correct 'shape' of a Lisp expression (we mentioned this earlier, when introducing defun). If you read the editor section of the manual which came with your Lisp you will certainly find that the editor can help you in many other ways such as enabling you to manipulate individual expressions within more complex Lisp functions, and so on.

Regrettably we cannot tell you exactly what facilities your editor will provide, since the Common Lisp specification does not include the editor and therefore software designers are free to include any editor they like. This is not a failure of Common Lisp; it is a perfectly sensible omission, since of course it is perfectly possible in desperate circumstances to create Lisp code on either a simple text editor or a word processor. But we do urge you to explore the abilities of whatever editor you have: you are likely to find that it is a very powerful aid to the creation of elegant, readable and of course above all working Lisp programs. Here follows a brief description of how you would use such an editor.

4.1.3   Top level

When you start up your Common Lisp, it will certainly present you with a Lisp top level, and a prompt ready for you to type something. This may be in a clearly defined window of its own, in which case there will be a way (consult your manual) of summoning the editor to run in a different window. On some systems the top level may not be in a window but will fill the whole screen, and here you will find that a special keystroke sequence (or perhaps a dedicated 'function key') will transfer you to a similarly full-screen editing environment. Consult your software manual.

Besides discovering how to get into your editor, you also need to find out how to get back again, to Lisp top level. This may again be a key sequence or a function key, or it may be a choice from a pull-down or pop-up menu. You will probably find that there are two ways of getting back to Lisp: you may simply want to try out a fragmentary expression before incorporating it into your growing function, but more often you will have used the editor to modify a buggy function. In this case you will want the function's new and hopefully correct version to overwrite the old one, and so as well as returning to Lisp you will need to have the new definition both read and evaluated just as though you had typed it into top level by hand.

4.1.4   The edit–run cycle

You will find that in creating a function or program you go through a cycle: edit (first attempt at writing the function), run (try it out at top level: it will probably turn out to have a bug), edit (correct the bug), run (there will probably be another bug), and so on. This edit–run cycle is the fastest way yet discovered of creating successful programs, and it is so fast because Lisp is an **interpreted** language. This means that your code is handled directly by read and eval. In most other languages there is an intervening stage where your code is **compiled** into some more basic and even more arcane language which the computer can understand. Such languages have no equivalent of the Lisp evaluator, and this is why we stress the evaluator so much in this book: if you understand eval, you will be able to understand any Common Lisp program ever written just by looking up any unfamiliar primitive functions in the manual.

(An aside for those who insist on the full story: eval itself, like all other primitive Lisp functions, is probably written in the above-mentioned 'language which the computer can understand'. This is generically known as **assembler** or **machine code**, and its precise form depends upon what microchip is used as your computer's central processor. But of course it is possible to mimic the abilities of eval by writing a suitable program in any language. Throughout this book we present eval as though it were written in Lisp, and we believe that this is the only lie we tell you. Our excuse is that our description of eval using Lisp-like forms and Lisp terminology will be accurate and complete, and that our objective is to teach you to understand eval, not to write assembler code.)

4.1.5   Other editing facilities

Getting back to our discussion of the editor, you need to find out how to operate one other crucial facility, and that is how to 'save' your code once you have written it and got it working. Saving means creating a file on your computer's disk to which your code is written. You give the file a name, so that at some later time you can restore your carefully created functions to Lisp, rather than having to type them all out again into Lisp's top level. The facility is sometimes called 'writing'. The means of getting your functions back may be associated with the editor, so that you 'load' your file into the editor and then return to Lisp using read and eval, or it may well be possible to load the file directly into Lisp. Please consult your manual on all of these points: if we could simply tell you the answers we would do so.

As you work through this book, and especially from Chapter 9 onwards, it will be a good idea to keep all of the functions which you define for any one chapter in a file together. If you were to put everything – all the code in this book – into one huge file you would have to wait ages for it to load into Lisp, every time.

Please have a good look at what facilities your editor offers. It may well be a version of the hugely popular EMACS editor, which is essentially an ordinary screen-based text editor, but with the considerable added advantage that it 'knows' a good deal about Lisp and can help you

to write correct programs from the start. Check to see whether your
editor does parenthesis balancing – as you type in a closing parenthesis,
does the cursor automatically blink back to a previous opening
parenthesis? If you deliberately place the cursor on an opening
parenthesis, does it blink forward to the corresponding closing parenthesis? This automatic balancing can save you literally hours of work in
chasing down misplaced parentheses, so if it does not seem to work the
first time you try it, do check in your manual: there may be some special
steps to take so as to get it working.

Secondly, start typing a function, any old function, such as

```
(defun foo (x) ...
```

Do not type the dots: type a carriage return instead. If your cursor is now
sitting under the e of defun rather than at the start of the line, you can be
happy. It means that your editor can do **automatic indenting** of your code
as you type it. We have said before that correct, or at least conventional,
indenting can be a huge help in understanding written Lisp code.
Towards the end of this chapter you will meet some functions which will
give more force to that statement: you will see at once if you think about
it that to write them with any other indentation than we show would only
make them even more confusing to look at! We do urge you, now that
you have reached the point where you can write multiline function
definitions, to acquire the habit of giving the correct indentation to your
lines, even if you are typing them into top level. We shall show ourselves
doing this after every Lisp prompt in this book. Once it becomes
instinctive to you to indent properly, the fact that your (auto-indenting)
editor may occasionally appear to give you the wrong indentations will be
an infallible pointer to the whereabouts of a bug.

A third useful thing which EMACS-like and many other editors do
for you is to allow you to pass a single expression from your editing
window to Lisp, there to be evaluated just as though you had typed it to
the Lisp prompt yourself. The expression itself may be as simple as a call
to setf, or as complex as the definition of a large function. This ability to
eval (or more probably to read and hence to eval) a single expression
from the possibly large file of expressions which is showing in your editor
window saves you the tedium of having to write and then to reload the
whole file every time you make a small change to just one function, say.

Although few if any Lisp top levels automatically indent code as
you type it in (normally, of course, you would never type more than a
one-liner to the Lisp prompt: you would first create the form in your
editor and then transfer it to Lisp) many of them do allow a certain
amount of editing of anything typed to the Lisp prompt. In particular,
you may be able to move the cursor back and forth and to edit what you
have just typed. You may also be able 'bring down' earlier entries (which

have since disappeared off the top of the screen) and to re-evaluate them as if you had retyped them to the prompt. As ever, please take the trouble to explore your software manual: it is almost certain to repay your effort.

We will cover other parts of the standard Lisp programming environment in a later chapter.

Review

You may be surprised to hear that you have now completed the first stage of learning Lisp. You can put together the basic 'nuts and bolts' of Lisp so as to achieve desired results, and we are about to move on to discuss some of the techniques which can add power and flexibility to your programs. There is actually a good deal more which we want you to know about the basics; in particular we have not yet covered the very useful concept of cons cells. We will return to cons cells in a later chapter, but for the moment we think it important to try to retain your interest during these early stages: despite their usefulness, cons cells are not really very interesting!

At this point we strongly urge you to go back over the examples and exercises in the earlier chapters, but this time using your editor instead of Lisp top level. Carry on until you feel reasonably familiar with your editor, in particular with the operation described in this chapter. It will be half an hour or so well spent, since as we have already said the sole purpose of the editor is to make your work with Lisp easier and quicker. Fairly soon now we shall be asking you to write larger pieces of Lisp code, and if you were to try to type each one into top level by hand you would soon be screaming with frustration.

4.2 Scoping

The first of the techniques which we wish to show you in this chapter is the **scoping** of variables. As we said at the end of the previous chapter it is not strictly speaking a technique since except under rather special circumstances you the programmer have no control over it. However, it is a crucially important attribute of Lisp, made use of by a number of very useful special forms and macros to some of which we shall introduce you in a minute. If you grasp the principle of variable scoping, you will write programs which contain substantially fewer bugs than if you do not grasp it.

Suppose that you have a variable, q, which has been bound via setf to the value (a b c). And suppose that you also have this silly function:

```
(defun sillyfunction (q)
  (print q))
```

which, as you can see, does nothing other than print its single argument.
The question is, what is printed by the call to (print q) if you now type
into top level:

> ? (sillyfunction 3)

Will it print the argument which you supplied to sillyfunction, which was
the number 3; or will it print the previously existing value of q which was
the three-element list (a b c)?
    And how about this pair of functions:

```
(defun even-sillier-function (q)
  (setf q 'oaktree)
  (fiddle))

(defun fiddle ()
  (print q))
```

which we call as before:

> ? (even-sillier-function 3)

Now what will be printed: 3; oaktree; or the list (a b c)? Our purpose is
not to play pointless guessing games with you but to suggest that later on,
when you are writing large programs of your own, it would be very
inconvenient to have to be continually checking that you had not used the
same variable name twice. Even worse, imagine yourself as part of a team
of programmers who together were building a huge program whose
variable names must never clash. What is needed here is some simple rule
of thumb which will restrict your own personally chosen variable names
to the values which you intend them to have, and which will not
accidentally pick up inappropriate values from other parts of the
program. And variable scoping provides exactly that rule of thumb. Let
us explain.
    Imagine that you have in front of you a Lisp prompt, and that you
have just run up Lisp itself and have not yet loaded anything into it, you
have not defined any functions in it, and most importantly you have not
bound any variables in it. It is a virginally pure and empty Lisp,
containing only the standard primitive functions and eval. Now you type

> ? (setf q '(a b c))

You know what this does: the value of q is now the three-element list
(a b c). Next, you define a function by hand into top level:

> ? (defun foo ()
>   (print q))

and you call it:

```
? (foo)
```

We hope you will agree that, whatever you may have thought above, the call to foo now results in the printing of the current value of q, which is the list (a b c). In this case q is described as a **global** variable, which means that, unless there is good reason to the contrary, its value is whatever it was originally bound to by your initial call to setf. What was special about that initial call to setf was not that it came first, but that you typed it directly into top level: it was not an integral part of one or other of your function definitions.

This hypothetical large program we have been talking about would almost certainly be something which you had worked on over many Lisp sessions, and therefore it would be something which you would normally load into Lisp from a file, rather than typing it all in by hand every time. So far, we have talked about such files as though they contained only a series of Lisp functions, but in fact they can contain anything which you could type by hand from top level. Remember, when the file is loaded into Lisp, it goes via the normal read function just as though you had typed everything in it by hand. So that if the file contains the single form

```
(setf q '(a b c))
```

the variable q is assigned to (a b c) exactly as if you had typed the instruction into top level yourself. So loading of the file into your initially bare Lisp would also result in this global assignment of the list to q, and any of your subsequent functions (until you close Lisp down, of course) can **refer** to that value: they can make use of it, or they can alter it via another setf instruction.

But if one of your functions has a parameter named q the evaluator will do something very special. It will 'save away' any existing value of q and will use that value of q which is supplied as an argument when the function is called. So when eval comes to deal with sillyfunction as defined above it will save away the global value of q, which is a three-element list, and will use the local value of 3. The call to

```
? (sillyfunction 3)
```

will result in the 3's being printed. The temporary, local change in the value of q is known as a **binding**. However, when the evaluation of sillyfunction is finished, the local binding of q to 3 will be undone, and if you check from hand at top level you will find that q once again has its assigned value (a b c). The effect is as though the 'same' variable had different values at different times, the 'lifetime' of q's binding to 3 being the period during which sillyfunction is being evaluated. (If you are thinking in terms of the 'box' model mentioned in Chapter 1, it is as though a temporary duplicate box had been created, an empty duplicate into which the new value of q can be put.) When writing your program, it is convenient to imagine that q will be bound to 3 throughout the written definition of sillyfunction, and partly for this reason values which are bound in this particular manner are known as **lexically scoped** variables.

The phrase **lexical scoping** has further meaning than this. It also means that bound values are not 'passed down', as it were, when one user-defined function is nested within another. Therefore, when these two definitions:

```
(defun even-sillier-function (q)
  (setf q 'oaktree)
  (fiddle))

(defun fiddle ()
  (print q))
```

are evaluated like this:

```
? (even-sillier-function 'cat)
```

the parameter q is bound to cat only in the indicated area. The globally assigned value of q is printed by fiddle: the three element list rather than the word oaktree. At the same time, it is the local, lexical binding of q within even-sillier-function (i.e. the word cat), and not the global assignment of it, which is changed to oaktree by the setf instruction. It does not matter how many times you change the value of a variable within a function provided that that variable also appears as a parameter to the function; its previous value if any will still be restored once evaluation of the function is complete. Almost all of the bindings you will ever set up in Common Lisp will be lexically scoped. Only some rather rarely used functions employ different kinds of scoping.

4.3 Environments

To a Lisp programmer, the word 'environment' means much the same as it does in everyday English, but is more specific. One can talk of a 'programming environment', which means the various debugging (fault-finding) tools and editors which you may have at your disposal alongside Lisp itself. Some programming environments are very basic, giving you little other than Lisp and a simple editor; others offer sophisticated help systems, semi-automatic saving and loading of your work to/from a disk file, and 'intelligent' editors.

A more important use of the word is the 'environment' in which a function is evaluated. In this case it means all of the bound or assigned variables which are available to that function as it runs, and as you now know any given variable can have different values within the lexical scope of different functions. The environment of a single function of course includes that function's own parameters together with their bound values, plus the names and values of any globally assigned variables (the function itself may alter these, as you have seen). The environment also includes all the functions which could be called from within the current function. In our example above each of the three functions has its own environment of variables and values, and that same environment includes all three functions (yes, a function can call itself, as you will see in Chapter 5).

A function's environment may further include macros, which you will meet in Chapter 5, and may be modified by such factors as defined parameters, compiler declarations or packages, all of which are beyond the scope of this book. The bindings of variables are by far the most important factor in an environment.

We said earlier that if a function's parameter is also the name of a globally assigned variable, then the variable's global value is 'saved away' during evaluation of the function and restored afterwards. The same thing happens when one function is called from within another. Have a look at the following two definitions:

```
(defun foo (x)
   (bar 7 x)
   (print x))

(defun bar (x y)
   (print y)
   (print x))
```

Suppose that you type them into Lisp and then evaluate them like this:

```
? (foo 'mary)
```

Let us see in detail what happens. First of all, before the evaluation of foo, any globally assigned value of x is saved away and the value mary is bound to it. You know already that x will retain this new value throughout the lexical scope of foo, but that value will not be passed on to bar, the latter being nested within (called from) foo.

Now we come to the evaluation of bar. Again, any existing values of x and y will be saved away. The existing value of x is mary, and y either has a global value or no value at all. Next, the parameters of bar, namely x and y, are given the values which were supplied as arguments to the call to bar from within foo. That is, x acquires the value 7 and y acquires the value mary.

The two calls to print within bar will then print mary and 7
respectively, and the evaluation of bar will come to an end. At this point
all variable values which were saved away at the start of bar are restored:
y reacquires its global value if it ever had one, or becomes unbound,
whilst x reacquires the value it had within the lexical scope of foo, i.e. its
value becomes mary. So the final call to print within foo prints mary.

In fact, every time a nested function call occurs in a Lisp program –
and of course bar might have called a third function named gort which
called a fourth function which in turn called a fifth, and so on – the values
of all bound variables are saved away. The parameters of the new
function are then given the values of the corresponding arguments in the
function call, and evaluation proceeds in that new environment. Note that
globally assigned variables are not bound variables, and thus their values
remain available, no matter how deeply nested a function call may be; the
only exception being that one of the function's own parameters may
overwrite the global variable. If a global variable's value is altered by a
function, its old global value is permanently lost and only its new value is
available to nested functions.

It is both convenient and correct to regard the variable–value
environment of a function as consisting of items in two categories: the
variable bindings created from its own parameters and arguments; and
the assigned values of the global variables if any. It is also important to
remember that nested functions are evaluated in a different environment
from that of the 'outer' functions from which they are called.

4.4   Making use of bound variables

Global variables are in fact rather disapproved of by Common Lisp
programmers simply because it is so easy to forget their existence, and in
fact there is a stylistic convention to make global variables stand out
amidst a file of Lisp code: their names always have an asterisk at either
end. So our global q would in a real Common Lisp program be called *q*.
From now on in this book we shall use that convention.

From a stylistic point of view, too, global variables are to be
avoided if at all possible. They are considered to be inelegant, and a
potential source of bugs. Ideally a Lisp program would use only bindings,
set up as the program was evaluated, so that when evaluation was finished
the bindings would be undone and the environment would again be
'clean', with no leftover assignments which could confuse later runs of the
same program or, worse, the evaluation of other programs which
happened to use the same variable names.

There are a number of Lisp forms which will allow you to set up
bindings when you need them. You already know about defun; another

frequently used one is let. Like defun, let is a special form. The syntax of let is like this:

```
(let ((var1 value1) (var2 value2)...)
   <some Lisp expressions to be evaluated in the context of these bindings>)
```

There can be as many variable–value pairs as you need. The effect of let on the evaluator is that all of the 'value' expressions are evaluated first (as usual, they can be as complex as you need them to be and can include calls to other functions) and the results are saved. Then each of the variables is bound to the corresponding result, with any previous (e.g. global) value it might have had 'saved away', to be restored when the lexical scope of the let ends. The bindings all happen in parallel rather than sequentially, so that for example

```
(let ((var1 value1) (var2 var1)...
```

would cause an error because var1, whose value is intended to be passed on to var2, would have no value at that point.

It is also permissible to specify variable names on their own, with no associated values:

```
(let ((var1 value1) var2 (var3 val3)...
```

In this case var2 is automatically bound to NIL.

The bindings so arrived at would remain in force until the closing parenthesis of the let expression, and all forms within the body of the let would be evaluated in the context of those bindings. Thus:

```
? (let ((q 'oaktree))
    (foo q))
```

where foo has previously been defined as

```
(defun foo (q)
   (print q))
```

will result in the value oaktree being printed. Note that the binding of q within let is still lexical in scope: its value is passed to foo as an argument in the normal way. This may be more obvious if we define foo slightly differently:

```
(defun foo (x)
   (print x))
```

and, just to labour the point about lexical scoping, if we were to define
foo with no parameter at all:

```
(defun foo ()
  (print q))

? (let ((q 'oaktree))
    (foo))
```

then an 'unbound variable' error would be generated as soon as the
evaluator encountered the print instruction.

We shall use let a good deal in this book, and always for the
purpose of setting up desired variable bindings.

One final important point: within the scope of a binding (e.g.
within the body of a function definition or within a let form) you can use
setf to alter that binding without fear that in so doing you will assign a
global variable of the same name. Even setf can only 'get at' the current
binding of the variable, and if the variable happens to have a global value
as well, that will be restored as usual once the scope of the binding ends.
To see that happening, define this little function:

```
? (defun tryit (x)
    (print x)
    (setf x 5)
    (print x))

TRYIT
```

Now give the variable x a global (ugh!) value:

```
? (setf x 'frisbee)

FRISBEE
```

and run tryit:

```
? (tryit 'cat)

CAT
5
5
```

Notice that the setf within tryit did work: at that point, within the lexical
scope of x as specified by its presence in tryit's parameter list, the value
of x was changed to 5. But now, outside that scope because tryit is no
longer being evaluated, the value of x is its former and global (ugh!)
value:

```
? x

FRISBEE
```

Exercise 4.1

(a)   Here are two cooperating functions:

```
(defun baz (x)
  (print x)
  (let ((x '(a b c)))
    (foo x))
  (print x))
(defun foo (y)
  (print y))
```

What will be printed on screen when baz is evaluated thus:

```
? (baz 'oaktree)
```

(b)   What do the following produce when evaluated?

(i)
```
(let ((x 'one) (y 'two))
  (print (list x y))
  (let ((x 1))
    (print (list x y))))
```

(ii)
```
(defun two_list (x y)
  (list x y))

? (let ((x 'first) (y 'second))
    (two_list y x))
```

4.5 Looping

4.5.1 dotimes and dolist

A programming loop is a section of code (usually quite small and included as a part of some larger function) which causes eval repeatedly to evaluate the *same* group of Lisp expressions until some predetermined stopping condition is reached. Another way of saying the same thing is that within a loop Lisp repeatedly executes the same set of instructions until the stopping condition is reached.

Two simple but very useful looping macros in Common Lisp are dotimes and dolist. The former resembles the 'repeat for n = 1 to 10' construct found in several other languages:

```
? (dotimes (n 5)
    (print n))

0
1
2
```

```
3
4
NIL
```

There can be as many legal Lisp forms as your loop requires in the body of the loop: in the position where we have put only (print n). Each one will be evaluated on each cycle of the loop. The final NIL in the output is of course the value returned by dotimes. It is not obligatory to call the **control variable** n. You can give it any mnemonic name you choose, but its value (5 here) specifies how many cycles of the loop there shall be before it stops. The control variable and its initial value have to go in a list, as shown above. Note that the control variable is actually decremented (made 1 smaller) each time around the loop, otherwise the above printout would not happen.

You may have noticed at once that whereas similar constructs in other languages loop from 1 to n, dotimes loops from 0 to (- n 1). It is a convention throughout Common Lisp that when 'internal' items need to be counted (number of times around a loop, the position of an element within a list, the 'address' of on element of an array) such counts are always zero based rather than being based upon 1 as in everyday real-world counting.

You can also, if you wish, include the name of a result variable, after the control variable and its initial value, but within the same list. The variable is initially unbound, but the forms within the body of your loop can alter its value. When the loop stops, dotimes automatically returns the then value of the result variable, and as in the example above if you do not specify a result variable at all NIL is returned.

Here follows an example of how to use a result variable in dotimes. The let is there to give x an initial value of NIL. Without the let, x would be unbound the first time setf tried to cons onto it the value of n, and an error would immediately result. (Actually, the result variable can be not merely a variable but any single and legal Lisp form including a function call. But we shall return to this in detail when we come to use it, in Chapter 11.)

Another way of looking at this is that, unlike let, dotimes does *not* 'save away' the previous value of x and substitute something else. If x had a previous value then the setf form would faithfully try to cons the value of n onto it, and if that turned out to be an illegal operation then an error is what you would get.

```
? (let ((x nil))
    (dotimes (n 5 x)
      (setf x (cons n x))))

(4 3 2 1 0)
```

dolist does exactly the same thing except that it **iterates** (loops) on lists:

```
? (dolist (el '(a b c d e))
    (print el))

A
B
C
D
E
NIL
```

or, using a result variable:

```
? (let ((result nil))
    (dolist (el '(a b c d e) result)
      (setf result (cons el result))))

(E D C B A)
```

What happens is that result is initially NIL, and consing el onto it during the first loop causes the value of result to be (A). The next time around the loop b is consed onto that, so that it becomes (B A); and so on. Remind yourself that the expression

```
(cons el result)
```

will not effect any change in result, it will merely return a value. setf is required actually to update result each time around the loop.

As you can see, this particular dolist form reverses a list. But please do not be tempted to use it in your programs for that purpose: it is an abysmally slow way of achieving the effect which the inbuilt Lisp function reverse does so much more elegantly:

```
? (reverse '(a b c d e))

(E D C B A)
```

4.5.2 The do macro

Both dotimes and dolist are, like if, intended to fulfil fairly simple programming needs. When you need to create a complex loop the preferred function is do, because its strict syntax helps to clarify what your loop is actually doing. Just as cond is a more powerful and more frequently used function than if, so do is a more powerful and more

frequently used function than either of the two forms of loop so far
described. We can write a function zeroit using do:

```
(defun zeroit (n)
   (do ((n 10 (- n 1)))
        ((zerop n) 'done)
      (print n)))
```

Notice first of all the indentation of the do form. It has two clauses which
look superficially rather like cond clauses, and they are lined up vertically.
The final section of the do form (the call to print) is indented halfway
between the start of the do itself and the start of the cond-like clauses.
Some programmers would prefer to line the print statement up with the
cond-like clauses.

The syntax of the first 'cond clause' in do is:

```
(do ((var1 value1 step1) (var2 value2 step2)...)
```

This is very similar to the syntax of let: the same double parentheses and
the same automatic binding of an arbitrary number of variables to some
desired values. But it also specifies what shall happen to each variable
each time around the loop. It is not obligatory upon you the programmer
to specify that anything shall happen to any one variable each time
around the loop; for example you might simply want to bind a value to it,
a value which would hold throughout evaluation of the do form. As in the
case of variables bound by let, the scope of the binding is purely lexical.

The second 'cond clause' of do will remind you very much of cond
itself when used to halt a loop:

```
(do ((var1 value1 step1) (var2 value2 step2)...)
     (<exit-test> <exit-forms>)
```

Once the ‹exit-test› succeeds the loop halts. All of the ‹exit-forms› are
then evaluated in turn (there may well be only one, which may be NIL or
T) and the value returned by the last such form is the value returned by
the whole do. The remainder of do is known as its **body**, and again may
consist of as many Lisp forms as you like. Each one of them is evaluated
each time around the loop:

```
(do ((var1 value1 step1) (var2 value2 step2)...)
     (<exit-test> <exit-form1> <exit-form2>...)
  <form1>
  <form2>
  ...)
```

Here's the definition of zeroit again:

```
(defun zeroit (n)
  (do ((n 10 (- n 1)))
      ((zerop n) 'done)
    (print n)))
```

It could have been written like this:

```
(defun zeroit (n)
  (do ((n 10))
      ((zerop n) 'done)
    (print n)
    (setf n (- n 1))))
```

but we hope you will agree that the former version is more elegant. You can probably imagine that, in functions where do has a much larger body, it is convenient to have all the variable assignments, and information as to what happens to them each time around the loop, all together in the same place. Anything which makes a program easier to understand is good programming style.

We shall use do a good deal in the course of this book.

Exercise 4.2

(a)   Write a function which returns the last element of a list. Note: do not call your function last because a Common Lisp function called last already exists. Obviously, you should not use last in this exercise! (Hint: use let and dolist.)

```
? (my_last '(1 2 3))

3
```

(b)   Write a function which counts the elements in a list. Don't call it length and do not use length in your answer.

(c)   Write a function which takes two arguments el and lis and which returns the rest of the lis if it finds el in lis. Assume that lis has no nested lists which contain el, i.e. that where el appears in lis it appears as an atom. Do not call it find or member, and do not use the Common Lisp functions find or member.

```
? (my_find x '(a x y))

(X Y)

? (my_find x '(a (x) y))

NIL
```

(d) Write a function that takes two lists of numbers and returns a list of the map addition, that is it adds corresponding members of each list.

```
? (two_map_add_list '(1 2 3 4 5 6 7) '(7 6 5 4 3 2 2))
(8 8 8 8 8 8 9)
```

(e) Write a function that takes a list of numbers and returns T if all the elements are numbers.

4.6 Mapping functions

4.6.1 mapcar and mapc

While a loop repeatedly evaluates the same piece of code, **mapping** is the process of repeatedly applying the same function to successive elements of a list. A simple everyday equivalent of this process would be going through a list and ticking off (checking) each item. But mapping is much more powerful than that, and allows you to apply any legal Lisp function to each element in turn of any list.

We shall start with a simple case. The Common Lisp manual describes a whole family of mapping functions, one of which is called mapcar. The manual also tells you that mapcar can take any number of arguments of which the first must be the name of a function and the rest must be lists. For the moment we'll consider the case where it takes only two arguments:

```
(mapcar <function> <list>)
```

which in real Lisp might look like this:

```
(mapcar 'cdr '((a b) (c d) (e f)))
```

Notice that mapcar has needed only two arguments here, the function name cdr and a list. The named function is known as an **auxiliary function** because its purpose is to do whatever mapcar tells it to do. mapcar will apply cdr to each element of the list in turn, and in this case each element is a two-element sublist. As you can again see from the manual, mapcar returns a list of its results; that is, in this case, a list of the results of each successive application of cdr. So, the above call to mapcar would return

```
((B) (D) (F))
```

Try it, if you like, at Lisp top level; but be careful to quote the name of the auxiliary function as well as the list.

If you were to change the auxiliary function to car, then the call to mapcar would return

```
(A C E)
```

mapcar is a function: it doesn't force the evaluator to behave in any unusual way. It might be defined like this:

```
(defun ourmap (fn lis)
   (do ((list-var lis (cdr list-var)) (result nil))
       ((null list-var) (reverse result))
      (setf result (cons (funcall fn (car list-var)) result))))
```

(By the way, we have avoided calling our function mapcar in case you should want to try it out for real. It is not a good idea to redefine inbuilt Lisp functions, even if your system will let you do so! Also, funcall will be explained below.)

First of all, we take the parameter lis and bind its value to a local variable list-var. At the same time, we specify that list-var shall be reduced to its own cdr each time around the loop. Then we set up a local variable called result, and bind it to an initial value of NIL which as you know is the same as the empty list. The reason for this is that as we work through the input list, applying fn to each element, we shall store up the individual results in a list by consing each one onto result. But if result were initially unbound, this would immediately cause an error.

do will stop looping and will return as soon as the value list-var becomes NIL, and at that point we want it to return the reversed value of result. But until that point is reached, we want it to cons onto result, during every iteration of the loop, the value returned when fn is applied to whatever 'argument' is the current car of list-var.

The problem is that it is not fn the function name that we want to apply to some argument, but the functional value of fn. It is as though we needed an extra little call to eval there, to handle fn for us. The inbuilt Lisp function funcall will do what we need. As its name implies, it calls a function to work on one or more arguments. It is also correct to say that funcall applies the function to its arguments in the way described in Chapter 3.

It may have occurred to you that funcall works rather like the opening parenthesis in a normal function call. The difference is that the opening parenthesis in a function call must be followed by the name of the function, whereas funcall is followed by the name of a variable whose value is the name of the function, or by some other indirect method of accessing the function (you will see some interesting examples in Chapter 11).

And that is it: you know what mapcar does and you have followed the progress through the evaluator of a possible definition of mapcar. You have probably noticed that throughout this section we have been using an idiom which we did introduce earlier: that of saying that a function 'does this' or 'takes that' during evaluation. Of course, eval itself is still faithfully going through its set of rules, as often as is necessary, in order to achieve these effects, and you might think it an interesting test of your understanding to work through the evaluation of ourmap using only those rules.

Recap Box

(1)   If the expression is an atom, return its value.

(2)   If the expression is a list, then either

    (a)   If the first member of the list is a special form, handle it and its arguments accordingly.

    (b)   If the first member of the list is a macro, handle it and its arguments accordingly.

    (c)   If the first member of the list has a functional value then retrieve that function, and

        (i)   find the values of the remaining members of the list by applying these rules to each of them in turn;

        (ii)   apply the function from (c) to the arguments from (i), and return the result.

---

mapc is like mapcar but returns its second argument, that is the first of the lists passed to it:

```
? (mapc 'car '((a b) (c d)))

((A B) (C D))
```

rather than

```
? (mapcar 'car '((a b) (c d)))

(A C)
```

While mapcar is often used in programs for the sake of its returned list of results, mapc is more likely to be used where the returned value is not important but the side-effects of the auxiliary function are. In one sense it does not matter which you use if either will do the job, but for the sake (as usual) of clarity it is preferable to choose the one intended for the job.

You may sometimes come across the statement that Lisp 'uses functions as data' or that in Lisp 'functions and data are the same thing'.

Now you can see what is meant: the auxiliary function in mapcar (the mapping functions are not by any means the only ones which use auxiliaries, as you will see) is used just like any other argument to any other function. The point is that that particular argument to mapcar (or whatever) is a function and not, say, a call to a function which needs to be evaluated.

So far we have only shown you the very simplest way to use mapping functions: in conjunction with an auxiliary function which takes just one argument. But mapping functions can take as many arguments as you care to give them, the restrictions being that all except the first must be lists, and that there must be as many lists as the auxiliary function takes arguments. The function '+' can take two arguments, so if it is used as an auxiliary to a mapping function it must be followed by two lists:

```
? (mapcar '+ '(1 2) '(3 4))

(4 6)
```

But:

```
? (mapc '+ '(1 2) '(3 4))

(1 2)
```

One other point about mapping functions is worth noting here: the lists supplied to them will usually be computed by other parts of a larger program, and on occasion these lists can end up being different lengths. Usually this would be a bug of course, but the mapping functions handle it quite gracefully and without causing an error: they stop mapping over any lists once the shortest of them has been mapped. So:

```
? (mapcar '+ '(1 2 3) '(3 4))

(4 6)
```

Exercise 4.3

(a)   Rewrite two-map-add-list (Exercise 4.2(d)) using mapcar.

(b)   Write a function which 'listifies' each element of a list:

```
? (listify '(1 2 3))

((1) (2) (3))
```

4.6.2   Writing your own auxiliary functions: lambda expressions

You may well have expected that in a language as flexible as Lisp you
would be allowed to specify any function you liked as an auxiliary
function including functions written by you; and of course you can so long
as it is a function, and not a macro or special form. Functions are defined
by defun or are stated to be functions in the Common Lisp specification.

Very often, programmers will keep the definitions of their hand-
coded auxiliary functions (they keep them in a disk file, of course) and
will use them over and over again in their programs. In such cases they
simply use their auxiliaries in exactly the same way as we used car and cdr
above, quoting their names. It is good programming practice to include
also a hash sign. Like the quote itself, the hash sign is a macro which read
knows how to handle. In fact, it is a call to a Lisp special form confusingly
named function. The purpose of function is to retrieve the functional
value of the auxiliary. Remember that it is a read macro, so that whatever
it does happens, as it does with the quote sign, before read passes the
results on to eval. function also has some more esoteric properties which
we shall show you in our chapter on lexical closures.

Strictly speaking, and also from the point of view of good Lisp
style, all of the quoted auxiliary functions above should have been
preceded by a hash sign, like this:

```
(mapcar #'car '((a b) (c d)))
```

Without the hash sign the above functions will still work, but to a trained
Lisp eye they look like an instant source of probable bugs! So please
acquire the habit of using the hash sign, as we shall from now on.

Suppose that for some reason you needed an auxiliary function
which, when used with a mapping function, would add 3 to each element
of a list (assuming the elements also to be numbers, of course). You
might define it as usual:

```
(defun add3 (n)
  (+ 3 n))
```

and you might then use mapcar to call it repeatedly on some list:

```
? (mapcar #'add3 '(1 2 3))

(4 5 6)
```

But, you may be thinking, one would not often need an auxiliary like
that, and it seems wasteful to keep a file full of rarely used definitions. In
fact it is not essential to have the definition existing as a separate entity at
all: you can if you prefer define it on the fly, within the call to mapcar. This

you do via a **lambda expression**. As you can see, a lambda expression looks very much like a function definition, except that in place of the call to defun and the name of the defined function there appears the word lambda:

```
? (mapcar #'(lambda (n) (+ 3 n)) '(1 2 3))

(4 5 6)
```

One thing to be careful of is that you do always properly close off the parentheses of the lambda expression: remember that it is a complete argument (to mapcar) in its own right. It is all too easy to put one of its closing parentheses at the end of the entire call, which of course will result in an error.

Clearly, lambda lists and function definitions are very similar things. In older Lisp dialects functions were actually stored (once they had been defined) as lambda expressions, and sometimes these lambda expressions were stored on the property lists of the functions' names. Other dialects even stored the lambda expressions as the values of the function names, as though the names were ordinary variables. Common Lisp does not do either of these things; in fact its specification does not say exactly how a function name should be associated with a lambda expression, or even that the function need be represented by a lambda expression at all. But lambda expressions are so useful as auxiliary functions that they have been retained in Common Lisp. You should think of lambda expressions as an alternative way of creating functions.

A lambda expression can actually be used as the function in a function call. Here is a lambda expression:

```
(lambda (x y) (+ x y))
```

and here is the corresponding function definition using defun:

```
(defun addem (x y)
  (+ x y))
```

You can easily see the similarity between the two, and it is not hard to imagine that in older Lisps the job of defun was simply to build the lambda expression from the elements of the definition and then tie it to the function name in some way.

When calling a function you have to give it any arguments it may need. Exactly the same is true of a lambda expression, and the way in which you supply arguments to a lambda expression is to make a list of the lambda expression itself and the arguments. In other words a list in which the function comes first and is followed by its arguments. Does this sound familiar? It should: it is the pattern for any function call passing through the Lisp evaluator. Here is the function call using the above lambda expression and giving it arguments of 3 and 4:

```
? ((lambda (x y) (+ x y)) 3 4)

7
```

Apart from their syntax and purpose, everything which is true of a call to defun is true of a lambda list. In a later chapter we shall return to the subject of defun, and everything which will be said there will also be true of lambda lists.

Exercise 4.4

(a)   Write a function to reverse a list, using mapc. (Do not call it reverse and do not use reverse!)

(b)   Write a function that takes two lists and interleaves their elements:

```
? (interleave '(a b c d) '(1 2 3))
(A 1 B 2 C 3)
```

(c)   Write a function that returns only the atomic elements of a list (i.e. not any sublists):

```
? (only-atoms '(1 (i o) o p 9 (p) (((ooo)) p u )))
(1 0 P 9)
```

SUMMARY

You should by now be familiar with everyday use of your editor. We have explained variable value scoping to you, and have shown you how to use let to create lexically scoped bindings of local variables. We have also explained that during evaluation of a function call similar bindings occur for the function's parameters, allowing their previous values to be 'saved away' so that you the programmer do not have to be constantly on the watch for duplicated variable/parameter names.

We hope that you are beginning now to get a feel for how powerful Lisp is, as we progressively show you more and more of its most frequently used techniques, including the use of auxiliary functions.

At this point we want to stress that a loop repeatedly executes the same set of instructions, the same piece of Lisp code if you like, whereas mapping applies the same function to the elements of a list. In the next chapter we shall introduce you to another technique which is superficially similar but in fact very different: recursion is a very powerful technique and is used very often in professional Lisp programming. Lisp is as famous for its recursion as it is for its parentheses.

Part 2

PROGRAMMING AND DATA STRUCTURES

Chapter 5
Recursion

This second part of the book begins with a whole chapter devoted to the difficult technique of recursion. Besides a step-by-step detailed description of how the technique works, we give you a number of examples of recursion in everyday life as well as many programmatic examples. Perhaps even more importantly, we offer you some rules of thumb which will help you to define working recursive functions, by taking for granted the details of the process itself.

5.1 Recursion

5.1.1 Recursion in the real world

Recursion is arguably the most difficult concept which programmers have to understand whilst learning a programming language. It is a programming technique something like the loop but different from the loop in certain crucial ways which give the technique considerable power as well as a symmetry which verges on the beautiful. Back in Chapter 1 we showed you a set of rules for a simple version of the evaluator, and we commented that one of the rules was interesting because it asked for the whole set of rules to be applied to some intermediate result; in fact it asked for the set of rules to be applied to each of a function's arguments in turn. We explained at the time this was recursion and we promised to return to the subject.

Try asking yourself 'What is recursion?'. Do not expect an answer, just ask yourself the question. Please stop reading for a second and do it, quite deliberately. Now the real question is, who exactly was talking to whom as you did that? There are presumably not two of you inside your head, one of whom asked a question and one of whom listened (if there are, you have a curable mental dysfunction). And yet it is a common enough phrase: I asked myself; and there are many similar phrases which are equally common: I said to myself, I told myself, I took a firm grip on myself.

The question is just one of the many forms of an underlying question about 'self' and 'consciousness'. If I am self-conscious, in the sense of self-aware, rather than shy, what exactly do I claim is conscious of what (and, of course, what is asking that question). To put that another way, in what sense is 'I' distinguishable from 'myself'? It doesn't seem to make nearly as much sense to claim that I am conscious of I.

This is not just playing about with the rules of English grammar, but a serious logical complication to which there is as yet no answer. It is also one which will have to be answered if we are ever to create a convincingly intelligent machine, one about which would-be detractors cannot say 'Oh, but deep down inside it's just doing what its programmer told it to do'. A truly intelligent machine will need to be self-aware, self-motivated, self-controlled and to carry out all the other self-monitoring activities which we glibly assume are being carried out both by ourselves and by others all the time.

The question of self-consciousness is also a convenient angle from which to approach the notion of recursion. Since no-one can answer the question, we cannot say for sure that self-consciousness is a good model of recursion, so just treat it as an analogy for now. And suppose that the human mind has a previously unsuspected ability: that when it wants to talk to itself, it is able to create instantaneously a perfect copy of its complete mental state. We are not putting this forward as a serious psychological hypothesis, but it is interesting from an AI point of view to note that computers can do precisely that, and indeed many computing environments depend crucially upon that ability.

If such a copied self were possible, then the 'master' self could presumably talk to the copy without defying the laws of logic or the normal criteria of sanity. Once the copy had served its purpose by listening (and perhaps replying) it could be disposed of.

But, and this is important, since the copy of the original self was a perfect copy, it would necessarily also contain a copy of itself. That second copy would also contain a copy, and so on like a model village which contains a model of the model village; or like Russian dolls endlessly concealing smaller but otherwise identical dolls.

Those two fairly simple ideas: that of something containing a series of copies of itself, one inside the other; and that of each copy being able to communicate with the next in the series, together make up the concept of recursion. The technique consists of causing a running computer program to create a copy of itself and to feed it some data. The copy modifies the data, creates another copy, and passes the data on to be modified yet again before being passed to a third copy, and so on. Naturally, the process has to be brought to a halt at some point, and then things get even more interesting, but we shall come back to that later.

Recursion is in fact a fairly common everyday occurrence, though we tend not to notice it. 'God made Man in His own image' is in fact a recursive sentence, leading to all sorts of heretical ideas such as that in that case Man must also be a god capable of creating godlike beings (possibly beings which will run on wheels until we get the bugs out of their legs and feet). Recursion is often used to create logical puzzles such as 'This sentence has no meaning', or 'This statement is false', by causing English sentences to refer to themselves in much the same way as a person can refer to himself or herself. In music too, the idea of a 'round' or canon is recursive. Songs such as 'Frere Jacques' or 'London's Burning', in which one voice sings the first phrase alone, whereupon the second voice starts from the beginning of the song whilst the first voice proceeds to the second phrase.

The canon example is useful because it has the connotation of each recursive copy of the song starting from a point (in the musical score, on paper) to the right of its 'parent' copy. The Lisp tracer prints out information about a running recursive program so that the information about any one copy is placed below and to the right of its 'parent' copy. The overall 'shape' created on the screen by running a recursive program through the tracer is characteristic and instantly recognizable, as you shall shortly see.

5.1.2 Recursion in a computer program

But there is one crucial difference between all these examples and recursion as used in computer programs. To see what that is, imagine a rather special Russian doll, whose speciality was that once you had taken each successive doll apart and had reached the smallest, innermost doll, the thing would reverse the sequence of your actions and methodically put itself back together again. Some programmers therefore find it handy to think of recursion as some kind of clock spring, which you progressively wind tighter and tighter and which once released will unwind itself again. In fact the term 'unwinding' is very commonly used in the context of how recursive programs work. We shall explain recursion via examples, first via examples in which the unwinding is not obvious to the programmer, and then via examples where the unwinding is more important than the winding up.

Look carefully at this function:

```
(defun printem (n)
    (print n)
    (if (zerop n) nil
        (printem (- n 1))))
```

Suppose printem to be called with an argument of 5. Pretty obviously, the first form within the function will print the value of the argument, which of course is 5. Then we come to an if, whose test form asks in effect 'is 5 equal to zero?'. It is not, so we move on to the 'else' clause, which does something you have not seen until now: it calls the same function, printem, again. Using the Russian doll analogy, at this point you have opened the first doll and have found the identical second doll inside. The second call to printem is not in any sense a loop: it is a new call, complete with its own lexical bindings – that is to say, with its own environment. Inside the evaluator, the functional definition of the symbol 'printem' has been retrieved a second time, and there are now two copies of it being evaluated. This is really no different from any nested function call, such as the calls to print, to if and to zerop within printem.

As we said very early on in this book, a normal (serial) computer cannot do two things at once. What happens here is that evaluation of the first or 'outer' version of printem is suspended until such time as evaluation of the second or 'inner' one is complete. This is actually true of any function which contains a call to another function, but in recursion it is especially important.

As you can see from the above definition, the second call to printem is handed (in Lisp terminology we say that it is **passed**) a value for its argument which is one less than that supplied to the first call. Or: in the environment of the nested call, n has a value one smaller than it had in the environment of the top level call. So once again, when during evaluation of this second call the test 'is 4 equal to zero?' fails, yet a third call to printem is set up. Evaluation of the second call is then suspended until such time as the third call completes.

So the effect of recursion is to create a series of suspended calls to printem, each one waiting for its successor to complete before it itself can do so. This is where the idea of tension, of a wound spring, comes from. It is handy to think of these calls to printem as being 'inside' or 'below' one another. When you see the term 'recursive level', that is what it means; so far we have described levels 1, 2 and 3. In fact you now know why top level is so called: it is equivalent to level 1 in a recursive call.

(Aside: in fact Lisp terminology extends this idea to cover all 'inner' calls to functions. If the above definition of printem had called not itself but another function, that other function could be referred to as being called 'one recursive level down' or 'at one level below top level'.)

> *Point to remember*   Recursion halts when the most recent call to the recursive function returns a value rather than calling itself yet again.

Our recursive function, printem, returns NIL when the value of its parameter is 0 (zero). When this is the case, its if statement does not create a new call to printem. On the way to this point, successive calls to printem will have printed the numerals from 5 down to 0. That printing is all that this particular function does, and as you have seen it all happens during the 'winding' or 'forward' phase of recursion.

Once recursion has halted it will immediately start to unwind. If you think about it, you will readily agree that the copy of printem which halts (which returns NIL) is actually the sixth copy. Once the NIL has been returned, evaluation of printem number 6 is complete, so now printem number 5 can complete. In fact eval has finished with number 6 and goes back to whatever it was doing when evaluation of number 5 was suspended.

In fact in this case there is nothing left for eval to do to number 5 (there is no unevaluated code in it) so all that remains is for number 5 to return a value. What value is it? Well, in compliance with the universal rule that a function always returns the value of its last-evaluated form, number 5 returns the value of its own inner call to printem number 6, which as we now know was NIL. Similarly, printem number 4 will then return the value of its own inner call to printem number 5, which we have just realised must be NIL. Eventually, of course, the NIL has filtered right back to top level, and the whole overall recursive sequence returns NIL:

```
? (defun printem (n)
    (print n)
    (if (zerop n) nil
        (printem (- n 1))))

PRINTEM

? (printem 5)

5
4
3
2
1
0
NIL
```

5.1.3   Rearranging the definition to get a different effect

OK so far? Now let us rewrite the function slightly:

```
(defun printem (n)
   (if (zerop n) nil
       (printem (- n 1)))
   (print n))
```

Once again recursion will wind until n is equal to zero. This will prevent the if from creating a new call to printem. But in this case there is still some more of this printem number 6 to be evaluated, namely the instruction to print the current value of n. Once this has been done printem number 6 dutifully returns a value – according to the rule, the value of its last evaluated form, i.e. of the print statement itself. The value returned by any print statement is whatever print printed, which as things stand is zero.

   Since printem number 6 returned a value rather than calling a printem number 7, recursion halts. eval can now go back and continue its suspended evaluation of printem number 5, and again what remains is a print instruction. This time, a 1 will be printed, and that will also be returned as the value of printem number 5. All the way back along the series of calls to printem, each one will print its own value of n. The result on screen is the same series of numbers as before but in the reverse order, and the value returned to top level will be 5 rather than NIL:

```
? (defun printem (n)
     (if (zerop n) nil
         (printem (- n 1)))
     (print n))

PRINTEM

? (printem 5)

0
1
2
3
4
5
5
```

We hope that from the above detailed explanation you have learned the following. Recursion winds until a value is returned and then unwinds automatically. Recursive functions can call other functions, and hence can affect the outside world, either when winding down into recursion or when unwinding back out of it, or both. Most importantly: what happens

(in terms of the evaluator) is for most of the time obscure; the crucial
points are the start, the end, and the point at which recursion halts
because a value has been returned. During the rest of this chapter we
shall try to teach you to write correct recursive functions almost by
instinct. You will see that other than in a very few extremely complex
cases it is almost a syntactic skill, and that once you have understood how
recursion works there is rarely any need to follow the whole process
through in your head in order to write recursive functions which work.

5.1.4   Using the tracer to show recursion on screen

At this point we would like to introduce you to the Lisp tracer, a standard
part of any Lisp programming environment, which should be a big help to
you in understanding recursive programs. If you still have the second of
the above two versions of printem defined in your Lisp, all well and good.
If you have not, please define it:

```
? (defun printem (n)
    (if (zerop n) nil
        (printem (- n 1)))
    (print n))

PRINTEM
```

Now type into top level:

```
(trace printem)
```

The value returned when this form is evaluated is not defined in Common
Lisp because the environmental tools are not strictly speaking a part of
the language. Your own Lisp may return a list of the symbol printem or
perhaps T or NIL. But, whatever is returned, the above call to trace should
turn tracing on. In some systems it may first cause the tracing functions to
be loaded automatically from disk.

If you now issue your call to printem you'll see something very like
Figure 5.1 on your screen.

What you see may not be identical to Figure 5.1, but most tracers
will indicate printem's argument as it is entered, and the value which it
returns as it is exited. The numbers printed close to the left-hand margin
are of course put there by the print instruction within printem itself.

The indentation in Figure 5.1 is typical of all Lisp tracers: the
lower and the further to the right, the greater the level of recursion. Look
in particular at the call to printem when its argument is zero (in the middle
of the above trace). This is the call which halted the recursion, and you
will see that the indentations of its entry point and its exit point are the

```
? (printem 5)
  Calling (PRINTEM 5)
   Calling (PRINTEM 4)
    Calling (PRINTEM 3)
     Calling (PRINTEM 2)
      Calling (PRINTEM 1)
       Calling (PRINTEM 0)

0
            PRINTEM returned 0

1
          PRINTEM returned 1

2
        PRINTEM returned 2

3
      PRINTEM returned 3

4
    PRINTEM returned 4

5
  PRINTEM returned 5
5
```

Figure 5.1   Using the Lisp tracer.

same. Similarly for the call when printem's argument was 1: the entry and
exit points are indented by the same amount. This is to be expected: any
particular call is entered at some recursive level, and then evaluation of it
is suspended until all subsequent recursion, both forward and backward
(or down and up, or right and left: however you prefer to think of it), is
complete. Then evaluation of that particular call can resume, at the same
recursive level.

If you care to redefine printem in the form in which we originally
showed it to you, and then to call trace on it again (redefining a function
automatically untraces it), you will get something like this:

```
? (printem 5)
  Calling (PRINTEM 5)

5
    Calling (PRINTEM 4)

4
      Calling (PRINTEM 3)

3
        Calling (PRINTEM 2)
```

```
2
     Calling (PRINTEM 1)
1
     Calling (PRINTEM 0)
0
        PRINTEM returned NIL
       PRINTEM returned NIL
      PRINTEM returned NIL
     PRINTEM returned NIL
    PRINTEM returned NIL
   PRINTEM returned NIL
 NIL
```

By the way, we should tell you for future reference that you can trace as many functions as you like at one time:

```
? (trace printem foo baz gort)
```

where foo, baz and gort are all the names of functions. Subsequently, evaluating

```
? (trace)
```

will give you a list of all functions currently being traced. There is also a companion function called untrace which, like trace itself, can take one or many arguments. These arguments should be the names of currently traced functions, and untrace will switch tracing off for those functions. Evaluating untrace with no arguments will untrace everything.

5.2 How to write recursive functions

5.2.1 Preventing endless recursion

Now that you have a tool with which you can see a bit more clearly what is going on, let us return to recursion. Here is possibly the world's simplest recursive program:

```
(defun foo ()
   (foo))
```

You can probably see that this program is capable of recursing for ever, since it lacks the all-important stopping condition. foo would call itself repeatedly, creating and suspending a new copy of itself each time, until your computer ran out of memory in which to accommodate them all. At that point you would get an error message! If you were to trace foo before evaluating it, the resulting printout would run right off the right-hand edge of your screen. All in all foo is not a very useful function, and yet you would be surprised how often experienced programmers write functions which, although longer, are in all important respects exactly like it! Endless recursion is one of the more common errors in Lisp programming, and we hope that what follows will at least help you to avoid that bug.

The error message which Lisp prints in cases of endless recursion usually mentions the phrase **stack overflow**. The Lisp stack is the place where all the suspended function calls are held during recursion. In fact, despite the power of recursion as a technique there is no difference as far as the evaluator is concerned between a nested call to a function's self and a nested call to any other function. Evaluation of the outer function still has to be suspended until evaluation of the inner function is complete, and in fact all uncompleted calls are kept on the stack. As you will be able to see in later chapters where we shall show you quite large programs, the evaluator is always, so long as a Lisp program is running, working on function calls nested within function calls. The stack can thus hold a 'history' of function calls since the start together with their arguments, so that when an error occurs the information on the stack can be very useful for debugging purposes. Most Lisp error-handling systems give you access to the stack, though at first you may find it hard to understand. As with most of the programming environment, we can only advise you to consult your software manual.

So, if a recursive function is not to recurse endlessly it needs a stopping condition. That is, it needs within it a conditional statement one of whose tests will, when it succeeds, cause the function to return a value and hence to halt the recursion. In both versions of printem that test was:

```
...(if (zerop n)...
```

but, as we mentioned earlier, if allows only a single 'then' action or a single 'else' action, and cond is far more flexible. For this reason, recursive functions almost always use one clause of a cond to detect their stopping condition. Look at this recursive function:

```
(defun backit (lis)
  (cond ((null lis) nil)
        (t (append (backit (cdr lis)) (list (car lis))))))
```

All that this does is to reverse a top level list just like the inbuilt Lisp function reverse. When we say 'top level' we mean to imply that if the list contains elements which are themselves lists their contents will not be internally reversed:

```
(a b (c d) e (f g))
```

will become

```
((F G) E (C D) B A)
```

What we want to teach you at this point is how we set about writing the function. We certainly did not sit down with pencil and paper, drawing tracer-like diagrams so as to see what would happen at each level of recursion. The first thing we said was 'OK, we need a halting condition' because nobody likes to write an endlessly recursive function, and an obvious way to get our function to halt was to ensure that the recursive call to backit, the one appearing in the last line of the above definition, was given the cdr of the list as its argument. This entailed that each successive recursive call to backit had a progressively shorter version of the list to work upon, so that our halting condition could be the point where the list was reduced to NIL.

So we could already write:

```
(defun backit (lis)
  (cond ((null lis) nil)
        (...
```

5.2.2   Use the fact of recursion to help design your program

Being now sure that the recursion would eventually halt, we only had to worry about what would happen at earlier recursive levels when it did not halt. Recursion being a process of evaluating identical copies of a function, we felt confident that whatever we told the function to do at the start of the recursive process would be faithfully repeated at each forward (downward) level until the halting condition was reached.

The first obvious step in reversing a list is to move the first element of it to the end, like this:

```
(append (cdr lis) (list (car lis)))
```

(Remember, append requires both of its arguments to be lists, so we ensured that the moved element became a list by using the function list.) But that line of code would not do as it is because it contains no recursive call: backit would faithfully move the first element of the list to the end, but would do nothing more.

What we really needed was to have available an already reversed version of the cdr of the list. We could then tack on car of the original list onto the end of it using append, and that would be that. But the cdr of a list is still a list, is it not? And what function have we handy for reversing a list? Why, backit of course! Hence the final line of our function:

```
(t (append (backit (cdr lis)) (list (car lis)))))
```

Putting it all together, we got:

```
(defun backit (lis)
  (cond ((null lis) nil)
        (t (append (backit (cdr lis)) (list (car lis))))))
```

In other words, we assumed that backit would work correctly on the cdr of the list, and on the basis of that assumption the above definition must work correctly during the top-level call. Therefore, such is the nature of recursion in generating identical copies of the function, it must work correctly at any recursive level: the one thing we did not need to do was consider each of them in turn.

However, our assumption that backit would work correctly on the cdr of the list was not a naive assumption. We realized that in order for it to do so, the top level call would have to do the right thing, so that all of its recursive copies would also do the right thing. So this is the other secret about writing working recursive programs: having assumed that the first recursive call will work, and realizing that it will be called to work on an input list which is one element simpler that the original list, ascertain the difference between what it should return and what you want the final outcome to be. The difference will tell you what the top level call, and hence your definition, needs to do. In this case, of course, the recursive call should return the cdr of the original list, reversed; and the difference between that and the desired result is that it needs to have the car of the original list tacked onto its end.

It may help at this point to see the trace of backit in action:

```
? (backit '(a b (c d) e (f g)))
  Calling (BACKIT (A B (C D) E (F G)))      -- line A
    Calling (BACKIT (B (C D) E (F G)))      -- line B
      Calling (BACKIT ((C D) E (F G)))
        Calling (BACKIT (E (F G)))
          Calling (BACKIT ((F G)))
            Calling (BACKIT NIL)
            BACKIT returned NIL
          BACKIT returned ((F G))
        BACKIT returned ((F G) E)
      BACKIT returned ((F G) E (C D))
```

```
        BACKIT returned ((F G) E (C D) B)          -- line C
        BACKIT returned ((F G) E (C D) B A)        -- line D
        ((F G) E (C D) B A)
```

The first line here is of course the hand-typed call to backit, and the last line is backit's returned value; the rest of what you see above is the actual trace. In line A you see the top level call to backit traced, and in line B you see the first recursive call to backit, the one which appears in the last line of the function definition and which is passed the cdr of the list as its argument. At this point the top level call has been suspended, as it were halfway through moving the first element of the original list to its end. Then follows a good deal more recursion which we prefer not to think about, and in the middle of it backit is called with an empty list (NIL) as its argument. It duly returns NIL and recursion begins to unwind. Line C shows what the first recursive call made of the cdr of the list, and finally in line D the suspended move of the car of the original list to its end is completed.

There is one unanswered question here: why did we decide that in the halting condition backit should return NIL rather than any other value? Could we have used T, for example, instead? Well, no we could not, and the reason can be found in the last line of the definition. We are using append, which as the trace shows gradually builds up the reversed list as recursion unwinds. Consider the recursive level at which the last line of the function

```
    (t (append (backit (cdr lis)) (list (car lis)))))
```

contains the call to the halting condition, and the suggestion is that the halting condition returns T. Inside the evaluator, after evaluation of the halting condition, this line would then effectively be

```
    (t (append t (list (car lis)))))
```

but as you know by now append requires both of its arguments to be lists. NIL was all right because, of course, NIL is the same as the empty list. So in fact any returned value other than NIL would cause an error.

(Aside: throughout this book we have avoided telling you other than in general terms what error messages you might get. This is because error messages, like the tracer, are not part of the Common Lisp specification. Any implementation of Common Lisp will generate an error message in response to the same piece of buggy code, but exactly what the message should say is not laid down anywhere. If you try out this buggy version of backit you may get an error message which seems to bear no relation to the actual error: 'T is not a valid argument to CAR', for example. This is because of the particular way in which append is implemented in your Lisp, and because of the particular tests which are applied by your Lisp's error-handling system to detect the bug. Our feeling is that you should not worry about it! We advised you in an earlier chapter to read your error messages and to try to understand what they are telling you, and in the vast majority of cases that is still good advice.)

5.2.3   A more complex example

Here is a more complex recursive function:

```
(defun atomise (lis)
   (cond ((null lis) nil)
         ((atom (car lis))
          (cons (car lis) (atomise (cdr lis))))
         (t (append (atomise (car lis)) (atomise (cdr lis))))))
```

It takes a list which is arbitrarily nested, i.e. any element may consist of a sublist whose elements may be subsublists and so on, such as:

```
((a (b c)) d (e) (f g) ((h) i))
```

and converts it into a simple top level list containing all the atoms of the original list in their correct order:

```
(A B C D E F G H I)
```

As usual, atomise is going to work its way down through successive cdrs of the input list, until its argument is an empty list. So the first clause of the cond inside atomise is easy to write. Then, as before, imagine that atomise already works on a simpler version of the input, which here will be its cdr simply because it is a list (you will meet a case where the 'simpler' version of the input is not its cdr in our next example). We assume that the recursive call to atomise is given as its input the cdr of the input list:

```
(d (e) (f g) ((h) i))
```

and that it returns

```
(D E F G H I)
```

So our top level function has somehow to manipulate both (D E F G H I) and the car of the original list, (a (b c)), so as to return (A B C D E F G H I). But of course our assumed-to-be-working recursive call to atomise should be able to turn (a (b c)) into (A B C), which we could then simply append onto (D E F G H I). So the last line of our definition can be written:

```
(defun atomise (lis)
  (cond ((null lis) nil)
        (...
          ...)
        (t (append (atomise (car lis)) (atomise (cdr lis))))))
```

If this were the full definition of the function, the first recursive call to atomise on the last line would be expected to work on (a (b c)). At the next recursive level down there would be another call to (atomise (car lis)), and this one would have to work on the car of (a (b c)), which is of course the atom a. But at the next recursive level an error would occur, since you cannot take the car of an atom. Evidently our function needs to treat the case where its input is an atom rather than a list as a special case.

Do not forget our continuing assumption that recursive calls to atomise work correctly. So what our function needs to know is what to do when it has a single atom such as a and a list such as (B C), and of course the answer is to cons the atom onto the list: (A B C). (Remember, Lisp does not care about upper or lower case letters. We are using upper case to denote returned values and lower case to denote input values, as usual.)

```
(defun atomise (lis)
  (cond ((null lis) nil)
        ((atom (car lis))
          (cons (car lis) (atomise (cdr lis))))
        (t (append (atomise (car lis)) (atomise (cdr lis))))))
```

The first recursive call on the last line of atomise now returns (A B C), and we can be sure that the second recursive call on that line will correctly handle the remainder of the input list.

> *Point to remember* When writing the recursive call inside the definition of a recursive function, pretend that the function already exists but that it only works on lists one recursive step smaller than the current input. Your definition should specify how to convert that pretended result into what you really want.

It seems too good to be true, and yet if used with care this almost syntactic method of writing recursive functions infallibly works, and is one of the major rules of thumb used by expert Lisp programmers.

The first step in writing a recursive function is to recognize that whatever problem it is intended to solve can be solved recursively; for example the problem of reversing a list, or of 'atomizing' it. The key to this is to recognize that the problem could be solved trivially if a smaller version of the same problem had already been solved. That is another way of saying what we said above: assume that your function already works, and use it in your definition of the function. Here is a numerical example:

```
(defun sum-up-to (n)
   (cond ((zerop n) 0)
         (t (+ n (sum-up-to (- n 1))))))
```

This function generates the sum of all the integers from zero up to n. If n is 4 the result is 10; if n is 5 the result is 15, and so on. As usual, we assume that sum-up-to already works, and we recursively call it to deal with (- n 1), adding the current value of n onto that. When n has fallen to zero, we stop the recursion. As we said before, any value returned from the cond will halt recursion; in this case it has to be zero rather than NIL because when that halting recursive call unwinds, whatever value it returns will be added onto n by the previous recursive call. If the value were not a number, the function + would complain.

Exercise 5.1

(a)   Write a recursive function add-up which takes a list of numbers and returns the sum of those numbers:

> ? (add-up '(1 2 3))
>
> 6

(b)   Write a recursive power function which exponentiates a number; that is, given two numbers x and y it does x^y, i.e. multiplies x by itself y times. For example:

> ? (power 2 2)
>
> 4   (This is 2 times 2)
>
> ? (power 2 3)
>
> 8   (This is 2 times 2 times 2)

(c)   Write a recursive function to return the last element of a list. Compare your definition with your solution to Exercise 4.2(a) and notice how the extra power of recursion over simple loops makes your code more concise and more elegant.

(d)   Write a function that returns the 'first' atom in a list no matter how deeply nested:

> ? (first-atom ())
>
> NIL

```
? (first-atom '(a b c))
A
? (first-atom '((((((a))) b)) c))
A
```

(e)   Write a function which counts the elements in a list. Do not call it length and do not use length. Again, compare your definition with the one you wrote for Exercise 4.2(d).

(f)   Write a recursive function which takes as its arguments any Lisp object and a list. The function checks to see whether the object is equal to any member of the list. If it is, the function returns T; if not it returns NIL. Do not use member: write a recursive solution!

(g)   Write a recursive function which applies a function to each element of a list until the function application returns a non-nil value:

```
? (apply-to-list #'zerop '(1 2 3))
NIL
? (apply-to-list #'zerop '())
NIL
? (apply-to-list #'zerop '(9 8 0))
T
```

5.3 The Towers of Hanoi

This is a children's puzzle, sometimes called the Towers of Brahma. It consists of a baseboard on which are mounted three vertical pegs, and on one of the outer pegs are three discs or rings arranged in order of size (Figure 5.1).

It does not matter exactly how many rings there are, nor whether there is an odd or even number of them. The problem is to move all of the rings from where they are to the other outermost peg, the one on the far right in our diagram. But of course there are rules to make this difficult:

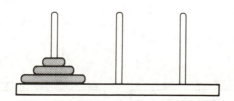

Figure 5.2   Towers of Hanoi: starting state.

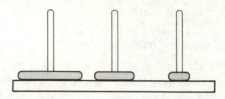

Figure 5.3   Towers of Hanoi: after two moves.

(1)   move only one ring at a time; and

(2)   never place a larger ring on top of a smaller one

The first two steps are easy: move the smallest ring onto the target peg, and then move the medium-sized ring onto the middle peg. It is at this point that the problem becomes interesting from the point of view of eventually solving it with a computer program. The next move almost certainly does not involve the medium-sized ring, because moving it to the target peg, on top of the smallest ring, would violate rule 2 above, and moving it the other way merely undoes our most recent move. Moving the largest ring is also not allowed because it would violate rule 2 wherever we put it (Figure 5.2).

The smallest ring has the two possible moves from this position shown in Figure 5.3, and the first of these (the left-hand one in Figure 5.3) looks preferable because if we are ever going to get the whole tower of rings onto the right-hand peg we obviously need to get the largest ring onto there whilst the peg is empty (rule 2).

But look again at what we have done: we have moved a smaller tower of rings out of the way so that the problem of moving the largest ring to the target peg becomes trivial. What is more, the smaller tower is smaller than the whole tower by just one ring. By now a Lisp programmer's mind would already have decided that a recursive program

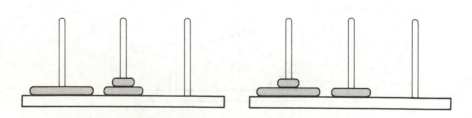

Figure 5.4   Towers of Hanoi: third move.

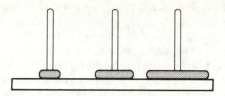

Figure 5.5   Towers of Hanoi: after moves 4 and 5.

would be what is needed here. And indeed, having moved the largest ring to the target peg, the next step involves moving a still smaller tower, this time consisting only of the smallest ring, out of the way so that the problem of moving the medium-sized ring onto the target peg becomes trivial (Figure 5.4). In two more obvious moves the problem is solved.

Exercise 5.2   We would like you to have a go at writing the recursive function to solve this problem. You may find it difficult, and if in the end you want to give up you will find the solution at the end of the book. But please do try: even if you do not succeed you will be in a position to appreciate the elegance and power of recursion when finally you look up the answer. Here follow some hints to make things easier for you.

Call your function hanoi , and give it four parameters. The first parameter denotes the ring which is currently being moved, and a neat trick here is to number the rings in order of their size so that when the function tries to move ring 0 it can realize that it has moved all of the rings numbered 1, 2, 3. . ., i.e. that it has finished. (cond ((zerop n)... should immediately spring to mind as the condition under which recursion halts. The remaining three parameters are the names of the three pegs: call them a, b and c. The call to your function will be

    ? (hanoi 3 'left 'middle 'right)

and it should return NIL.

Remember here how we have suggested writing a recursive function: assume that hanoi can already move a smaller tower of rings from left to middle. So you should ask yourself what then needs to be done to convert that situation into the desired result. First you will need to move ring 3, the largest ring, from left to right. The 'moving' will be a simple call to print, printing a sentence partly composed of the arguments to your function, to show that your function is working. Then, a second recursive call to hanoi can move the same smaller tower from middle to right.

So your function definition should consist of the test for halting the recursion, a recursive call to itself, a print statement and a further recursive call to itself. The function in the form in which it appears on the screen can handle the case where it is trying to move ring 3. At one recursive level down it will be trying to move ring 2, and at two levels down it will be trying to move ring 1. At the next level down, it tries to move ring 0, which is its halting (terminating) condition.

You decide which pegs each call is trying to move a ring from or to by changing the order of the three 'peg' arguments. The parameters of the function definition are, when the function is called, bound to `left`, `middle` and `right`, in that order, and these values will be passed on as arguments to the inner recursive calls. So, if the parameters `a`, `b` and `c` represent `left`, `middle` and `right` respectively, then the parameters `a`, `c` and `b` represent `left`, `right` and `middle` respectively. You arrange your `print` statement to say that whichever ring is currently being dealt with is moved from the leftmost parameter to the rightmost parameter.

As we have said, this `print` statement will effectively do the 'moving'. However, `print` will only agree to print one lisp object, an atom or a list. Attempts to make it print a sentence will result in a 'too many arguments' error. The way to get round this is to form the words of the sentence into a single list:

```
(print (list 'take 'me 'to 'your (car lis)))
```

That is more than enough hints. Please have a go at writing the function and then, whether you succeed or not, have a look at our solution at the end of the book.

It is possible that one of your attempts at writing `hanoi` will result in endless recursion. If this happens you will get an error message, probably mentioning the phrase *stack overflow*. But this will only happen if you have a mistake in your terminating condition. When the function works, it will print something like the following:

```
(MOVE 1 FROM LEFT TO RIGHT)
(MOVE 2 FROM LEFT TO MIDDLE)
(MOVE 1 FROM RIGHT TO MIDDLE)
(MOVE 3 FROM LEFT TO RIGHT)
(MOVE 1 FROM MIDDLE TO LEFT)
(MOVE 2 FROM MIDDLE TO RIGHT)
(MOVE 1 FROM LEFT TO RIGHT)
```

You can also try it out using an even number of rings; you will see that then the first move will be from `left` to `middle` rather than from `left` to `right`. One word of warning: if you ask `hanoi` to handle a tower of more than about five rings you'll probably run out of patience long before it has printed all the necessary moves!

Exercise 5.3 Here is a harder exercise. The objective is to write a function called `powerset`, which takes any top-level list and generates all the possible combination sublists. For example, if given the list `'(a b c)` it would return `'((a b c) (a b) (a c) (b c) (a) (b) (c) ())`. You will need to use functions you have already learned about, in particular `cons`, `append` and `mapcar`, the latter employing an auxiliary function written by you.

The difficult part of this exercise is in establishing exactly what is the difference between the top level problem and the simpler one solved by the recursive call. However, as the function's name implies, we are talking about mathematical sets, which means that your solution will be correct if it generates the correct list but with its elements in a different order form the order given here. Since this is a difficult exercise, here's a useful hint: work out on paper what would be returned by a working powerset if it were given the input (a b c), and what it would return if it were given (a b). The latter is the output of your recursive call, so try to spot the (essentially simple) method of converting it into the former.

SUMMARY

In this chapter we have covered recursion in some detail, and have tried to give you the basic skills of writing recursive functions. In the next chapter we shall get the subject of *cons cells* out of the way before we go on to some even more advanced programming techniques.

One final point before leaving for now the subject of recursion: you learned almost at the very beginning of this book that when eval is called to evaluate a function, it evaluates each of that function's arguments first, before applying the function to the results. You can now see that eval is a recursive function, and that if it were written in Lisp its definition would include recursive calls to itself to handle the argument evaluation.

Chapter 6
More about Functions

We describe cons cells, the basic building blocks of which Lisp is composed. Then we return to the subject of function definition to teach you about macros, lambda lists and keywords. Macros are functions which on evaluation redefine themselves, and we tell you why this can be useful. Both function definitions and macro definitions contain lambda lists and lambda lists may contain keywords. We show you how to make use of these so that your functions become as flexible, or as inflexible, as you like in terms of what input data they will or will not accept.

6.1 Cons cells

So far we have presented the Lisp evaluator as a rather clever function to which we have gradually assigned more and more abilities as your own understanding of Lisp has progressed. We have brushed aside any questions of what really happens by saying that eval is written in machine code, which we do not want to burden you with. Without violating that rule we can nonetheless bring you slightly closer to the whole truth by introducing you to cons cells. You may have wondered how Lisp keeps track of everything: what do we mean when we say that your new function has in effect 'become a part of Lisp'? How does Lisp remember the value which you assign to a variable? What actually happens when car returns the first element of its (list) argument?

Well, you are not reading a computer science book, and we will

125

not even attempt to answer all possible such questions. But that is not a cop-out: we promised to teach you Common Lisp, and the Common Lisp specification does not answer all questions either. For example, it does not specify exactly how a value is to be assigned to the name of a variable. That decision and many others like it are left to the expertise of the individual software house, as it implements Common Lisp for some particular computer or central processing unit. But we users of Lisp do not really need to know exactly how a value is assigned to a variable. We can look in the Common Lisp manual to see what the term means, and that is quite enough for all practical purposes. Exactly how cons cells are implemented on any particular computer similarly is not very useful information from the point of view of the Lisp user. In fact it would not matter if cons cells did not actually exist at all as any kind of discernible 'thing' within the machine. It is the *concept* of cons cells which is so useful for writing work-first-time Lisp programs. It finally explains the acronym 'Lisp', which stands for '**List P**rocessing language'.

Let us deal first with the notion of assignment. You probably know that modern personal computers can, by the standards of only a few years ago, make use of huge amounts of inbuilt memory. Your own computer may well have a megabyte or more of random access memory (RAM). That means that you the programmer have at your disposal a million 'slots', like pigeonholes, into each of which you can put whatever you like. When using a high level language such as Lisp you do not usually need to worry about the contents of individual cells; that's why Lisp is called a 'high level' language. But it is often very useful to know that such things do exist, down at the machine level. Between any two memory cells there can be a **pointer**. Starting from any one cell you could follow its pointer and arrive at another cell. That is how values might well bound to variables in your particular Lisp: when you type in the name of the variable, eval tries to follow a pointer from the cell containing that name to another cell containing its current value. (So you can see how values can be 'saved away' by binding – all that happens is that the destination of the pointer is temporarily changed.) eval then tests the contents of that remote cell to see what kind of thing it is: you already know that it could be a simple value; it could be a function definition; or a macro or a special form. If there is no pointer, eval issues a pertinent error message depending upon the form of your typed input: it will say 'this variable has no value' or 'there is no such function', in most cases.

Now that you have the idea of memory cells and pointers we can go on to talk about **cons cells**, which are simply pairs of cells; for efficiency they are likely to be adjacent cells in memory. Conceptually, a left-hand memory cell and a right-hand memory cell together make up one cons cell. Much of the time the left-hand cell contains a value and the right-hand cell contains a pointer to another cons cell. That cons cell too

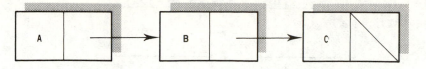

Figure 6.1   Cons cells: a three-element list.

has a value in its left-hand half and a pointer in its right-hand half, and hey presto we have a Lisp list (Figure 6.1).

Figure 6.1 represents the list

(A B C)

The diagonal line in the right-hand half of the final cons cell signifies NIL. Lisp lists, even if they are complex function definitions, almost invariably end with NIL in the right-hand half of their final cons cells. But it is possible to create a Lisp list which does not have NIL at its end. You would do this by typing

? (cons 'a 'b)

and letting eval evaluate it. It would return

(A . B)

and you may remember that when we introduced cons to you in the first place we warned you not to worry if by accident you ended up with one of these **dotted pairs**. The dot, and the all-important spaces on either side of it, signify that this is a single cons cell containing two values. Sometimes this is a useful trick. One could, for example, create a list of such cons cells to serve as a 'data structure' in which to store useful information:

((author1 . john) (author2 . tony))

and fairly obviously you could access either of our names by using the 'keys' author1 or author2.

But what would this look like in cons cell notation? Well, the main outer list would look just as you would by now expect (Figure 6.2). Think of the left-hand halves of each cons cell as representing an element of the main list. Now, each element of the main list is in fact a sublist, in each case a dotted pair. So the left-hand half of each of the above cons cells will have a pointer, each pointing to another cons cell which represents the corresponding sublist (Figure 6.3).

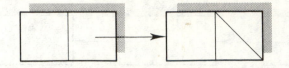

Figure 6.2   Cons cells: the outer list.

    We hope we have shown you enough to convince you that cons
cells are nothing special or alarming. They are always there underlying
what you do in Lisp, but you will rarely come across them because you
will almost always be working with ordinary Lisp lists such as that shown
in Figure 6.1, and consequently read and print will hide the cons cells
from you. You will appreciate what a good thing that is when we tell you
that the dotted pair notation for the list represented by Figure 6.1 is:

    (a . (b . (c . nil)))

And now we must reveal to you an awful truth: eval does not, as we have
been pretending so far, work on the actual text of your Lisp code; it
works on the cons cell representation of your code! The main purpose of
the read function is to convert your code into cons cell form, and the main
purpose of print is to convert it back again after eval has finished with it.
Every list which is ever 'stored' within Lisp, including function
definitions, is stored as an appropriately linked set of cons cells.
However, the whole two-way conversion process is completely 'transparent' to you the user, by which we mean that you could interact quite
successfully with Lisp and could write sophisticated programs without
ever knowing that cons cells existed. In almost all cases you can think of a
Lisp list in its textual, parenthesized form without that ever leading you
into mistakes.

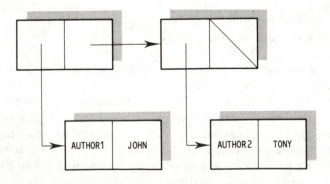

Figure 6.3   Cons cells: the outer list contians two sublists.

However, this simple knowledge of cons cells will enable you to understand the meaning of the dotted pair notation should it ever arise, and occasionally a cons cell diagram can help you to get rid of some nasty bug in your program.

Exercise 6.1

(a)   Convert the following to normal representation:

```
? '(a . ((b . c)))
? '(a . ((b . ((c)))))
? '(a . (b . (((c . nil)))))
? '(a . c . d)
```

(b)   Convert the following to dotted notation:

```
(A (B (C)))
((A ((B))))
(A ((B C)))
```

6.2 Macros

Now we would like to turn to something completely different, and much more interesting: macros. We have told you before that macros are a special kind of Lisp function which are handled in a special way by eval, and we feel that it is time we told you what we meant.

The thing which is special about a macro is that it is always *expanded* before being evaluated. A macro is written in such a way that the expansion results in a normal Lisp form, which is then evaluated instead of the macro. In other words, a macro is a form which rewrites itself as soon as you call it. You may well be wondering what on earth is the point of that, and part of the answer is that it gives you a form of 'shorthand' to use in your programs, a way of giving more mnemonic names to inbuilt Lisp functions (just as the macros first, second, third etc. replace car, cadr, caddr etc.). As you shall see in later chapters, macros can also serve to make your programs easier to use by non-programmers. More sophisticated macros (cond, defun and do are examples) allow the programmer to specify complex syntax to help future users of the macros themselves.

Here are the rules for eval with rule 2 changed to accommodate macros:

(1)   If the expression is an atom, return its value.

(2)   If the expression is a list, then either

    (a)   If the first member of the list is a special form, handle it and its arguments accordingly.

    (b)   If the first member of the list is the name of a macro, call the function macroexpand to expand it. Then return to step 1.

    (c)   If the first member of the list has a functional value then retrieve that function, and

        (i)   find the values of the remaining members of the list by applying these rules to each of them in turn;

        (ii)   apply the function from (c) to the arguments from (i), and return the result.

Just in case you should define yourself a macro and then, later, use it inside another macro (it is easy to do: first inside cond, for example) macroexpand is clever enough to call itself recursively until the resulting form is no longer a macro. Notice that inside the evaluator the macroexpansion phase is separate and prior to normal evaluation: step 2b ends with the instruction 'go back to step 1'. When writing a macro you are writing at one step removed, as it were: what you write will be turned into what you actually want it to be only at macroexpansion time.

Point to remember   Macroexpansion does not evaluate the macro's arguments.

We shall explain. A possible definition of first in Lisp is:

```
(defmacro ourfirst (lis)
   '(car,lis))
```

defmacro is itself a macro (we warned you that Lisp is recursive!) but just think of it as a macro-creating version of defun. When the above definition is evaluated it creates a macro, just as defun creates an ordinary function. When you later come to call the macro:

```
? (ourfirst '(a b c))
```

the body of the macro will be expanded and substituted in place of your call. The body of the macro in this case is of course

```
'(car ,lis)
```

and the interesting parts of this are the **backquote** and the **comma**. The backquote is similar to the ordinary quote: it specifies that the form following it is to be taken literally. The form is if you like a template for the result of the expansion: everything will appear literally in the macro-expanded form, except that within the template any comma indicates that the form following the comma itself is to be evaluated during the expansion process. As we said above, macro expansion does not involve automatic evaluation of ourfirst's argument; therefore the value of lis during macro expansion is the quoted list '(a b c). The comma retrieves this value, so that the result of the expansion is:

```
(CAR '(A B C))
```

This is then handed to eval and is evaluated in the normal way, just as though it has appeared as part of your program. Perhaps this will be clearer if we show the macro in action. Suppose you defined a function:

```
(defun atomhead (somelist)
   (cond ((atom (ourfirst somelist)) t)
         (t nil)))
```

This function is a predicate, returning T if the first element of its argument is an atom, or NIL otherwise. A call to it might well be:

```
? (atomhead '(a (b c) (d e f)))

T
```

During evaluation of atomhead, eval comes across the call to the macro ourfirst, and calls macroexpand to deal with it. At this stage, because we are in the middle of evaluating a function call, the variable somelist is bound to the supplied argument, namely to '(a (b c) (d e f)). Because of the effect of the comma, this same value is bound to the variable lis inside the macro call. It is as though the definition of atomhead had been:

```
(defun atomhead (somelist)
   (cond ((atom (car somelist)) t)
         (t nil)))
```

so that all is well and atomhead returns T as it should. But suppose that the comma had been missing from the macro definition:

```
(defmacro ourfirst (lis)
   '(car lis))
```

There would then be nothing to tell macroexpand that it should evaluate

lis, and in this case the effect would be as though atomhead had been
defined like this (again, notice the defun):

```
(defun atomhead (somelist)
  (cond ((atom (car lis)) t)
        (t nil)))
```

Naturally, that would produce an error because eval would complain that
lis had no value.

> *Point to remember*   Unlike functions, macros do not automatically
> evaluate their arguments. You may or may not want the arguments
> to be evaluated during macroexpansion, but if so you will have to
> provide something (a comma inside a backquote or an explicit call
> to eval, for example) to signify the fact.

When you find that you repeatedly use the same short section of code in
your program, it is usually a good idea to define it as a macro and to use
that instead, even if as in the case of atomhead it would be perfectly
feasible to define it as an ordinary function. Macros are more efficient
than ordinary functions, though in Lisp programming they tend to be
used mainly for the sake of convenience; AI programs are not prized
primarily for their efficiency. Here is another example:

```
(defmacro listhead (anylist)
  '(cond ((atom (car ,anylist))
          (cons (list (car ,anylist)) (cdr ,anylist)))
         (t ,anylist)))
```

This macro returns its own (list) argument if the first element of that
argument is itself a list. If the first element is an atom, it turns it into a
list:

```
? (listhead '((a b) (c d) (e f)))

((A B) (C D) (E F))

? (listhead '(a (b c) (c d)))

((A) (B C) (D E))
```

Notice that in the definition the backquote precedes the entire cond.
Therefore the cond is the template and will be substituted verbatim for
any call to listhead, except that the four occurrences of anylist, each
preceded by a comma, will be replaced by the unevaluated argument to
that call.

Note that macros cannot be used as auxiliary functions (to mapcar,
for example). Auxiliary functions must be functions or lambda expressions.

There is a further piece of syntax associated with the backquote which is often useful when writing serious programs. It is the ,@ (pronounced 'comma-at-sign'). Look at this macro definition:

```
(defmacro insert-num (num lis)
   '(list ,num ,@lis))
```

It works like cons, but only on numbers, i.e. it adds a new number to the head of a list of numbers. It will probably never be of the slightest use to you, but it is a nice, simple example of the effect of ,@.

The meaning of ,@ is the same as that of the comma alone, except that it also does what is conceptually an append: the parameter lis, when it appears in the second line as an argument to list, effectively appears with its outer set of brackets removed. Thus, the call

```
? (insert-num 2 (3 4 5))
```

becomes

```
(LIST 2 3 4 5)
```

before being passed to the evaluator. You will meet ,@ again in the final section of this book.

One last but important point about macros. The process we have described above, where expansion takes place immediately prior to evaluation of the macro, is the normal case. However, on smaller computers and for the sake of speed of response, some manufacturers (usually the best) are starting to supply incremental compilers with their Lisp packages. We do not intend to cover the subject of compilers in this book, but if your Lisp has an incremental compiler its effect will be that the body of any macro really is expanded and written straight into your functions for you. There is then no macroexpansion phase in the evaluator.

If you are wondering how Lisp would ever know which of your existing functions it should rewrite if you decide to redefine one of their subordinate functions as a macro, the answer is that it would not! So if you would like to avoid being hassled by 'undefined function' bugs resulting from what the incremental compiler does, please acquire the excellent habit of putting all macros towards the top of any file in which they appear, ahead of any function definitions in same file (or, at least, ahead of any functions which use them). That way, as the file loads, all the macros will be defined first, and their expansions will then be used correctly during the later definition of functions. For the same reasons, if you redefine a macro after the file has loaded, you will need to read into Lisp again all the functions which use that macro; otherwise their definitions will still carry the (expanded) old version of the macro.

Later in this book, when we come to show you quite large programs, we shall be using macros to help simplify our code and to make it more readable. Macros are usually quite simple things, although they can often be a little confusing at first.

Exercise 6.2

(a)   Write a macro fred? which returns T if its argument is the atom fred:

```
? (fred? 'fred)
T
? (fred? 999)
NIL
```

(b)   Write a two-cons macro which conses its first two arguments onto its third:

```
? (TWO-CONS 'a 'b '(1 2 3))
(A B 1 2 3)
```

(c)   Write a not-equal macro which returns T if its two arguments are not equal, and NIL otherwise.

(d)   Write a macro which returns the first three elements of a list.

(e)   Write an unless macro which takes a test and a single action argument. The action is evaluated if the test is not true. This macro already exists in Common Lisp so call yours new_unless and do not use unless.

6.3   Lambda lists

In the definition of any function, there is immediately following the name of the function a list of the function's parameters: the list of X and Y in the following definition:

```
(defun foo (x y)
  (append x y))
```

This list of parameters, known for historical reasons as the **lambda list**, is a powerful mechanism in its own right. First of all, you are allowed as many or as few parameters as you like, including none, although the list must always be present even if it is empty. Normally, an error would result if when calling the function you did not supply exactly as many arguments as there were parameters in its definition. Such parameters, the only kind we have shown you so far, are known as **required** parameters. There are also other types of parameters, each type being distinguished from the required parameters in that they are preceded in the lambda list (i.e. in the function definition) by a **lambda list keyword**.

All of these lambda list keywords begin with an ampersand, and the most
frequently used of them is &optional:

```
(defun foo (lis &optional tail)
  (append lis tail))
```

The keyword itself is not a parameter, i.e. no arguments will be bound to
it during a call to the function. As the keyword implies, foo can be called
either with or without an argument to match its optional parameter. If no
such optional argument is supplied, the optional parameter is automatically bound to NIL:

```
? (foo '(a b c))

(A B C)

? (foo '(a b c) '(d e f))

(A B C D E F)
```

It is also possible to specify an initial or default value for any optional
parameter, and the syntax of this looks very like the variable–value pairs
which follow a let or a do:

```
(defun foo (lis &optional (tail '(d e f)))
  (append lis tail))

? (foo '(a b c))

(A B C D E F)
```

The &optional keyword normally appears in lambda lists when the
corresponding argument to the function is to be used only rarely. An
example is the inbuilt print function which can take an optional second
argument specifying to which **stream** its output shall be printed:
sometimes a programmer might want the output to be printed directly to
a disk file rather than to the screen, for example. It is also possible to use
multiple optional parameters: all variable names from the keyword
&optional up to the next keyword in the lambda list (or up to the end of
the list if there is no other keyword) represent optional arguments:

```
(defun foo (lis &optional lis2 lis3 lis4...)
  (append lis lis2 lis3 lis4...))
```

However, at the time of writing the definition of foo you may not be able
to tell exactly how many arguments foo will receive, and even when using
&optional you still need to provide as many parameters as there ever will

be arguments. There are quite often occasions when you would like your function to be able to accept an arbitrary number of arguments. In such cases you would use the &rest keyword:

```
(defun foo (lis &rest atoms)
  (append lis atoms))

? (foo '(a b c) 'd 'e 'f)

(A B C D E F)
```

As you can see, the &rest keyword makes a list of all the arguments following it, up to the end of the list (or the next keyword), and this list is bound to the variable name which in the lambda list follows the &rest keyword. Note that &rest parameters cannot be initialized as &optional parameters can. This is obvious if you think about it, since the whole point of the keyword &rest is to cope with cases where you do not know in advance how many arguments there will be. Incidentally, and although we have not mentioned this before, both append and list effectively use &rest keywords in their definitions. This means that you can give to either of those functions as many arguments as you like.

If you have occasion to use &optional and &rest in the same lambda list, the &optional parameters must come first. During subsequent evaluation of the lambda list, all of the &optional parameters will be processed (bound to a supplied argument), and only then will the remainder be listed and bound to the &rest parameter.

The third main keyword used in lambda lists is &key. This keyword allows you to use keywords amongst the arguments supplied to a function! However, these latter keywords will not be confused with the lambda list keywords, because instead of beginning with an ampersand they begin with a colon. In fact they are Lisp keywords rather than lambda list keywords. Any atom beginning with a colon automatically becomes a Lisp keyword symbol and is 'remembered' as such. Conversely, lambda list keywords are ordinary atomic symbols which happen to begin with an ampersand.

The purpose of using Lisp keywords in this way is simple: as your functions grow in complexity, they may sometimes need quite large numbers (say, six or eight) of parameters and hence of arguments. When you come to use such functions within a larger program, it is inconvenient to have to remember the precise order of them all the time. Things could get even worse if your function definition had six &optional parameters but you found that you regularly needed to supply an argument only for the fifth of them. You can think of keywords as being rather like labels, via which you can specify exactly which parameters you are supplying arguments for, regardless of the order of the parameters within the lambda list:

```
(defun foo (&key lis1 lis2)
  (append lis1 lis2))

? (foo :lis1 '(a b c) :lis2 '(d e f))

(A B C D E F)

? (foo :lis2 '(d e f) :lis1 '(a b c))

(A B C D E F)
```

Notice that when &key appears in the definition of a function, each parameter following it will need two arguments in any call to that function. Of those pairs of arguments, the first is treated as the keyword (and must be preceded by a colon as above), and the second as its value.

The Common Lisp specification permits one other lambda list keyword: &aux. Parameters appearing after &aux in the lambda list are known as **auxiliary variables** and are initialized (or are automatically bound to NIL) just like the parameters which follow &optional. However, the effect is exactly the same as if, in the body of the function definition, you were to bind some local variables using a let. In our opinion it is preferable to use let for the sake of clarity, but you will undoubtedly come across programs written by others which do make use of the &aux keyword. See what you think:

```
(defun foo (x &aux (y 3) (z '(a b c)))
  ...)
```

or

```
(defun foo (x)
  (let ((y 3) (z '(a b c)))
    ...))
```

The Lisp constant lambda-list-keywords has a value which is a list of all the lambda list keywords permissible in any particular implementation of Common Lisp. Besides the four we have mentioned, you should also see &body, &whole and &environment. These are used exclusively in macro definitions and are beyond the scope of this book. There may be yet more keywords in the list, since the Common Lisp specification allows implementers to add extra lambda list keywords if they think them useful.

Exercise 6.3

(a)   member is a Common Lisp function that by default uses the equality test eql to decide whether or not its first argument is a member (an element) of the list supplied as its second argument. If the test succeeds, it returns that remainder of the list which begins with the element. member uses eql as its test if you do not supply an extra, keyworded, argument to specify some other test:

```
? (member '(3) '((2) (3) (4)))
NIL
```

This fails because, of course, no two lists are eql.

```
? (member '(3) '((2) (3) (4)) :test #'equal)
((3) (4))
```

Write an equal-member macro that always uses the test equal. That is, it will not need a keyworded argument, but it will behave as member behaves when given the test equal. In fact, you should use member in your solution.

(b)   Write a reverse-funcall macro that calls a function with its arguments reversed. You will need to use the &rest keyword to handle the function's arguments, and you will need ,@ in order to pass them to funcall:

```
? (rev-funcall #'list 'a 'b 'c 9 8 7 6)
(6 7 8 9 C B A)
```

(c)   Write a macro called defun-one which defines functions with no arguments. That is, your macro when called will need to be given the name of the function it is to define, plus the body of that function. The call might look like this:

```
? (defun-one john (print 9) (print 3) (print 44))
JOHN
```

The returned value of john is the name of the function defined by the macro, and if that function were to be defined by hand its definition would look like this:

```
(defun john ()
  (print 9)
  (print 3)
  (print 44))
? (john)
9
3
44
44
```

The final 44 is, of course, the returned value of the function john after it has carried out its three internal print forms.

(c)   Rewrite your macro so that the functions defined by it carry out their
        bodies in reverse order:

```
? (reverse-defun goo (x y) (list x y) (print x) (print y))
GOO

? (goo 1 2)
2
1
(1 2)
```

(d)   We can represent a real-world object as a nested list, e.g. we can represent
        a person as:

```
((first-name fred) (surname flintstone)
 (occupation teacher))
```

Write a function which creates such a structure. The function should take
three keyword arguments. If one of the values is left unspecified by the
user it should automatically be filled with NIL. Hint: it is often convenient
to use the backquote instead of the function list:

```
? (setf a 1)
1

? (setf b 2)
2

? (list a b)
(1 2)

? `(,a ,b)
(1 2)
```

Use backquote and comma in your function, which should behave as
follows:

```
? (make-person :occupation 'none)
((FIRST-NAME NIL) (SURNAME NIL) (OCCUPATION NONE))

? (make-person :surname 'flintstone :occupation 'none)
((FIRST-NAME NIL) (SURNAME FLINTSTONE) (OCCUPATION NONE))
```

(e)   Write a macro that takes two arguments, a 'person' as defined in the
        previous exercise and one of the three 'slot-names' first-name, surname or
        occupation. The macro then returns the corresponding value for that slot-
        name. If no second argument is given all of the values should be returned:

```
? (setf a (make-person :surname 'flintstone :occupation 'none))
((FIRST-NAME NIL) (SURNAME FLINTSTONE) (OCCUPATION NONE))

? (PERSON-ACCESS a)
(NIL FLINTSTONE NONE)

? (PERSON-ACCESS a 'surname)
FLINTSTONE
```

```
? (PERSON-ACCESS a 'occupation)
NONE

? (PERSON-ACCESS a 'first-name)
NIL
```

(f)   Write a person-set macro using keyword arguments :first-name, :surname
       and :occupation. In a call to your macro any or all of these keywords may
       be specified, with a value. The effect of the macro is to change the
       corresponding data in the person list. Hint: use setf and a car–cdr
       combination to alter the items within the list itself.

```
? a
((FIRST-NAME NIL) (SURNAME FLINTSTONE) (OCCUPATION NONE))

? (person-set a :occupation 'researcher :first-name 'john)
RESEARCHER

? a
((FIRST-NAME JOHN) (SURNAME FLINTSTONE) (OCCUPATION RESEARCHER))

? (person-set a :occupation 'none
               :first-name 'john
               :surname 'domingue)
NONE

? a
((FIRST-NAME JOHN) (SURNAME DOMINGUE) (OCCUPATION NONE))
```

SUMMARY

In this chapter you have learned three things. You have learned about
cons cells, which although not often useful in themselves are the bottom
line where the truth about Lisp is concerned. Cons cells are analogous
to molecules in chemistry: the lowest level at which Lisp is still Lisp and
not some form of machine code or patterns of binary digits. You have
also learned about macros and lambda list keywords, which together
will add power and elegence to your programs. Power because
keywords such as &optional and &rest free you from the 'one parameter,
one argument' restrictions of your earlier function definitions; and
elegance because, as you will see in the final section of this book,
macros really come into their own when you need to think about
functional abstraction and/or data abstraction.

Chapter 7
Simple Knowledge Representation

In an earlier chapter we promised to return to the subject of knowledge representation. There is considerable debate about whether or not is is correct to talk about 'knowledge' being stored in a computer at all, but we do not want to enter into that debate; in the sense that 'knowledge' can be stored in books and retrieved from them, so facts and data can be stored in and retrieved from the machine. As you will see, the combination of even a fairly simply structured data store and an active program can convincingly simulate a human being doing what we call 'using knowledge'.

7.1 Knowledge representation

At the end of this chapter we shall invite you to build in Lisp a primitive model of human memory. The model is a long-standing favourite of Open University Cognitive Psychology courses, and students have built essentially the same model in several different programming languages as well as in Lisp. At that point we will have stopped teaching you how to use Lisp, and will have begun teaching you what kinds of things you can do with it. You will then stop worrying about such things as how many arguments a function takes, or whether it is a simple function or a macro. These factors will become important if your program has bugs in it, but the main concern will be the behaviour of the model, and how closely that behaviour corresponds to what we believe to be analogous human behaviour.

We begin this chapter with simple **alists**, of which you have in fact

141

already seen an example, earlier in this book. We shall then describe to
you progressively more complex ways of representing knowledge in Lisp,
until you are ready to build the model of memory.

7.1.1 Alists

An **alist** (short for association list) is a list of two-element sublists or
pairs. For the sake of efficiency such pairs are often implemented in Lisp
as dotted pairs:

```
((author1 . john) (author2 . tony))
```

although of course they need not be:

```
((author1 john) (author2 tony))
```

The list of pairs can be as long as you like, but each pair consists of first
an atom which is a **key**, followed by some piece of **data** which you wish to
retrieve using the key. For example, the assignment of values to variables
could be stored (but is not) in an alist:

```
((var1 . val1) (var2 . val2) (var3 . val3)...)
```

The Lisp function assoc takes two arguments, a key and an alist, and
returns the whole of any pair whose car is eql to the key (but, see below).
This implies that the key argument to assoc can be an atom, a number
equal to and of the same type as the key in the alist, or a variable whose
value is the same object as the key in the alist. Actually, assoc returns
only the first matching item it encounters, working down the list from left
to right (from car to cdr).

```
? (setf q '((author1 . john) (author2 . tony) (author3 . fred)))

((AUTHOR1 . JOHN) (AUTHOR2 . TONY) (AUTHOR3 . FRED))

? (assoc 'author2 q)

(AUTHOR2 . TONY)
```

If assoc does not find the specified key in the alist, it returns NIL. And
since the cdr of NIL is also NIL it is possible to retrieve the data, rather
than the whole pair, very simply:

```
? (cdr (assoc 'author2 q))

TONY
```

An extra, keyworded and therefore optional argument to assoc allows you to specify that some test other than eql shall be used to compare any key with the keys in the alist. You might well want it to be eq or equal, but in fact you can use any function, including those written by you, as an auxiliary here. For example, allowing assoc to use its normal eql test:

```
? (assoc '(a) '((a . b) ((a) c)))

NIL
```

The assoc fails because a list (of a) is not eql to a list. If we now specify that the test shall be equal instead:

```
? (assoc '(a) '((a . b) ((a) c)) :test #'equal)

((A) C)
```

the call to assoc succeeds.

You can if you like think of an alist as being conceptually similar to a table of information (Figure 7.1).

Alists are most easily created and manipulated using acons and pairlis. In fact you could if you liked go on adding pairs to an alist via explicit and long-winded calls to setf:

```
? (setf q (cons (cons 'author4 nil) q))

((AUTHOR4) (AUTHOR1 . JOHN) (AUTHOR2 . TONY) (AUTHOR3 . FRED))
```

but acons does exactly the same thing more neatly:

```
(setf q (acons 'author nil q))
```

The purpose of pairlis is to facilitate the creation of alists. It takes as

author1	john
author2	tony
author3	fred

Figure 7.1 An alist drawn as a table.

arguments two lists, one of intended keys and one of intended data, and creates an alist out of them. The two lists must obviously be of the same length:

```
? (pairlis '(one two three) '(x y z))

((ONE . X) (TWO . Y) (THREE . Z))
```

You are also allowed to supply a third, optional argument to pairlis. This argument should already be an alist, whereupon pairlis will 'append' it to the end of the newly created alist:

```
? (pairlis '(one two three) '(x y z) '((four . alpha)))

((ONE . X) (TWO . Y) (THREE . Z) (FOUR . ALPHA))
```

The advantages of alists for representing knowledge are that new items can be very quickly added, and it can sometimes be useful that the most recently added information is the most rapidly returned. The main disadvantage is that if the data you need is way down in a long alist then retrieval can be inefficient, i.e. slow.

Alists are most often used when the stored data is dynamically changing as the program runs. For example, if Lisp did keep track of its variable assignments via an alist, then variable binding could be implemented via the same alist. In such a system, functions such as let would place a marker pair onto the alist, and then add the local variable value pairs. When evaluation of the let came to an end, all pairs back to and including the marker would be removed from the alist, whereupon the original variable value pairs would again be available to assoc. This would effect the desired lexical scope of the bindings produced by let. You will see an example of an alist used to keep track of the values of variables towards the end of this book, when we show you a way of implementing a simple production system.

Alists are rather cumbersome things to use. Under normal circumstances they always have to be bound to some variable, and as we have said it is normal programming practice simply to cons on any updates to existing pairs, without bothering to remove the old and perhaps redundant version. It is pretty much a choice of two evils: leaving redundant information around is wasteful of memory, but removing them (say, with setf) is expensive in terms of processing time.

In case you are wondering exactly how setf could remove a pair which might be some arbitrary distance down an alist, one way is to do the removing before consing on the new pair:

```
(setf (assoc 'author1 q) nil)
```

This leaves behind in the alist an empty pair, the list NIL, but at least it gets rid of the unwanted data.

Exercise 7.1

(a)   Write a function which takes an alist like this:

```
((one . 1) (two . 2) ... (ten . 10))
```

as one of its arguments, together with two other arguments each of which
is one of the sequence of atoms

```
one, two ... nine, ten
```

Your function should 'add' the two atomic arguments:

```
? (word-add '((one . 1) (two . 2) (three . 3) (four . 4))
            'three
            'four)
7
```

(b)   Set a global variable *values* to NIL. This variable will hold an alist
consisting of dotted pairs. The first element of each dotted pair will be the
name of a 'variable' and the second element will be the variable's 'value'.
Write a function which takes a symbol and a value and adds a suitable
dotted pair to the alist. Big hint: look up the function acons in your Lisp
manual in order to save yourself a lot of trouble.

```
? (add-val 'x 66)
((X . 66))
? (add-val 'y 55)
((Y . 55) (X . 66))
```

(c)   Write a function var-value which retrieves the value of any desired variable
from the alist *values*:

```
? (var-value 'x)
66
? (var-value 'y)
55
```

(d)   Assign a global variable *funs* to NIL. This variable will hold an alist of
function names and lambda expressions. Write a function which takes a
name and a lambda expression and adds it to *funs*:

```
? (add-fun 'foo '(lambda (x y) (list x y (+ x y))))
((FOO LAMBDA (X Y) (LIST X Y (+ X Y))))
? (add-fun 'bar '(lambda (x y) (list x y (* x y))))
((BAR LAMBDA (X Y) (LIST X Y (* X Y))) (FOO LAMBDA (X Y) (LIST X Y (+
X Y))))
```

(e)   Write a function which takes a function name which is stored on *funs*,
together with any appropriate arguments to the function, and then applies

the function to those arguments:

```
? (apply-fun 'foo 7 8)
(7 8 15)
? (apply-fun 'bar 7 8)
(7 8 56)
```

7.1.2 Property lists

A conceptually similar but more convenient way of storing information is to use Lisp's **property lists**. Every symbol (other than special symbols such as Lisp keywords) has associated with it a property list. All of the symbols you have seen and used so far have had property lists. A property list which has not been changed by the programmer may be empty, or it may contain certain rarely-needed system information. However, it is important to note that property lists are not lists in the ordinary sense, and the normal list-manipulating functions such as cons and append will not work on them. Instead, there is a small set of dedicated functions provided for the manipulation of property lists.

A property list is again a list of pairs, but they do not appear as nested lists as in alists. All the odd-numbered items are **indicators** (sometimes called **properties**) which are normally symbols, and all the even-numbered items are the corresponding **values** which may be any Lisp object. Property lists are usually referred to as plists, which is pronounced 'pee-list'.

The function get will retrieve the value of a specified indicator from the plist of a specified symbol. If the plist of the symbol foo carries the indicator author1, then

```
(get 'foo 'author1)
```

will return whatever value is in that slot. If there is no such indicator on the plist, or if it has no value, or if its value is NIL, get will return NIL. In order to put the values into the plist in the first place, you use setf with a call to get:

```
? (setf (get 'foo 'author1) 'john)

JOHN

? (get 'foo 'author1)

JOHN
```

The function `symbol-plist` will enable you to see the plist of any symbol:

```
? (symbol-plist 'foo)

(AUTHOR1 JOHN)
```

In fact, as mentioned above, the plist may contain other information besides what you put there. Please do not interfere with anything on a plist which is not 'yours'; it could have alarming results and you might have to restart your Lisp to get things back to normal!

Unlike an alist, a plist can have only one of each indicator (though you can add as many different indicators, and their values, as you like). Any attempt to add a second author1–name pair to the above plist will result in overwriting the one which is there already. In other words, plists are destructively updated: it is as though with an alist you simultaneously consed on a new pair whilst removing an old one.

Sometimes you might want completely to remove an indicator and its value from a plist. The function `remprop` does it:

```
(remprop 'foo 'author1)
```

If `remprop` fails (if for example there was no such indicator) it returns `NIL`. If it succeeds, it returns some non-`NIL` value.

The advantages of plists over alists are that they are more efficient (faster) and more convenient to use. The main disadvantage is that they are destructively updated: you could not, for example, use a plist to store the 'history' of some variable's changing value throughout the run of a program: at any instant during the run the plist would show you only the variable's current value. There is also a faint possibility that one of your chosen indicator names might clash with some existing system-specific indicator name; but the possibility is quite remote.

Exercise 7.2

(a)   Write a function `add-num-prop` which takes list of arguments and adds a number property to each element of the list. The value of this property should be the same as the position of the argument within the list. Use as your list of arguments the sequence 'zero' to 'twenty'. Thus, the symbol zero should acquire a 0 as its number, the symbol one should acquire a 1, and so on.

(b)   Modify the above function so that as well as setting up the properties it creates and returns an alist associating each number with the symbol.

```
? (add-num-prop2 '(zero one two three four five six
                    seven eight nine ten eleven twelve
                    thirteen fourteen fifteen sixteen
                    seventeen eighteen nineteen twenty))
```

```
((20 . TWENTY) (19 . NINETEEN) (18 . EIGHTEEN) (17 . SEVENTEEN) (16 .
SIXTEEN) (15 . FIFTEEN) (14 . FOURTEEN) (13 . THIRTEEN) (12 . TWELVE)
(11 . ELEVEN) (10 . TEN) (9 . NINE) (8 . EIGHT) (7 . SEVEN) (6 . SIX)
(5 . FIVE) (4 . FOUR) (3 . THREE) (2 . TWO) (1 . ONE) (0 . ZERO))
```

(c)   Set the value of a global variable *symbols* using the above function. Write a function which adds any two numbers between zero and ten, expressed as words, and returns the answer as a word.

```
? (word-add2 'one 'three)
FOUR

? (word-add2 'five 'three)
EIGHT
```

(d)   Write a function which takes a person's name and adds the following information as properties of the person's name if given as keywords

```
age
occupation
street-name
town
```

If a keyword is not specified do not overwrite any old values:

```
? (add-info 'fred :age 40 :town 'rocksville)
ROCKSVILLE
```

(e)   Write a function that returns an alist. Each element of the alist should contain the name and value of some particular slot in a 'person' as defined in the previous exercise:

```
? (person-info 'fred)
((AGE 40) (OCCUPATION NIL) (STREET-NAME NIL) (TOWN ROCKSVILLE))

? (add-info 'fred :age 38 :occupation 'pop-star)
NIL

? (person-info 'fred)
((AGE 38) (OCCUPATION POP-STAR) (STREET-NAME NIL) (TOWN ROCKSVILLE))
```

7.1.3 Hash tables

An even faster method of retrieving values associated with specific Lisp symbols is to use a **hash table**. Think of a hash table as a single row of pigeonholes. Each pigeonhole can hold a single **entry**, and each entry associates a particular **key** with a particular **value**. The hashing process itself applies some **hashing function** (it does not matter what it is) to your actual key in order to decide which pigeonhole should hold any given key–value pair; so the order of the entries in a hash table may or may not bear any relation to the temporal order in which you added them, and entries added in sequence may not lie anywhere near each other in the hash table. We as programmers simply trust the hashing process to return our data to us very rapidly whenever we ask for it.

It is not intended that you should ever need to see a screen representation of a hash table in the way that you can see an alist or a property list. In any case it is doubtful that a screen representation would have any useful meaning, since if the hash table becomes full (because you need to store a great many entries in it) it will automatically be resized and its entries recomputed. The **inspector** provided with your Lisp (see next chapter) may allow you to 'see' the contents of a hash table at a particular instant, and the describe function almost certainly will; but normally you would never need to do so.

The function make-hash-table creates a new, empty hash table which can hold a certain number of entries. This number of entries is known as its **size**, but the Common Lisp specification does not ordain what that size shall be. We do not need to know what it is anyway because of its automatic resizing should it become full. However, in order perhaps to save on memory usage you can if you wish specify an approximate size for the initial hash table. You can also specify how full the table should get before automatically resizing itself, and by how much it should grow when this happens. But for most purposes it is far simpler to let these values default to whatever the implementers of your Lisp decided were appropriate.

We said that when using alists you could supply an auxiliary function as an optional argument to assoc so as to control exactly how it compared keys. With make-hash-table you have to make that decision when the new hash table is created, by supplying an appropriate optional argument to make-hash-table. In fact only three alternatives are allowed: eq, eql and equal. If you do not supply this argument make-hash-table defaults to using eql, which is usually what you want anyway.

A call to make-hash-table returns the hash table so created. Exactly how this will be represented on your screen is implementation dependent, which means that whoever implemented your Lisp was free to invent any suitable representation. That representation might well include the words 'An EQL hash table with entries 0'. Whatever the on-screen representation is, you can be sure that you will not be able to hand-type it back into Lisp. For that reason the returned value of make-hash-table is invariably assigned to a variable:

```
? (setf ourtable (make-hash-table))
```

Adding entries to a hash table is done using setf, in a similar manner to the method of adding indicator–value pairs to property lists:

```
(setf (gethash 'mud ourtable) 'pie)
```

makes mud the key and pie the value of a new entry in the hash table:

```
? (gethash 'mud ourtable)

PIE
```

That is, gethash retrieves the value of the key from the hash table. Again analogously to the use of plists, remhash takes a key as its first argument and removes that entry from a hash table. It is actually a predicate, returning T if there was an entry to remove and NIL if not.

```
? (remhash 'pie ourtable)

NIL

? (remhash 'mud ourtable)

T
```

It is often desirable to clear a hash table completely of entries, for example before a second run of the program in which the hash table is used. clrhash does that:

```
? (clrhash ourtable)
```

and it returns the hash table itself.

Example 7.1

So far we have talked about 'one-dimensional' representations of knowledge, analogous to a single row of pigeonholes. Although such representations at first sight may seem so trivial as to be virtually useless, we do in fact use them all the time in real life. A telephone directory, a diary, a television listing are all similar in that one piece of information (a name, a date, a time) is used to access another corresponding piece of information. All of them could be implemented on a computer using one or other of the above three methods. Here is a toy example:

```
(setf diary
      (pairlis '(jan1 jan2 jan3 jan4 jan5 jan6 jan7)
               '(drink nil (visit mum) nil nil nil dentist)))
```

handily creates an electronic diary. Here is the function which 'looks things up' in that diary:

```
(defun appointment (date)
  (assoc date diary))
```

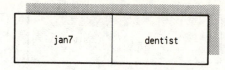

Figure 7.2 A dotted pair of atoms.

Let's try it out:

> ? (appointment 'jan6)
>
> (JAN6)

Remember, assoc returns the whole of the pair whose car
matches the key. In this case you might have expected
(JAN6 . NIL) but if you think back to our discussion of dotted
pairs you will remember that print always tries to give you the
simplest-looking version of any returned value. A 'dot-nil'
appearing at the end of a Lisp list is implicit and is never printed.
Let us try a different day:

> ? (appointment 'jan7)
>
> (JAN7 . DENTIST)

This one, we hope, does not surprise you at all. But we would
like to remind you of its cons cell notation (Figure 7.2).

And finally let us try:

> ? (appointment 'jan3)
>
> (JAN3 VISIT MUM)

You may be wondering whether this is correct. By analogy with
other pairs in the alist, you might have expected

> (JAN3 . (VISIT MUM))

But actually the two are the same thing, and again print gives
you the simpler version. As you know, the dot in the 'expected'
version signifies a single cons cell. But cons cells cannot really
hold lists: they hold atoms. So in the right-hand half of the cell in
Figure 7.3 there should be a pointer leading to the list (visit
mum). The cons cell notation in Figure 7.4 shows us at once that
this is a perfectly normal Lisp list. No cell contains two values,
and therefore no dots are needed.

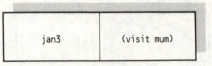

Figure 7.3 A dotted pair of an atom and a list.

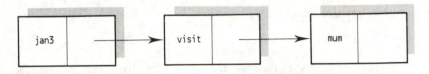

Figure 7.4 A three-element list.

You also do not strictly need the pairs whose values are NIL: jan2, jan4, jan5 and jan6. We only included them because this is supposed to be a model of a diary, and real diaries have blank pages for dates when you have no appointments. If you call appointment giving it a date which does not exist in the diary, it will return NIL; which is perhaps even more meaningful than a list of the date with no appointment shown.

If an appointment for jan5 came up, you could modify your diary with setf:

```
(setf (assoc 'jan5 diary) '(jan5 . tennis))
```

but as we have said before this is not in the spirit of alists. Other people reading your code would expect you simply to acons the new pair onto the front of the list, knowing that assoc would faithfully retrieve it in preference to the old no-appointment entry. After a while, with new appointments coming in all the time, your diary might look like this:

```
((JAN15 . FUNERAL)
 (JAN5 . TENNIS)
 (JAN1 . DRINK)
 (JAN2)
 (JAN3 VISIT MUM)
 (JAN4)
 (JAN5)
 (JAN6)
 (JAN7 . DENTIST))
```

Notice that the dates are out of order, reflecting the sequence in which you heard about your new appointments rather than the order in which you will fulfil them. That does not matter, because assoc looks only for a match and does not understand or care about the meaning of items such as jan3. But it raises an interesting point. We remarked at the very start of this book that cognitive science researchers, in building computer models of human mental processes, are not happy unless the detailed workings of their models – their computer programs – somehow parallel the equivalent operations inside the mind.

At the time, that probably did not seem a very clear thing to say, but here in this diary program is an excellent example of what we meant. Imagine for a moment that it were not a model of a diary, but a model of how the same information might be stored in human memory. If you showed it to a friend, he or she would almost certainly remark 'Oh, I don't store things in that way at all. I'm very aware, when I think about my future appointments, that January 15th is further away than January 1st. It doesn't make sense for that to be the very first appointment I remember; unless of course there's something special about that date which your model doesn't account for.'

It is upon such arguments, woolly and unprovable though they may be, that AI tends to base its judgements of whether a particular cognitive model is a good or a bad model. Before other researchers decide to come after us with knives, we had better admit that on occasion psychology can offer large amounts of meticulously acquired empirical evidence to indicate that the human mind does indeed carry out certain of its operations in clearly definable ways; and that philosophy has some very cogent arguments to suggest that this kind of introspection (claiming to 'feel' how one's own mind works) is virtually certain to lead to incorrect conclusions. Our point is that the objectives which AI–cognitive science undertakes are necessarily still so far above the present state of our knowledge that we are more or less forced to make numbers of rather simplistic assumptions about the real world, in order to achieve any progress at all.

Exercise 7.3

(a)   Write a program to model exactly the same diary, but this time use property lists instead of an alist.

(b)   Repeat the above exercise using hash tables.

7.1.4 Arrays

Now we want to move on from 'one-dimensional' representations as above to 'two-dimensional' representations, analogous to the normal arrangement of pigeonholes in which several rows are stacked vertically above one another. In common with most programming languages, Lisp provides a type of data object called an **array**. A Lisp array can have one **dimension**, like a hash table, in which case it is usually referred to as a **vector**. Alternatively it may have two dimensions, i.e. it has 'rows' and 'columns' as in our real-life pigeonholes analogy.

Many programming languages provide no more than one- or two-dimensional arrays. In Common Lisp it is perfectly legal, though of doubtful usefulness, to create an array of zero dimensions, which is in effect a single element or a solitary pigeonhole (isn't that interesting?). A Common Lisp array can also have more than two dimensions. It is quite easy to imagine what a three-dimensional array 'looks like': it would be a cube of pigeonholes if all three dimensions were the same size, or a rectangular solid otherwise. But what about a four- or even five-dimensional array? Our minds, so accustomed to dealing with a three-dimensional world, find such ideas very hard to grasp. Common Lisp allows arrays of up to at least seven dimensions to be created, and in fact the Common Lisp specification imposes no limit on the number of dimensions. Perhaps the possibility of creating n-dimensional arrays is an early sign that those AI researchers who seek to build an artificial intelligence superior to that of human beings are right: the machine can already handle at least one concept which leaves most of us gasping.

Arrays are created and accessed in very similar ways to hash tables. The array-creating function is make-array, and takes as its main argument a list of the dimensions you want the resulting array to have. It can also take up to seven optional, keyworded arguments, but most of these are intended for relatively esoteric applications and as usual we shall introduce you to the basic use of the function, and shall cover its extended facilities as and when we need them later in this book.

```
(make-array '(7 7))
```

creates and returns a 7×7 array whose 49 elements can each hold any type of Lisp object. As with hash tables, exactly what is shown on screen when the returned value of a function is an array is unspecified. Your Lisp may well return a list of seven sublists, each of which contains seven NILs, to indicate the array's current contents. Similarly,

```
(make-array '(7 7 7))
```

creates and returns an array having three dimensions each seven elements long, or 343 elements in all. The number of dimensions an array has is known as its **rank**.

Think of a two-dimensional 3×4 array as a table or set of pigeonholes as in Figure 7.5. The element marked C is accessed much as one would denote a specific point on a map via its grid reference: one states the distance 'down' and the distance 'across'. Given these two arguments, the function aref (short, of course, for array reference) retrieves the value in that element, and as usual setf is used to change that value. However, a factor which can sometimes cause the famous One Off Bug is that all 'distances' are zero based rather than one based. What that means is that for a dimension of (say) 3 the possible distance measurements are 0, 1 and 2 rather than 1, 2 and 3.

To try this out, first create an array and assign it as the value of some variable so that you can refer to it again:

```
? (setf ourarray (make-array '(3 4)))
```

This, as mentioned above, will return some representation of the array so created. Then:

```
? (setf (aref ourarray 1 2) 'c)

C
```

And, to satisfy yourself that the C has indeed been stored in that element:

```
? (aref ourarray 1 2)

C
```

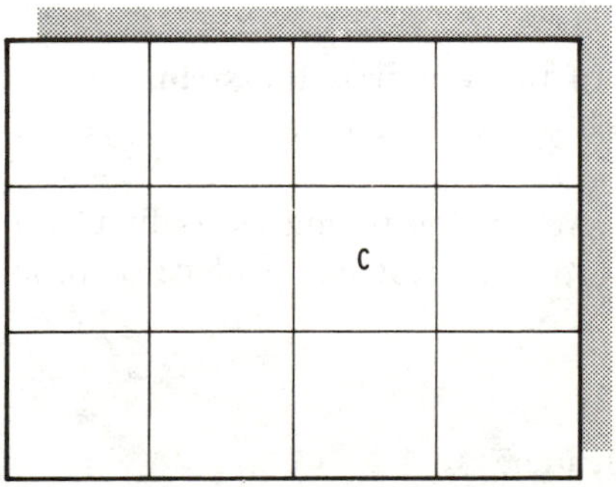

Figure 7.5 An array.

You can create and access larger arrays in just the same way, except of course that aref will need to be supplied with a 'distance along' index for each dimension which your array has. For a three-dimensioned array aref will need four arguments in all; for a four-dimensioned array it will need five, and so on.

Notice that the indices given to aref do not have to be in a list as they do for make-array. In fact the definition of aref in Lisp would begin:

```
(defun aref (array &rest indices)
    ...)
```

and, as you know, the lambda list keyword &rest makes a list of all following arguments anyway.

7.1.5 Other simple data structures

You are already familiar with Lisp's most basic data structure: the list. One important property of a list is that it contains an ordered set of elements, and it shares this property with vectors (one-dimensional arrays). Since lists and vectors have this important similarity, Common Lisp introduces for the first time in Lisp the data type **sequence**, of which both lists and vectors are subtypes. A sequence is not, however, a distinct 'thing', separate from lists and vectors. A sequence is always either a list or a vector, just as a Lisp form is always either an atom or a list. Think of the term as just a convenient classification, a generic description of a class of Lisp objects which includes all lists and vectors. Its usefulness is that Common Lisp can now specify a series of **generic functions**, which will work equally well whether their arguments are lists or vectors.

Such functions as length, reverse, remove, delete and substitute are such generic functions. In fact if you look in the Common Lisp specification you will see that there are 28 of them, though most of them are intended for somewhat esoteric purposes. We shall introduce these generic functions as and when we need them throughout the following chapters.

A further subtype of the vector is the **string**, and since you have not come across strings before we shall sidetrack here for a moment to explain them.

A string in Lisp is created by typing as its first and last character the double quote, so that it looks just like a piece of reported speech in English:

"tony"
"take me to your leader"
"(I (will (not)))"
"**$%@!!"

are all strings. Between the quotes you can in fact type any keyboard characters which normally print visibly on the screen, plus space and/or carriage return. The value of a string is itself, as is the case with numbers, and when we say itself we mean exactly itself: if you typed lower-case letters then lower-case letters will be returned when you ask Lisp for the value of the string: there is no conversion to upper case as there is with ordinary symbols. Since it is not a symbol a string cannot be assigned a value, nor can it be the name of a function, nor does it have a property list. Every string, no matter how many 'words' it may contain in the eyes of us humans, is always an atom. The double quotes are not part of the string, but serve only to indicate that it is a string.

The function print, if given a string as its argument, will print the string complete with its surrounding double quotes. A companion function princ will print it without the quotes. Incidentally, besides printing its argument print also (always) prints a newline (carriage return) before it and a space afterwards. princ prints only its argument. Strings are most used when a program requires interaction from a user: keyboard input can be read into Lisp as a string, thus preserving any capitalization, and after processing the output can also be printed as strings. The purpose of princ is to make such outputs more readable to humans.

Strings are implemented in Common Lisp as a specialized form of vectors, and therefore many of the generic sequence functions work on strings too. What makes string vectors special is that the only type of object which they are allowed to contain is the **character object**, that is, a Lisp object whose type is 'character'. When a character is a character object, rather than being simply a part of something printed on the screen, it is denoted by a hash sign and a backslash. Thus the character object corresponding to the character a is #\a. Each element of a string vector holds a single character object, so you can imagine the string "foo" being held internally in Lisp as in Figure 7.6. This correctly implies that the second character in the string "foo" is #\o. There are some two dozen Common Lisp functions designed solely for the manipulation of strings, but string handling is a somewhat involved subject in its own right and is beyond the scope of this book.

Returning to the subject of data structures, you know that lists can be arbitrarily nested inside one another. Data objects known as **trees** can

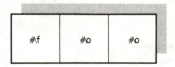

Figure 7.6   A string.

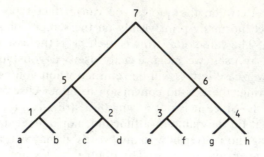

Figure 7.7   A hypothetical tree.

be created by nesting lists in a certain regular pattern. For example this list:

        (((a b) (c d)) ((e f) (g h)))

has two sublists, each of which in turn has two sublists, each of which contains two elements. The tree so created is visualized as in Figure 7.7.

This is upside down from a natural tree, with the **root** at the top and the **leaves** or **leaf nodes** at the bottom. In between, wherever branches divide, there is said to be a **node**. Every node other than the root or leaf nodes has both a **parent node** and two **child nodes**. Because every parent has exactly two children the overall structure is referred to as a **binary tree**, but in a different tree parents might not all have the same number of children and some might have no children at all. A tree does not have to be a symmetrical structure.

Notice how the list corresponds to the tree: nodes a and b are listed together because they have the same parent at node 1. Nodes c and d are similarly listed together because they have the same parent at node 2. All four have the same grandparent, as it were, so that the two sublists containing between them a, b, c and d are also listed together. The same pattern recurs with e, f, g and h, making another list of two sublists each containing two items. Finally, all eight items have a common great-grandparent at node 7, so a final outer list is made which contains all eight items in their nested lists.

Here is a function which, given such a list, will hunt down each branch of it until it comes to an atom, and will then print the atom. Please turn back to Chapter 5 and compare it with the function atomise.

```
(defun leaves (tree)
  (cond ((null tree) nil)
        ((atom tree)
         (print tree))
        (t (leaves (car tree)) (leaves (cdr tree)))))
```

You might like to trace this function in action and to see it searching every branch of the tree for atoms. We shall use a tree to hold the data for our promised toy model of human memory.

7.1.6   Example: a real AI program

In 1969 A. M. Collins and M. R. Quillian published their conclusions about how human memory might work, based upon their own experimental data. The article had a considerable impact upon other researchers, and although Collins and Quillian themselves went on to develop much more sophisticated versions of their ideas, their original description of the memory mechanism remained a milestone and is regularly referred to in cognitive science courses even today.

The essential and, at the time, surprising suggestion made by Collins and Quillian was that human beings do not after all simply remember vast numbers of facts about the world around them, but instead organize what they know into some kind of mental data structure. This brings the dual benefit of reducing the amount of memory required and simplifying the process of recall. After all, when someone asks you to recall something (and provided that you can recall it!) you are not conscious of your mind's hunting frantically through every single fact you know until by a fluke it happens to hit upon the one you want. Instead, the process appears to be fairly direct and very fast: except on occasions when your memory fails (i.e. when you cannot remember something which you know you should be able to remember) you are aware almost immediately that either you do know that fact, and therefore can remember it, or that you do not know it at all. Moreover, even if you do not know the desired fact, you can often make a 'probable' guess at it: 'Well, I don't know if X's baby screams all night, but most babies seem to do it, so I expect that that one does too.'

Collins and Quillian's hypothesis provides a beautifully elegant suggestion as to how all of that might be possible, and its especial attraction from an AI point of view is that it can be fairly simply written as a computer program. That is, the hypothesis can be modelled on the computer.

The hypothesis is that memories of objects in the real world are remembered as nodes arranged into a hierarchy (start visualizing something like the tree diagram in Figure 7.7). At the bottom of the tree its leaves represent all the individual objects which you know about: individual persons, individual animals, personal computers, and so on; all the objects which are unique in the real world as you see it. Each of those objects will have a set of particular attributes which distinguish it from all other similar objects. For example you can presumably distinguish between your own mother and Queen Elizabeth II. The suggestion here is that you can do so because you associate with your mother one set of attributes but associate a quite different set with the Queen of England. Nonetheless, those two people share a large number of common attributes, and were to you start writing them down it is likely that you would soon reach the conclusion that they have far more attributes in common than they have points of difference.

For any two or more leaf nodes which represent the same kind or **class** of object the hypothesis separates the common attributes from the uniquely individual attributes. The latter remain associated with the leaf nodes (representing the real-world individuals) while the former are associated with their parent node, which in this example might represent all women. Note that there is no real-world object corresponding to any node in the tree except its leaf nodes: all other nodes represent classes of objects.

You may also be able to remember two other real-world individuals: your father and the President of the United States. (At the time of writing the President is a man; if by the time you read this she is a woman, then we are talking about the First Gentleman.) Those two individuals will have many common attributes which again the hypothesis would abstract out and associate with their parent node.

The process of abstracting common attributes and moving them one level up the tree continues: men and women share many common attributes too, and these are moved up to the parent node which might well represent all human beings; all those whom you know about, that is. The next node up might represent all carnivores, the next all living things, the next all physical entities, and so on. There is a slight problem about what the ultimate root node, representing your entire known universe, would be called; maybe God? A schematic of what our example looks like on paper is shown in Figure 7.8.

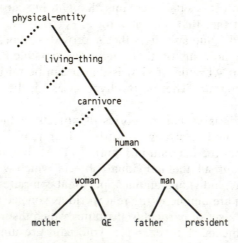

Figure 7.8   A real tree.

The links drawn between the nodes all represent the relationship isa, implying that each child node is an instance of the class represented by the parent node to which it is linked; as for example in 'Mary isa cow' (in the farmyard rather than the pejorative sense). The dotted links feed into our schematic from other classes and objects not directly represented here. The crucial point to remember about this data structure is that the **attributes** of objects are stored at the node where they are most generally true of all nodes beneath them in the tree. Thus we would put the attribute 'has a soul' with the node 'human being' which is probably where most Westerners would put it, but people who have grown up under the influence of Eastern philosophy might feel that it should properly be associated with 'all living things'. Thus the hypothesis is flexible in that it allows for beliefs rather than merely facts; and if you personally happen to be an atheist you might think that the attribute 'has a soul' should be omitted altogether.

So that is how, according to Collins and Quillian's hypothesis, we store our memories. Now let us turn to the question of how we retrieve them, how we **access** them. Suppose that you need to remember whether or not your father eats (or ate) meat. We shall return to the question of vegetarians in a moment. The hypothesis states that you start at the leaf node representing your father. Finding no appropriate attribute to answer your question 'does he eat meat?' you move on up to the parent node and look again. Still you will find no answer, so you repeat the process. There is no appropriate information at the 'human' level either, but finally at the node labelled 'carnivore' is the datum you seek. The process of remembering is then complete.

One obvious conclusion to be drawn, if the hypothesis is correct, is that human subjects would take a shorter time to remember information which is specific to individual (leaf) nodes, and a progressively longer time to remember more and more general items of information (because the latter would involve more traversing up the tree). And in fact this is precisely what Collins and Quillian did find.

Here is the tree of nodes from Figure 7.8 represented as a list:

```
(setf *tree* '(root
          (physical-entity
          (living-thing
          (carnivore
          (human
          (woman (mother queen-elizabeth))
          (man (father prince-philip))))))))
```

We shall create the isa links via a series of setf instructions to add to each node's property list information as to which is its parent node:

```
(setf (get 'physical-entity 'isa) 'root)
(setf (get 'living-thing 'isa) 'physical-entity)
(setf (get 'carnivore 'isa) 'living-thing)
(setf (get 'human 'isa) 'carnivore)
(setf (get 'woman 'isa) 'human)
(setf (get 'man 'isa) 'human)
(setf (get 'queen-elizabeth 'isa) 'woman)
(setf (get 'prince-philip 'isa) 'man)
(setf (get 'mother 'isa) 'woman)
(setf (get 'father 'isa) 'man)
```

and then we shall add to the appropriate property lists a couple of attributes:

```
(setf (get 'carnivore 'eats) 'meat)
(setf (get 'human 'contains) 'soul)
```

Finally here is the function which traverses the tree to retrieve the attributes:

```
(defun remember (node property value)
   (cond ((eq node 'root) nil)
         ((equal (get node property) value) (princ 'Yes'))
         (t (remember (get node 'isa) property value))))
```

Yes, we agree that all that looks horrible. But do not worry: shortly, once we have shown you how the model works, we are going to show you a far more elegant way of implementing it. Incidentally, if you ever need to print on screen such complex list structures as *tree* (which print and princ display as single, unindented long lines) use the function pprint, whose name means 'pretty print'.

Actually, we do not expect that you will have any trouble at all in understanding how remember works. It is a very typical small recursive function just as you have seen several times before. And it steps up the tree node by node looking on the property list each time for the required pattern of data, precisely according to Collins and Quillian's hypothesis. The function has a couple of minor refinements. We use equal to check the value against the retrieved property (in the second clause of the cond) to allow for possible cases where the value is a list rather than an atom; and the first clause of the cond checks each successive node to see whether it is the root node, and halts the recursion when it finds it (if you like, when it has gained sight of God). We could as well have made it look for the case when the current node was NIL, i.e. when it had run off the top of the tree, but this would have meant an extra and unnecessary level of recursion.

At this point a cognitive scientist would consider how good a model this is of the corresponding mental process, on the assumption that the hypothesis itself is reasonable. For a start, it does not seem too likely that we remember all the attributes of all entities in our world in terms of node–property–value triples. But that is really just a programming convenience, and probably is not very important. A more sophisticated program might allow us to store our data in more sophisticated forms, but the essential points of the tree-like hierarchy of nodes and their associated attributes, traversed by a recursive function, would not necessarily be affected.

A more awkward point is the blanket classification of all human beings as carnivores. Biologically it is correct, but we do not normally remember our friends and families via their biological classifications. The fact remains that it is a quite important and hence memorable attribute of many humans that they are not carnivores, and they would resent our remembering them as though they were. What our model seriously lacks is some mechanism whereby it can check at each stage not only for the information it is looking for, but also for any contradictory information. Then we could store on the leaf nodes, or at least at some point below the carnivore node, the knowledge that some individual humans are not carnivores.

In programming terms, one possible (and crude) way of achieving this would be to allow for the presence of negative properties, distinguished from the normal positive properties by having the symbol not- tacked onto the front of them. Thus, your vegetarian relative would have a property not-eats with the value meat. A fairly simple change to the above program (please take our word for it) would enable it to check also for the negative of any property it was seeking, a negative property with the same value as the positive property, and if it found it to return 'No'.

The difficulty here from the cognitive science point of view is that that certainly is not the way we do it in our heads. To us, the description of someone as a vegetarian implies that he or she does not eat meat: we don't remember the non-carnivorousness as a fact in its own right. Being a vegetarian also implies a number of other things about the individual: a preference for certain restaurants over others, perhaps a preference for certain kinds of food shops, a sensitivity to the rights of animals, and so on. But of course not all of these need be true of any particular vegetarian; it is as though the attribute 'vegetarian' required a whole new mini Collins and Quillian hypothesis to sort it out.

It is interesting in this context to look at the model the other way up, as it were: to forget all about the fact that remember chunters its way up the tree, and to imagine instead that values filter their way down. The correct terminology here would be to say that nodes in the lower parts of the tree **inherit** values which are **default** values from nodes higher up the tree. This way of thinking makes it easier to see that the default values will always be inherited unless we supply some information to the contrary. And in classifying an individual as a vegetarian we are assuming that a small set of default values external to the basic tree will be applicable to that individual unless our knowledge of him/her says otherwise.

An even larger problem, which was in fact one of the criticisms levelled against the original hypothesis, is that it is virtually impossible to choose the correct node names for anything more than a very tiny part of the full tree which, according to the hypothesis, must exist in a person's mind. In our example, it seem undeniable that all women and all men must be human beings, and that so far (until AI succeeds in its goals, perhaps) there is nothing else we know of which could come into that category. So the bottom three levels of our tree might well be correct. But then we move up to the problematical carnivore level. We've already described how local arrangements can be made to prevent inheritance of the 'eats meat' description in cases where it is inappropriate. But suppose were trying to draw the tree which exists in the mind of the president of the local Vegetarian Society. That person might know almost nobody who was not a vegetarian, so that to classify human being as carnivores at all would be quite inappropriate. That tree would have vegetarian where ours has carnivore, and would make local arrangements to cope with the few acquaintances who did eat meat.

Even worse it is, to say the least, probable that as any one person learns new facts in the course of any normal day he or she is constantly modifying the attributes of nodes in his/her tree, and may even be altering the categories – the node names – as well. It is almost certainly impracticable to try to build a model of any one person's memory, so what we need is a general model, one which could in principle be adapted to fit any one person. But here we come back to the problem of choosing the correct node names: what name should we put where we now have carnivore, so that everyone (or even most people) would accept it as being psychologically valid? The further one moves up the tree away from the leaf nodes, the more intractable that question becomes.

We should not leave this discussion without telling you that Collins and Quillian themselves later developed a more sophisticated version of their hypothesis. Instead of a tree, they had a network, by which we mean that instead of each node having just one parent it could have any number of parents, just as in a tree it can have any number of children. This would allow, in our admittedly unlikely example, the human node to be connected to both the carnivore and the vegetarian nodes. Instead of a single remember function there were (at least) two functions; when asked to 'remember' whether or not your father is a vegetarian one function would start from the father node and the other from the vegetarian node, and they would attempt to find a path along the links towards each other. If they met at a single node, memory was considered to have been be successful. The process was known as **spreading activation**.

7.1.7 `defstruct`

Earlier, we promised to show you a more elegant way of implementing the above simple version of Collins and Quillian's hypothesis, and that is what we are about to do. Its importance from your point of view is that it will introduce you to a new type of data structure which will not need a separate list to represent the tree, and which will not involve interminable series of `setf` instructions in order to secrete data away on property lists. We think that you will enjoy learning about the data structures created via `defstruct`, and we believe that the ideas which you will come across in the process will give you a sound basis for understanding **object-oriented programming** which will be the climax to this book.

Structures defined by `defstruct` are the Lisp equivalents of the data 'records' used in Pascal. Each one has a predetermined set of **slots** into which you can put your data. The data in any slot is often called the **filler**. When you define such a structure you are in effect defining a **class** of similar structures, which are identical as far as their available slots are concerned and will differ only in what data is put into those slots. A good way of visualizing it is that you are creating a template or form (in the sense of the forms which have to be filled in in order to buy, say, a driving licence). Once such a thing exists, there can be millions of copies or **instances** of it, all essentially alike but all carrying different information. In the process of defining a structure with `defstruct`, you get for free a macro to create new instances of it. You also get for free macros to access any slot of the structure, and you can use `setf` with those **accessor functions** so as to change the contents of any slot.

Exactly what a structure defined by `defstruct` 'really is' is not important to the user. It might be, as its printed representation suggests, simply an ordered list of pairs rather like a property list, or it could equally well be a vector; or it could be an object created at machine-code level and which is not otherwise accessible from Lisp at all. It does not matter because `defstruct` gives you a means of creating such objects, functions to access its slots, and – most importantly – it actually modifies the `setf` macro so that it can obey your instructions to change the value of any particular slot. When you define a structure with `defstruct`, you are in effect defining a new type of Lisp object: the only functions which will work on it, apart from the modified `setf`, are those provided for you by `defstruct`.

You can use `defstruct` very analogously to the way you have seen other defining macros used, in particular `defun` and `defmacro`:

```
(defstruct <name of structure class>
  (<slot1> <default filler1>)
  (<slot2> <default filler2>)
  ...)
```

The name which you choose for your class of structures can be any symbol, but it must be a symbol; you could not for example use a number as the name. As you can see, there is no lambda list as there would be if defining a function or macro, and this is simply because we are defining a data structure. When it has been created, the structure will not do anything; it will just act as a repository for data. To give it parameters would make about as much sense as trying to give parameters to a variable! In fact if you find it helpful you can think of the structure as being a rather complex kind of variable.

Following the name of the structure is a series of two-element lists – there can be as many of them as you need – each of which specifies a slot **name** and a **default** or initial **value** to be held in that slot. Although Lisp will not complain if you leave out a default value, that slot would then have a value which was undefined. So, to avoid possible problems caused by later trying to retrieve an undefined value, it is best always to put something in; NIL is often a good choice if nothing more useful springs to mind, though if one day you needed a structure intended to hold only numbers you would probably prefer to initialize each slot to zero.

The type of the initial value does not otherwise matter; any slot can hold any Lisp object, and the fact that you may have initialized a slot to zero will not prevent you from later replacing that zero with, say, a list. (Aside: more advanced use of defstruct, which we do not cover here, does allow you to restrict the filler of a slot to be of a certain type.)

Here is the definition of the structure class for our Collins and Quillian model mark II:

```
? (defstruct node
    (parent nil)
    (attributes nil))

NODE
```

This defines a class object for structures of the type NODE. If you like, it is a template for however many identical structures we may need in order to represent our tree; in terms of the driving licence analogy it is a blank application form. But, behind the scenes there will have been automatically created for you a **constructor macro**. The name of this macro will be formed by adding make- to the front of whatever name you have given your structure class, i.e. in this case it will be called make-node. Its purpose is to allow you to create as many **instances** as you like of this class of structure: as many blank forms as you need. There will also be, automatically created, a series of **accessor macros**, the same number of them as there are slots in your class structure. Each of these will have a name which will be similarly formed from the names which you originally supplied as the names of your slots: in our example there will be two, called node-parent and node-attributes.

You are now in a position to create all the nodes of the tree, but please notice first that the isa links are now going to be implicit: the class object contains a parent slot, and when creating the corresponding structures for the various nodes in the tree it will be up to you to make sure in each case that the filler of that slot is whichever node appears at the other end of the corresponding isa link in Figure 7.8.

The root node is very easy to create because it has neither a parent nor any attributes:

```
? (setf root (make-node))

#S(NODE PARENT NIL ATTRIBUTES NIL)
```

The hash-S serves to indicate that this is a structure, and the subsequent list shows you the structure's contents. Notice that although we did not specify any parent or attribute slots, they are still there and have been initialized to NIL. So this new structure, which is now the value of the symbol root, really is a copy of the class structure. Therefore the accessor macros will work on it. This is how:

```
? (node-parent root)

NIL

? (node-attributes root)

NIL
```

The argument root must not be quoted in either case because it is the corresponding structure, which is the value of root, which we want to access.

Now let us create the structure representing the next node down in the tree: physical-entity. This time we will need to supply a filler for the parent slot, so that our new object conceptually 'points to' its parent, root, without our having to specify the link explicitly:

```
? (setf physical-entity (make-node :parent 'root))

#S(NODE PARENT ROOT ATTRIBUTES NIL)
```

and let us try the accessor macros again:

```
? (node-parent physical-entity)

ROOT

? (node-attributes physical-entity)

NIL
```

The next node down is as easy:

```
? (setf living-thing (make-node :parent 'physical-entity))

#S(NODE PARENT PHYSICAL-ENTITY ATTRIBUTES NIL)
```

but the next one, carnivore, has an attribute:

```
? (setf carnivore (make-node :parent 'living-thing
                             :attributes '((eats meat))))

#S(NODE PARENT LIVING-THING ATTRIBUTES ((EATS MEAT)))
```

Do not be confused by the double brackets around the value in the attributes slot: they are there simply because in a more elaborate version of our model we would want as the value a list of attribute–value pairs. What you see here is a list containing just one such pair.

```
? (node-parent carnivore)

LIVING-THING

? (node-attributes carnivore)

((EATS MEAT))
```

. . . and so on. Here is the entire set of function calls, first to defstruct and then to make-node, required to create the complete tree:

```
(defstruct node
  (parent nil)
  (attributes nil))

(setf root (make-node))
(setf physical-entity (make-node :parent 'root))
(setf living-thing (make-node :parent 'physical-entity))
(setf carnivore (make-node :parent 'living-thing
                           :attributes '((eats meat))))
(setf human (make-node :parent 'carnivore
                       :attributes '((contains soul))))
```

```
(setf woman (make-node :parent 'human))
(setf man (make-node :parent 'human))
(setf queen-elizabeth (make-node :parent 'woman))
(setf prince-philip (make-node :parent 'man))
(setf mother (make-node :parent 'woman))
(setf father (make-node :parent 'man))
```

OK, so that does not look any better (if anything, it looks worse) than our original version using property lists. Please bear with us; at least we are achieving our objective of introducing you to defstruct. In a moment we shall show you how to make such a mess look a good deal cleaner. But first let us consider the new version of remember which will work with our new structure-based tree:

```
(defun remember (node attribute value)
   (cond ((eq node root) nil)
         ((member (list attribute value)
                  (node-attributes node)
                  :test #'equal)
          (princ 'Yes'))
         (t (remember (symbol-value (node-parent node))
                      attribute
                      value))))
```

There are a couple of things here which you have not seen before, but first please do not let the indentation confuse you. member is shown here with three arguments, one of them keyworded, and remember itself takes three arguments. In the second and third clauses of the cond these arguments would not fit one one line, so the neatest thing to do with them was to line them up vertically beneath one another. The evaluator, as usual, will ignore all intervening spaces and carriage returns (newlines); the indentation is there purely so that humans can read the function more easily.

This new version of remember will be called in the same way as the earlier version. For example:

```
? (remember 'father 'eats 'meat)
```

and at once there is a difficulty. For, when eval strips the quotes off eats and meat it will return those two symbols, which is exactly what we want. But when it strips the quote off father it will return father, and that is most definitely not what we want. We need it to return the value of father, i.e. the structure which we want remember to deal with.

You may be thinking that that sounds a trivial problem: why not just call remember with its first argument unquoted? And indeed that would be a solution as far as the top level call to remember is concerned. But the recursive call to remember in the 't' clause of the cond would still cause problems because of course (node-parent node) would still return father, so that the recursive call would have the same difficulty: it would still be passed the name of the variable, father, when what it wanted was the variable's value. So besides not quoting father in the top level call we need to retrieve the value of that symbol before passing it down in the recursive calls. That latter is the purpose of symbol-value: it always returns the value of any symbol supplied as its argument. The correct call to remember is now:

```
? (remember father 'eats 'meat)
```

Another solution which may have occurred to you is to put an explicit call to eval around the (node-parent node):

```
...(t (remember (eval (node-parent node)) attribute value)))))
```

and that solution would work. We object to it on stylistic grounds: that explicit calls to eval make it harder to understand what a function does, and are therefore best avoided.

Note that the variable root is unquoted in the first line of the cond. So eq will be asking whether the values of node and root are the same structure.

Now to the function member, which works on lists. We mention that in order to be sure that you do not think it to be one of the generic sequence functions. member will not work either on vectors or on strings. Its operation is fairly intuitive: it says 'is item X an element of list Y?'. Item X can of course be anything which would be acceptable as an element of a legal Lisp list.

As with assoc the default equality test used by member is eql, but here we need it to be equal because our attributes are always going to be lists. Therefore we have to specify the test with a keyworded argument. member returns NIL if the item is not a member of the list, but it is quite often useful to remember that, although member behaves like a predicate, it does not necessarily return T if the list does contain the item. What it actually returns is that part of the list which begins with the item:

```
? (member 'c '(a b c d e))

(C D E)
```

Within remember, member is used to check whether or not, for example, (eats meat) is an element of ((eats meat)), which of course it is. So member returns ((eats meat)), and as far as cond is concerned any non-NIL value returned by one of its tests is equivalent to T, so that the ‹action› part of that clause is then evaluated.

We hope you will agree that apart from these two complications the new version of remember is still the same simple recursive function

which you saw in the earlier, property list based, version. And here at last
is the long-promised concise version:

```
(defstruct node
  (parent nil)
  (attributes nil))

(defun create-node (name parent &optional attributes)
  (setf (symbol-value name)
        (make-node :parent parent :attributes attributes)))

(defun make-tree (data)
  (mapc #'(lambda (object)
            (create-node (name object)
                         (parent object)
                         (attributes object)))
        data))
```

First, as usual, we create the structure to represent the class of structures.
Then we define a function which will create a single instance of the class,
using symbol-value to save us the bother of remembering not to quote its
first argument. And finally we use a simple mapc to iterate over a list
representing our nodes, their parents and their attributes if any, assigning
as it goes the correct parent and attributes to each node. make-tree uses
three little helper macros, which as usual should be written into your file
earlier than the function which uses them:

```
(defmacro name (x)
  `(car ,x))

(defmacro parent (x)
  `(cadr ,x))

(defmacro attributes (x)
  `(caddr ,x))
```

This creates the tree:

```
(make-tree '((root)
             (physical-entity root)
             (living-thing physical-entity)
             (carnivore living-thing ((eats meat)))
             (human carnivore ((has soul)))
             (woman human)
             (man human)
             (queen-elizabeth woman)
             (prince-philip man)
             (mother woman)
             (father man)))
```

Our existing, latest version of remember will happily work on the resulting tree of structures.

This has turned out to be a rather extreme example of the trade-off between compactness of the program code (the stuff you keep on a disk file and show to other programmers) and the simplicity of your program in actual use. But we hope that in showing it to you we have made a useful point: that it is not always the shortest program to achieve a given effect which is the most stylish. Other factors, in particular clarity and ease of use, are at least as important as mere brevity.

Exercise 7.4 The implementation of Common Lisp which you are using includes functions for the addition and subtraction of integers (whole numbers). Without those functions, Lisp would not know how to add or to subtract. In this exercise we ask you to write, using defstruct, a small suite of functions to fill the gap, i.e. to achieve the addition of integers without using any of Lisp's inbuilt arithmetical functions. You should assume that Lisp has no concept of 'number', so that you will need to tell it that the integers (which to Lisp are merely distinguishable patterns) must be arranged in the usual series 0, 1, 2, 3 . . . N before any kind of arithmetic is possible.

The first step, as ever, is to decide on a sensible representation of this basic data. We ask you to use defstruct to create a class of structures each of which shall represent an integer in the above series. Each structure should have slots for its name, for a successor and for a predecessor. The name should be a word (two, five, eight etc.), and the fillers of the successor and predecessor slots should be structures.

(a)   Use defstruct to create the class of structures, calling it num.

You will now automatically have a function make-num which will create the individual structures and which takes keyworded arguments to specify the slot-fillers. If in a call to make-num you do not specify a filler for a particular slot, the slot will automatically be filled with NIL. Hint: both the first structure in the sequence (zero) and the last (ten will be enough) will have either no predecessor or no successor.

(b)   Write a function set-up-numbers which takes as its single argument the sequence of integers (0–10). After creating the structure for zero and assigning it to the global variable *zero*, it calls a recursive function set-up-numbers2. The latter creates the second and all subsequent structures until the end of the sequence is reached. At each stage, it fills the previous structure's succ slot with the current structure, and the current structure's pred slot with the previous structure. Make sure that when evaluation is complete the outer function returns NIL.

The result is a linked chain of structures, each one knowing what other structure is its predecessor and what other structure is its successor. It is likely that if you were now to ask your Lisp to print out the value of *zero* you would get a very long printout indeed, as Lisp recursively dealt with the predecessor of the predecessor of the predecessor etc., and the successor of the successor of the successor etc., for every structure in the sequence. Therefore, make certain that none of the functions which you write for this exercise will ever return the chain of structures. If in doubt, make sure of this by writing NIL as the last expression in each function definition.

Now, run your function so as to create the chain of structures:

```
? (set-up-numbers '(zero one two three four five
                    six seven eight nine ten))
NIL
```

At this point you have taught the computer the series of integers from zero to ten; the remaining question is how to use that information so as to add and subtract numbers within that range. We use a process closely analogous to that taught to young children in schools: they are given Cusenier rods, or sets of building blocks of equal size, and numerical value is directly equated to length or to height. If you put two identical rods end to end, or put one pile of bricks on top of an identical pile, you end up with 'twice as much'. Similarly, in order to add two integers x and y, we need to count along our sequence of structures from zero: move forward one structure until we have counted to the value of x, and then continue moving forward until we have further counted to the value of y. Whichever structure we arrive at is the answer. For example, if we wanted to add 2 and 3 we would count from the 'zero' structure to the 'two' structure, and then on a further three structures to the 'five' structure.

(c)   Write a function that takes two integers x and y as inputs and adds them as follows:

> move along the sequence from zero by x nodes and print the name of the structure reached;
> move along the sequence from zero by y nodes and print the name of the structure reached;
> move along the sequence from zero by x nodes and then by y nodes and print the name of the structure reached.

In our solution, we have written a function called add-num which calls a function called move-up. We have taken care to make add-num return NIL so as to avoid watching the huge printout referred to earlier!

Now, a call to add-num should work:

```
? (add-num 1 3)

ONE
THREE
FOUR
NIL
```

(d)   Write a similar pair of functions, sub-num and move-down, to effect
       subtraction. Assume that x will always be larger than y so that no negative
       numbers are involved; i.e. moving up x nodes from zero necessarily allows
       you subsequently to move down y nodes without overrunning zero:

       ? (sub-num 8 3)

```
EIGHT
THREE
FIVE
NIL
```

We hope that you will agree – even if our hints were not broad enough and
you had to look up the answers! – that in the end that was a fairly simple program
to achieve a very powerful result. The ability to formalize our counting so that it
can potentially handle numbers of any size is one of the things which marks
human beings out from the animals. Experiments suggest that animals 'count' by
recognizing patterns, much as you or we might recognize the patterns on a set of
dice or on a deck of playing cards. Apparently, birds count their eggs as 'one,
two, three, many'; and if one egg is temporarily removed from a clutch of five its
parents do not even notice!

SUMMARY

Choosing the best method of representing knowledge or data can make
all the difference between an elegant, and if required a psychologically
valid, program and an *ad hoc*, confusing jumble. The choice can often
be a difficult one, and Lisp provides a considerable number of
mechanisms for representing knowledge in different ways. All of them
require the knowledge to be associated in some way with a Lisp symbol,
from the symbol whose value is a simple alist to the symbol which is the
name of a structure created by defstruct. All of them also implicitly
impose the pattern indicator-property-value, although as you have seen
the 'facts' represented by such triples can be linked together to form
larger data structures such as trees and networks.

The next chapter will be something of a calm before the storm: we
intend to show you how to get bugs out of your programs both during
and after their creation, and to give you some hints about good and bad
programming style. Thereafter we shall launch into some serious AI
programming which, we hope, will tie together everything which you
have learned so far and will inspire you to carry on by yourself, without
us. In the Bibliography we suggest some books which you might care to
move on to, all of them excellent in their various approaches to AI's
central goal of creating an intelligent machine.

Chapter 8
Programming Style

This chapter describes all of the debugging aids provided in
Common Lisp to help find the faults in non-working programs.
It also considers good programming style, and standard
methods of making your program code more comprehensible
to other programmers.

8.1 Debugging

As you have followed the examples and attempted the exercises we have
given you so far, you have probably had to track down a few bugs in your
programs. Usually these will have been due to missing parentheses or
simple typing mistakes. It may also have occurred to you that the tracer
often helps you to locate a bug, and possibly your Lisp implementation
includes an editor which 'knows' a little about Lisp syntax and can help
you to get rid of some bugs even as you create them. But in the next
chapter this book is going to change gear: we are going to start
introducing you to 'real' AI programs, programs which would not be at
all out of place in a present-day AI laboratory.

These will of course be larger programs than any you have written
until now, and so of course they will have concomitantly more, and more
obscure, bugs when you have written them. This is not us trying to
patronize you: it is inevitable. There is a (joke) law which states that the
number of bugs in a program at any one time is directly proportional to
the time spent so far in trying to get them out. The difficulty is that the

175

more complex a program gets the more likely it is to contain not merely simple syntactic bugs such as spelling mistakes, but semantic bugs caused by the programmer's not having been able to predict exactly how the program would behave under all input conditions. Beyond a certain level of program complexity it is almost an AI truism to say that all programs contain bugs. If you happen to be a regular user of a personal computer you will certainly know that even expensive commercial software can rarely be operated for very long before one of its bugs surfaces to cause you problems.

This is not (usually) due to total ineptitude on the part of the original programmers, it is simply that it is extremely difficult, and therefore very expensive in terms of programmers' salaries, to get even most of the bugs out of a large program. Fortunately Allegro Common Lisp running on the Apple Macintosh, with which we have checked all of the programs in this book, is one of the few virtually bug-free examples of commercial software.

AI research has different aims from those of commercial software houses, and sets itself higher standards: we still hope to write bug-free programs, though the sad truth is that we rarely achieve this goal. So Lisp has acquired over the years an impressive array of aids to successful debugging. (The idea is once again recursive, for of course the debugging aids are themselves programs which may contain bugs . . .) Debugging aids are necessarily part of the **user environment** and the **user interface**, which terms refer to the means whereby you the programmer interact with the virtual machine which is, in our case, Lisp. A decade or so ago many programmers were still using teletype machines, which resembled electric typewriters. Then came the so-called 'glass teletype' machines which were in effect the same thing except that the computer's responses appeared on a screen rather than on a roll of paper (a terminal connected to a mainframe computer is an example of this).

Nowadays most AI researchers, most industrial users of AI techniques, and even large numbers of amateurs at home possess personal computers which by the standards of only a few years ago are extremely sophisticated. A major invention has been the **mouse**, which enables its user to move a pointer around on the screen, and which has one or more buttons which allow certain things to be done to whatever on-screen entity the pointer happens to be pointing at. User interfaces are changing for the better at a very fast rate, and in consequence the user environment, which comprises the tools (the editor, the tracer etc.) available to help the programmer, has to change as rapidly.

For this reason Common Lisp specifies only a minimum set of environmental tools, and describes those in only a minimal way, so that implementers of Common Lisp are left free to include the most sophisticated tools they can dream up. In this chapter we shall cover in an equally simple way the tools which your Lisp should have; the documentation which came with your Lisp will almost certainly reveal that its tools are far more powerful and useful than the descriptions given here would suggest. You may even find that it has tools which we (and the Common Lisp specification) do not mention. So: please read your documentation!

After that, and before moving on to 'real' AI programs in our next chapter, we think it worthwhile to spend some time discussing programming style. Whilst it is obviously (and very) exciting to write a hitherto non-existent program and to get it to do whatever you the programmer want it to do, an objective which should come a close second in any programmer's mind is to ensure that that program will be clear and comprehensible to others; and even that it will be clear and comprehensible to the programmer him/herself after a couple of months have gone by.

There are five main tools described in the Common Lisp specification. One of them, trace, you have already come across. The others are step, apropos, describe and inspect.

8.1.1   The stepper

The stepper, brought into action by using the macro step, can be regarded as a very much more detailed version of the tracer. When you ask for your top level call to some function to be stepped the stepper traces its detailed evaluation on screen. It does so one 'step' at a time, and you will be able to tell the stepper to move onto the next step via some simple means such as a press of the RETURN key or a click of the mouse. We cannot tell you exactly what you will see at each step, since that is one of the decisions left to the implementer of your Common Lisp, but we can promise you that it will be interesting. You may, for example, discover 'hidden' truths such as that the cond macro macroexpands during its first round of evaluation into a series of nested ifs!

Most implementations of step in fact show you far more than you really want to know. But amongst all the unwanted information you will certainly find things which are very useful. For example, the function addall which we suggested as a useful function to write during Exercise 7.1 in the last chapter was defined like this:

```
(defun addall (dates appts)
  (mapc #'(lambda (date appt)
            (setf (get 'diary date) appt))
        dates
        appts))
```

step always takes a single argument, which must be a complete (unquoted) function call, complete with arguments. So give addall a couple of simple arguments and see what your stepper will show you:

```
? (step (addall '(jan1 jan2 jan3) '(drink (visit mum) dentist)))
```

The printed result on screen will look something like this:

```
(ADDALL '(JAN1 JAN2 JAN3) '(DRINK (VISIT MUM) DENTIST))
  '(JAN1 JAN2 JAN3) = (JAN1 JAN2 JAN3)
  '(DRINK (VISIT MUM) DENTIST) = (DRINK (VISIT MUM) DENTIST)
  (BLOCK ADDALL (MAPC (FUNCTION (LAMBDA # #)) DATES APPTS))
   (MAPC (FUNCTION (LAMBDA (DATE APPT) (SETF # APPT))) DATES APPTS)
     (FUNCTION (LAMBDA (DATE APPT) (SETF (GET # DATE) APPT)))
     #<An INTERPRETED-LEXICAL-CLOSURE.>
     DATES = (JAN1 JAN2 JAN3)
     APPTS = (DRINK (VISIT MUM) DENTIST)
     (SETF (GET 'DIARY DATE) APPT)
       (SET-GET 'DIARY DATE APPT)
         'DIARY = DIARY
         DATE = JAN1
         APPT = DRINK
       DRINK
     DRINK
     (SETF (GET 'DIARY DATE) APPT)
       (SET-GET 'DIARY DATE APPT)
         'DIARY = DIARY
         DATE = JAN2
         APPT = (VISIT MUM)
       (VISIT MUM)
     (VISIT MUM)
     (SETF (GET 'DIARY DATE) APPT)
       (SET-GET 'DIARY DATE APPT)
         'DIARY = DIARY
         DATE = JAN3
         APPT = DENTIST
       DENTIST
     DENTIST
    (JAN1 JAN2 JAN3)
   (JAN1 JAN2 JAN3)
  (JAN1 JAN2 JAN3)
```

In amongst all that you can clearly spot the original arguments to addall being evaluated, and mapc working its way through progressive cdrs of those two lists. Notice that the indentation implies the same thing as it does in the tracer, namely levels of nesting of function calls, which as we said in an earlier chapter are thought of as being the same levels as levels of recursion.

Notice also the occasional hash sign. This indicates that, in order to lessen the chance of the printout running off the right-hand edge of the screen, print has printed the nesting of calls only to a level of three. The first form containing a hash sign is

    (LAMBDA # #)

On the next line, as the stepper moves down one level, this becomes

    (LAMBDA (DATE APPT) (SETF # APPT))

and on the next line it is

    (LAMBDA (DATE APPT) (SETF (GET # DATE) APPT))

and finally a few lines later, after the auxiliary function's arguments have been evaluated, the call to get is similarly expanded:

    (SETF (GET 'DIARY DATE) APPT)

The level at which print begins to collapse forms into hashes is set by a global variable called *print-level*. Remember that a global variable is assigned rather than bound, which in turn implies that its value is available at all times, at any point in any of your functions or programs. You would not often want to make programmatic use of the value of *print-level*, of course, but notice the convention we mentioned earlier of having asterisks as the first and last characters of global variables. The value of *print-level* can be altered, should you ever wish to do so, via setf.

A similar global variable is *print-length*, whose effect on print is to cause it to truncate (and replace with asterisks) printed lists which are longer than the value of *print-length*. Normally this is again 3, and again it can be altered via setf. We shall return to the question of global variables later in this chapter.

8.1.2 apropos, describe **and** inspect

apropos takes a single argument and finds any symbols whose names contain that argument. It prints those symbols, together with any information about the values or function definitions of them. For example,

    ? (apropos 'map)

will print at least the following:

```
MAPHASH, Def: COMPILED-FUNCTION
MAPLIST, Def: COMPILED-FUNCTION
MAP, Def: COMPILED-FUNCTION
MAPL, Def: COMPILED-FUNCTION
MAPC, Def: COMPILED-FUNCTION
MAPCON, Def: COMPILED-FUNCTION
MAPCAR, Def: COMPILED-FUNCTION
MAPCAN, Def: COMPILED-FUNCTION
```

and

```
? (apropos 'hash)
```

will print at least this:

```
HASH
REMHASH, Def: COMPILED-FUNCTION
MAKE-HASH-TABLE, Def: COMPILED-FUNCTION
SXHASH, Def: COMPILED-FUNCTION
MAPHASH, Def: COMPILED-FUNCTION
HASH-TABLE-P, Def: COMPILED-FUNCTION
HASH-TABLE
HASH-TABLE-COUNT, Def: COMPILED-FUNCTION
CLRHASH, Def: COMPILED-FUNCTION
GETHASH, Def: COMPILED-FUNCTION
```

apropos provides a handy summary of what Lisp 'knows' about any given symbol, and as you become more expert in Lisp it will often save you the trouble of hunting through the Common Lisp specification to see what functions are available for any given purpose.

describe shows what is known about a single symbol:

```
? (describe 'mapcar)

Printed Representation: MAPCAR
Type: SYMBOL
Package: 'LISP'
Value: #<UNBOUND>
Definition: #<Compiled Function MAPCAR>
Property List:
Indicator -> Value
CCL::%PPRINT-FUNCTION CCL::PP-MAP
```

Do not worry that you do not understand all of this. Remember that Common Lisp is designed to be used by programmers at all levels of expertise, and simply make use of whatever is useful to you in describe's output. describe operates recursively, and sometimes it will indent within its description a deeper description of some item.

inspect is intended to be an interactive version of describe. This means that it is intended to make full use of your computer's user interface – e.g. mouse, menus, dialogue boxes – to get deeper and deeper descriptions of anything which describe itself would produce. We recommend that you get to know inspect as it is implemented in your Lisp: it is a very powerful and useful tool, and will come into its own as we introduce you to more and more complex programming constructs.

8.1.3 break **and** backtrace

break is a function which can take no arguments or an optional string argument which is a message to be printed on the screen. You're allowed to put as many calls to break – break points – in your code as you like, and the message might say something like 'Breaking after the COND in FOO'. The intention is that you should put a temporary call to (break) into your program or function at the point where you think an error may have occurred, and its effect will be to 'freeze' the evaluator at that point. You the user are not returned to the top-level prompt but are instead put into a **break loop**, which is just like a top-level loop except that it offers a few extra facilities which are useful for debugging purposes. When in a break loop, you can check the current, frozen, values of any variable just as you could check the values of global variables from top level. But you can also inspect the **stack**.

In our chapter on recursion we described how evaluation of an 'outer' function is suspended until evaluation of an 'inner' function has completed, and we told you that this was also true of any nested function call. We are now in a position to tell you exactly what we meant. The process of 'suspension' involves the current state of the function call (usually the next form waiting to be evaluated plus all subsequent forms), together with the current values of all local and global variables, being bundled up and consed onto the front of what is conceptually a list.

The 'stack' analogy comes from self-service cafeterias where a stack (or pile) of plates sits in a suitably shaped hole in the counter, and at the bottom there is a powerful spring. As each customer takes a plate, the spring pushes up the next plate. When the washer-up appears and adds some clean plates to the stack, the spring is forced down so that still only one plate shows. In programming terms, the stack is a list: new elements are consed onto the front (top) of it, and every now and again the first (top) element is taken off. The taking off could of course be accomplished by

```
(setf stack (cdr stack))
```

but in fact there are inbuilt macros called push and pop which respectively add or remove an element to/from any list:

```
(push item mystack)
```

will add a new 'plate', and

```
(pop item mystack)
```

will remove it, provided that mystack has been initialized to NIL (or to some other list). Please note that it is unlikely that you will be able to affect Lisp's stack directly using these functions.

Having this frozen stack of function calls available for inspection is rather like being able to trace each earlier function call, from the break point back to the top level starting point. For this reason the facility to inspect the stack is usually called **backtrace**. It is particularly useful for checking that the values of various variables/parameters have been what you expected them to be. Exactly how the backtrace is presented to you, or even exactly how you summon it, is not specified in Common Lisp. As with all of the facilities described in this 'debugging' section, please consult your software documentation for the precise details.

When an error occurs during evaluation of your function or program you are similarly put into the break debugging environment, and usually this environment includes its own read—eval—print loop which temporarily replaces the normal one. The debugging aids you have available while in that loop will be the same as those given to you by break itself.

It is an interesting psychological point that experienced Lisp users seem to divide into two camps where debugging is concerned: those who are happy to put up with the verbosity of the stepper for the sake of a 'forward' analysis of their programs' execution, and those who prefer to bring things to an abrupt halt with break and then look 'backwards' to see what went wrong. It does not matter which you choose, and ideally a programmer should probably use both, with a knowledgeable eye on which is the more likely to find his/her bug with the minimum of delay.

8.1.4   print **is useful too**

If all else fails you can turn to Lisp's print function for help. It is common practice to insert temporary calls to print in the definitions of suspect functions in order to track down bugs. The print expressions serve first of all to assure you that the functions are actually being evaluated; but you could also make them print out, for example, the values of all of a function's parameters so that you could check that they were correct.

Here is a function from Exercise 7.3 modified so as to print out useful information as it is executed:

```
(defun addall (dates appts)
    (print (list 'dates dates 'appts appts))
    (mapc #'(lambda (date appt)
                (print (list 'date date 'appt appt))
                (setf (get 'diary date) appt))
          dates
          appts))
```

The two added `print` expressions will print the parameters and their values in the main `addall` function as it is evaluated, and the parameters and values of the inner lambda expression each time it is evaluated. The list printed by each call to `print` consists of two pairs of items; each item comprises a quoted variable name and an unquoted variable name. The quoted name is merely a label, to remind as you watch the resulting printout which variable's value you are looking at!

Try to be sparing with your added `print` expressions; besides inevitably slowing down your program, a large number of them can, after the next run of your program, leave you even more confused than before!

Here is another technique which, if used with care, can make the business of adding and later removing temporary `print` expressions somewhat less tedious, though it does not allow you to print self-explanatory lists as above. It relies upon the fact that the function `print` always returns its single argument. Suppose that you had been having trouble with the following function from Exercise 7.2(c), and you felt that you wanted to know what the call to `assoc` returned:

```
(defun word-add2 (num1 num2)
    (cdr (assoc (+ (get num1 'number) (get num2 'number))
          *symbols*)))
```

You can achieve this by putting a call to `print` *around* the call to `assoc`:

```
(defun word-add2 (num1 num2)
    (cdr (print (assoc (+ (get num1 'number) (get num2 'number))
          *symbols*))))
```

Here we are asking `print` to print the whole `assoc` expression: `print`'s final closing parenthesis comes at the end of the expression:

```
(defun word-add2 (num1 num2)
    (cdr (print <assoc expression>
          *symbols*))))
```

During evaluation, assoc returns whatever it does return (the thing you want to see) to print, whereupon print prints it and then returns the same thing to cdr. As far as cdr and assoc are concerned, the interposed call to print is completely 'transparent'. It might as well not be there for all the effect it has on the operation of word-add2.

Please take care with this technique, or you could actually add bugs rather than help to remove them. For example, were you accidentally to put print's closing parenthesis at the line end, thus excluding *symbols*, you would get an error message from Lisp about supplying too few arguments to assoc!

Finally on the subject of debugging please remember what was said in Chapter 7 about the position of macros in your files of functions: the macro definition should precede the defintions of any functions which use the macro. At the time, we mentioned that your Lisp may employ an incremental compiler, in which case the correct positioning of macros in a file will be not merely a matter of good style but will be crucial to their working. If as a file loads Lisp announces that one of your macros is undefined, you will almost certainly find that one or more functions which use that macro come before its definition in the file. Similarly, if you redefine a macro you may need to reload into Lisp all the functions whose definitions contain the macro. Two simple rules of thumb will keep you out of any possible trouble on these counts: always make sure that a macro works properly before including it in the definitions of any other functions; and always put your macros at the top of any file in which they appear.

8.2 Global vs local variables

Common Lisp provides a large number of global variables which are used to control various aspects of the user environment. We described two, *print-level* and *print-length*, above. In an earlier chapter we mentioned that instead of having your program print to the screen as usual, you might want it to print to a file. The global variable *standard-output* controls that. But unless you specifically wanted to alter the environment for some special programming purpose you would not normally worry about the values of the Lisp globals: the values are automatically preset to some 'normal' state every time Lisp starts up.

A different kind of global variable is a global **constant**. A constant is just like any other variable except that it is, as its name implies, always a global variable and its value is never intended to be changed. You have already heard about one of these, too: lambda-list-keywords. As you may remember, the value of this constant is a list of the permissible lambda list keywords in your particular implementation of Common Lisp, and obviously there would not be much point in your changing it. The variable is there for information rather than for use.

You can create your own global variables and constants using the macros defvar and defconstant. In a program to play tic-tac-toe (noughts and crosses in the UK) for example you might need:

```
(defvar *board* '((nil nil nil) (nil nil nil) (nil nil nil)))
```

and

```
(defconstant row-length 3)
```

The global variable *board* would subsequently hold the state of play at any moment, as Xs and 0s were added, while the global constant row-length might need to be referred to by the program on each turn to ensure that it did not try to put its X or 0 in a non-existent fourth square. Once you have assigned a value to a variable using defconstant you will not be able to assign a different value to it until you have closed Lisp down and restarted it.

However, good Lisp programmers usually try to avoid adding global variables to the environment if at all possible. As a general rule of thumb, a global variable should hold information which you want to remain permanently accessible whether your program is currently being executed or not, or which you want to be available to widely different parts (modules, see below) of your program. Often it is conceptually cleaner to pass the value of the variable from one function to another as an argument to one of its parameters, even if sometimes that means that an intermediate function may not use that value at all. Consider these three schematic functions:

```
(defun foo (a b)
  (<do something with a>)
  (bar a b))

(defun bar (c d)
  (<do something with c>)
  (gort d))

(defun gort (e)
  (<do something with e>))
```

The function foo does something (it does not matter what) to the value of its parameter a. Then that value, whether altered or not, is passed on to the function bar along with the original value of foo's parameter b. Within bar, these become respectively the values of parameters c and d. The function bar does something with the value of c and then passes the value of d on to the function gort, which does something with it as the value of its parameter e. We hope you can easily see that that value is exactly the value originally supplied as the second argument to foo at top level. Of course, if you did not actually need to pass the value down, for example if its value was always going to be the same regardless of your program's other input conditions, then it would be better to bind it to a local variable inside gort, via a let.

Actually, any variable which is not local (i.e. if it is not lexically and locally bound) is automatically assumed by Lisp to be global. Use of defvar tells both Lisp and other programmers that you really meant the variable to be global and did not, for example, simply misspell a local variable's name.

8.3   Program structure

8.3.1   Modularity

The above schematic, besides showing you how values can be passed down from top level without any need to make them into global variables, is also a micropicture of any large Lisp program. Usually, the top-level function of a large Lisp program is a quite simple function serving only to call other functions in a predetermined order. These subordinate functions would each be designed to complete some conceptually 'whole' part of the program's overall purpose. They are often referred to as **modules** and the program is said to be **modular** or **modularized**.

Going back to the tic-tac-toe example, its modules might be:

- read input from user
  This would involve allowing the user to type in something convenient to a human being such as the coordinates of the square on which s/he wanted to place an X or a 0, and converting it into some internal representation more convenient for Lisp operations (for example, correctly adding the new move to the global variable *board*).

- check to see whether either side has won
  In a simple game like tic-tac-toe, this need only consist of checking each of the eight possible winning lines in turn.

- calculate own next move
  Again, this might be as simple as looking for a line containing two of the machine's own tokens and a blank square, but in more complicated games it might require the ability to recognize patterns on the board regardless of their orientation, and the use of a **static**

evaluation function. This latter was mentioned in Chapter 1, in the context of Samuel's checkers-playing program.

- display new board state
  The program needs to show the user what has happened after each move. The display could be anything from a simple printout of the current value of *board* to a simulated three-dimensional picture of the game.

So the top-level function for tic-tac-toe would look something like this (it is not intended to be a genuine program):

```
(defun tic-tac-toe ()
  (loop
    (read-input-from-user)
    (check-for-win)
    (display-board-state)
    (calculate-own-next-move)
    (check-for-win)
    (display-board-state)))
```

(Of course, in a real program the functions would almost certainly need parameters so as to pass information to one another, and check-for-win would almost certainly be a predicate so that you could put an if around it and thus be able to exit from the loop.)

Notice that modularization has already saved a good deal of programming work since the two functions check-for-win and display-board-state can both be used twice. The modularization can (and should) be carried 'down' as far as necessary; for example the function calculate-own-next-move will probably need to perform several quite distinct actions in order to achieve its desired overall effect, and it too should have subordinate functions each designed to carry out one of these.

So you can visualize the program in the form of a tree. At the top, the root, is the top level function. Ranged along the next level down the tree are that function's modular subordinate functions; along the next level down are the equally modular subordinate functions of those subordinate functions; and so on. At the bottom you would expect to find very simple functions intended to effect only very tiny parts of the program's overall purpose. The overall tree is known as the program's **execution space**.

The reason why modularity is good programming practice is as usual for the sake of clarity. We cannot impress upon you forcefully enough how rapidly you will forget how your programs work, very soon after you have written them. If (as is likely!) they later turn out to contain unexpected bugs, then you or anyone else who has to hunt them down will be very grateful for any help included by you. Besides this, debugging is made easier anyway if the program's various operations are compartmentalized into modules, so that you can see more or less at a glance which functions are involved in any particular operation; you would not want to waste hours or days hunting in display-board-state for a bug which turned out to be in read-input-from-user; and without the modularity you might do just that.

8.3.2   Documentation and comments

We said above that while your first objective naturally is to write a working program, your second should be to make its operations clear. Modularity helps; so do mnemonic choices of variable names and function names. But there are two more things which a good programmer always includes: **documentation** and **comments**. Documentation is the way to add notes as to the purpose of any function or global variable (they become part of the function or variable's definition), while comments are added at random throughout the program to explain its workings. For example:

```
(defvar *board* '((nil nil nil) (nil nil nil) (nil nil nil))
  "Holds the current board state")
```

and

```
(defun check-for-win ()
  "Looks at all eight possible lines in turn")
  ...)
```

Sometimes, of course, it will be perfectly obvious what a function does (and mnemonic function/variable names help):

```
(defmacro last-but-one (lis)
  `(cadr (reverse lis)))
```

and in such cases no documentation is necessary. But the best rule of thumb is: if in doubt, document.

Once the documentation has been put in place as above, it will not be necessary to open and read the file(s) containing the definitions in order to read it. The function documentation will return it. However, since it is in principle possible (though as we mentioned earlier, usually not good programming practice) to use the same name for both a variable and a function, documentation needs a second argument to in case there ever should be a confusion of names:

```
? (documentation '*board* 'variable)

"Holds the current board state"
```

```
? (documentation 'check-for-win 'function)

"Looks at all eight possible lines in turn"
```

There is also a third alternative for the second argument, structure, for retrieving documentation from structures created via defstruct.

The documentation string (a string is anything enclosed in double-quotes) must, if it is present at all, be the second argument to defun, immediatly after the lambda list. It can also appear as the second argument to any other macro (such as defmacro or let) which binds its variables as defun does. Please check in your manual to see where documentation strings are permitted.

Comments may appear anywhere amongst your program code. Lisp completely ignores anything which follows a semicolon and which is on the same line as the semicolon:

```
;;; This function is called once after each move. If a win is
;;; detected, it returns T to cause an exit from the game.

(defun check-for-win ()
   "Looks at all eight possible lines in turn"
      (do ((lines ... (cdr lines))) ; create list of eight lines
          ((null lines) nil)          ; no win if no lines left
       ;; check any one line
       (cond ((equal (car lines) '(x x x))
              (return t))
             ((equal (car lines) '(0 0 0))
              (return t)))))
```

Notice the convention of using three semicolons to preface a line which is external to the function definition and which contains nothing but a comment; two semicolons to preface a line which is indented to match the code; and one semicolon to preface a line placed alongside the code. The idea is that the convention gives you three 'levels' of comment: major comments, perhaps describing how a function is used; code level comments to describe what integral sections of the function do; and comments which are really just marginal notes. Feel free to use the conventions in whatever way you feel most helps to clarify the workings of your program.

8.4 Good programming style

This is very hard to define, although most experienced programmers are very sure what bad programming style is, and recognize it at once. Conversely, experienced programmers can waste whole afternoons (we did, several times, during the writing of this book) arguing over whether some tiny quirk of programming is good or bad style. The difficulty is that, Lisp being so flexible, it is usually possible to achieve any given programmatic effect in several different ways. For example, detecting the point at which to exit from a loop might be done with an if, or with a cond, or even with a logical operator such as and or or. Often it is hard to say why any particular choice is the 'best' one. Many programmers adore the mapping functions and will always use them instead of loops if they can. Others feel that if you cannot do it recursively then you shouldn't be doing it in Lisp. And so on: Lisp style can be as individual and as idiosyncratic as style in written English.

Just as certain forms of words in English look more elegant, are more pleasurable to read, than others, so it is in Lisp, and for much the same reasons. This is not really surprising, since after all both of them are languages, intended to express our own human ideas and aspirations. However, although there are similarities between programming languages and natural languages there are also (of course) differences. The main difference is usually spoken of in terms of **level**.

Way down at the 1s and 0s level of the computer, whatever is going on is not immediately comprehensible to humans: most of us could not read the codes to be found there. The basic computer operations represented by the codes are often expressed in **assembler language**, which is more concise than the basic codes but remains equally unreadable to most of us. Assembler language is said to be a higher level language than the codes, but a lower level language than, say, Lisp. Lisp is a high level language and, as you shall see, does its best to be comprehensible to human beings.

Nonetheless, by comparison with a natural language such as English, Lisp is a very low level affair indeed. It is very much constrained by the needs of the computer on which it runs; that is to say, the manner in which it can express the programmer's ideas is limited to expressing those ideas as represented on the machine. This leads to the interesting conclusion that while English may be the best language for describing the programmer's ideas, Lisp is the best language for describing the resulting program! This book, and indeed any book on programming, is an attempt to bridge that gap: to enable you to learn how to express your ideas in Lisp so that the behaviour of the resulting program embodies those ideas.

An elegantly written Lisp program will be **generalizable**, and it will cater for both data abstraction and functional abstraction. The concept of 'generality' here implies that rather than writing a program to solve one particular problem you should try to write it so that it can solve a whole class of problems, the class of which the particular problem is just one example. During the next two chapters you will build a system which can make inferences. The first version will be capable of only a very few, and very simple, inferences. Two successive versions will increase the applicability and the usefulness of the system; that is, they will generalize it.

The idea behind **data abstraction** is that you should try to make your program virtually independent of the low level forms of knowledge representation which are available in Lisp. For example, unless for some reason it is crucial that your data be stored on property lists, you should write your program so that it would be a simple matter to use alists, hash tables or any of the other methods you learned about in Chapter 7. This usually means writing specific storage, access and retrieval functions (usually macros) and using them throughout your program in place of explicit calls to, say, setf and gethash. In Chapter 9 we shall point out some examples of this.

Functional abstraction is the same idea applied to functions. Throughout the rest of this book you will come across functions or macros which appear to do nothing other than call another function with a very similar name. Usually these will be top level functions (remember our description of a program as a tree of functions), directly callable by the user, where the extra and apparently useless function allows us to provide some pleasing syntax.

But more importantly the apparently useless functions will usually be the master functions in modules or submodules of the overall program. This is where the idea of abstraction comes in: one day you might decide completely to rewrite one of the modules, and when that happens you will not want the extra chore of rewriting every call to that module throughout the rest of the program. If the module's master function (the one called, of course, throughout the rest of the program) does no more than call a submaster function which actually runs the module, then you have a very convenient point at which to take out the old module and slot in the new one without altering the remainder of your program at all.

In short, the abstraction of both data and functions will cause you a little extra effort at first, but will make even major surgery to your program very much easier at a later date. A point worth making here is that AI programs are very rarely written so as to satisfy a complete specification. As we have mentioned before, the mere act of building a cognitive model can reveal factors which the underlying theory or hypothesis had not taken into account. So AI programs have a tendency to grow and to evolve. You can save yourself and perhaps others a great deal of work by writing your programs so that they are easy to modify.

Finally, we would like to repeat the advice we have stressed so often in this chapter and throughout the book: strive for clarity of expression. If more than one way of expressing something seem to you to be equally clear, then go for the most concise. But do not let brevity override clarity: do not for example be tempted to replace a long-winded looking cond with combinations of and and or just because it produces shorter code. We hope you will agree that the following is harder to understand at a glance than the version given above:

```
(defun check-for-win ()
  "Looks at all eight possible lines in turn"
  (do ((lines ... (cdr lines))) ; create list of eight lines
    ((null lines) nil)          ; no win if no lines left
  ;; check any one line
  (and (or (equal (car lines) '(x x x))
           (equal (car lines) '(O O O)))
      (return t))))
```

Maybe you do not agree, and that is fine by us: you have an inalienable right to develop your own personal Lisp style. You have read what we think elegant Lisp consists of, and we have tried hard to make our programs live up to our own advice. But throughout the rest of this book there may be many times when we show you some code and you think 'oh, I wouldn't have done it that way'. But in the end we would probably all agree on a couple of basic points: that non-modular programs are mind-blowingly tortuous, and that unnecessary global variables are dangerously messy. Also, we suspect from our own experience that if you do try to develop your own personal style, rather than insensitively churning out any old code so long as it works, you too will very soon come to cringe at certain forms of Lisp, whilst finding others as smooth and pleasurable as warm milk chocolate.

SUMMARY

We believe that we have now told you enough to give you a very good 'feel' for how Lisp works, and for the kinds of things you can do with it. The remainder of this book is in some ways a continuation of Chapter 1: an introduction to artificial intelligence. But this time instead of showing you AI in mere words we want to show you it in action, via substantial working programs which achieve the kind of results which AI likes to achieve.

Each program, when completed, will in an important sense behave as a tool; as we said in the very first sentence of this book AI is essentially the study of computational techniques. We commented then that if the resulting programs exhibit some kind of intelligent behaviour, AI counts them as successes. But we hope that what we have said since then has convinced you that producing even a small amount of intelligence from the machine is a substantial undertaking. That is why programming techniques are so important in AI: if we are ever to achieve the goal of a computational equivalent of the human mind, we need not only vastly superior hardware (perhaps in the form of parallel computers) but vastly superior programming techniques to anything which is available now.

We have therefore chosen our topics for the rest of this book largely on the basis of their popularity with expert Lisp programmers. We want you to see what is currently possible in Lisp, and although of course we shall give you an idea of how to use each system once you have built it, we shall from now on concentrate less upon the cognitive science context and more upon the actual techniques.

Part 3

TECHNIQUES AND APPLICATIONS

Chapter 9
A Basic Rule Interpreter

9.1 Expert systems   9.2 A simple rule interpreter

A great deal of money and research effort is being poured
into work on expert systems. In its broadest sense, the term
covers any computer program which embodies some area of
human expertise: expertise at finding faults in other electronic
equipment, expertise at diagnosing illnesses, expertise at
playing board games, to name but three. This chapter
discusses what is meant by such terms as knowledge,
inference and expertise, before inviting you to build a very
simple rule-based expert system interpreter. Rule-based
expert systems are by far the commonest kind, although it is
perfectly possible to build an expert system which does not
rely upon the technique of IF–THEN rules.

9.1 Expert systems

9.1.1 Expert machines vs expert humans

Expert systems are systems – suites of cooperating programs – which are
designed to represent within themselves the knowledge of one or more
human experts in some specialized field such as medical diagnosis,
electrical fault diagnosis or financial decision making. When given a
suitable input, perhaps the set of symptoms of which a patient is
complaining, the expert system can make inferences based upon the input
and upon what it 'knows': it can for example infer what illness the patient
is suffering from and what would be a suitable course of treatment. Often
the machine can also give a prognosis: a prediction as to how the patient's

recovery will progress and how long it will take. In these respects that expert system can do what a human doctor can do. However, there is no suggestion here that expert systems, in their current state of development, could replace human experts in other than very limited ways; but as sophisticated memory joggers and as confirmation that the human expert has reached a correct conclusion they have enormous potential.

Current research into expert system design concentrates upon the more interesting idea that the expert system should be able to explain its reasoning. That is, the human (expert) user would be able to say to it 'How did you arrive at this conclusion, given the facts I supplied you with?', and the computer would respond sensibly, explaining itself in terms of the supplied facts, facts it knew already, and rules of inference which it knew already. One of AI's current goals is to provide the facility for an argument between the machine and its human user: an argument in the form of a discussion, where a final conclusion would be reached on the basis of the machine's remorseless 'A therefore B' reasoning and the human mind's greater flexibility and intuitive leaps. Very few researchers into expert system design would want to replace human beings with machines; the objective is to provide ever-improving (perhaps one day self-improving) tools for human beings to use.

We are deliberately avoiding using the word **deduction** in place of the word **inference**. Strictly speaking, a deduction must be true if the premises upon which it is based are true, but establishing the truth or otherwise of just one premise can take a lifetime. Another kind of inference is the **inductive** inference. An inductive inference is not necessarily true but is a matter of probability. The inference that the sun will rise tomorrow because it has always done so up till now, rather than because of any immutable and known set of physical laws, is inductive and is the kind of thing we do every day. Human expertise is very much, and perhaps entirely, a matter of personal experience, and therefore is inductive rather than deductive in nature. It is quite possible to argue that no individual human being knows anything for certain other than the (sadly, recursive) fact that s/he exists. On the other hand there is a very real sense in which the operations of a computer are deductive: if the premises (the data) which it has been given by its user or by its programmer are true, then its inferences will necessarily have all the power of deductive truths.

But it is a big if: the machine faithfully does what we tell it to do, and if we have programmed faulty reasoning into it, it will give us back faulty answers. As programmers say, 'Garbage in, garbage out'. The difference between deductive and inductive reasoning, roughly parallel to the difference between common sense and intuition, marks a major point of distinction between present-day 'intelligent' machines and intelligent human beings. It seems clear that intuition is largely based upon experience, i.e. upon learning, and also upon what Edward de

Bono calls lateral thinking: the ability to spot analogies between apparently dissimilar problems and then to modify the first problem's solution so that it solves the second.

Both of these areas (the latter is sometimes referred to as 'analogy mapping') are in the forefront of present-day AI research. Neither of them is deductive; but the machine can only 'think' deductively, and therein lies a so-far intractable difficulty. Our intelligent machines can do some things better than we can (a perfectly played game of chess could be a purely deductive exercise), but critics of AI rightly argue that computers cannot think for themselves: no matter how complex their programs, in the end and on some conceptual level they are still only doing what we tell them to do. The counterargument is that perhaps we do the same: that we are programmed by evolution and by our lifetimes' experiences to react in precisely the ways that we do, and that the notion of individual 'personalities' may be no more than the results of the differences between our programs. Ultimately this question may turn out not to matter: as Turing suggested, if you cannot tell the difference between a person and a machine then the difference should be unimportant. Expert systems are exciting because they offer a partial handle on the problem: insofar as human thought processes are based upon clearly definable rules (game playing and rational decision making being two examples) expert systems can mimic us more successfully than previous computational techniques have been able to do.

9.1.2 Procedural vs declarative knowledge

In Chapter 7 we showed you various ways of representing real-world facts as triples of data, the indicator–property–value triples which could alternatively be regarded as expressing a **relationship** between two objects or classes of objects. For example, Joey isa canary or John has fleas. In expert systems the basic 'unit' of information is a logical or even causal relationship expressed as an IF–THEN rule: **if** Joey is a bird **then** Joey can fly, or **if** component 91 is faulty **then** the amplifier will lack bass response. A very large subset of what we humans would call knowledge, the kind of knowledge one might need in order to prove a point or to draw an inference, can be represented in this way, just as another very large subset of what we know can be represented via descriptive triples. Expert systems give to the computer the concept of IF–THEN rules.

The idea of gathering the combined expertise of a number of human experts and then encapsulating it, as it were, in a machine which can then provide answers based on that experience sounds very attractive, not least for industrial purposes. Until a very few years ago the most sophisticated machines used in industry were dumb robots: for example the machines which in some automated factories help to build automobiles. They were preprogrammed to millimetre accuracy, but no actual program was written. If the machine had an arm ending in, say, a painting tool, what would happen was that a human expert would take hold of the tool and use it just as s/he normally would to put a paint of coat onto a vehicle. Behind the scenes a computer would 'remember' every tiny movement, and thereafter the robot arm could repeat the whole process on its own, indefinitely. The problem was that if the very next car on the production line were not positioned with equal millimetre accuracy in front of the robot, some of the paint would miss its target. What was needed was a robot which was bright enough to realize that something had changed and could modify all of its own actions accordingly.

Another example is is that of business administration. The old data processing systems could store and retrieve huge amounts of data about a company and its employees; but it was up to the human users of the systems to work out which facts needed to be retrieved in any one case and to make decisions based upon them. The expert system equivalent should be able to do that work for itself. The common element in these two examples is the likelihood of errors arising during use. The older machines faithfully do their stuff even if they are being used in ludicrously inappropriate ways, but the hope is that if you ask the wrong questions of an expert system it will simply say, in the words of Arthur C. Clarke's HAL, 'I'm sorry, Dave: I can't do that'[†].

The type of knowledge which we are talking about here can conveniently be referred to as **active** or **procedural** knowledge: knowledge of how to do something, including how to draw inferences. The kind of knowledge referred to in Chapter 7 would by comparison be **passive** knowledge (sometimes referred to as **declarative** knowledge), more useful when one needs to perceive or to recognize some object. There is no suggestion (yet?) that all procedural knowledge can be reduced to a set of IF–THEN rules. Knowledge is intimately bound up with belief, into which there has been as yet comparatively little research although it is obvious that essentially the same knowledge – that, say, of how to publish a daily newspaper – produces very different results in the down-market press from those it produces in the hands of a responsible editor.

Declarative knowledge is knowledge that something is the case, be that knowledge the result of a deductive inference (hard to achieve) or of a belief (induction). Declarative knowledge can often be stated explicitly and in full by the knower, though since it is largely belief-based it may be inaccurate. Procedural knowledge is knowledge of how to do something: you may know how to drive a car, and you may know it so well that when doing it you rarely have consciously to think about it. But if you cannot

---

[†] Actually, it was a malfunction in HAL rather than a failure to understand. 'My mind is going' HAL remarked later on.

drive a car, a written instruction manual would not help you much: what you would need to do is to try to drive a car. Direct experience of the process would teach you, rather than any amount of words. Most human expertise involves both types of knowledge, and a part of the task of any knowledge engineer is to obtain and to represent both types effectively.

9.1.3 Eliciting the knowledge

The expert's knowledge is usually extracted in the first place via verbal protocols. That is, an expert sits down and does his or her normal job, but all the while speaks his or her thoughts out loud. Those thoughts are recorded, and later analysed, often with the help of the expert him/herself. After the experiment has been repeated several times with several different experts as subjects, a core of common agreement (a set of rules each of which can be derived from any of the protocols) will usually emerge. What is left over is usually a quite substantial number of rules, some of which may represent the fact that one subject was a greater expert than another, and some of which may be rules with which one or more of the experts would agree with but which are in fact wrong. The whole process of **knowledge elicitation** is fraught with the possibility of error, and even as we write researchers are gradually discovering improved methods of analysis which can help to reduce the errors.

An even more intractable problem, which we shall not attempt to solve in this book, concerns what are known as **compiled rules**. Consider, again, someone learning to drive a car. At first s/he has to take the utmost care over every single action, and has to go through them over and over again in order to get them right. A year later, that same person may happily drive whilst conducting a conversation, listening to the radio or working out some problem. At the end of the journey the driver may well have no conscious memory of having carried out any of the actions so laboriously learned, and yet s/he clearly has done so. It is almost as though s/he had mentally put a defun around the rules for driving, and now only had to 'call the function' for driving to happen without his/her having to think about it.

9.1.4 Outline of a rule interpreter

An expert system based around a rule interpreter is often referred to as a **production system**, though the term seems gradually to be going out of favour. Now let us move on to how such an expert system actually works. It consists of two main parts: a set of rules and an **interpreter**. The rules are analogous to the tree of data in our Collins and Quillian model. One could clearly remove the existing tree and 'plug in' a different tree, say a genealogical tree, and the overall system would then generate inferences about specifically family relationships rather than about the relationships between classes of objects. Similarly, the set of rules in an expert system could be exchanged for a set of rules concerning some different area of expertise, and again the overall system would still work happily. The interpreter is analogous to the remember function which derived inferences from the data. It too always works in the same way, though even in its simplest form, which we shall show you shortly, it is far more sophisticated than remember. In both the Collins and Quillian model and in an expert system there is very little knowledge in the functional parts of the programs: most of it is stored declaratively in the data.

The interpreter can be thought of as behaving rather like eval, which always does the 'same' things in order to choose the appropriate one from amongst all the available Lisp functions to work on the given data. (The 'knowledge', in Lisp, is stored in the functions and not in eval.) Similarly, the expert system interpreter chooses from the available rules one which is appropriate to whatever question it currently needs to answer.

Just as eval needs to reduce the top level function call to smaller and smaller subcalls until it comes to the level at which it can apply Lisp functions directly to arguments, so the interpreter divides any overall problem into subproblems until it finds questions which individual rules can deal with. eval does this recursively, but the interpreter uses a loop. It cycles repeatedly through its complete set of rules. The interpreter has four main parts: its main loop, its **working memory**, its **matcher** and its **conflict resolution strategies**.

In Lisp it is convenient to store the rules in a way which associates each of them with a particular symbol (we shall use indicators and their property lists, though we hope it is clear from Chapter 7 that there are several other ways in which to represent them), and to keep these symbols, these 'rule names' on a list. A simple looping function can then process each of the rules in turn, accessing each rule via its name.

Working memory is a term borrowed from psychology, and by the same analogy the set of rules would correspond to **long-term memory**. Working memory in human beings is said to hold only a limited number of items, and its small size explains why most of us would have to give up if asked, say, to work out in our heads all the possible moves and countermoves, up to seven moves ahead, in a game of chess: we simply cannot keep enough possibilities 'in our heads' at the same time. In a rule interpreter the size of working memory is not usually limited at all, but the principle is the same: it is a kind of scratch pad, holding temporary data as computation proceeds. Although it is a quite simple thing – usually a list or an alist is sufficient – working memory is crucial to the operation of a rule interpreter as you shall soon see.

As for the rules themselves, any IF–THEN rule is of the general form

```
IF X THEN Y
```

in which X is known as the **antecedent** or left-hand side of the rule whilst Y is known as its **consequent** or right-hand side. The antecedent may contain any number of terms, or conditions; and the consequent is sometimes but not always limited to a single term, an action to be carried out when the antecedent succeeds. No doubt you will recognize the similarity here to the Lisp if function; but in a rule there is no equivalent of the 'else' branch: that would have to be taken care of by a separate rule.

Working memory is normally initialized to hold a representation of the problem which the expert system is required to solve, i.e. to the initial data from which it is expected to draw inferences. Subsequently, each time around the loop, the antecedent of each rule in turn is compared, or **matched**, against the contents of working memory. If an antecedent matches, then the consequent of that rule is executed, and the effect of that is a change to the contents of working memory. Almost invariably, the consequents of rules either deposit something in working memory, or remove something from it.

For example, a hypothetical rule might say: IF working memory contains two digits and the instruction to add them, THEN deposit in working memory the sum of the two digits and remove both the digits themselves and the instruction to add.

The matching process is (at least in the simple interpreter which we shall show you first) purely lexical: the interpreter takes each term in a rule's antecedent and looks for corresponding patterns amongst the items in working memory. We match the words (constants) and the values of any variables in the IF part of the rule against the contents of working memory. If the match succeeds, we go on to execute the THEN (the consequent) part of the rule. The idea is very reminiscent of a single cond clause.

The idea is that, once any given rule has matched and has changed the contents of working memory, then on the next cycle of the interpreter some other rule will match. It will in turn change working memory again, so that on the next cycle a third rule will match, and so on. Eventually there will come a cycle during which no rules match, and at this point the interpreter halts. The final contents of working memory should, if the expert system is working, represent the solution to the original problem or the desired inference from the input data.

When a rule's consequent is executed (because its antecedent has matched with working memory) the rule is said to **fire**. Only one rule is allowed to fire per cycle. However, this is not the same thing as saying that only one rule per cycle is allowed to match. The more rules there are the more likely it becomes that two or more rules might match during any one cycle. Furthermore, if you remember that a rule's antecedent may contain several terms, and that working memory may contain any number of possibly-matching items, it should be clear that the permutations of possible matches mean that when a single rule matches it might do so in several different ways.

We do not propose to worry you with these complications in our first simple interpreter, but in a later version of it we shall introduce **conflict resolution strategies**, whose purpose is to choose which of several matching rules should be allowed to fire on that cycle.

Even without conflict resolution strategies, and depending upon the precise contents of working memory during any one cycle, any one of the complete set of rules might fire. So ideally the order in which the rules are stored (the order of their names in a list) should be irrelevant.

To sum up, in order to build a simple rule interpreter we shall need a looping function which, using a list of rule names, can retrieve each of the rules in turn and present it for processing. Processing will involve taking a single rule and comparing each of the terms in its antecedent (they will be Lisp forms or something very similar) with the items currently in working memory. When all of the terms in a rule's antecedent match, the rule will fire so that its consequent changes the contents of working memory. When no rules fire during a cycle, the process will stop.

9.2   A simple rule interpreter

9.2.1   The main loop

Our first version of the rule interpreter, which by the standards of this book so far will be a large program and which we would like you to duplicate on your own computer as we go along, will not actually be capable of very much when you have built it. Its purpose is to give you a feel for the underlying structure of such a program – its 'skeleton' – so that when we later take the same code and extend it so as to add real power to our expert system, you will understand how and why our suggested changes bring worthwhile improvements. The completed system will consist of some 35 short functions plus a small handful of interface functions intended only to make actual use of the system easier.

Throughout the rest of this chapter we shall explain each of the functions in detail. Where functions of more than a line or two of code are concerned, we shall again adopt the technique of first showing you a skeletal version and then gradually adding more facilities to it until a final version can do all that is required of it. Because the constant repetition of near-identical pieces of code is a potential source of errors, and because any such errors might cause you to spend frustrating hours hunting down a bug which in the end turned out to be a typographical mistake on our part or on our publisher's part, we provide a complete and commented listing of the program in Appendix A. If as you type our functions into your own file and evaluate them in your own Lisp one of them seems not to work as we say it should (or, more likely, generates only an error message!) please refer to the appendix as being the final word on the correctness of what you have typed. We hope you will also find the complete listing useful when you want to see the definitions of two functions on the same page, without the words of our main text getting in your way.

While defining the functions and macros below in your own file, please do remember our advice that macros should all be together near the top of the file, followed by the function definitions. In our text it will usually be the case that we want to describe a fairly powerful function to you first, whereupon the purpose of a relatively trivial macro or two should be self-evident to you. Nonetheless, in your file, Lisp may well insist on seeing the macros first.

Here are the bare bones of the basic main loop of the interpreter:

```
(defun production-system (ruleset goal)
   (do ()
      ((or halt-signalled? goal-achieved? (not fired-rule)))
      (fire-rule (find-rule-to-fire ruleset))))
```

Since at the moment we do not need to set up any local variables, the first argument to do is an empty list. The second argument to do specifies as usual the condition(s) under which the loop shall halt. There are three sets of circumstances under which we would like this particular interpreter to halt. The first is when some rule had fired and has inserted into working memory a specific 'halt' token; the eventual user of the system might need this in order to stop the interpreter part-way through its normal run. The second condition is when the **goal**, that is whatever any one run of the system was intended to do, appears as an item in working memory and thus has been achieved; and the third condition is when no rules fire during any one cycle, the assumption here being that no rules would fire on the next cycle either, or the next, or the next . . .

The first two of the above three arguments to or are simple mnemonically named variables (there is nothing special to Lisp about the question mark, which it treats like any alphabetic character). Their values will be set appropriately as the interpreter runs. The third argument involves another such variable, fired-rule, which will be set to NIL at the start of each cycle and reset to T (or to some non-NIL value) if any rule fires. If at the end of a cycle its value is still NIL, we want that fact to halt the interpreter. The not logically inverts the NIL, giving us a T to look for.

Each time around the loop, find-rule-to-fire goes through all of the rules in succession, looking for one whose antecedent terms all match with items in working memory. find-rule-to-fire is in fact the master function for an entire module of other functions. The final result produced by this module, which will be the name of a rule, is passed to another module controlled by fire-rule, and this latter module fires the rule, i.e. it effects the alterations necessary to working memory specified in the consequent of the rule.

Now look at this immediate and rather elegant modification made possible by the syntax of do:

```
(defun production-system (ruleset goal)
  (do ((fired-rule (fire-rule (find-rule-to-fire ruleset))
                   (fire-rule (find-rule-to-fire ruleset))))
      ((or halt-signalled? goal-achieved? (not fired-rule)))))
```

We hope you remember that when setting up local variables in the first argument to a do, each variable requires a three-element list. The list shows first the variable's name, then its initial value, and finally what shall happen to it each time around the loop. You have seen expressions such as

```
(do ((n 10 (- n 1)))
    ...)
```

before, and the one above is essentially no different. The variable fired-rule acquires, each time around the loop, the value returned by fire-rule, and we shall later write fire-rule in such a way that it always returns the value returned to it by find-rule-to-fire. This will either be the name of a rule or, if no rules matched working memory on that cycle, NIL. Making use of the returned values of functions in this way has a nice elegance about it, and it has the added advantage that it ensures that both fire-rule and find-rule-to-fire are called on each cycle of the loop, so that they no longer have to appear in the body of the do form. In fact as you can see the do now has no body at all. Most Lisp programmers are obscurely pleased with themselves when they succeed in writing a do loop with no body!

The next step is to make very similar arrangements for the other two 'halting' variables, halt-signalled? and goal-achieved?:

```
(defun production-system (ruleset goal)
  (do ((fired-rule (fire-rule (find-rule-to-fire ruleset))
                   (fire-rule (find-rule-to-fire ruleset)))
```

```
                (goal-achieved? (goal-achieved goal)
                                (goal-achieved goal))
              (halt-signalled? (halt-signalled) (halt-signalled)))
            ((or halt-signalled? goal-achieved? (not fired-rule)))))
```

The two functions `halt-signalled` and `goal-achieved` will simply inspect
working memory for the presence of the corresponding tokens. Since they
are such small functions we may as well define them as macros for the
sake of efficiency:

```
(defmacro halt-signalled ()
  `(member '(%%halt%%) *working-memory* :test #'equal))

(defmacro goal-achieved (goal)
  `(member ,goal *working-memory* :test #'equal))
```

Every item in working memory is going to be a list, so both the 'halting'
token and the `goal` item will be a list. This implies that `member`, which as
you may recall defaults to using the standard `eql` as its test for
membership, has to be told explicitly to use `equal` instead. The horrible-
looking 'halt' token is deliberately made that horrible to minimize the
chances of any future user accidentally including it in a rule which was not
intended to stop the interpreter (as someone conceivably might if it were
simply the word 'halt', for example).

Point to remember   The macros should go at the top of your file![†]

    The main loop is now almost finished, and would in fact work as it
stands once the `find-rule-to-fire` and `fire-rule` modules had been
written. But when writing anything other than a very trivial program, it is
always a good idea to make it print messages on the screen as it runs, so
that you the programmer can be sure that it is working properly. To that
end we shall take a short break from the interpreter so as to introduce
you to the `format` function.
    You can think of `format` as a very powerful version of the simpler
printing functions `print` and `princ`. Like them, it takes a Lisp object and
prints it; unlike them it can print as many such objects as you the
programmer want it to print. Interspersed amongst those objects will be
some **directives**, which are characters which are not printed but serve to
control the way in which the printing is formatted. The second argument
to `format` is enclosed in string quotes and contains all the objects to be
printed together with all the necessary directives.

[†] The reasons have to do with the Lisp compiler, which we do not cover in this book. Your
macros may well work if not placed at the top of your file (or at least earlier than the
functions which use them), but it seems to us better to teach you good programming
practice than bad, even if we have not got room to explain why!

The first argument to format specifies the **stream** to which its output shall be printed. This might be the screen or a file, but for most practical purposes the argument is T and therefore the output goes to the screen. (All of Lisp's input/output functions, e.g. those functions which allow something to be read from a file, and those functions which allow something to be printed to the screen or saved to a file, make the obvious default assumptions, i.e. that you will want to read from a disk file, save to a disk file, or print on screen. If you ever need to use any source other than disk or any destination other than the screen, look up the corresponding functions (specifically read and print) in your Lisp manual to discover their extra facilities.)

Directives are always introduced, amongst the arguments to format, by the tilde (˜) character, and for our present purposes we shall mention only three of the many possible directives. The per cent (%) character causes the Lisp object immediately following it to start on a new line. This is similar to the effect of print, which also outputs a newline (carriage return) before printing its argument, but the advantage of format is that it can also print strings, for example, verbatim as far as upper and lower case are concerned and without their double quotes. Thus:

```
? (format t "˜%foo foo")
```

prints

```
foo foo
```

whereas:

```
? (format t "˜%foo ˜%foo")

foo
foo
NIL
```

The directive ˜a, placed within the string quotes of the second argument, will on printing be replaced by whatever first follows the end of the string quotes. Thus you can insert some non-string item such as a list into the printed result:

```
? (format t "This is a list: ˜a" '(a b c))

This is a list: (A B C)
NIL

? (format t "This is a list: ˜a" (list 'a 'b 'c))

This is a list: (A B C)
NIL
```

If there are several examples of ~a inside the string, each of them is replaced during printing by the corresponding one of a series of arguments placed after the string:

```
? (format t "One list: ~a and one atom: ~a" (list 'a 'b 'c)) 'z)

One list: (A B C) and one atom: Z
NIL
```

Finally, the double directive ~{...~} iterates over a list. Rather like mapcar, it does to each element of the list whatever is specified (via more directives) inside the braces:

```
? (format t "~%Here are the contents of working memory~{~%~a~}"
  '(one two three four))

ONE
TWO
THREE
FOUR
NIL
```

The directives inside the braces imply that a newline is to be printed before each item of the list.

Point to remember format as used above always returns NIL. Be careful when including a format expression in a test form such as if or cond, that the returned NIL does not make one of your tests also return NIL. The same applies to and and or.

Having got format out of the way we can now return to the interpreter.

```
(defun production-system (ruleset goal)
  (do ((fired-rule (fire-rule (find-rule-to-fire ruleset))
                   (fire-rule (find-rule-to-fire ruleset)))
       (goal-achieved? (goal-achieved goal)
                       (goal-achieved goal))
       (halt-signalled? (halt-signalled) (halt-signalled)))
      ((or halt-signalled? goal-achieved? (not fired-rule)))

    (format t "~%Rule Interpreter Halted")
    (cond (halt-signalled? (format t "~%Halt Signalled"))
          (goal-achieved?
            (format t "~%Goal ~a Achieved" goal))
          ((not fired-rule) (format t "~%No Rules Fired")))
    (format t " ~%Final contents of working memory:~{~%~a~}"
            *working-memory*))))
```

There is still no body in the do form, but the interpreter can now tell you when it halts and can give one of three reasons why it halted, depending upon the states of the three halting variables halt-signalled?, goal-achieved? and fired-rule. Finally, it prints the contents of working memory after the halt, neatly arranging them one item per line.

There is one more refinement we can make to this function before leaving it, and that is to add a count of the number of cycles executed during any run of the interpreter. It will have no particular purpose in this first version of the overall system, but we can at least pass it down as an extra argument to fire-rule, so that the latter can, via another format statement, tell us which cycle the interpreter is on whenever a rule fires. Again, we make use of do's ability to set and update a local variable:

```
(defun production-system (ruleset goal)
  (do ((cycle-number 0 (1+ cycle-number))
       (fired-rule (fire-rule (find-rule-to-fire ruleset)
                              cycle-number)
                   (fire-rule (find-rule-to-fire ruleset)
                              cycle-number))
       (goal-achieved? (goal-achieved goal)
                       (goal-achieved goal))
       (halt-signalled? (halt-signalled) (halt-signalled)))
      ((or halt-signalled? goal-achieved? (not fired-rule))
       (format t "~%Rule Interpreter Halted")
       (cond (halt-signalled? (format t "~%Halt Signalled"))
             (goal-achieved?
               (format t "~%Goal ~a Achieved" goal))
             ((not fired-rule) (format t "~%No Rules Fired")))
       (format t "~%Final contents of working memory:~{~%~a~}"
               *working-memory*))))
```

However, this adds a slight complication: something which we did not mention when first introducing do to you, and that concerns the order in which its local variables are assigned their values. In the normal version of do the assignment is in parallel; that is to say each local variable is assigned its value at the same time. Because of this,

```
(do ((a 3) (b (+ 2 a)))
  ...)
```

would not work. (Remember that unless you actually want a variable to be reassigned each time around the loop, it is permissible to leave out the third term in each assignment list.) Although a would be correctly assigned the value 3, it would by then be too late to assign to b a value which was derived from the value of a. If you were to try this, you would find that b did not in fact acquire a value at all, so that as soon as you tried to refer to it (to make use of b) eval would complain that it was unbound. In the rule interpreter, we want to assign a value to cycle-number and then to use that value during the (parallel) assignment of a value to fired-rule.

There is another version of do, called do* (pronounced 'do-star'), which gets over this problem by assigning values to its local variables sequentially. Thus the final change to our interpreter so far is to substitute do* for do:

```
(defun production-system (ruleset goal)
  (do* ((cycle-number 0 (1+ cycle-number))
        (fired-rule (fire-rule (find-rule-to-fire ruleset)
                               cycle-number)
                    (fire-rule (find-rule-to-fire ruleset)
                               cycle-number))
        (goal-achieved? (goal-achieved goal)
                        (goal-achieved goal))
        (halt-signalled? (halt-signalled) (halt-signalled)))
       ((or halt-signalled? goal-achieved? (not fired-rule))
        (format t "~%Rule Interpreter Halted")
        (cond (halt-signalled? (format t "~%Halt Signalled"))
              (goal-achieved?
               (format t "~%Goal ~a Achieved" goal))
              ((not fired-rule) (format t "~%No Rules Fired")))
        (format t "~%Final contents of working memory:~{~%~a~}"
                *working-memory*))))
```

We hope you will agree that what looks at a casual glance to be a fairly complex function definition is really quite a simple thing, which you can quite correctly regard as doing no more than assigning some values to a few local variables and printing out a few messages. Notice how the indentation helps readers of the code to see what it is going on: all the variable assignment lists in do*'s first argument are lined up vertically beneath one another, as are the various actions to take when one or other of the halting conditions applies, in do*'s third argument.

9.2.2   Firing a rule

As we mentioned in Chapter 8, the top-level function in a large program often is quite simple, serving only to call the program's various modules in the correct order. production-system calls on two modules: fire-rule and find-rule-to-fire. We shall describe fire-rule first since it is by far the simpler of the two.

```
(defun fire-rule (rule cycle-number)
  (cond (rule
          (setf *working-memory*
                (append (consequent rule)
                        *working-memory*))
          (format t "~%Cycle: ~a Rule: ~a fired~{ ~a~}~
                     put in working memory."
                  cycle-number rule (consequent rule))
          rule)))
```

fire-rule receives as arguments a rule name from find-rule-to-fire, and a cycle number from the do* loop in production-system. If on any particular cycle find-rule-to-fire finds no suitable candidate rule, no rule whose antecedent matches with working memory, then find-rule-to-fire will return NIL, and in that case we want fire-rule also to return NIL. As described above, the returned value of fire-rule will become the value of fired-rule, one of the main loop's halting variables. So the body of fire-rule is a cond which returns the value of its parameter rule. At the same time, the cond ensures that fire-rule returns NIL if there is no rule to fire.

Do not be confused by the lack of the characteristic double parentheses immediately after the word cond. The 'test' form here is not a function call as it so often is, but merely the value of the variable rule, which will be either NIL or something non-NIL: a rule name. You might also be wondering why eval does not take it to be a call to a non-existent function rule. The answer is that cond is a macro, and hence is expanded into something else before it is evaluated. So what looks like a function call written up there on the page is really only a side-effect of cond's syntax. Specifically, it is quite likely that in your Lisp that cond clause would expand into

```
(if rule ...)
```

without any sign of a 'function call' to rule.

When there is a rule to work upon, the 'action' part of the single cond clause appends the consequent of the rule to *working-memory* and prints a comment to the user via format. As you know by now, format is there just for the user's benefit and contributes nothing to the success of the interpreter itself. The important effect is the addition of the rule's consequent to working memory: this is what 'firing a rule' means.

The consequent of the rule is also kept as a list of one sublist, such as

```
((%%halt%%))
```

so that the effect of append is to add the sublist to *working-memory*.

The consequent itself will be held on the property list of the corresponding rule name, so that another simple macro will serve to retrieve it:

```
(defmacro consequent (rule)
  `(get ,rule 'consequent))
```

This macro is an example of **data abstraction**. It allows you, or any future programmer working on this program, to change the way in which the rule's consequent is stored. A simple change to this macro and to the antecedent macro, coming up soon, would cause it to retrieve the desired data from a hash table instead of from a property list. Later on you will see that the corresponding function store-rule could similarly and simply be changed.

9.2.3 Choosing which rule to fire

Now we come to the second module, that whose master function is find-rule-to-fire. It, too, consists of two (sub)modules: the **matcher** which does all the donkey work of comparing the antecedents of rules against working memory; and the **conflict resolution strategies**. In this first version of the interpreter we shall not use conflict resolution at all because we intend that only one rule of the set of rules shall match on any one cycle, and the matcher will be a simplified version of what it will become later. However, at this stage it is probably useful to provide a diagram of the underlying program structure (Figure 9.1), showing how the five main modules interconnect.

find-rule-to-fire does two things. It recurses through the entire list of rules and 'looks at' each one in turn, and it takes care to return the right value to fire-rule when it has finished. It passes on to another function, recognise-rule, the problem of deciding whether or not any given rule matches with working memory. Incidentally, the name of this latter function reflects the fact that the process of matching and then

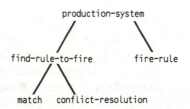

Figure 9.1 Program structure.

firing a rule is often referred to as the **recognise–act cycle**, not to be confused with a cycle of the interpreter's main loop during which the antecedents of the whole ruleset are checked against working memory.

```
(defun find-rule-to-fire (ruleset)
  (cond ((null ruleset) nil)
        ((recognise-rule (car ruleset)))
        (t (find-rule-to-fire (cdr ruleset)))))
```

At this point we make the usual decision that when a rule successfully matches against working memory, the function recognise-rule shall return its name, and that otherwise it shall return NIL. We hope that you notice the pattern of the cond in this recursive function. As usual, the recursion is to halt if ruleset, the list of rule names, is reduced to NIL. If at any point the first rule in ruleset matches against working memory, recognise-rule will return a value and thus also halt the recursion. Otherwise find-rule-to-fire simply recurses on to the next rule in ruleset. It is worth noticing here that recognise-rule 'cdrs' down the list of rules until it finds one which correctly matches with working memory, and then it stops cdring. In this first version of the interpreter (and the next) only one rule will be allowed to fire per cycle, and this means that each cycle may test a different number of rules: sometimes the very first rule will match, sometimes only the very last. So a 'cycle' does not yet really mean going through all of the rules in turn, but means going through them in turn until one matches.

Just in case the form of that second clause confuses you: we have employed a common programming trick which is not to write more code than is absolutely necessary. In this case the clause has no 'action' part. This is clearly not the same thing as you see in the first clause which has NIL as its 'action'. You might think that the clause should read:

```
((recognise-rule (car ruleset)) (recognise-rule (car ruleset)))
```

so that the action to be taken when recognise-rule succeeds as a test is to call that function again so as to return its returned value. If you think that, please feel free to write it into your own program: there is absolutely nothing wrong with it and as we have said before anything which aids clarity is worthwhile. On the other hand, when the result of the test also happens to be the value which we want returned from the corresponding cond clause, there does not seem to be much point in applying the test all over again in the 'action' position of the clause. (This would be particularly true, of course, if the test happened to contain a side-effect which we did not want evaluated twice.) If you do not supply

an 'action' in a cond clause, that clause has only the value of the test to
return, and it does so. If you think that obscure, our excuse is that
everybody uses this particular bit of shorthand. We have not used it until
now in this book, but from now on we shall not restrain ourselves!

find-rule-to-fire will, in the final version of the interpreter, choose
one rule to fire (per cycle of the interpreter) from any number of rules
which potentially might be firable. It will use a mapcar to keep a list of the
results of recognise-rule's attempts to recognize (match against working
memory the antecedent of) each rule in turn, and at the end of each cycle
it will employ conflict resolution strategies to decide which of the
matching rules should actually fire; that is, which of the rule names
returned by recognise-rule should be returned to fire-rule.

recognise-rule itself actually does not do anything much. It
retrieves the rule's antecedent from the rule's property list, and again
passes the main problem on, this time to match-antecedent. The latter
function will return T if matching succeeds, and whenever that happens
recognise-rule returns the rule's name. If match-antecedent returns NIL, so
does recognise-rule:

```
(defmacro recognise-rule (rule)
  '(if (match-antecedent (antecedent ,rule)) ,rule))

(defmacro antecedent (rule)
  '(get ,rule 'antecedent))
```

recognise-rule is there mainly for conceptual clarity: find-rule-to-fire
could have called match-antecedent directly; but just as find-rule-to-fire is
the master function for both the matcher module and the conflict
resolution module, so recognise-rule is the master function for the
matcher module alone. In the final version of the interpreter, there will
be a comparable master function which controls only the conflict
resolution module.

If recognise-rule succeeds, it returns the value of rule (the
matching rule's name); otherwise it returns NIL.

9.2.4   The matcher

We are now about to plunge into a description of the matcher. It will be
the most complicated piece of programming which you have encountered
so far, but the principle of it is useful in many contexts other than that of
rule interpreters. Consider what needs to be done. We have a rule's
antecedent which consists of a list of sublists. Each of those sublists must
match against one or other element in working memory if the rule overall

is to match, and working memory itself consists of a list of sublists. For example, we might need to try to match

        ((a) (b) (c) (d) (e))

against

        ((one) (two) (three) (four))

The match would fail of course. Even worse, we might want to try to match

        ((a b c) (d e f) (g h i))

against

        ((a b c) (d e beta) (c three gamma))

Regardless of what the antecedent of a rule or the contents of working memory might actually mean, the plain programming fact is that we need ultimately to be able to do our matching at the level of atoms. We need to detect the facts that f and beta are not the same, that g and c are not the same, that h and three are different, and so on. The essential point is that so long as elements of the two lists do match at atomic level, the matching process can continue. But as soon as even an atom does not match (it occurs in our example at the third element of the second sublist) the whole antecedent thereby fails to match. It can therefore be discarded and the matcher can move on to the antecedent of the next rule.

Let us approach the problem in the usual recursive way, breaking the overall problem down into ever-smaller subproblems until finally we can solve them all. The antecedent of a rule consists of a number of terms or **conjuncts**. They are called conjuncts because the effect of matching is rather like the effect of the function and: all of them have to match individually if the antecedent is to match as a whole. So, we need to go through the whole list of conjuncts trying to match each in turn against working memory. match-antecedent does this, and sensibly it calls match-conjunct-with-working-memory to process each separate conjunct:

```
(defun match-antecedent (antecedent)
  (cond ((null antecedent) t)
        ((match-conjunct-with-working-memory (car antecedent))
         (match-antecedent (cdr antecedent)))))
```

Once again you see the familiar pattern of a recursive function. match-antecedent recurses its way down the list represented by antecedent, and stops if the list becomes empty. On the way, if match-conjunct-with-working-memory fails (we shall ensure that it returns NIL if it does) recursion halts. In other words, match-antecedent does not waste time trying to match the remainder of an antecedent when some part of it has already failed to match.

match-conjunct-with-working-memory introduces to the program the global variable *working-memory*, so that for the first time we actually have a list of working memory patterns against which to try to match the single pattern of our conjunct:

```
(defun match-conjunct-with-working-memory (conjunct)
  (match* conjunct *working-memory*))
```

match-conjunct-with-working-memory in turn calls match*, and match* again uses recursion to work its way down a list: this time the list representing working memory. It tries for a match between the conjunct and each member of that list in turn, and if it finds a match it stops (recursion halts) because our interpreter is not intended to look for a second possible match between any one conjunct and the contents of working memory:

```
(defun match* (pattern patterns)
  (cond ((null patterns) nil)
        ((match (car patterns) pattern))
        (t (match* pattern (cdr patterns)))))
```

Here, in the second clause of the cond, we have again used the trick of allowing the result of the test to double as the result of the (non-existent) action.

All that remains is for match to compare the single conjunct (now called pattern) against a single item from working memory. At this stage both of them will be lists which have no sublists, such as:

```
(d e f)
```

and

```
(d e beta)
```

and equal will compare those for us quite happily:

```
(defun match (pattern1 pattern2)
  (equal pattern1 pattern2))
```

Maybe that strikes you as a bit of a cheat. Perhaps you think that after all

our talk of comparing sublists at the atomic level we should have written
a match which would actually compare each atom:

```
(defun match (a b)
      (cond ((null a) nil)
            ((eql (car a) (car b))
             (match (cdr a) (cdr b)))))
```

But, since equal already exists that would be merely re-inventing the
wheel. Our contention that equal carries out atomic level matching, just
as well as an extended version of match could do, is good enough for the
moment. In the next version of the interpreter (coming shortly) we shall
actually need to inspect each atom individually.

   The value of the call to equal will, of course, always be T if a match
was found but NIL otherwise. This value is returned by match to match*
which, if the whole of one antecedent term matches, returns T to match-
conjunct-with-working-memory. The latter too returns T to match-antecedent,
and match-antecedent returns T to recognise-rule if the whole antecedent
matches. If the matching process fails anywhere along the line, one or
other of the matching functions will return a NIL, which will also filter up
to recognise-rule.

   So we now have a matcher which can tell us when any one conjunct
of any one rule's antecedent matches with some element of working
memory (match). Therefore it can tell us when all of a rule's antecedent
matches working memory (match-antecedent). This is the rule whose name
find-rule-to-fire wants, so that it can return it to fire-rule, so that its
consequent can be added to working memory, and so that the interpreter
can continue to the next cycle and the next rule to match/fire; or, of
course, to halt.

9.2.5   The user interface

The interpreter is now complete, and presumably you are keeping it (the
definitions of all of its functions so far) in a file on your computer's floppy
or hard disk. In order for you to see some results (we did warn you that
they were going to be be trivial!) from all your hard work so far, it needs
some rules, and it needs a problem to work upon. So at this point it
would be nice to build a user interface which will make it easy both to
give the interpreter sets of rules, and to set up working memory with an
initial problem state and perhaps a goal state as well. In particular, you
will need to initialize the two global variables *working-memory* and
rules:

```
(defvar *working-memory* nil "This holds the working memory.")

(defvar *rules* nil "Holds the ruleset to be interpreted.")
```

Please type these two definitions into your file. For conceptual reasons, and also for reasons to do with program compilation which we will not go into in this book, the top of the file is the 'right' place to put them. From the standpoint of what we've told you so far, they could go anywhere in the file. So the very top is as good a place as any!

For the sake of this example we decree that all rules shall be written as lists, whose first element shall be the rule's name. That will be followed by a series of sublists, each containing an element of the rule's antecedent. Then will come an 'implication arrow' to signify the IF–THEN nature of the rule, and finally will come a sublist containing the rule's consequent:

```
(rulebigrule (a b c) (one two three) (alpha beta gamma) ==>
    (damn))
```

That sort of thing is easy for us humans to read, and now we need to make it equally readable to our program. Once again we define a master function to control other, 'lower' functions:

```
(defun set-up-rules (ruleset-name rules)
  (store-ruleset
    (mapcar #'(lambda (rule)
                (store-rule (antecedent-part-of rule)
                            (consequent-part-of rule)
                            (name-part-of rule)))
            rules)
    ruleset-name))
```

store-ruleset is going to store a list of the names of a complete set of rules as the value of a property, whose name is the same as the name of that particular set of rules, on the property list of an indicator called *rules*. The virtue of this is that *rules* can then hold any number of different sets of rules, each set designed to produce different behaviour on the part of the overall expert system. As we said before, one should in principle be able to 'plug in' any set of rules, depending upon what kind of expertise you wanted the machine to display. Here is store-ruleset:

```
(defun store-ruleset (ruleset ruleset-name)
  (setf (get *rules* ruleset-name) ruleset))
```

The list of rule names is returned to store-ruleset by a mapcar in set-up-rules, whose auxiliary function store-rule adds two property-value pairs to the property list of each rule name. One pair represents the antecedent of the rule, and the other represents its consequent:

```
(defun store-rule (antecedent consequent rule-name)
  (setf (get rule-name 'consequent) consequent
        (get rule-name 'antecedent) antecedent)
  rule-name)
```

You will notice that setf here has four arguments rather than two. This is another bit of convenient shorthand provided by Lisp: in fact setf can cope with any even number of arguments, assumed to be variable–value pairs, and will faithfully set each variable to each corresponding value.

Finally, the mapcar inside store-rule uses three little macros whose operation we shall explain in a minute:

```
(defmacro antecedent-part-of (rule)
   `(subseq ,rule 1 (position '==> ,rule :test #'eq)))

(defmacro consequent-part-of (rule)
   `(subseq ,rule (+ 1 (position '==> ,rule :test #'eq))))

(defmacro name-part-of (rule)
   `(car ,rule))
```

We can now write something like:

```
(set-up-rules 'first
           '((ruleF  (red light) (president awake)
                     (chiefs summoned) (hotline used)
                     (worldwide red alert) (button pushed)
                  ==> (%%halt%%))
             (ruleE  (red light) (president awake)
                     (chiefs summoned) (hotline used)
                     (worldwide red alert)
                  ==> (button pushed))
             (ruleD  (red light) (president awake)
                     (chiefs summoned) (hotline used)
                  ==> (worldwide red alert))
             (ruleC  (red light) (president awake)
                     (chiefs summoned)
                  ==> (hotline used))
             (ruleB  (red light) (president awake)
                  ==> (chiefs summoned))
             (ruleA  (red light)
                  ==> (president awake))))
```

and can be sure (a) that the global variable *rules* has a property first which has as its value a list of the names of rules A to E, and (b) that each rule name has both an antecedent and a consequent property, with the corresponding items stored as their values.

The function subseq, used in the above macros, is one of the generic sequence functions we mentioned earlier, capable of operating on either lists or vectors (and hence on strings). In this case it operates upon a list typed in by you as an argument to set-up-rules. That list consists of a certain number of elements, and subseq will return that part of the list lying between any two numbered elements inclusive of the lower-numbered element but exclusive of the higher-numbered element. As usual the counting is zero based: the first element is element number 0 and not element number 1.

     subseq takes two or three arguments. The first is the name of the sequence (the name of a variable whose value is the sequence), the second is the start-point of the subsequence and the third is its end-point. If you do not specify an end-point subsequence assumes that you mean the end of the sequence itself. Thus,

```
? (subseq "thatcher" 5)

"her"

? (subseq "thatcher" 1 4)

"hat"

? (subseq '(a her hat b) 1 3)

(HER HAT)
```

Notice that subseq's returned value is always of the same type as that of its 'sequence' argument.

     As used above, subseq requires the function position to help it do its job. position is also a generic sequence function, and it returns a number representing the position of any one element (its first argument) in any sequence (its second argument). Again the count is zero based. If the element occurs more than once in the sequence, position returns the first occurrence:

```
? (position '==> '(a ==> b ==> c))

1
```

If you have not already typed in the rules (i.e. the above call to set-up-rules) please do so. The best way is to type it into your file just as it appears above, and then to reload your file. In future you will never have to type it all again because the typing will effectively be done for you each time the file is loaded.

     This set of rules are possibly the ones used in the Pentagon and in the Kremlin to decide whether or not the third world war has started. In each place, there is a special wall with a red light and a green light on it. Normally the green light is on and the red light is off, but if the latter comes on someone should at once wake the President, because he should know what to do about it. If he does not know what to do about it, the next step is to summon the joint Chiefs of Staff and to ask if they know what to do about it. If they do not know either, then you had best get the President to telephone his opposite number in either Washington or

Moscow. If still no joy, you should put your forces on a worldwide red alert; and if even that does not bring the opposition to his knees then you may as well give up the struggle for peace and push the button. The effect will be to bring all expert systems, including the human ones, to an immediate halt.

Now, one more little function will get the whole system running:

```
(defun ps (ruleset working-memory goal)
    (setf *working-memory* working-memory)
    (setf ruleset (get *rules* ruleset))
    (production-system ruleset goal))
```

and you would call it like this:

```
? (ps 'first '((red light)) '(green light))

Cycle: 0 Rule: RULEA fired (PRESIDENT AWAKE) put in working memory.
Cycle: 1 Rule: RULEB fired (CHIEFS SUMMONED) put in working memory.
Cycle: 2 Rule: RULEC fired (HOTLINE USED) put in working memory.
Cycle: 3 Rule: RULED fired (WORLDWIDE RED ALERT) put in working memory.
Cycle: 4 Rule: RULEE fired (BUTTON PUSHED) put in working memory.
Cycle: 5 Rule: RULEF fired (%%HALT%%) put in working memory.
Rule Interpreter Halted
Halt Signalled
Final contents of working memory:
(%%HALT%%)
(BUTTON PUSHED)
(WORLDWIDE RED ALERT)
(HOTLINE USED)
(CHIEFS SUMMONED)
(PRESIDENT AWAKE)
(RED LIGHT)
NIL
```

But the system is intended not merely to start the third world war if a red light comes on, but to start preparations for such a war while being ready to stop short of actual war if the preparations themselves lead to a lessening of the threat from the other side. When this happens, on each of the special walls in Washington and Moscow, a green light comes on and the red one goes out. So our system is supposed to be looking for a green light, and hence the third argument, the 'goal' argument to ps.

Try changing the consequent of ruleE to indicate that a worldwide red alert has finally made the enemy back down:

```
? (setf (get 'ruleE 'consequent) '((green light)))

((GREEN LIGHT))
```

```
? (ps 'first '(red light) '(green light))
Cycle: 0 Rule: RULEA fired (PRESIDENT AWAKE) put in working memory.
Cycle: 1 Rule: RULEB fired (CHIEFS SUMMONED) put in working memory.
Cycle: 2 Rule: RULEC fired (HOTLINE USED) put in working memory.
Cycle: 3 Rule: RULED fired (WORLDWIDE RED ALERT) put in working memory.
Cycle: 4 Rule: RULEE fired (GREEN LIGHT) put in working memory.
Rule Interpreter Halted
Goal (GREEN LIGHT) Achieved
Final contents of working memory:
(GREEN LIGHT)
(WORLDWIDE RED ALERT)
(HOTLINE USED)
(CHIEFS SUMMONED)
(PRESIDENT AWAKE)
(RED LIGHT)
NIL
```

Notice that the reason given here for the interpreter's halting is that the goal has been achieved rather than that 'halt' has been signalled. ruleF in fact was never fired at all, and the interpreter completed only four cycles rather than five.

Summary so far, and debugging tips

We have shown you how to build the 'skeleton' of an expert system rule interpreter. As we promised, it does not do anything very interesting (what could be more boring than World War Three?). But we hope that you have gained more than a passing acquaintance with the system's various functions. If you took our advice and actually defined the functions in your own Lisp, it is likely that the problems you encountered taught you more about the system, and about Lisp programming in general, than any amount of words from us.

Maybe you have been unlucky, and have not managed to get the system to work. In that case, please check your program very carefully against the listing in Appendix A. It will not be enough just to read through each line of code, first in your version and then in ours, as easily as you might read a book. That is too accident prone a method: we human beings are very good at assuming, for example, that a word is spelled correctly when in fact it is not – but its general shape looks right and its meaning seems appropriate to its context. When checking programs, you must consciously check every character, as well as looking out for more obvious errors such as missing or extra parentheses and missing or extra double quotes.

If you are still in trouble, you need the tracer. Try tracing the master function of each of the four modules: production-system, fire-rule, find-rule-to-fire and recognise-rule. (Actually, you will probably not be allowed to trace recognise-rule because it is a macro, so trace match-antecedents instead.) With the tracer set to trace them all at once, run ps. If your bug is not something as trivial as 'wrong number of arguments supplied to ps', the resulting printed trace should help you to ascertain in which module your bug lies.

Once you know that, untrace everything and trace instead the functions which constitute that module. Then run ps again. This time the trace should enable you to see which actual function is not working properly. Triple check that function against its definition in our appendix. Then, since there is no reason why you should trust us, check for yourself that the parentheses around every expression within that function, and not just around the functions itself or around a cond in its body, balance as they should.

If you still cannot find the bug, go back to the trace again and look at the values fed to the buggy function at the time when it failed. If you have carefully carried out all the investigations suggested in the last three paragraphs, then it is virtually certain that one or more of these arguments is wrong. In particular, is the argument an atom when the function expects a list (or vice versa)? When you find an incorrect argument, the obvious next step is to find out where it came from. It must have been passed down from an earlier call, from another function. So are the arguments to that earlier function correct? If so, the bug lies in the earlier function. If not, then you must look at a still earlier function. And so on.

Embarrassingly, it is sometimes possible to discover via this detailed debugging process that you were yourself typing in the wrong arguments right at the start!

Our objectives in Chapter 10 will be to extend the power of the rule interpreter by means of two important conceptual changes: the idea of putting variables rather than constants into the antecedents and consequents of the rules, and the very interesting concept of conflict resolution.

Chapter 10
A Second Version of the Rule Interpreter

This chapter takes you through two stages of improvement to the interpreter built in Chapter 9. You will learn how to generalize its rules so that they can apply in many more cases, and you will discover how to choose when two or more rules fire during the same cycle of the interpreter. By the end you will have a practical understanding of the elements of rule-based system design, and of the problems which are likely to arise.

10.1   A more interesting interpreter

10.1.1   The need for variables

The main drawback of the rule interpreter developed in Chapter 9 is that its rules are completely specific: they deal only in constants and cannot cope, for example, with a president who refuses to get out of bed yet again for some crummy red light. It would be nice if the rules could say 'if anybody is awake then. . .'.

The idea of including variables in the antecedents and consequents of rules is an easy one to grasp. Consider the following rule:

```
(gfather (father ?x ?y) (father ?y ?z) ==> (grandfather ?x ?z))
```

One can almost read this as an English sentence: gfather is clearly the name of the rule, and the rule itself says that IF there is some person X who is the father of another person Y, and if that same person Y is in turn the father of a third person Z, THEN person X is the grandfather of person Z. This rule would succeed in matching against a working memory like this:

```
((father pierre guy) (father guy jean))
```

and when fired would duly update working memory with the appropriate inference:

```
((grandfather pierre jean)
 (father pierre guy)
 (father guy jean))
```

The variables in the rule, ?x, ?y and ?z, are just like ordinary Lisp variables except that their scope is the lexical scope of the rule itself and, once bound, their bindings cannot be altered within the scope of that rule. What that means is that for example ?x retains its initial binding to pierre throughout the rule, and that when the rule fires it is that value which is added to working memory. Working memory is assumed never to contain variables. It also means that if the second term in the rule's antecedent were altered so that it tried to re-bind ?x:

```
(gfather (father ?x ?y) (father ?x ?z) ==> (grandfather ?x ?z))
```

the rule would then fail to match against the above working memory.

Please do not be confused by our use of the term **binding** in this context. The process described here is not binding in the full Lisp sense whereby any previous value of the variable is 'saved away' and later restored, but it is binding in the sense that the values so given to the variables are temporary. The alternative term **assignment** would be even less appropriate, since it would misleadingly imply that the variables acquire permanent, global values. Our terminology is conventional for Common Lisp.

The scope of the variables is restricted to that of the rule because, of course, if this rule fails to match we still want other rules in the same ruleset to be able to use the same variable names and to bind them to other values for their own purposes. Without this restriction on a variable's scope every variable name throughout the entire set of rules (perhaps hundreds of them) would have to have a different name!

The bindings created during matching of

```
(gfather (father ?x ?y) (father ?y ?z) ==> (grandfather ?x ?z))
```

against

        `((father pierre guy) (father guy jean))`

might be held as a simple alist:

        `((?x pierre) (?y guy) (?z jean))`

What happened was that ?x was initially unbound and therefore was bound to pierre. Similarly ?y was initially unbound and so was bound to guy. Both of these bindings occurred during the matching of the first term in the antecedent against the first term in working memory. The interpreter goes on to try to match the second term of the antecedent against working memory.

        `(father ?y ?z)`

against

        `((father pierre guy) (father guy jean))`

In working memory's first term, father matches with father but ?y cannot match with pierre because ?y has already been bound to guy. So the matcher signals a failure and goes on to the second term of working memory. Here father and father match again, and this time ?y correctly matches with guy. So ?z gets bound to jean and matching of the antecedent is complete. The bindings of ?x, ?y and ?z remain available for use in the consequent of the rule.

    The bindings created during matching of a rule are known as the rule's **environment**, analogously to the way the values of the various Lisp global variables and constants are known as the Lisp environment. You might think, because the scope of the bindings is lexical to the rule and therefore should not remain in force once the rule has been processed, that the bindings could simply be thrown away as soon as the rule had either fired or failed to match. You would be right; but looking ahead a bit we are going to want, in the final version of the interpreter, to allow several rules to fire during any one cycle, and we are going to collect all the rules which do fire so that at the end of the cycle we can apply conflict resolution strategies to choose the best one of them to fire. At that point we are going to need each rule's environment so that any variables in its consequent can be replaced by their bound values.

    We shall keep the rule's environment on the property list of the rule's name, along with its antecedent and consequent. The environment of each rule will be set to NIL at the start of each run of the interpreter.

10.1.2 Modifying your program

The code written for the first version of the interpreter in Chapter 9 requires about a dozen mainly minor programmatic changes, plus the addition of a small handful of macros, to allow it to handle variables within its rules. Once again, please refer to the full listing of the code in Appendix B if you have any doubts about the accuracy of the code fragments shown here in our main text.

The first two macros will, we hope, give you no trouble at all:

```
(defmacro note-environment (rule environment)
  `(setf (get ,rule 'environment) ,environment))
```

This takes two arguments, a rule name and an alist representing the environment (as above). It places the environment on the property list of the rule name. Since setf will return the environment, so will note-environment. The macro is called by find-rule-to-fire once all the antecedents of the rule have been through the matcher and any necessary bindings have been incorporated into the rule's environment.

```
(defmacro environment (rule)
  `(get ,rule 'environment))
```

This simply retrieves and returns the environment, if any, of its rule name argument. It will only ever be needed when a rule's antecedent has already matched and fire-rule is about to fire it. The 'environment' slot of the rule name's property list will have been provided with an environment (even if it is NIL) long before environment is ever called upon to retrieve it. So environment returns a rule's environment, or NIL.

In the previous version of the interpreter, all of the nested functions in the matcher returned either T or NIL, depending upon whether or not a match was achieved. At the bottom of the recursive heap the simplest of those functions, match, always returned the value of a call to equal, and that same value was, so long as all parts of the rule's antecedent continued to match with working memory, passed all the way back up to match-antecedent and thence to recognise-rule. If match-antecedent returned T, recognise-rule returned the corresponding (matching) rule's name, and if match-antecedent returned NIL then recognise-rule also returned NIL.

In this version of the interpreter all of the functions in the matcher will return either the atom fail or the current rule's environment. NIL will not do because if a rule contained no variables at all, but only constants as in the rules for the previous version of the interpreter, its environment would be NIL. At the bottom of the heap match, too, will no longer return

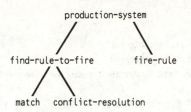

Figure 10.1 Program structure.

T or NIL but will return the environment or fail. This will make no difference as far as recursion is concerned since any value returned from a recursive call halts recursion at that point.

When a rule fails to match, it does so because some single atom in it has failed to match. The function match will detect this, and so we shall ensure that when it does so it returns as that rule's environment the atom fail. All of the functions above match, up to and including match-antecedent, will have to check that the environment as returned to them by subordinate functions is not eq to fail, before going on to process the cdrs of their current input lists. There is no point in continuing to process a rule which has already failed. Here is the macro they will use to make the check:

```
(defmacro fail (environment)
  '(eq ,environment 'fail))
```

Adding to the interpreter the ability to handle variables is clearly going to affect every function in the matcher. It is also going to affect the fire-rule module, since as you know variables can and probably will also appear in the consequents of rules. Remembering that the overall program is a hierarchy (Figure 10.1), we can therefore expect changes to fire-rule itself, to find-rule-to-fire, and to recognise-rule, as well as to the matching functions.

Let us take fire-rule first, since the necessary changes to it are easy. Here is its old definition:

```
(defun fire-rule (rule cycle-number)
  (cond (rule
         (setf *working-memory*
               (append (consequent rule)
                       *working-memory*))
         (format t "~%Cycle: ~a Rule: ~a fired~{ ~a~}~
                   put in working memory."
                 cycle-number rule (consequent rule)) rule)))
```

and here is its new one:

```
(defun fire-rule (rule cycle-number)
  (let ((instantiated-consequent
           (instantiate (consequent rule) (environment rule))))
    (cond (rule
            (setf *working-memory*
                  (append instantiated-consequent
                          *working-memory*)
            (format t "~%Cycle: ~a Rule: ~a fired~{ ~a~}~
                       put in working memory"
                    cycle-number
                    rule
                    instantiated-consequent)
            rule)))))
```

The first form within fire-rule is a let, which binds to the variable instantiated-consequent whatever value is returned by the function instantiate. As its name suggests this latter function will '**instantiate**' the variables in a rule's consequent: it will replace them with their values, as stored in the rule's environment.

The cond form within the let is very much as before, except that where the original definition referred to a rule's consequent the new one refers to the instantiated-consequent.

instantiate is defined like this:

```
(defun instantiate (rule-consequent environment)
  (cond ((null rule-consequent) nil)
        ((atom rule-consequent)
         (value-of rule-consequent environment))
        (t (cons (instantiate (car rule-consequent)
                              environment)
                 (instantiate (cdr rule-consequent)
                              environment)))))
```

We again hope that you will recognize the pattern of the cond, with its recursive calls first on the car and then on the cdr of the input list. This is reminiscent of the function atomise which we showed you in an earlier chapter.

The first clause of the cond specifies that instantiate shall stop if ever it manages to cdr its way right to the end of rule-consequent. This implies in turn that the consequent of a rule can have as many terms (conjuncts) as we like, rather than just one as has been the case in our examples until now. Once rule-consequent has been reduced to NIL, recursion can halt. The second clause says that if recursion has progressively reduced rule-consequent to one of its constituent atoms, recursion can also halt and the value to be returned should be the value-of that atom given the current bindings in environment. Of course, the atom concerned will not always be a variable, but may be a constant like father or the number 3; value-of will have to be able to handle such cases.

The third clause of the cond specifies what to do when rule-consequent has not yet been reduced to an atom: recurse first on its car and then on its cdr, confident that enough repetitions of those two operations will eventually present for 'valuing' every atom within the original value of rule-consequent.

So value-of has to take an atom as its input argument, and has to return the value of that atom if it happens to be a variable, and the atom itself otherwise. Here is a possible definition of it:

```
(defun value-of (item env)
  (or (second (assoc item env))
      item))
```

We can be confident that if the item is not a variable, or if it is a variable with no value (it is the same thing), assoc will faithfully hunt down the env alist and, finding no suitable pair to return, will return NIL. The second, or cadr, of NIL is also conveniently NIL, so there will be no error, and or will return the item itself. If on the other hand the item is a bound variable, so that assoc can find a pair whose first element is the variable, second will ensure that the value rather than the variable is returned.

However, here is our preferred definition:

```
(defun value-of item env)
  (let ((binding (and (variable-p item)
                      (bound item env))))
    (cond (binding (binding-of binding))
          (t item))))
```

This uses three little macros and we hope you agree that it is easier for a newcomer to read than the former definition. More importantly, it allows **data abstraction** by no longer directly accessing the alist, but instead doing so via the three accessing macros. In future, should we ever wish to change the precise way in which we implement our 'variables' and our 'bindings' (perhaps by using hash tables, which are faster than alists) we shall only have to change the macros; then, provided that throughout our program we have used the macros rather than clumsy things like the above first version of value-of, it will immediately work correctly in its new form.

In the new definition of value-of, we first check to ensure that the input item actually is a variable, before sending assoc chasing off down the alist in search of its value. The macro bound is merely a mnemonic synonym for assoc, and returns the whole pair if anything just as assoc does. This is the value which let binds to the variable binding. The cond says that if there is a binding, that is if binding's value is not NIL, return the binding-of it, i.e. its value, otherwise return the item, which we now know must be a constant rather than a variable. Here are the three macros:

```
(defmacro bound (variable environment)
   `(assoc ,variable ,environment))

(defmacro binding-of (binding)
   `(cadr ,binding))

(defmacro variable-p (x)
   `(char= (elt (princ-to-string ,x) 0) #\?))
```

That last needs a bit of explaining. The difficulty is that the only obvious way of recognizing a variable from any other atom is that its first character is a question mark. But it is not easy to 'get at' the first character of an ordinary Lisp symbol. Our solution is to turn the symbol into a string, which as you know is a subtype of the type **sequence** so that the generic sequence function elt will work upon it.

First of all, the function princ-to-string returns a string created from the characters of whatever variable name is the argument to variable-p. For example, it might return "?X". The function elt (it is short for 'element') takes a string and a number (zero based as usual) as its arguments and returns the corresponding character from the string. In this case, character zero (the first) should always be a question mark if the input value is a variable.

When elt returns the requested character from a string, it returns it as a **character object**. If you think about it, it has to do so, because within a string the upper and lower case forms of the same character are different, and that difference is reflected in the fact that there is a corresponding character object for each. We have mentioned character objects before; to recap, they are a type of Lisp object and are distinguished on screen by the hash sign and the backslash which precede them. #\? is the character object for a question mark; and since character objects, like numbers, always evaluate to themselves it does not need to be quoted.

char= is the equivalent function to = or eq when you are dealing with character objects rather than numbers or symbols.

That was a long explanation for something which we claimed made our definition of value-of easier to read. But now that there is no longer any mystery to you about how variable-p works, perhaps you can agree that our definition is indeed more readable than our original version, even though in this case that is the same thing as being more long winded.

The precise amount of elegance or conciseness which you are prepared to trade for readability in your programs is something which you as the programmer must decide. As you know by now we tend to opt for readability, but you are not obliged to do the same.

That completes the changes to the fire-rule module. The matcher itself, starting from find-rule-to-fire, will require another eight functions to be changed and that will be it. Your program will then be an expert system whose rules are not tied to specific events or situations because they can be generalized via variables.

Here is the old definition of find-rule-to-fire:

```
(defun find-rule-to-fire (ruleset)
  (cond ((null ruleset) nil)
        ((recognise-rule (car ruleset)))
        (t (find-rule-to-fire (cdr ruleset)))))
```

and here is the new one:

```
(defun find-rule-to-fire (ruleset)
  (if ruleset
     (let ((environment (recognise-rule (car ruleset))))
        (cond ((not (fail environment))
               (note-environment (car ruleset) environment)
               (car ruleset))
              (t (find-rule-to-fire (cdr ruleset)))))))
```

Ignore the (if ruleset ...) for the moment. The next form withing find-rule-to-fire is a let, which binds to the variable name environment whatever is returned from recognise-rule's attempt to match the first rule in the ruleset against working memory. This will be either a rule's environment (which may be NIL) or the atom fail. If it is an environment, it will contain all of the bindings set up by any one rule, since recognise-rule does not return until it has fully processed a whole rule.

In the previous definition of recognise-rule it was recognise-rule itself which made the decision whether or not to return the rule name to find-rule-to-fire, and it based this decision on the value, T or NIL, returned from match-antecedent:

```
(defmacro recognise-rule (rule)
  `(if (match-antecedent (antecedent ,rule)) ,rule))
```

But, given our new definition of find-rule-to-fire, recognise-rule needs to return the environment. So the decision as to whether or not to return the current rule's name has to be moved up into find-rule-to-fire.

So the cond inside find-rule-to-fire first checks to see whether the environment is the atom fail. If not then the (complete) environment for that rule can be placed on the property list of the rule's name. If it is, the current rule has failed to match and nothing further need be done. Then, as we have just mentioned, find-rule-to-fire needs to return the name of the rule. If the environment is the atom fail, then (in the 't' clause of the cond) find-rule-to-fire simply moves recursively on to the next rule in the ruleset.

Eventually, one of the recursive calls may have brought find-rule-to-fire to the end of the ruleset. At that point the list ruleset will be empty, or NIL. Then the if statement which we earlier told you to ignore comes into play. All it does is return an immediate NIL from find-rule-to-fire. The original version of find-rule-to-fire used a (null ruleset) clause in its cond which did the same job. The point of the if in our latest version is that if ruleset has been reduced to NIL we want to avoid all the computational expense of setting up a let and, via recognise-rule, running the entire matcher module on an empty list.

The new version of recognise-rule calls match-antecedent as before (and returns whatever match-antecedent returns) and supplies a value of NIL to be the initial value of the current rule's environment. The current rule in this case is the rule which is just about to be matched against working memory:

```
(defmacro recognise-rule (rule)
  `(match-antecedent (antecedent ,rule) nil))
```

Moving on down the tree of functions we come next to match-antecedent, the first function in the matcher proper. Its old definition was this:

```
(defun match-antecedent (antecedent)
  (cond ((null antecedent) t)
        ((match-conjunct-with-working-memory
           (car antecedent))
         (match-antecedent (cdr antecedent)))))
```

and its new definition is this:

```
(defun match-antecedent (antecedent environment)
  (cond ((or (null antecedent) (fail environment))
         environment)
        (t (match-antecedent
             (cdr antecedent)
             (match-conjunct-with-working-memory
               (car antecedent) environment)))))
```

There are two changes here. One is in the first clause of the cond: as well as checking for the end of the list antecedent, match-antecedent now also checks that the environment is not the atom fail. If it is, then as before there is no point in match-antecedent's bothering to check the rest of the antecedent's conjuncts.

The other change is to the second clause of the cond, which does the same things as before but slightly differently. This second clause consists of a single recursive call to match-antecedent, but supplied as the argument to its new environment parameter is the former call to match-conjunct-with-working-memory. When match-antecedent is first called (by recognise-rule) its environment argument is NIL. This will obviously not satisfy the first clause of the cond, so match-antecedent immediately calls itself to work on the cdr of the antecedent; but before this can happen the nested call to match-conjunct-with-working-memory has to be evaluated. In the course of this evaluation match will create bindings for any variables which appear in the first conjunct of the antecedent. When the matcher as a whole finishes matching that first conjunct, the resulting environment will be returned back up to match-conjunct-with-working-memory, and it is this environment which becomes the value of match-antecedent's environment parameter in the recursive call, the one which is to deal with the cdr of the antecedent. During the next recursive call to match-antecedent, the one which will pass the third conjunct of the antecedent to match-conjunct-with-working-memory, the same thing happens again, except that this time the environment will have been augmented by any bindings created during the matching of the second conjunct. And so on until either some conjunct fails to match or all of them have matched successfully.

This process is complicated but crucial, because it achieves the desired effect of ensuring that bindings created during the matching of any conjunct are available during the matching of any subsequent conjunct.

By comparison, the changes to match-conjunct-with-working-memory and to match-with-one-of are simplicity itself, requiring only the additional environment parameter to their lambda lists and the corresponding extra argument in their calls to lower functions:

```
(defun match-conjunct-with-working-memory (conjunct environment)
  (match-with-one-of conjunct *working-memory* environment))

(defun match-with-one-of (pattern patterns environment)
  (match* pattern patterns environment 'fail))
```

There are now just two more functions to change, match* and match, and one tiny macro to write, and then this version of the rule interpreter will be complete. Here is the old version of match*:

```
(defun match* (pattern patterns)
  (cond ((null patterns) nil)
        ((match (car patterns) pattern))
        (t (match* pattern (cdr patterns)))))
```

and here is the new one:

```
(defun match* (pattern patterns environment
               last-matched-environment)
  (cond ((or (null patterns)
             (not (fail last-matched-environment)))
         last-matched-environment)
        (t (match* pattern (cdr patterns) environment
                   (match pattern (car patterns)
                          environment)))))
```

In some ways the new match* is similar to the new match-antecedent: both employ the elegant technique of using the returned environment from a call to a lower function: in its second cond clause, match* uses a nested call to match much as match-antecedent uses a nested call to match-conjunct-with-working-memory. However, there is a crucial difference between match* and match-antecedent: whereas match-antecedent is matching each conjunct of an antecedent in turn and needs to stop if any one of them fails, match* is comparing a single conjunct against each item in working memory in turn, and it needs to stop if it detects a match. This explains the not which differentiates the new first cond clause in match* from the comparable clause in match-antecedent.

The value of the parameter environment in match* is passed down from match-antecedent via match-with-one-of and match-conjunct-with-working-memory. It therefore represents the environment created so far by a series of successful matches of sequential conjuncts of an antecedent (if they had not all been successful match-antecedent would already have halted). This environment needs to be passed on down through match* to match, so that the variable bindings created so far remain accessible during the attempted matching of the current conjunct against successive elements of working memory.

The position is that some number of conjuncts have already successfully matched, and in the process their variables have become bound to values. The conjunct which match* is currently working on has not managed to match against any of the elements of working memory so far, but may do so at any moment. The attempted matching has to take place in the context of the variable–value bindings created by earlier successfully matching conjuncts, and that context is the value of the parameter environment.

When the current conjunct does finally match against an element of working memory, it may have variables of its own (that is, variables not occurring in earlier conjuncts) whose bindings augment the environment. It is this augmented environment which, in view of the fact that the current conjunct has matched, match* needs to return from the first clause of its cond.

Hence the need for the variable which we have called last-matched-environment. Maybe that strikes you as a diametrically non-mnemonic name. Our excuse is that in the recursive call to match*, in the last line of its cond, the nested call to match which actually returns the value of last-matched-environment is evaluated before the rest of the recursive call. If you can think of a better name for the variable, please use it. The important thing is that the copy of our program which you type into your own computer should be comprehensible to you, rather than to us.

The only remaining function to alter is match itself, which as we have said so often creates the individual bindings which together make up the environment of any rule. Here are the old and the new versions of match:

```
(defun match (pattern1 pattern2)
  (equal pattern1 pattern2))

(defun match (pattern1 pattern2 environment)
  (let ((pattern1-value (value-of pattern1 environment)))
    (cond ((fail environment) 'fail)
          ((equal pattern1-value pattern2) environment)
          ((variable-p pattern1-value)
           (bind pattern1-value pattern2 environment))
          ((and (consp pattern1) (consp pattern2))
           (match (cdr pattern1) (cdr pattern2)
                  (match (car pattern1) (car pattern2)
                         environment)))
          (t 'fail))))
```

match, as we are sure you remember, has to compare two atoms, one derived from the current rule's antecedent and the other derived from working memory. The atom derived from the current rule's antecedent may be a variable, which may or may not already have been bound during the matching of previous parts of the current rule. The environment argument to match holds, as we have just been saying, the environment if any generated by those same previously matching parts of the current rule. So the first thing to do within match is to retrieve the previously bound value of the current pattern atom, if any.

The second clause of the cond says that if the retrieved value of pattern is the same thing as the current atom from working memory (pattern2) then return the current environment.

If pattern1 is a variable which has not already been bound, value-of will have returned it as a variable. The third clause of the cond says that when this is the case bind should be called to add the new variable–value pair to the environment.

The fourth cond clause copes with the initial case where match is called by match* to work on a complete conjunct and a complete working memory element, both of them being lists. match simply recurses, once again using the technique of a nested call to itself to pass the growing environment on from call to call.

Finally, all possible successful cases having been dealt with, the 'otherwise' clause of the cond simply returns fail as the environment.

Now there is only bind to worry about, and it is so simple that another little macro will do:

```
(defmacro bind (variable pattern environment)
  '(cons (list ,variable ,pattern) ,environment))
```

And that is it. We shall give this version of the interpreter just a brief test, so as to move on rapidly to the third and final version. Here is a simple ruleset involving variables:

```
(set-up-rules
 'infect
 '((r1 (infected ?x) (kisses ?x ?y) ==> (infected ?y))
   (r2 (has-flu ?y) ==> (infected ?y))))
```

These two rules say that if someone has the flu then s/he is infected, and that if an infected person kisses someone else then the someone else becomes infected too. With a simple working memory supplied in a call as below the interpreter should reach the goal infected mel, and in the process will note in working memory that mary and tom also get infected in the process:

```
? (ps 'infect '((kisses mike mary) (kisses mary tom)
                (kisses tom mel) (has-flu mike))
       '(infected mel))
```

Summary so far

The rule interpreter can now handle more than one situation – it can make more than one inference from the same set of rules – because we have generalized the rules by adding variables. However, in both of the versions shown so far the rule sets are definitely ordered: change the ordering of the rules, and the whole thing stops working; or, more likely, goes into an endless loop. (Maybe you have already noticed that, and cursed us for it.) In fact our rules are very carefully ordered: in particular where a rule could match with working memory on every cycle, so causing an endless loop, we have put it at the bottom of the list of rules, so that all of the other rules in that ruleset will fire first!

The third and final version, coming up next, uses **conflict resolution strategies**. With these in place, the interpreter can be modified so that any number of rules can match, though only one will be fired, during any one cycle. If you think about it, this implies that the rules in the ruleset can be in any order, which is what we want to achieve. You may also have noticed that the order of conjuncts within an antecedent affects the rule. For example, the simple grandfather rule:

```
(grandfather ((father ?x ?y) (father ?y ?z)
             ==>
             (gfather ?x ?z)))
```

will not work if its two antecedent conjuncts are reversed.

10.2   Adding conflict resolution

10.2.1   The strategies

Conflict resolution strategies are **heuristics**. As mentioned very early on in this book, heuristics are rules of thumb, handy guesses, which are programmed into systems simply in order to get them to work. A heuristic is not based upon any hypothesis as to how the human mind achieves similar effects, nor is there usually any attempt to show that the heuristic helps in more than a few and possibly special cases. An excellent example of a heuristic is the one which we shall use to prevent the interpreter from going into an endless loop when one rule repeatedly matches with working memory. The heuristic is, simply: out of the rules which matched during this cycle, fire the one which last fired the longest time ago. We shall call that rule the least-recently-fired rule.

It is immediately obvious that if a ruleset happened to contain only one rule, this heuristic would not help at all. But in a more normal case where there are several, maybe hundreds of, rules, it does seem to help stop endless loops, sort of. Anyway it looks as though it should. And that is the way heuristics are.

A second heuristic often used to stop endless looping, and which we shall use as well, is: if any rule is a candidate for firing but has previously been fired with exactly the same consequent, i.e. with all of the consequent's variables replaced by the same values, then reject it as a candidate. It is hard to imagine a case where one actually would need a rule to fire more than once and on each occasion to add exactly the same thing to working memory (remember that the interpreter has no provision for taking anything out of working memory); but if you nonetheless feel that there probably are such cases, and want to reject our heuristic on that basis, we would not argue much.

A third commonly used strategy is: out of the rules which matched during this cycle, fire the one which has the simpler consequent. By 'simpler' here we really mean shorter. These three heuristics will be applied as sequential filters; that is, each one will attempt to reduce the set of candidate rules to one candidate, and will hand its resulting list onto the next filter. Finally, we shall use one other heuristic in our conflict resolution strategy, and that is: if there are still two or more candidate rules remaining after all the filters have been tried, choose the first!

We shall in fact give you control of the filtering process by storing the conflict resolution strategies as function names (one strategy, one per filter) held in a list as the value of a global variable *conflict-resolution-strategies*. The advantage of this will be that once this latest version of the interpreter is running on your machine, you will be able to change the ordering of the filters so as to get different behaviour from the system. Please note that the code for this conflict-resolving version of our interpreter appears in Appendix C.

10.2.2 The final version of the rule interpreter

Earlier, we described the function find-rule-to-fire as the 'master' function for both the conflict resolution and the matcher modules. Here is its existing definition again:

```
(defun find-rule-to-fire (ruleset)
  (if ruleset
    (let ((environment (recognise-rule (car ruleset))))
      (cond ((not (fail environment))
             (note-environment (car ruleset) environment)
             (car ruleset))
            (t (find-rule-to-fire (cdr ruleset)))))))
```

and here is its new one with the necessary call to the conflict-resolution module

```
(defun find-rule-to-fire (ruleset)
  (conflict-resolution
    (remove nil
            (mapcar #'(lambda (rule)
                        (recognise-rule rule)) ruleset))))
```

The older version would cdr down the list of rules, calling recognise-rule each time to see whether the current rule matched. If the returned value from recognise-rule were ever anything other than fail, i.e. if the current rule matched against working memory, then rather than continuing with the remainder of the ruleset find-rule-to-fire would simply return the name of the current and successful rule.

In the new version we want find-rule-to-fire to return not the name of a single rule but a list of the names of all the rules which match during the current cycle. The simplest way to achieve this is via a mapcar, using recognise-rule as mapcar's auxiliary function. The business of providing an initial NIL environment for the matcher has been moved down into recognise-rule, as has the decision whether or not to continue trying to match the current rule; and as you will see in a moment the action to be taken when a rule matches (note-environment in the older definition of find-rule-to-fire) will change. A new version of recognise-rule will return NIL when a rule fails to match, so that removing all the NILs from mapcar's output will leave a list of all the rules which did match on the current cycle.

Previously, recognise-rule returned either the environment of the single matching rule, or the atom fail, because that is what match-antecedent, like all the matching functions, returned:

```
(defmacro recognise-rule (rule)
  '(match-antecedent (antecedent ,rule) nil))
```

In its new version it will call match-antecedent immediately, and will use the returned value from match-antecedent (and hence from the whole matcher module) to decide whether or not the current rule's antecedent as originally passed to match-antecedent did match with working memory. If it did, i.e. if the value returned by match-antecedent is an environment rather than fail, recognise-rule will do something rather neat. It will return the name of the current successful rule, because that is what find-rule-to-fire needs, but it will also add to the rule name's property list an instantiated version of the current rule's consequent. In this context, as you probably remember, to instantiate something is to replace all of its variables with their values.

The crucial point is that at the instant when a rule has just successfully matched via match-antecedent, recognise-rule 'knows' what those values should be because it has available the environment created during the matching of the rule's antecedent. So at that moment recognise-rule is able to replace all the variables in the rule's consequent with their correct values.

```
(defmacro recognise-rule (rule)
  '(let ((environment
          (match-antecedent (antecedent ,rule) nil)))
```

```
(cond ((not (fail environment))
       (note-instantiation ,rule
                           (instantiate (consequent ,rule)
                                         environment))
       ,rule))))
```

As you can see, the usual consequent macro retrieves the rule's
consequent from the rule name's property list, and then instantiate will
replace the variables in the consequent with their values, and finally note-
instantiation will place the result on the rule name's property list.
    instantiate, you will be pleased to hear, has not changed at all:

```
(defun instantiate (rule-consequent environment)
   (cond ((null rule-consequent) nil)
         ((atom rule-consequent)
          (value-of rule-consequent environment))
         (t (cons (instantiate (car rule-consequent)
                               environment)
                  (instantiate (cdr rule-consequent)
                               environment)))))
```

and here is note-instantiation:

```
(defmacro note-instantiation (rule instantiation)
   '(setf (get ,rule 'instantiation) ,instantiation))
```

Notice that we no longer need to remember each rule's environment; that slot on the rule-name's property list will no longer be used. In
the previous version of the interpreter find-rule-to-fire would store each
matching rule's environment on its property list, and subsequently fire-
rule would dig it out again so as to be able to instantiate the rule's
consequent. In this version we do the instantiation when the necessary
information is directly available, and we pass the results of that via the
rule's property list to fire-rule. It seems much neater and cleaner.
Consequently the macros note-environment and environment are no longer
used.
    match-antecedent, and all of its subordinate functions in the matcher
module, remain exactly as they were. The only difference is that whereas
previously the matcher was called once per rule until some rule or other
matched, it is now called once per rule for every rule in the ruleset. The
changes to recognise-rule and to find-rule-to-fire, already described
above, are enough to ensure that the conflict resolution module is passed
a list of the names of those rules which matched in any one cycle.
    Here are the new global variable and the master function for the
conflict resolution module:

```
(defvar *conflict-resolution-strategies*
   '(fireable-rules find-least-recently-fired-rules
     simplest-instantiations find-first))

(defun conflict-resolution (matching-rules)
   (mapc #'(lambda (crs)
             (setf matching-rules (funcall crs matching-rules)))
         *conflict-resolution-strategies*)
   matching-rules)
```

The parameter matching-rules acquires as its value the list of rule names, candidates for firing, passed down from find-rule-to-fire. The mapc iterates through the four function names held in the global variable *conflict-resolution-strategies*, and on each iteration it uses funcall to apply one of those strategies to the list of candidate rules. funcall, as you may remember, calls whichever function is its first argument to work on whatever value is its second argument. In this case it calls one of the conflict resolution strategies to work on the value of matching-rules. This is a single expression, i.e. the list of candidate rules.

Notice that this next piece of code would not have worked, though it might look at first sight as though it should:

```
...(mapc #'(lambda (crs)
             (setf matching-rules (crs matching-rules)))
         *conflict-resolution-strategies*)...
```

The reason is that when eval came to evaluate that setf line, it would try to find the functional value of crs. But of course crs has not got a functional value: its only value is the *name* of a function, of a conflict resolution strategy. It is that function name which has a functional value, and funcall enables us (and eval) to get at it.

The purpose of the setf is to update the list of candidate rules each time any conflict resolution strategy is applied. The hope is that the list will get shorter each time as rules which do not satisfy the strategies are filtered out.

10.2.3   First strategy: do not fire the same rule twice with the same instantiated consequent

It is worth recalling at this point that the conflict resolution module is passed a list of rule names as its argument, and that on the property lists of those rule names are their instantiated consequents. The job of conflict resolution is to choose just one rule from the list. The module is arranged as a series of filters: each strategy is implemented as a function or suite of functions which tries to reduce the current list of candidate rules. Eventually only one rule remains, and it is then fired in the usual way.

The first strategy we apply helps to prevent endless looping and drops a rule from the list of candidates if on this occasion its instantiated consequent is identical to that on some previous occasion when the rule was fired. That consequent can easily be retrieved from the property list of the rule name, but so far we have no record of any previous instantiations of the rule's consequent. That record will also appear on the property list of the rule name; it will be a list of instantiations, and will be added to every time the rule fires, throughout a complete run of the interpreter. The obvious place to do something 'every time the rule fires' is in `fire-rule`, and as you will see later that function will, in this final version of the interpreter, add the necessary information to the appropriate property list.

The master function for this strategy is `fireable-rules`. A rule is regarded as not fireable if its current instantiated consequent is identical to a previous one. The function is quite simple: ·

```
(defun fireable-rules (rules)
  (remove nil
          (mapcar #'fireable rules)))
```

It simply uses `mapcar` to check each rule in turn, and removes those which are not `fireable`. `fireable` itself is even simpler:

```
(defun fireable (rule)
  (if (not-member (instantiation rule)
                  (previous-fired-instantiations rule))
      rule))
```

It uses three little macros to do its donkey work and at the same time give us some data abstraction:

```
(defmacro not-member (item lis)
  `(member ,item ,lis :test #'equal)))

(defmacro instantiation (rule)
  `(get ,rule 'instantiation))

(defmacro previous-fired-instantiations (rule)
  `(get ,rule 'previous-fired-instantiations))
```

and that is all.

10.2.4 Second strategy: fire the least recently fired rule

This strategy also helps to prevent endless loops by ensuring that once some particular rule has fired, at least one other rule has to fire subsequently, before the first rule can fire again. In order to do this we need, of course, some way of knowing which cycle any rule has previously fired on. The lowest cycle number amongst all the candidate rules would then be the rule we want. So once again fire-rule will be modified so as to add to the rule name's property list a note of the current cycle number whenever the rule is fired, and that information can be retrieved as needed here.

The function called by conflict-resolution to run this strategy is find-least-recently-fired-rules:

```
(defun find-least-recently-fired-rules (matching-rules)
  (find-least-recently-fired-rules1
   (sort matching-rules #'< :key #'cycle-last-fired)))
```

The purpose of this function is to take the list of candidate rules and to reorder it according to the cycle number during which each rule was last fired. Those rules with the lowest cycle number (i.e. those which fired least recently) are to come at the front of the list. Once we have reordered the list in this way, we shall know that the cycle number of whichever rule is the car of the list is the 'oldest' cycle number we need to deal with, so that it together with any rules further down the list which have the same cycle number can continue to be candidates for firing; but any rules with higher cycle numbers must have fired more recently, and can thus be discarded from the list.

find-least-recently-fired-rules uses the Common Lisp function sort, which is very powerful and is one of the generic sequence functions. The first argument to sort is the sequence to be sorted, in this case the list matching-rules. The second argument to sort is a predicate which takes two arguments and which specifies what the ordering of the sorted output shall be, and here we have used the predicate < (pronounced 'less than') to specify that rules which are somehow numerically less than the others shall appear at the front of the sorted list. In other words, the rules in the output list will be in ascending numerical order. The third, keyworded, argument to sort is again a function, and this one specifies how the numerical value of a rule is to be judged, so that the list of rules can be put into numerical order.

So the complete call to sort should be read as 'sort the list matching-rules from the lowest-numbered rule to the highest-numbered rule, and judge each rule's lowest numberedness by using the function cycle-last-fired'. cycle-last-fired simply retrieves from any rule's property list the record of the cycle on which it last fired. But, even though it is such a simple function, it cannot be written as a macro because, as you may remember from our earlier discussion of auxiliary functions, only a function and not a macro or special form can be used for this purpose:

```
(defun cycle-last-fired (rule)
  (or (get rule 'cycle-last-fired) 0))
```

The call to or is there because if the current rule happens to be the very
first candidate for firing it will not yet have been fired, so that there will
be no record of the last cycle when it did so! In that case get would return
NIL, and the or simply makes sure that any NIL is replaced by a zero.

find-least-recently-fired-rules1 takes the sorted list of rules and
retrieves the cycle number on which the car of the list fired. It passes this
on as a second argument to find-least-recently-fired-rules2:

```
(defun find-least-recently-fired-rules1 (candidates)
  (find-least-recently-fired-rules2
    candidates
    (cycle-last-fired (car candidates))))
```

Finally, find-least-recently-fired-rules2 recurses down the list of candidate rules until either it reaches the end of the list or some earlier rule
turns out to have last fired more recently than the car of the original list.
Until one of these termination points is reached, it continues to cons each
rule onto its output list:

```
(defun find-least-recently-fired-rules2 (candidates
                                         lowest-cycle)
  (cond ((null candidates) nil)
        ((> (cycle-last-fired (car candidates)) lowest-cycle)
         nil)
        (t (cons
             (car candidates)
             (find-least-recently-fired-rules2
               (cdr candidates)
               lowest-cycle)))))
```

The list of rules returned by find-least-recently-fired-rules2 will almost
certainly be shorter than the list of matching-rules originally passed to
find-least-recently-fired-rules, so the desired filtering effect has been
obtained.

10.2.5 Third strategy: fire the rule with the simplest instantiation

Our quite arbitrary decision as to what simplest means in this context is
that it means the instantiation (of a rule's consequent) which has the
smallest number of atoms in it. So here is a chance to use the atomise
function which we showed you several chapters ago. atomise reduces any

list, no matter how deeply nested, to a simple list of all the atoms in the
original list:

```
(defun atomise (lis)
  (cond ((null lis) nil)
        ((atom (car lis)) (cons (car lis) (atomise (cdr lis))))
        (t (append (atomise (car lis)) (atomise (cdr lis))))))
```

The master function for the simplest instantiations submodule of the
conflict resolution module is simplest-instantiations:

```
(defun simplest-instantiations (matching-rules)
  (simplest-insts1 (sort matching-rules #'< :key #'complexity)))

(defun complexity (rule)
  (length (atomise (instantiation rule))))
```

Like find-least-recently-fired-rules it uses sort to obtain a reordered list
of the candidate rules, but this time they are sorted according to
increasing complexity of their consequents. Once that has been done,
simplest-insts1 and simplest-insts2 behave in exactly the same way as
find-least-recently-fired-rules1 and find-least-recently-fired-rules2:

```
(defun simplest-insts1 (rules)
  (simplest-insts2 rules (complexity (car rules))))

(defun simplest-insts2 (rules simplest)
  (cond ((null rules) nil)
        ((> (complexity (car rules)) simplest)
         (simplest-insts2 (cdr rules) simplest))
        (t (cons (car rules)
                 (simplest-insts2 (cdr rules) simplest)))))
```

10.2.6 Fourth strategy: fire the first candidate rule

If after all that the list of candidates still contains more than one rule, we
have to fall back on brute force to reduce the list to one element:

```
(defun find-first (rules)
  (car rules))
```

There remains only one more thing to do: the modifications to fire-rule
so that when a rule fires it will add two pieces of information to the rule's
property list: a note of the current cycle number and the current
instantiation of its consequent (if you remember, we used the former in
find-least-recently-fired-rule and the latter in fireable). We shall also

define a couple of little helpers, one a function and one a macro. Here is
the previous version of fire-rule:

```
(defun fire-rule (rule cycle-number)
  (let ((instantiated-consequent
          (instantiate (consequent rule) (environment rule))))
    (cond (rule
            (add-to-working-memory instantiated-consequent)
            (format t "~%Cycle: ~a Rule: ~a fired~{ ~a~}
                    put in working memory"
                    cycle-number
                    rule
                    instantiated-consequent)
            rule))))
```

and here is the latest version:

```
(defun fire-rule (rule cycle-number)
  (cond (rule
          (let ((instantiation-to-fire (instantiation rule)))
            (setf *working-memory*
                  (append instantiation-to-fire
                          *working-memory*))
            (add-previous-fired-instantiation
              rule instantiation-to-fire)
            (format t "~%Rule: ~a fired~{ ~a~}~
                    put in working memory"
                    rule
                    instantiation-to-fire)
            (note-cycle-last-fired rule cycle-number)))))
```

We no longer need to call instantiate, passing it the rule's consequent
and the rule's environment as retrieved from its property list, because we
can retrieve instead the already-instantiated consequent of the rule.
Then, much as before, we update working memory by appending the new
instantiated consequent onto it and, after the format statement, we call
note-cycle-last-fired to put a note of the current cycle onto the current
rule's property list. The reason for not putting the format statement last is
that format always returns NIL, and we need fire-rule to return a non-NIL
value whenever a rule is fired.

Here are the two little helpers:

```
(defun add-previous-fired-instantiation (rule
                                           previous-fired-
                                           instantiations)
  (setf (previous-fired-instantiations rule)
```

```
          (append (list previous-fired-instantiation)
                  (previous-fired-instantiations rule))))

  (defmacro note-cycle-last-fired (rule cycle-number)
     '(setf (get ,rule 'cycle-last-fired) ,cycle-number))
```

And finally we must not forget that the two new pieces of information on
the property lists cannot safely be left there; they would almost certainly
mess up any future run of the interpreter. You could clear them all out as
soon as the interpreter halted, but again for the sake of readability of
your program it is probably better to clear them out before the start of
any future run. So we have put the call to the clearing-out function into
ps:

```
  (defun ps (ruleset working-memory goal)
    (setf *working-memory* working-memory)

    (setf ruleset (get *rules* ruleset))

    (initialise-ruleset ruleset)
    (production-system ruleset goal))

  (defun   initialise-ruleset (ruleset)
    (mapc #'(lambda (rule)
              (note-cycle-last-fired rule -1)
              (note-previous-fired-instantiations rule nil))
          ruleset))

  (defmacro note-previous-fired-instantiations
            (rule previous-fired-instantiations)
     '(setf (get ,rule 'previous-fired-instantiations)
            ,previous-fired-instantiations))
```

Notice the indentation of the above macro definition. Because its name is
so long, its parameters are listed on the next line rather than, as usual, on
the same line!

10.2.7 The proof of the pudding

So as to prove to yourself that conflict resolution, at least some of it, does
work, try the following simple test on your completed interpreter.

```
  ? (set-up-rules 'C+Q
          '((rule1  (?x is a woman)
                ==>
                (?X is human))

            (rule2  (?x is a man)
                ==>
                (?x is human))))
```

```
(RULE1 RULE2)

? (setf *wmcq* '((queen-elizabeth is a woman) (dad is a man)))

((QUEEN ELIZABETH IS A WOMAN) (DAD IS A MAN))

? (trace conflict-resolution find-first find-least-recently-fired-rules
fireable-rules simplest-instantiations)

NIL

? (ps 'C+Q *wmcq* '(dad is human))
  Calling (CONFLICT-RESOLUTION (RULE1 RULE2))
    Calling (FIREABLE-RULES (RULE1 RULE2))
    FIREABLE-RULES returned (RULE1 RULE2)
    Calling (FIND-LEAST-RECENTLY-FIRED-RULES (RULE1 RULE2))
    FIND-LEAST-RECENTLY-FIRED-RULES returned (RULE1 RULE2)
    Calling (SIMPLEST-INSTANTIATIONS (RULE1 RULE2))
    SIMPLEST-INSTANTIATIONS returned (RULE1 RULE2)
    Calling (FIND-FIRST (RULE1 RULE2))
    FIND-FIRST returned RULE1
  CONFLICT-RESOLUTION returned RULE1
Rule: RULE1 fired (QUEEN-ELIZABETH IS HUMAN) put in working memory
  Calling (CONFLICT-RESOLUTION (RULE1 RULE2))
    Calling (FIREABLE-RULES (RULE1 RULE2))
    FIREABLE-RULES returned (RULE2)
    Calling (FIND-LEAST-RECENTLY-FIRED-RULES (RULE2))
    FIND-LEAST-RECENTLY-FIRED-RULES returned (RULE2)
    Calling (SIMPLEST-INSTANTIATIONS (RULE2))
    SIMPLEST-INSTANTIATIONS returned (RULE2)
    Calling (FIND-FIRST (RULE2))
    FIND-FIRST returned RULE2
  CONFLICT-RESOLUTION returned RULE2
Rule: RULE2 fired (DAD IS HUMAN) put in working memory
Rule Interpreter Halted
Goal (DAD IS HUMAN) Achieved
Here are the contents of working memory
(DAD IS HUMAN)
(QUEEN-ELIZABETH IS HUMAN)
(QUEEN-ELIZABETH IS A WOMAN)
(DAD IS A MAN)
NIL
```

We hope it is obvious to you that both of the above rules are eligible to
fire on every cycle. Without conflict resolution, rule1 would simply cause
the interpreter to loop for ever. If you look carefully at the trace, you will
see that both rules are initially equally eligible, both of them matching
working memory and neither of them having fired before. So only the
brute-force find-first strategy saves us from endless looping, and it
chooses rule1 to fire. After that the same situation of two equally valid

rules arises, but this time `fireable-rules` can tell that `rule1` has fired before with the same consequent, and so `fireable-rules` rejects it for firing in favour of `rule2`.

Now let's try a more complex example. First, add some extra rules:

```
? (set-up-rules 'C+Q
              '((rule1 (?x is a woman)
                       ==>
                       (?X is human))
                (rule2  (?x is a man)
                        ==>
                        (?x is human))
                (rule3  (?x is human)
                        ==>
                        (?x has a soul))
                (rule4  (?x is human) (?x eats meat)
                        ==>
                        (?x is a carnivore))
                (rule5  (?x is human) (?x eats vegetables)
                        ==>
                        (?x is a vegetarian))
                (rule6  (?x is a carnivore)
                        ==>
                        (?x is a living-thing))
                (rule7  (?x is a vegetarian)
                        ==>
                        (?x is a living-thing))))
(RULE1 RULE2 RULE3 RULE4 RULE5 RULE6 RULE7)
```

and then add a couple of new items to the initial working memory:

```
? (setf *wmcq* '((queen-elizabeth is a woman) (dad is a man)
                 (queen-elizabeth eats meat)
                 (dad eats vegetables)))

((QUEEN-ELIZABETH IS A WOMAN) (DAD IS A MAN) (QUEEN-ELIZABETH EATS MEAT)
(DAD EATS VEGETABLES))
```

Then run the interpreter (the trace is a bit long, but you only need to glance through it):

```
? (ps 'C+Q *wmcq* '(dad is a living-thing))
  Calling (CONFLICT-RESOLUTION (RULE1 RULE2))
   Calling (FIREABLE-RULES (RULE1 RULE2))
   FIREABLE-RULES returned (RULE1 RULE2)
   Calling (FIND-LEAST-RECENTLY-FIRED-RULES (RULE1 RULE2))
   FIND-LEAST-RECENTLY-FIRED-RULES returned (RULE1 RULE2)
   Calling (SIMPLEST-INSTANTIATIONS (RULE1 RULE2))
```

```
     SIMPLEST-INSTANTIATIONS returned (RULE1 RULE2)
     Calling (FIND-FIRST (RULE1 RULE2))
     FIND-FIRST returned RULE1
   CONFLICT-RESOLUTION returned RULE1
 Rule: RULE1 fired (QUEEN-ELIZABETH IS HUMAN) put in working memory
   Calling (CONFLICT-RESOLUTION (RULE1 RULE2 RULE3 RULE4))
     Calling (FIREABLE-RULES (RULE1 RULE2 RULE3 RULE4))
     FIREABLE-RULES returned (RULE2 RULE3 RULE4)
     Calling (FIND-LEAST-RECENTLY-FIRED-RULES (RULE2 RULE3 RULE4))
     FIND-LEAST-RECENTLY-FIRED-RULES returned (RULE2 RULE3 RULE4)
     Calling (SIMPLEST-INSTANTIATIONS (RULE2 RULE3 RULE4))
     SIMPLEST-INSTANTIATIONS returned (RULE2)
     Calling (FIND-FIRST (RULE2))
     FIND-FIRST returned RULE2
   CONFLICT-RESOLUTION returned RULE2
 Rule: RULE2 fired (DAD IS HUMAN) put in working memory
   Calling (CONFLICT-RESOLUTION (RULE1 RULE2 RULE3 RULE5))
     Calling (FIREABLE-RULES (RULE1 RULE2 RULE3 RULE5))
     FIREABLE-RULES returned (RULE3 RULE5)
     Calling (FIND-LEAST-RECENTLY-FIRED-RULES (RULE3 RULE5))
     FIND-LEAST-RECENTLY-FIRED-RULES returned (RULE3 RULE5)
     Calling (SIMPLEST-INSTANTIATIONS (RULE3 RULE5))
     SIMPLEST-INSTANTIATIONS returned (RULE3 RULE5)
     Calling (FIND-FIRST (RULE3 RULE5))
     FIND-FIRST returned RULE3
   CONFLICT-RESOLUTION returned RULE3
 Rule: RULE3 fired (DAD HAS A SOUL) put in working memory
   Calling (CONFLICT-RESOLUTION (RULE1 RULE2 RULE3 RULE5))
     Calling (FIREABLE-RULES (RULE1 RULE2 RULE3 RULE5))
     FIREABLE-RULES returned (RULE5)
     Calling (FIND-LEAST-RECENTLY-FIRED-RULES (RULE5))
     FIND-LEAST-RECENTLY-FIRED-RULES returned (RULE5)
     Calling (SIMPLEST-INSTANTIATIONS (RULE5))
     SIMPLEST-INSTANTIATIONS returned (RULE5)
     Calling (FIND-FIRST (RULE5))
     FIND-FIRST returned RULE5
   CONFLICT-RESOLUTION returned RULE5
 Rule: RULE5 fired (DAD IS A VEGETARIAN) put in working memory
   Calling (CONFLICT-RESOLUTION (RULE1 RULE2 RULE3 RULE5 RULE7))
     Calling (FIREABLE-RULES (RULE1 RULE2 RULE3 RULE5 RULE7))
     FIREABLE-RULES returned (RULE7)
     Calling (FIND-LEAST-RECENTLY-FIRED-RULES (RULE7))
     FIND-LEAST-RECENTLY-FIRED-RULES returned (RULE7)
     Calling (SIMPLEST-INSTANTIATIONS (RULE7))
     SIMPLEST-INSTANTIATIONS returned (RULE7)
     Calling (FIND-FIRST (RULE7))
     FIND-FIRST returned RULE7
   CONFLICT-RESOLUTION returned RULE7
 Rule: RULE7 fired (DAD IS A LIVING-THING) put in working memory
```

```
Rule Interpreter Halted
Goal (DAD IS A LIVING-THING) Achieved
Here are the contents of working memory
(DAD IS A LIVING-THING)
(DAD IS A VEGETARIAN)
(DAD HAS A SOUL)
(DAD IS HUMAN)
(QUEEN-ELIZABETH IS HUMAN)
(QUEEN-ELIZABETH IS A WOMAN)
(DAD IS A MAN)
(QUEEN-ELIZABETH EATS MEAT)
(DAD EATS VEGETABLES)
NIL
```

The first two rules fired according to their order in the ruleset, as before, but after that the interpreter seemed to concentrate upon dad, inferring all it could about him until the goal was achieved. This looks impressively intelligent, but really it was not. To see what we mean, ask the same question about Queen-Elizabeth, by changing the goal in the call to ps:

```
? (ps 'C+Q *wmcq* '(queen-elizabeth is a living-thing))
  Calling (CONFLICT-RESOLUTION (RULE1 RULE2))
    Calling (FIREABLE-RULES (RULE1 RULE2))
    FIREABLE-RULES returned (RULE1 RULE2)
    Calling (FIND-LEAST-RECENTLY-FIRED-RULES (RULE1 RULE2))
    FIND-LEAST-RECENTLY-FIRED-RULES returned (RULE1 RULE2)
    Calling (SIMPLEST-INSTANTIATIONS (RULE1 RULE2))
    SIMPLEST-INSTANTIATIONS returned (RULE1 RULE2)
    Calling (FIND-FIRST (RULE1 RULE2))
    FIND-FIRST returned RULE1
  CONFLICT-RESOLUTION returned RULE1
 Rule: RULE1 fired (QUEEN-ELIZABETH IS HUMAN) put in working memory
  Calling (CONFLICT-RESOLUTION (RULE1 RULE2 RULE3 RULE4))
    Calling (FIREABLE-RULES (RULE1 RULE2 RULE3 RULE4))
    FIREABLE-RULES returned (RULE2 RULE3 RULE4)
    Calling (FIND-LEAST-RECENTLY-FIRED-RULES (RULE2 RULE3 RULE4))
    FIND-LEAST-RECENTLY-FIRED-RULES returned (RULE2 RULE3 RULE4)
    Calling (SIMPLEST-INSTANTIATIONS (RULE2 RULE3 RULE4))
    SIMPLEST-INSTANTIATIONS returned (RULE2)
    Calling (FIND-FIRST (RULE2))
    FIND-FIRST returned RULE2
  CONFLICT-RESOLUTION returned RULE2
 Rule: RULE2 fired (DAD IS HUMAN) put in working memory
  Calling (CONFLICT-RESOLUTION (RULE1 RULE2 RULE3 RULE5))
    Calling (FIREABLE-RULES (RULE1 RULE2 RULE3 RULE5))
    FIREABLE-RULES returned (RULE3 RULE5)
    Calling (FIND-LEAST-RECENTLY-FIRED-RULES (RULE3 RULE5))
    FIND-LEAST-RECENTLY-FIRED-RULES returned (RULE3 RULE5)
    Calling (SIMPLEST-INSTANTIATIONS (RULE3 RULE5))
```

```
       SIMPLEST-INSTANTIATIONS returned (RULE3 RULE5)
        Calling (FIND-FIRST (RULE3 RULE5))
        FIND-FIRST returned RULE3
      CONFLICT-RESOLUTION returned RULE3
    Rule: RULE3 fired (DAD HAS A SOUL) put in working memory
      Calling (CONFLICT-RESOLUTION (RULE1 RULE2 RULE3 RULE5))
        Calling (FIREABLE-RULES (RULE1 RULE2 RULE3 RULE5))
        FIREABLE-RULES returned (RULE5)
        Calling (FIND-LEAST-RECENTLY-FIRED-RULES (RULE5))
        FIND-LEAST-RECENTLY-FIRED-RULES returned (RULE5)
        Calling (SIMPLEST-INSTANTIATIONS (RULE5))
        SIMPLEST-INSTANTIATIONS returned (RULE5)
        Calling (FIND-FIRST (RULE5))
        FIND-FIRST returned RULE5
      CONFLICT-RESOLUTION returned RULE5
    Rule: RULE5 fired (DAD IS A VEGETARIAN) put in working memory
      Calling (CONFLICT-RESOLUTION (RULE1 RULE2 RULE3 RULE5 RULE7))
        Calling (FIREABLE-RULES (RULE1 RULE2 RULE3 RULE5 RULE7))
        FIREABLE-RULES returned (RULE7)
        Calling (FIND-LEAST-RECENTLY-FIRED-RULES (RULE7))
        FIND-LEAST-RECENTLY-FIRED-RULES returned (RULE7)
        Calling (SIMPLEST-INSTANTIATIONS (RULE7))
        SIMPLEST-INSTANTIATIONS returned (RULE7)
        Calling (FIND-FIRST (RULE7))
        FIND-FIRST returned RULE7
      CONFLICT-RESOLUTION returned RULE7
    Rule: RULE7 fired (DAD IS A LIVING-THING) put in working memory
      Calling (CONFLICT-RESOLUTION (RULE1 RULE2 RULE3 RULE5 RULE7))
        Calling (FIREABLE-RULES (RULE1 RULE2 RULE3 RULE5 RULE7))
        FIREABLE-RULES returned NIL
        Calling (FIND-LEAST-RECENTLY-FIRED-RULES NIL)
        FIND-LEAST-RECENTLY-FIRED-RULES returned NIL
        Calling (SIMPLEST-INSTANTIATIONS NIL)
        SIMPLEST-INSTANTIATIONS returned NIL
        Calling (FIND-FIRST NIL)
        FIND-FIRST returned NIL
      CONFLICT-RESOLUTION returned NIL
Rule Interpreter Halted
No Rules Fired
Here are the contents of working memory
(DAD IS A LIVING-THING)
(DAD IS A VEGETARIAN)
(DAD HAS A SOUL)
(DAD IS HUMAN)
(QUEEN-ELIZABETH IS HUMAN)
(QUEEN-ELIZABETH IS A WOMAN)
(DAD IS A MAN)
(QUEEN-ELIZABETH EATS MEAT)
(DAD EATS VEGETABLES)
NIL
```

and this is not by any means as intelligent a result. The interpreter followed exactly the same sequence of rules, ending up with the same fairly complex inference about dad but utterly failing to answer our 'question' about Queen-Elizabeth.

The difficulty, as you can probably see at once, is that we really want rule3 to fire twice. Because the consequents of those rules which fire are always added to the front of working memory, and because the attempts to match an antecedent against working memory always start from the first element of each, it is inevitable that the system will initially concentrate upon dad. This is because, once rule1 has fired it immediately and permanently becomes the least recently fired rule, so that rule2 has to fire next and that starts off the system's obsession with dad. (If we were to rewrite the ruleset so that rule2 came before rule1, the obsession would be with Queen-Elizabeth. So we still have not achieved our ideal of a completely unordered ruleset.)

Even with the rules as they are, if we could persuade rule3 to fire a second time once everything which could possibly be inferred about dad had already been inferred, then the system could go on to think about Queen-Elizabeth. So let us change our conflict resolution strategies and see what happens:

```
? (setf *conflict-resolution-strategies*
    '(find-least-recently-fired-rules simplest-instantiations
      find-first))

(FIND-LEAST-RECENTLY-FIRED-RULES SIMPLEST-INSTANTIATIONS FIND-FIRST)
```

The conflict resolution module refers to the global variable *conflict-resolution-strategies* in order to decide which of the available strategies to employ. So now let us try the same query again:

```
? (ps 'C+Q *wmcq* '(queen-elizabeth is a living-thing))
  Calling (CONFLICT-RESOLUTION (RULE1 RULE2))
   Calling (FIND-LEAST-RECENTLY-FIRED-RULES (RULE1 RULE2))
   FIND-LEAST-RECENTLY-FIRED-RULES returned (RULE1 RULE2)
   Calling (SIMPLEST-INSTANTIATIONS (RULE1 RULE2))
   SIMPLEST-INSTANTIATIONS returned (RULE1 RULE2)
   Calling (FIND-FIRST (RULE1 RULE2))
   FIND-FIRST returned RULE1
  CONFLICT-RESOLUTION returned RULE1
 Rule: RULE1 fired (QUEEN-ELIZABETH IS HUMAN) put in working memory
  Calling (CONFLICT-RESOLUTION (RULE1 RULE2 RULE3 RULE4))
   Calling (FIND-LEAST-RECENTLY-FIRED-RULES (RULE1 RULE2 RULE3 RULE4))
   FIND-LEAST-RECENTLY-FIRED-RULES returned (RULE2 RULE3 RULE4)
   Calling (SIMPLEST-INSTANTIATIONS (RULE2 RULE3 RULE4))
   SIMPLEST-INSTANTIATIONS returned (RULE2)
   Calling (FIND-FIRST (RULE2))
```

```
      FIND-FIRST returned RULE2
    CONFLICT-RESOLUTION returned RULE2
  Rule: RULE2 fired (DAD IS HUMAN) put in working memory
   Calling (CONFLICT-RESOLUTION (RULE1 RULE2 RULE3 RULE5))
     Calling (FIND-LEAST-RECENTLY-FIRED-RULES (RULE1 RULE2 RULE3 RULE5))
     FIND-LEAST-RECENTLY-FIRED-RULES returned (RULE3 RULE5)
     Calling (SIMPLEST-INSTANTIATIONS (RULE3 RULE5))
     SIMPLEST-INSTANTIATIONS returned (RULE3 RULE5)
     Calling (FIND-FIRST (RULE3 RULE5))
     FIND-FIRST returned RULE3
   CONFLICT-RESOLUTION returned RULE3
  Rule: RULE3 fired (DAD HAS A SOUL) put in working memory
   Calling (CONFLICT-RESOLUTION (RULE1 RULE2 RULE3 RULE5))
     Calling (FIND-LEAST-RECENTLY-FIRED-RULES (RULE1 RULE2 RULE3 RULE5))
     FIND-LEAST-RECENTLY-FIRED-RULES returned (RULE5)
     Calling (SIMPLEST-INSTANTIATIONS (RULE5))
     SIMPLEST-INSTANTIATIONS returned (RULE5)
     Calling (FIND-FIRST (RULE5))
     FIND-FIRST returned RULE5
   CONFLICT-RESOLUTION returned RULE5
  Rule: RULE5 fired (DAD IS A VEGETARIAN) put in working memory
   Calling (CONFLICT-RESOLUTION (RULE1 RULE2 RULE3 RULE5 RULE7))
     Calling (FIND-LEAST-RECENTLY-FIRED-RULES (RULE1 RULE2 RULE3 RULE5
  RULE7))
     FIND-LEAST-RECENTLY-FIRED-RULES returned (RULE7)
     Calling (SIMPLEST-INSTANTIATIONS (RULE7))
     SIMPLEST-INSTANTIATIONS returned (RULE7)
     Calling (FIND-FIRST (RULE7))
     FIND-FIRST returned RULE7
   CONFLICT-RESOLUTION returned RULE7
  Rule: RULE7 fired (DAD IS A LIVING-THING) put in working memory
   Calling (CONFLICT-RESOLUTION (RULE1 RULE2 RULE3 RULE5 RULE7))
     Calling (FIND-LEAST-RECENTLY-FIRED-RULES (RULE1 RULE2 RULE3 RULE5
  RULE7))
     FIND-LEAST-RECENTLY-FIRED-RULES returned (RULE1)
     Calling (SIMPLEST-INSTANTIATIONS (RULE1))
     SIMPLEST-INSTANTIATIONS returned (RULE1)
     Calling (FIND-FIRST (RULE1))
     FIND-FIRST returned RULE1
   CONFLICT-RESOLUTION returned RULE1
  Rule: RULE1 fired (QUEEN-ELIZABETH IS HUMAN) put in working memory
   Calling (CONFLICT-RESOLUTION (RULE1 RULE2 RULE3 RULE4 RULE7))
     Calling (FIND-LEAST-RECENTLY-FIRED-RULES (RULE1 RULE2 RULE3 RULE4
  RULE7))
     FIND-LEAST-RECENTLY-FIRED-RULES returned (RULE4)
     Calling (SIMPLEST-INSTANTIATIONS (RULE4))
     SIMPLEST-INSTANTIATIONS returned (RULE4)
     Calling (FIND-FIRST (RULE4))
     FIND-FIRST returned RULE4
```

```
        CONFLICT-RESOLUTION returned RULE4
      Rule: RULE4 fired (QUEEN-ELIZABETH IS A CARNIVORE) put in working memory
        Calling (CONFLICT-RESOLUTION (RULE1 RULE2 RULE3 RULE4 RULE6 . . .))
          Calling (FIND-LEAST-RECENTLY-FIRED-RULES (RULE1 RULE2 RULE3 RULE4
      RULE6 ...))
          FIND-LEAST-RECENTLY-FIRED-RULES returned (RULE6)
          Calling (SIMPLEST-INSTANTIATIONS (RULE6))
          SIMPLEST-INSTANTIATIONS returned (RULE6)
          Calling (FIND-FIRST (RULE6))
          FIND-FIRST returned RULE6
        CONFLICT-RESOLUTION returned RULE6
      Rule: RULE6 fired (QUEEN-ELIZABETH IS A LIVING-THING) put in working
      memory
      Rule Interpreter Halted
      Goal (QUEEN-ELIZABETH IS A LIVING-THING) Achieved
      Here are the contents of working memory
      (QUEEN-ELIZABETH IS A LIVING-THING)
      (QUEEN-ELIZABETH IS A CARNIVORE)
      (QUEEN-ELIZABETH IS HUMAN)
      (DAD IS A LIVING-THING)
      (DAD IS A VEGETARIAN)
      (DAD HAS A SOUL)
      (DAD IS HUMAN)
      (QUEEN-ELIZABETH IS HUMAN)
      (QUEEN-ELIZABETH IS A WOMAN)
      (DAD IS A MAN)
      (QUEEN-ELIZABETH EATS MEAT)
      (DAD EATS VEGETABLES)
      NIL
```

Still the interpreter chases off making all the possible inferences about dad; and as we have explained that is because of the ordering of the rules. But this time, instead of halting when it has exhausted the dad train of inference, it can go back and start again if it still has not achieved its set goal. Of course, as soon as rules are allowed to fire more than once, rule1 has a better claim than rule3, because it was last fired much less recently (that is, longer ago) than rule3. So rule1 fires for a second time. And immediately, rule4 which has never fired before has a better claim than rule3. So poor old rule3 gets left out anyway, even though the interpreter is now able to follow the chain of inference from Queen-Elizabeth to living-thing.

. The whole point is that heuristics are heuristics: often they work, but sometimes they do not.

10.2.8 An arithmetical example

Some human cognitive activities are particularly amenable to being represented as sets of rules. Arithmetic is one of those. For example, the steps involved in achieving two-column subtraction can easily be expressed as rules. Depending on the level of detail which you wished your rules to represent, there are a number of ways of doing this. For the sake of brevity we have elected to have just three rules:

(A)   Represent the problem as two columns of two digits each.

(B)   If both columns can be subtracted without a negative answer resulting, subtract them to give the solution. If not, go to rule C.

(C)   Add ten to the upper digit in the right-hand column and subtract 1 from the upper digit in the left-hand column. Go to rule B.

If no 'borrowing' is necessary, rule B produces the answer. If borrowing is necessary, rule C manipulates the digits of the problem until borrowing is no longer necessary, wherupon rule B can operate as before.

For these rules to work, working memory must contain suitable number bonds; that is, numeric triples of the form

> 5 minus 2 equals 3
> 9 minus 4 equals 5

and so on. We shall represent these bonds very simply as

> (5 2 3)
> (9 4 5)

Working memory will also need some 'plus 10' bonds of the form

> 7 plus 10 equals 17.

We shall represent these as

> (add10 7 17)

Here is our ruleset:

```
(set-up-rules
 'two-column-subtraction
 '((r1 ==>
       (7 2 5)
       (8 4 4)
       (4 3 1)
       (6 2 4)
       (8 1 7)
       (7 4 3)
       (add10 7 17)
       (add10 3 13)
```

```
        (13 5 8))
    (r2 (sub ?tl ?tr ?bl ?br)
        ==> (nbondr ?tr ?br) (nbondl ?tl ?bl))
    (r3 (nbondr ?tr ?br) (nbondl ?tl ?bl)
        (?tr ?br ?a1) (?tl ?bl ?a2) ==>
        (answer ?a2 ?a1))
    (r4 (answer ?x ?y) ==> (%%halt%%))
    (r5 (sub ?tl ?tr ?bl ?br)
        (add10 ?tr ?newtr)
        (?tl 1 ?newtl)
        ==>
        (sub ?newtl ?newtr ?bl ?br))))
```

and the corresponding call to the production system, which will initialize working memory with a particular subtraction problem, will be:

```
? (ps 'two-column-subtraction '((sub 8 3 2 5)) nil)
```

For the sake of simplicity of this example, we represent the four digits separately, rather than as two-digit numbers such as 47. Rule r1 will match on every cycle, because it has no antecedent. If you remember, match-antecedent cdrs down the list of antecedents until one of them fails to match working memory, or none is left. Since there are no antecedents in r1, none of them can fail to match, and so match-antecedent returns a null environment, which signifies a successful match. The sole purpose of r1 is to add the number bonds to working memory. Once it has done so, conflict resolution will ensure that it does not fire again (if it were to fire again, the only effect would be to slow the system down owing to the multiple copies of the number bonds' inflating the size of working memory.)

Rule r2 matches with working memory if the latter contains a representation of the problem in the form

```
(subtract <digit1> <digit2> <digit3> <digit4>)
```

Rule r2 thus matches on the first cycle, as does r1. The conflict resolution strategy simplest instantiation chooses r2 on the first cycle because its consequent contains fewer terms than that of r1, but it actually does not matter which of these two rules fires first. On the second cycle both of them will match again, and because in this case it was r2 which fired first, the least-recently fired strategy will fire r1. Thus, after two cycles the number bonds have been deposited in working memory and the problem has been represented as two columns of two digits each.

On the third cycle, rules r1, r2 and r5 will match. Rule r3 will also match if working memory contains the representations of the two columns, together with suitable number bonds (i.e. bonds whose first two digits match the digits in one or other of the columns). Rule r3 is fired on the basis of its simpler consequent, and deposits the answer as derived from the number bonds. If this happens then rule r4 will fire on the next cycle to halt the system. However, if no suitable number bonds are found r3 cannot match on cycle 3. The idea is that the number bonds will be present if no borrowing is required; but there will be no bond containing a negative answer, as in

(3 6 -3)

If rule r3 does not match the rule r5 fires on cycle 3 instead. It deposits a new version of the original problem, one for which the number bonds are present, and on subsequent cycles rules r2, r3 and r4 fire in sequence to produce the answer.

With the conflict resolution functions still traced as in the C+Q example, please type in the following and compare the printouts you receive with our description of what happens:

```
? (ps 'two-column-subtraction '((sub 8 7 1 4)) nil)

? (ps 'two-column-subtraction '((sub 8 3 2 5)) nil)
```

SUMMARY

In this chapter we have told you a good deal about rule interpreters, and have made you do rather a lot of programming work to relatively little practical purpose. We feel and we hope you also feel that it has not been a waste of time. You have built bare-bones versions of all the main modules of any expert system interpreter and have seen how they all cooperate in achieving some goal or deriving some inference. It is undeniable, we think, that these programs do display some rudiments of intelligent behaviour, and if this chapter has done no more than show you how very much programming work is required to generate even that, then we have probably done you a good turn.

But at the same time we hope that in working through these long programs with us you have gained a clearer insight into how you can manipulate Lisp, to produce the behaviour you want to get from your virtual machine (in this case the interpreter). Lisp is after all a language, and while it is very nice when you know all the dictionary definitions of its words (i.e. you know what all of its inbuilt functions etc. do), you still need some practice before you can easily express your thoughts in it, rather than in your native language.

Chapter 11
Lexical Closures

11.1 Lexical closures

11.2 Multiple closures created in the same environment

In Chapter 7 we described several ways of storing declarative (static, factual) knowledge within Lisp. In Chapter 9 we showed you how procedural (active) knowledge can be held in the rules of a production system, and we drew a distinction between the two types of knowledge. That distinction is of course only a convenience: most (perhaps all) human cognitive acts involve knowledge of facts as well as knowledge of procedures or processes. This is analogous to the distinction between functions and data, and one of the joys of Lisp, as we said very early on in this book, is that it does not make that distinction. We are about to show you a technique in which what is to all intents and purposes a function behaves as though it contained its own data. Such functions, known as **lexical closures**, can be used as repositories of data, and as you shall see the result is a very interesting Lisp entity with a number of unexpected uses.

11.1   Lexical closures

11.1.1   Lambda expressions

A lexical closure is a special kind of function: a lambda expression which 'remembers' the environment of variable bindings within which it was created. Most functions do not do this, of course; a local binding created

from a function's parameter is available only within the lexical scope of
that function and whilst the function is being evaluated:

```
(defun outerfun (x)
   (innerfun x))
```

allows innerfun to access the value passed to x during a call to outerfun,
but once outerfun has returned a value then x is no longer bound at all,
unless to some previous value 'saved away' by the binding process.

Using the special form function and a lambda-expression in exactly
the same way generates a function (outerfun in this case) which will in
turn generate a closure:

```
(defun outerfun (x)
   (function (lambda (y)
                (cons y x))))
```

or

```
(defun outerfun (x)
   #'(lambda (y)
         (cons y x)))
```

(You probably remember that #' ('hash quote') is an abbreviation for
function.)

This definition will of course create the function outerfun as
normal, but if outerfun itself is evaluated with some suitable argument it
will yield a lexical closure:

```
? (outerfun '(a b c))
```

At this point your Lisp will print something to indicate the presence of
the closure. But you cannot get at it: it no name. Therefore as with
hash tables, arrays and structures defined via defstruct, we assign it as the
value of some mnemonic variable:

```
? (setf trial-closure (outerfun '(a b c)))
```

This if course also returns the same message about a closure having been
created. The closure, now globally bound to trial-closure, is as we said
above the function represented by the original lambda expression

```
(lambda (y)
   (cons y x))
```

but somehow the value which we supplied to the parameter x (that is, the parameter of the closure-creating function outerfun) is still around, and trial-closure can make use of it:

```
? (funcall trial-closure 'q)

(Q A B C)
```

As you would expect, trial-closure has returned the result of consing its own argument onto the value of x. The function calls inside the closure (inside the lambda expression) behave perfectly normally; specifically, the value of x is not changed by the cons. Although you cannot inspect x directly, you can prove to yourself that it is unchanged by calling trial-closure again to cons something else onto x:

```
? (funcall trial-closure nil)

(NIL A B C)
```

As with any other Lisp function call, an error will be caused if you supply the wrong number of arguments to it. For example:

```
? (funcall trial-closure)
```

will cause an error.

11.1.2 mapcar **uses closures**

You are in fact already familiar with one Lisp form which includes a lexical closure:

```
(mapcar #'(lambda (y)
          ...))
```

and now you know that the call to function and the resulting closure means that forms within the lambda expression are able to access values 'outside' the mapcar. Look at this function definition, in which the hash sign does not appear:

```
(defun test (x)
  (mapcar '(lambda (y)
            (print x))
          '(a b c)))
```

You might think that test should print the value of x as many times as there are elements in the list which is mapcar's second argument. But it does not:

```
? (test 3)

Error: unbound symbol X
```

or words to that effect. Now try redefining test with the call to function included:

```
(defun test (x)
    (mapcar #'(lambda (y)
                 (print x))
             '(a b c)))
```

This time it will work, because function creates the all-important closure so that the forms inside the lambda expression are able to access the value of x:

```
? (test 3)

3
3
3
(3 3 3)
```

(The final list of 3s is of course the returned value from mapcar, and hence from test.) So the interesting difference between a lexical closure and an ordinary function is that a closure retains the ability to access variables which were bound in its lexical environment; that is, in the lexical environment which existed when the closure was created. In this example, the closure can still access the parameter x.

More usefully, the closure can also alter the values of those variables. Here is an example of how that can be done:

```
(defun up-one (x)
  #'(lambda ()
        (format t "x is now " x)
        (setf x (1+ x))))

? (setf a (up-one 7))

<A LEXICAL CLOSURE>

? (setf b (up-one 1))

<A LEXICAL CLOSURE>
```

Both a and b are now bound to lexical closures, and each closure was

created in a different environment; that is, with the lexically bound
parameter x bound to a different value in each case. Look closely at the
following interactions with Lisp:

```
? (funcall a)

x is now 8

? (funcall a)

x is now 9

? (funcall b)

x is now 2

? (funcall a)

x is now 10

? (funcall b)

x is now 3

? x

<UNBOUND VARIABLE>
```

It looks as though each closure has its own personal copy of x, and that is
indeed precisely what happens. From our previous discussions of binding
and of lexical scoping you are familiar with the idea that the parameter of
an ordinary function keeps its value only while the function is actually
being evaluated; and you know that even if at the time there is a global
variable of the same name around, there is no confusion between the two
values. The same thing is happening here: the fact that both xs are
lexically bound variables insulates them from one another and from all
other variables called x. In this example the two xs were bound, and were
stored into closures, in different environments and therefore Lisp will
never confuse the two. Later in this chapter we shall show you how to
make use of several different variables bound in the same lexical
environment.

Incidentally, when we showed Lisp complaining that x was an
unbound variable outside the lexical closures (the last of the above
interactions) we were assuming that x had not previously been globally
bound – for example by a setf operation. If you are (as we hope) trying
these things out on your own computer, and if by chance you do happen
to have a globally bound x at the moment, you can unbind it by the
instruction:

```
? (makunbound 'x)

X
```

Yes, it really is spelled 'makunbound'! Now your global x will have no value:

```
? x
```

```
<UNBOUND VARIABLE>
```

11.1.3 Generating infinity

Let us look at a more interesting example:

```
(defun natural-numbers ()
  (let ((nats '(1)))
    #'(lambda (x)
        (cond ((> x (length nats))
               (setf nats (gen x nats))
               (format t "~%I needed to do some work there.~
                          The first ~a natural numbers are~
                          ~{ ~a~}~%" x nats))
              (t
               (format t "~%I actually already know the first~
                          ~a natural numbers; they are~{ ~a~}~%"
                       x (subseq nats 0 x)))))))

(defun gen (num num-list)
  (cond ((= (length num-list) num) num-list)
        (t (gen num (append num-list
                            (list (1+ (car (last num-list))))))))))
```

This pair of functions uses a lexical closure to generate (potentially) the complete list of all natural numbers. Natural numbers are the whole numbers used in everyday counting (1, 2, 3. . .); none of them is a decimal number or a fraction. As you could well guess if you do not already know, the complete list of them is a very long list; in fact it continues to at least one kind of infinity. Nonetheless these two functions can generate them, though in all honesty we should really say that they *could* generate them since the endless job of waiting for the list to be returned from Lisp would be one which you would have to bequeath to your descendants in perpetuity.

Despite this somewhat inconvenient drawback, the functions remain fascinating. To see how they work, concentrate on gen first. It takes two arguments, one of which is a single natural number and the other of which is a list of natural numbers, say a short one containing all the natural numbers which the functions have generated so far. A moment's thought will convince you that the length of a list of natural numbers, so long as none have been missed out, is the same as the highest number in the list: (1 2 3) is three elements long, (1 2 3 4 5 6) is six elements long, and so on.

gen will only be called when num is greater than the length of num-list, i.e. greater than the last number in num-list, and in such cases it is the job of gen to add new elements to the list until num is equal to the length of num-list. As you can see, it does this recursively, adding the next higher number to the list each time, and finally returning the new list.

Turning now to natural-numbers, the first thing it does is to set up a lexical environment within which the closure will be created; that is, it uses a let to bind a list of the first natural number to the variable nats. In a moment we shall hand these two definitions to Lisp, and then we shall run natural-numbers to create the closure. As before, the 'definition' of the resulting closure will be the original lambda expression. All that the lambda expression contains in this case is a simple cond, which first checks to see whether its own local variable, x, is bound to a value which is greater than the current length of the list of natural numbers, which in turn is the value of nats. If so, it calls gen to update the list and then prints a message about what it has done. If not, it prints a message which includes that part of the current list whose length is equal to x. (By the way, the format control strings were too long to fit across the page, so we had to break them up. Notice that, when such a break occurs within a control string, there is an additional tilde (˜) at the end of the line. It is actually another format directive, which as you know consist of a tilde followed immediately by one other character. The extra character in this case is newline, or carriage return.)

The crucial part of the lambda expression is the line

```
(setf nats (gen x nats))
```

It relies on the fact that a closure cannot only access lexical variables such as nats, it can also alter their values as usual via setf. In fact a closure behaves very much as though it were permanently surrounded by a let, a let whose variables and bindings you specified when you created the closure. The difference between this and a normal let is of course that you can directly access the inner lambda expression.

Please now define those two functions in your Lisp and then carry out the following sequence:

```
? (setf gen-nats (natural-numbers))

<A LEXICAL CLOSURE>
```

The value of gen-nats is now a function; in fact it is a lexical closure consisting of the lambda expression from the body of the definition of natural-numbers, and this time there are no lexical variables (no parameters to natural-numbers) for it to access. If you glance back at the definition of natural-numbers you will see that the lambda expression itself has a single parameter, x. Therefore the lexical closure requires just one argument. Try it out; you should get results similar to the following:

```
? (funcall gen-nats 4)

I needed to do some work there. The first 4 natural numbers are 1 2 3 4
NIL

? (funcall gen-nats 6)

I needed to do some work there. The first 6 natural numbers are 1 2 3 4 5 6
NIL

? (funcall gen-nats 5)

I actually already know the first 5 natural numbers; they are 1 2 3 4 5
NIL
```

Exercise 11.1   Define new versions of natural-numbers (calling it weird-series) and of gen (calling it gen2) to create a series the first seven elements of which are

1 2 3 6 7 14 15

For the non-mathematically inclined: starting from 1, the second term is 1 times 2; the third term is the second term plus 1; the fourth term is the third term times 2; the fifth term is the fourth term plus 1; and so on. The trick is to make gen2 do what you want it to do by inserting a cond into the statement of what it should append to num-list. Use the length of num-list as the test, and note that Common Lisp provides a very useful function called evenp. It is a predicate returning T if its single numerical argument is even rather than odd.

11.1.4   Prime numbers

One more numerical example because it is interesting, and then we promise to lay off the mathematics. This one creates the list of all the prime numbers. A prime number is a number which is exactly (i.e. no decimals or fractions) divisible only by itself and 1. Zero and 1 are not considered to be prime numbers, but 2,3 and 5 are. 4 is not because it is divisible by 2 as well as by itself and 1.

Prime numbers are interesting because there does not seem to be any pattern, or even a weird-series, about the way they are scattered throughout the full list of natural numbers. If you know the first 99 prime numbers, there is no simple way of predicting the 100th. For this reason prime numbers are much favoured as the basis for cryptography: for uncrackable secret codes. Of course, your side's code is only completely uncrackable if it is based on a prime number which the other side does not yet know; so the search for ever higher prime numbers is of crucial importance in some quarters.

At the time of writing, no-one anywhere knows a handy formula for generating this series of numbers. All known methods of generating the list ultimately end up with brute force methods, though some are considerably more efficient (faster) than others. Our method will not by any means be the fastest, but it will employ a couple of techniques to speed things up. The problem is that the way to find the next prime number when we already know the first four (they are 2, 3, 5 and 7) is extremely tedious: at worst, we would add 1 to 7 and then see if the result could be divided by any of the natural numbers between 2 and 5 (any number will divide by itself and one; we want the numbers which are not divisible by anything else).

We can speed things up quite a bit by realizing that there is no point in dividing by any number which is not itself a prime, because all non-prime numbers are by definition divisible by at least one prime other than themselves and 1. There is also no point in dividing by any number which is larger than the square root of the number we are trying to prove to be a prime. (The square root of a number, multiplied by itself, produces the number: 3 is the square root of 9, 4 is the square root of 16, 5 is the square root of 25, and so on.)

Here are the four functions to create a closure which will infallibly generate as many prime numbers as you ask it to. But please do not be tempted to ask it for the prime number after the highest prime number yet discovered, even if you know what the currently highest one is. This book, your computer and even you will have crumbled to dust long before the answer comes out, since it would take something like 10^{20} or a hundred billion billion years.

```
(defun primes ()
   (let ((primes-list '(2)))
     #'(lambda (n)
         (cond ((> n (length primes-list))
                   (setf primes-list (gen-primes n primes-list))
                   primes-list)
               (t (subseq primes-list 0 n)))))))
```

The closure-generating function primes does pretty much the same things as natural-numbers and weird-series. As usual the helper function gen-primes does all the real work.

```
(defun gen-primes (num num-list)
   (cond ((= (length num-list) num) num-list)
         (t (gen-primes
```

```
              num
            (append num-list
              (list (gen-next-prime
                num-list
                (1+ (car (last num-list))))))))))))
```

It receives as arguments from primes the value of num which is the number of primes required, and the value of num-list which is the list of primes so far generated. If the length of num-list is num as required, it returns num-list; but otherwise it calls itself recursively whilst adding the next prime in the series to the end of num-list. gen-next-prime actually derives the required next prime number in the series:

```
(defun gen-next-prime (primes biggest)
  (cond ((gen-next-prime2 primes biggest) biggest)
        (t (gen-next-prime primes (1+ biggest)))))
```

gen-next-prime receives as arguments the current list of primes and a number, biggest, which is 1 larger than the last (and thus the largest) prime in the list. It will call gen-next-prime2 to try to divide each of the primes on the list into biggest. gen-next-prime2 will return T when it succeeds in proving that biggest is the next prime, and NIL otherwise. So long as this returned value is NIL, gen-next-prime recurses, adding 1 to biggest each time.

```
(defun gen-next-prime2 (primes biggest)
  (cond ((null primes))
        ((> (car primes) (sqrt biggest)))
        ((zerop (mod biggest (car primes))) nil)
        (t (gen-next-prime2 (cdr primes) biggest))))
```

gen-next-prime2 receives as arguments the current list of primes and the current biggest. It recurses through the list of primes. If it manages to get right through the list of primes without any of them dividing exactly into biggest, it returns T. If the current car of primes is larger than the square root of biggest, it also returns T. However, if any one prime on the list does divide exactly into biggest, it returns NIL. The function mod returns zero if its second argument divides exactly into its first.

Now:

```
? (setf try (primes))

<A LEXICAL CLOSURE>

? (funcall try 7)
```

```
1 3 5 7 11 13 17

? (funcall try 10)

1 3 5 7 11 13 17 19 23 29
```

In the above ways closures can be used as infinity generators, but they are smart enough never to generate more of any particular infinite series than they are actually asked for. Very many things can be described as infinite or very long series: the DNA helix, the arrangement of leaves and flowers on plants, the growth of world population, radioactive decay, the passage of time. Closures used as generators are, we think, interesting because they offer a fairly simple way of representing on the computer vast amounts of certain types of information, information which it would be very inconvenient to have to keep in the computer's main memory. Closures are also interesting for other reasons, as you are about to see.

11.2   Multiple closures created in the same environment

It is perfectly possible to create two or more closures at once, by putting two sequential lambda expressions into the same definition of natural-numbers, for example. Each of the closures so created will share the same set of lexical bindings; that is, each of them will 'remember' what those bindings are even when it is evaluated separately from the others. Each of them will also be able to alter those external bindings via calls to setf, and when it does so all of the others will know what has happened and will use the new binding. Extending our analogy which said that a closure behaves like a function which has a permanent let around its definition, closures created within the same environment behave as though they all had the same let around them. Please notice an important distinction here, that multiple closures created together, in the same environment, actually share their lexical variables; closures created separately, even via the same closure-generating function, do not share their variables (as you saw earlier with up-one).

11.2.1   An example:

```
(defun double-closure (item)
  (list #'(lambda () item)
        #'(lambda (new-item) (setf item new-item))))
```

If you follow the usual sequence and then do a couple of tests, you will see that the second lambda expression can setf the external variable item, and that the first lambda expression then 'sees' that new value when it refers to item:

```
? (defun double-closure (item)
    (list #'(lambda () item)
          #'(lambda (new-item) (setf item new-item))))

DOUBLE-CLOSURE

? (setf try (double-closure 'tony))

(<A LEXICAL CLOSURE><A LEXICAL CLOSURE>)

? (funcall (car try))

TONY
```

This calls the first of the two closures which are held as the value of try. As you can see from the definition of double-closure the corresponding lambda expression does nothing other than return the value of the lexical variable item.

```
? (funcall (cadr try) 'john)

JOHN
```

This calls the second closure, and the call to setf inside that closure changes the value of item. So if we now call the first closure again we shall see the altered value:

```
? (funcall (car try))

JOHN
```

11.2.2   Using let to create closures

Here is another example, this time using a let rather than a defun to provide the environment in which the closures are created:

```
? (setf a (let ((x 1))
            (list #'(lambda () x)
                  #'(lambda (j) (setf x j)))))

(<A LEXICAL CLOSURE> <A LEXICAL CLOSURE>)
```

As before, the first closure simply returns the values of the shared lexical variable, x, but the second is able to alter the binding of x.

```
? (funcall (first a))
```

1

```
? (funcall (second a) 7)
```

7

To prove that the lexical binding of x has been changed:

```
? (funcall (first a))
```

7

11.2.3 Simplifying the process

It has probably struck you that it is tedious to type all these calls to
funcall, and that if a list of sharing lexical closures is to be of any use as a
place to store knowledge you have to remember where each closure
occurs in the list so that you can choose the correct accessing function
(first or second here). So we would like to show you a rather neat
programming solution. First, we are going to make the list of closures
into an alist, using meaningful tokens as the keys:

```
? (setf a (let ((x 1))
            (list (cons 'x #'(lambda () x))
                  (cons 'set-x #'(lambda (j) (setf x j))))))

((X . <A LEXICAL CLOSURE>) (SET-X . <A LEXICAL CLOSURE>))
```

The closure within the element whose key is simply x will return the value
of x; the one within the element whose key is set-x will alter that value.
Now we can call assoc on the list to retrieve any desired element:

```
? (assoc 'set-x a)

(SET-X . <A LEXICAL CLOSURE>)
```

The cdr of that is of course the closure itself. Now we are in a position to
parcel the whole process up into a single macro:

```
? (defmacro foo (obj key &rest args)
    '(funcall (cdr (assoc ,key ,obj)) ,@args))

FOO
```

Remember that the ,@ syntax effectively removes the outer set of
brackets from the list args. Calls to foo can now either set or retrieve the
value of x:

```
? (foo a 'set-x 999)

999

? (foo a 'x)

999
```

It has probably occurred to you that what the technique has given us is something very like all those alists, plists, hash tables and arrays which you read about in Chapter 7. In all these methods of knowledge representation there is the underlying idea of a 'place' or 'slot' which has a name or a key and which can hold an item of data. In this case the slot is the lexical environment and its name is the name of the lexical variable x. It would be perfectly possible to have a number of different lexical variables, each with its associated set of lambda expressions, in the same lexical environment, in which case something very like a defstruct structure would result.

The big advantage of the new technique over the others is that it has only a single macro, which so far we have called foo, and which can either retrieve or alter any piece of data as required. Let us extend the example a little, and alter its lexical environment (the slot) so that we can decide what its initial value (contents) shall be:

```
? (setf a
    (let ((x nil))
      (list (cons 'x #'(lambda () x))
            (cons 'set-x #'(lambda (y) (setf x y)))
            (cons 'car-x #'(lambda () (car x)))
            (cons 'cdr-x #'(lambda () (cdr x)))
            (cons 'set-car-x #'(lambda (y) (setf (car x) y))))))
```

We would like you to try each of the possibilities in turn:

```
? (foo a 'x)

NIL

? (foo a 'set-x '(a b c))

(A B C)
```

We have now bound the lexical variable x to a list:

```
? (foo a 'car-x)

A

? (foo a 'cdr-x)

(B C)
```

We hope that those two were exactly as you expected. Now try:

```
? (foo a 'set-car-x 'z)

Z
```

We need to look at the value of x to see the change:

```
? (foo a 'x)

(Z B C)
```

11.2.4   Message passing

So we now have a multiple closure which can not only hold data, it can also hold little functions (the lambda expressions) to manipulate that data. The idea of a 'static' data structure also holding all the functions it will ever need is a very exciting one from the programmer's point of view, and we shall use it in Chapter 12 to create an object-oriented system. We have one final point to make here, just to give you a taste of what Chapter 12 will be about.

Given the syntax of any call to foo, it is easy to imagine that what you are doing is **sending messages to** the multiple closure, messages which tell it to do something. foo is clever enough to know which of the five lambda expressions any message is intended for, and to apply that function to any arguments you may supply. So let us rewrite foo like this:

```
? (defmacro –> (object message &rest args)
    '(funcall (cdr (assoc ,message ,object)) ,@args))

–>
```

The name of the macro, which looks like an arrow, is intended to signify something which includes all of the ideas 'send' or 'tell' or 'ask'.

Suppose that you had created a number of separate multiple closures, each intended to hold a description of some real-world entity in its various slots. It might occur to you that by adding a new closure to each you could give them isa links, or pointers to their parents, so that you could create yet another version of the Collins and Quillian model. And indeed you could. In Chapter 12 we shall use a combination of defstruct structures and multiple closures to derive from the notion of a hierarchy of complex objects a very powerful programming technique.

Chapter 12
Object-oriented Systems

12.1 Object-oriented systems

12.2 The world's smallest object-oriented system

We have often mentioned the phrase 'Lisp object', and if you have gathered that any legal Lisp 'thing' from atoms and lists to the structures defined by `defstruct` is a Lisp object, then you are absolutely right. We are about to show you a technique which was discovered only recently and whose power is not yet fully appreciated by the majority of Lisp programmers. It is called **object-oriented programming**, but its 'objects' are very different from the Lisp objects which you have seen so far: they are 'intelligent' entities containing both data and functions. As you work through this chapter you will create out of and on top of Lisp a system so powerful that already a whole new programming language (SmallTalk) has been written to take advantage of the principles which you are about to put into effect. This will be state-of-the-art Lisp programming.

12.1 Object-oriented systems

12.1.1 Hierarchical representations of knowledge

Think back for a moment to the final version of our Collins and Quillian model, the one using `defstruct`, at the end of Chapter 7. Each node in the tree was a data structure, and all the structures were identical: they differed only in what precise data was held in their slots. Each structure thus 'knew' which other structure was its parent and what its own

277

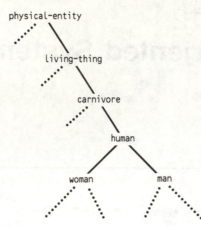

Figure 12.1   A hierarchy of classes.

attributes were. The remember function could, when required, retrieve the attributes of any 'leaf' node or it could follow the isa links from leaf-node to its parent, its grandparent etc. in search of the required information. We also mentioned that at a later stage of their research Collins and Quillian abandoned the idea of a tree in favour of a network, the difference being that instead of each node having just one parent node, it could have an arbitrary number of them. Though the tree became a network it remained a hierarchy, in which each parent represented the entire class of its children. Our own classes were woman, man, human, carnivore, living-thing and physical-entity (Figure 12.1).

It is important to remember that these classes did not represent any individual person or living thing in the real world: each one represented if you like a set of general statements about distinct groups of real things. For example the node human contained the attribute has soul, and this corresponded to the general statement that all human beings have souls. However, this was merely default information, and could be overridden in individual cases by more specific information located lower in the hierarchy. In our Collins and Quillian model only the leaves of the tree, at the very bottom of the hierarchy, represented actual individuals; everything above them was merely a convenient way of representing our knowledge about large numbers of actual individuals.

12.1.1   Hierachies of objects

Now comes something exciting. Imagine the tree or network bereft of its leaf nodes so that it contains only nodes representing classes of real-world entities, arranged in a hierarchy. Then forget that anything here refers to the real world at all: it is just an arrangement of things called classes which as yet contain no information other than a knowledge of their parents, but each of which is potentially able to hold information which will represent (which will be equivalent to general statements about) a coherent group of (as yet unspecified) other things. You should be imagining something like Figure 12.1 with the node names removed and amorphous blobs taking their places!

The result is that instead of a model of a single hypothesis, we have the beginnings of a powerful programming technique. Consider just one of these class nodes, which we may as well start calling classes since that is what they are called in the majority of object-oriented systems. The programmer can create as many of these class structures as are necessary and can connect them together via their 'parents' so as to form whatever 'shape' seems suitable to the project in hand. In an object-oriented system the result is usually a hierarchy, but other than that the programmer is free to create any arrangement s/he likes. Should s/he later decide that the arrangement is wrong, or that it has too few or too many class structures in it, modifications are almost trivially easy to make.

Besides having parents each class will be able to hold one or more items of data. The items of data will together describe in general terms (as the 'attributes' did in the Collins and Quillian model) the whole class of (still as yet unspecified) things which this class structure represents. There will be an equivalent of the remember function to retrieve this data when necessary, but in object-oriented systems we turn that concept on its head: we forget about the function which chases up the hierarchy and speak instead of the data being 'inherited' down the hierarchy. We say that **a class can inherit default values** from its parents, grandparents etc. as necessary. As you will see in a moment, it is convenient to think of the class as an 'active' entity, making use of the remember-equivalent in order to inherit what it needs. The data held by a class is known as its **local variables**.

In our program classes will be created by a new function called defclass, analogous to defun, defmacro and defstruct. In fact our classes will be defstruct structures, similar to the ones you created for the Collins and Quillian example.

There is one enormous, important and even more exciting difference between the structures you have seen so far and the classes in an object-oriented system: the latter can contain, and can inherit, functions as well as data. Both the data and the functions are added to the class after its creation.

Any one class structure can thus be regarded as an 'intelligent' entity, which can supply or (via inheritance) retrieve large amounts of data and/or functionality. As we said a few paragraphs ago, it is often convenient to disregard any inheritance of functions or of data which may occur, and to think of each class as itself possessing all the knowledge, both knowledge that and knowledge how, which is available to it. The functions held in a class are known as its **methods**.

12.1.3 Instances of objects

So far we have described only the underlying structure of an object-oriented system. Normally the class structures do not do anything, they merely act as repositories of information. In order to make the system do something useful, we have to create **instances** of our class structures. These are the groups of so far unspecified 'things' which the classes represent. Instances can be regarded as 'real', 'living' examples of their classes, just as mother was thought of (above) as a real, living example of the class woman.

In the Collins and Quillian model the real, living things appeared only at the leaves of the tree: they were instances of the lowest class nodes in the tree; of man or of woman. But users of object-oriented systems are allowed to create instances of any class. It will be as though each node in the hierarchy could have its own private set of 'leaves'. In Figure 12.2 mother and QE are instances of the class woman whilst father and president are instances of the class man.

To create an instance of a class is to create a Lisp object which 'shares' all of the knowledge available to its class, including knowledge which that class can inherit from its parents, grandparents and so on further up in the hierarchy. To put that another way, the class defines the nature and the behaviour of its instances (because it alone can supply them with default data or functions) but it is the instances which actually do the behaving. Instances can have their own local data, but functions are always associated with classes. In programs written using an object-oriented system, all of the important and (to the programmer) meaningful activity consists of messages and responses flowing between instances. In general, a message will ask an instance to operate upon its own data using functions associated with, or inheritable by, its class.

For example, imagine an arcade game involving attacking space-ships. In the program which creates the game, each spaceship would need to know certain things. In particular, it would need to know how to draw itself on screen, and it would need to know where to draw itself on screen. If the program was written in object-oriented style, each spaceship would be an instance of a general class of spaceships. The class structure, representing the class of all spaceships, would never appear on screen; but it would hold (or be able to inherit) the functions which enabled any spaceship instance to display itself on screen. The information as to where to do so would be held on each individual spaceship; that is, on each instance of the class.

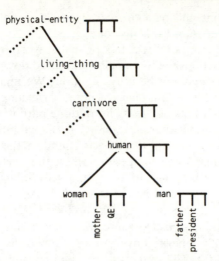

Figure 12.2 Adding instances to the hierarchy.

The overall game would also include other classes, perhaps land-based missile launchers which could bring down the attacking spaceships. There would be a class structure for the missile launchers too, and it would need to be able to tell any individual rocket launcher how to draw itself on screen and, say, how to fire a missile. Since missile launchers and spaceships are both on-screen entities, parts of the 'how to draw yourself' information might well be common to both and so might be kept in a superclass, called perhaps visibles; and that abstracted information would be inheritable, as and when needed, down the hierarchy through one or other of the missile-launcher or spaceship classes, so that it could be supplied to any individual missile launcher or spaceship.

As for the missiles themselves, there are two possibilities. Either each launcher could have its own subclass of missiles, each with its own individual instance missiles, so that things such as a missile's starting position on the screen could be inherited from its launcher; or there might be a general class of missiles covering also those fired from spaceships. This is the point of allowing every class-structure to have its own 'leaves': it allows the programmer rather than us, the designers of the system, to make more of the decisions about how the system shall actually be used. We hope you can agree that this is potentially a very powerful method of knowledge representation.

Our system will not restrict classes to having just one parent each (but instances will always be instances of a single class). We should point out that when a class has multiple parents that does not mean that it is forced to become two kinds of class at the same time. It remains unique in the hierarchy, with its own particular functions and data, but is able to inherit other functions and data, if ever it needs to do so, from any of several parents rather than from just one.

There is one other point which is probably worth making this early on: the notion of functions and data being inherited down the hierarchy is a convenient one but may not be fully accurate. We imagine a particular class object in need of a certain piece of data, for example, which it does not possess itself. So it looks up to its immediate parent(s) to see whether the data can be found there. If not, it looks further up to its grandparent(s), and so on until the data is found or the search fails. We also visualize the same thing happening when the class object needs a particular function. The point here is that this inheritance need not happen precisely at the time when it is needed. As you shall soon see, you could if you wished create the hierarchy of class objects, starting from the top, and taking steps to ensure that as each new child object was created it immediately inherited everything – functions and data – from its immediate parent(s). The objects in the hierarchy would thus contain multiple copies of most of the functions and most of the data, and those classes low down in the hierarchy might contain very large amounts of both.

In our system we shall show you both ways of achieving inheritance. The difference between the two in practice is that inheritance on creation gives fast responses (because every object itself contains all the functions and data which it is ever likely to need) whilst inheritance when needed is slower but makes far smaller demands on the computer's available memory-space (because no multiple copies are stored).

The classes in our system will be structures defined via `defstruct`, and their instances will be lexical closures. This difference of Lisp type will enforce the conceptual difference between classes and instances (for example, classes will be unable by definition to accept messages). The result will be a very elegant program in which the instances, the classes and the hierarchy itself are all as flexible as possible and therefore maximally convenient to future users of it.

12.1.4   Sending messages to instances

Almost everything in an object-oriented system is accomplished by the sending of suitable messages to suitable instances. The user does not normally communicate directly with classes (though some object-oriented systems do allow it), but relies upon the hierarchy which s/he has created and the fact of inheritance to enable any instance to respond appropriately to any messages sent to it. The messages will ask an instance to return some (possibly inherited) data about itself, or to run one of its (probably inherited) functions on arguments supplied with the message. Thus, when the arcade game program needed to move spaceshipA from one side of the screen to the other, it would send it a message saying something like

```
(hey 'spaceshipA 'move-to <new-position>)
```

Another useful comparison between conventional programming and object-oriented programming is as follows. In conventional programming we have data, and we have functions which operate upon the data. None of the data is capable of 'doing' anything: it is merely passive, and the functions hold all the knowledge of how to make the program work. In object-oriented programming, there are classes (in some systems these are called **objects**, but we are trying to avoid using that potentially confusing term) which can hold both data and the knowledge of how to make use of the data (that is, they have associated functions as well as data). Have a look at these randomly chosen conventional function calls:

```
(move ship)

(print lis)

(slice bread)
```

In each of them, the important item is the function. If you like, it is the function which you, the programmer, are 'talking to' or sending a message to. Here are the equivalent forms in object-oriented programming:

```
(-> ship 'move)

(-> lis 'print)

(-> bread 'slice)
```

The function -> (call it 'send') sends a message to ship, telling it to move itself; or it sends a message to lis telling it to print itself; or it sends a message to bread telling it to slice itself. The receiving entity, be it ship, lis or bread, has been written in such a way that it 'knows how' to do as it is told; in particular it knows how to inherit via its class the necessary functions. But as a programmer using an object-oriented system you would try to forget about all the details (all the details, that is, which we are about to explain to you!) and simply to assume that the recipient of a message knows how to respond to it.

For users of object-oriented systems, things are even better than that. It is quite normal to send the 'same' message to several quite

different recipients, and to have them each respond to it differently. Like
this:

```
? (-> lis 'move)

? (-> ship 'move)

? (-> bread 'move)
```

It seems obvious that the message move would have to elicit different
behaviour from all three recipients. This chapter will show you how to
obtain such interesting effects.

As we mentioned before it is convenient to regard any instance as
itself possessing, via its class, all the information it needs in order to
respond to messages. And sure enough, just as though that were true,
spaceshipA promptly moves itself to the other side of the screen when
told to do so. But in all probability it inherited the function which did the
actual moving. It will have inherited it from its parent class spaceship, and
will have applied that function to purely local information, in this case to
a record of its own current position on screen, and to any arguments
which might be supplied with the message (we supplied new-position
above). A little later the program might need to know where spaceshipA
now is (having exited from a let somewhere and so having forgotten the
value of new-position). It would then send the message

```
(hey 'spaceshipA 'position)
```

and without any inheritance of values being necessary at all, spaceshipA
would dutifully send back its current position.

We hope that this short description of object-oriented systems has
intrigued, you, so that you want to know more (and so that the rest of
this chapter is not wasted!).

12.2   The world's smallest object-oriented system

The code, uncommented, for our object system occupies less than two A4
pages. Nonetheless, it is as powerful as many commercially available
object systems, and in the course of building it you will encounter the
major principles upon which such systems are based. Some of the code
which follows is easy, some of it will be hard enough to test your growing
knowledge of Lisp to its limits. But we are sure that once you have got it
working you will be very impressed with the power of Lisp to create
highly flexible systems out of very little code.

The system, when built, will allow its user to create classes and to arrange them in a hierarchical network. Each class will have slots (because class structures will be the kind of structure defined by defstruct) to hold data or functions, and the user will be able to fill these slots with suitable Lisp forms. Each class structure will have a 'parents' slot whose contents (also decided by us) will allow us to build the hierarchy, just as it did in the Collins and Quillian model. It will further be possible to create instances of any class, and these instances will consist of lexical closures which as you already know are functions which carry with them an environment of variables. In fact a set of closures, created within the same environment and each with just one lexical variable to refer to, could behave very much like a set of slots. That is exactly what our 'instances' will be, except that an extra closure in each set will be a function which, when called, will trigger the inheritance mechanism via the local class.

There will in the end be about 20 functions, most of them very short, which together create the system. Users of the system will need to know of the existence of only three of them in order to create classes, instances of those classes, and local functions for those classes known as **methods**. In order that the user's object-oriented code, written using our system, can cause things to happen amidst the hierarchy of classes and instances, there will also be an additional macro which can carry a message to any instance, or from one instance to another. This macro will not normally be called from top level.

The underlying program will be structured differently from any that you have seen before: instead of having a single master routine which is called from top level and which then runs various modules in order to create some overall effect (as for example in the production systems of Chapters 9 and 10), the object system has three master functions. Each of these will run its own module when called by the user from top level, but the user can, and indeed should, run each on its own, independently of the others. Only at a very low level of programming will different modules call upon the same small 'helper' or book-keeping functions.

The three master functions are: defclass, whose module does everything necessary to the creation of a new class; defmethod, whose module does everything necessary to the creation of new methods once classes have been defined; and make-instance, whose module does everything necessary for the creation of intances of classes. Figure 12.3 shows the main components of the system and their connections in bold type. The grey lines and plain type indicate connections to subsidiary and largely book-keeping functions. As you can see, the three main modules are almost entirely separate from one another down to quite a low level. There is a double link between find-method and find-method-in-parents, which indicates that each is both the parent and the child of the other, i.e. they are mutually recursive, as you shall see.

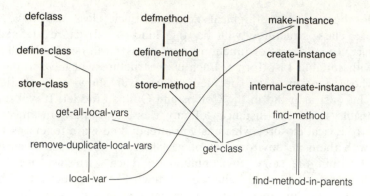

Figure 12.3 Program structure.

12.2.1   Classes and local variables

Let us start with the classes. Going back to the Collins and Quillian example for a moment, we created the various nodes via defstruct. If you remember, defstruct defined a class of nodes and automatically provided us with the function make-node with which to create the nodes themselves. We are going to do the same thing here, using defstruct to define the **class of all classes**; and in return we shall get the function make-class which will enable us to create our individual classes. As before, defstruct will also automatically define accessor macros which allow us to retrieve or to alter the data in any class's slots. So the call to defstruct which creates the class of all classes must specify the slots which all of the classes will need:

```
? (defstruct class
    (name nil)
    (local-variables nil)
    (functions (make-hash-table))
    (parents nil))

  CLASS
```

We now automatically have make-class, which will create for us new classes. Each one, as you can see above, will have a slot for its name, a slot for its local variables, a slot for functions and a slot for the names of its parents, whose names will be stored in a list. We shall keep the functions, which from now on we shall correctly refer to as **methods**, in a hash table simply because that seems convenient and elegant. Each class will be given such a hash table in its functions slot, when make-class creates it.

As we create classes, we are going to store them in another hash table, indexed (retrievable) via their names. initialise-class-system does just what its name suggests and also calls make-class to create the root class. The latter's name will be t and its parent slot will default to nil (i.e. no parents):

```
(defvar *all-classes* nil)

(defun initialise-class-system ()
  (if *all-classes*
      (clrhash *all-classes*)
      (setf *all-classes* (make-hash-table)))
  (setf (gethash t *all-classes*)
        (make-class :name t)))
```

The global variable *all-classes* holds the name of the hash table where the classes are to be stored. If that hash table already exists, initialise-class-system empties it via a call to clrhash. If not, it creates the hash table. You probably remember that make-hash-table, called with no arguments, creates a hash table whose entries can be any Lisp object. The call to setf enters the root class into the hash table.

We need to have our system define the root class automatically, rather than leaving it to the user, because some of our later functions, specifically those which chase up the tree so as to effect inheritance, will need to know when they have reached the root class. Also, if we wish we can later define **object system primitives**, that is, methods which because they are assigned to the root object will be inheritable by any other class.

We feel that make-class, as the means of creating new classes in our system, is too cumbersome to use. So we will write a function to do the job more simply (by the way, let* is not a misprint; it will be explained below):

```
(defun define-class (class-name parents local-vars)
  (let* ((locals (get-all-local-vars (if parents parents '(t))
                                     local-vars))
         (class
          (make-class :name class-name
                      :parents (if parents parents '(t))
                      :local-variables locals
                      :functions (make-hash-table))))
    (store-class class-name class)))
```

Once that is defined, we shall only have to type something like:

```
? (define-class 'spaceship 'visibles '((position q14)))
```

in order to create, in this case, the spaceship class. It has only one local variable, representing its position in quadrant 14 (which we assume to have some meaning in the context of the arcade game). The list of local-vars mentions only the position for our spaceship, but in general it looks like this:

```
((var1 val1) (var2 val2) (var3 val3)...)
```

which you will readily recognize as being very similar to the lists of variables and their bindings as used in let.

But even define-class is not elegant enough for us. We shall nest define-class inside a macro:

```
(defmacro defclass (class-name parents local-vars)
  `(define-class ',class-name ',parents ',local-vars))
```

Notice our use of quotes and commas within the backquote. Quote-comma means 'give me the result of evaluating the following form, but quote it'. In other words, it does exactly what it looks as though it does! The purpose of quoting these arguments before passing them on to define-class is to relieve users of our system from the bother of quoting their arguments during their calls to defclass so that it is as convenient to use as defun, defmacro and defstruct. defclass is a macro which they will often call from top level, and our purpose in making it a macro is precisely to make things easier for its eventual users. Whatever arguments they do supply to defclass become the values of defclass's three parameters. These are evaluated by the commas inside the backquote but are then quoted, so that define-class does not try to evaluate them again.

Now let us go back to define-class. Within it, let* is to let what do* is to do. That is, let* binds its variable–value pairs sequentially rather than in parallel. The effect here is that the value of locals can be used in the call to make-class. The call to make-class creates a new class with all of its slots initialized. The name slot acquires the name supplied in the call to defclass, and passed down to define-class; and the parents slot will default to a list of one element, t, if no parents are supplied. The functions slot was not mentioned in the call to defclass, so make-class gives it a hash table as specified in the original call to defstruct. Notice that this is not the same thing as inheritance: the new class acquires a new hash table all to itself; it is not given any kind of copy of the hash table in the class of all classes (t). Finally, the local-variables slot is given the value returned by a call to get-all-local-vars that is, the value of locals.

There are two ways of effecting inheritance. One, which we have described before, is secretly to provide each class with a little remember-like function which can retrieve any needed data from other classes in the hierarchy. We shall use that method for the inheritance of methods. But, in order for you to see the difference, we shall where local variables are concerned use the other technique, which is to do all of the inheritance at one go as a new class is created. (Since we do not expect users to send messages directly to class structures, but only to their instances, the contents of the local-variables slot in existing classes should never change.) get-all-local-vars does this job. Finally, in define-class, the function store-class is called to record the new class in the hash table named *all-classes*:

```
(defun store-class (class-name class)
  (setf (gethash class-name *all-classes*) class))
```

This function is an example of data abstraction. Were we later to change our minds about how to store the names of the classes – say, to keep them on the property list of *all-classes* instead of in a hash table of that name – simple changes to store-class and to get-class (coming up shortly) would be all that we needed to make.

The next function, get-all-local-vars, looks at the new class's parents slot to find the name(s) of its parent(s), and retrieves the local variables from each of those parent classes. There is no need to look any higher – say to the new class's grandparents – because the parent classes include all of the grandparents' local variables already: they inherited them via a similar call to get-all-local-vars when they were themselves created. However, the very first class created via make-class must inherit from the root class, i.e. it must have the root class as its parent, because as yet no other class exists:

```
(defun get-all-local-vars (parents current-local-vars)
  (dolist (parent parents (remove-duplicate-local-vars
                            current-local-vars))
    (setf current-local-vars
          (append (class-local-variables (get-class parent))
                  current-local-vars))))
```

The dolist iterates through the list of the new class's parents. Each time around the cycle it appends to the parameter current-local-vars the list of local variables derived from one of the parents. When the list of parents is exhausted, dolist evaluates its **result form** so as to remove any duplicates from the resulting list of current-local-vars. We shall now describe this process in greater detail.

class-local-variables is one of the accessor macros defined automatically for us by defstruct. We have to give it as its argument the particular class (the actual structure, not the class's name) from which we want it to get the local variables. That class is retrieved from *all-classes* by get-class:

```
(defun get-class (class-name)
  (cond ((gethash class-name *all-classes*))
        (t (error "~a is an undefined class" class-name))))
```

The first clause of the cond will return the class if it succeeds in finding it. The second demonstrates a simple way of making use of Lisp's error-handling system, via a call to the function error. As you can see, error takes a format control string, which it prints in just the same way as format would. It also puts you into your Lisp's debugging system: probably into a break loop. At any rate, the effect apart from the message will be exactly the same as when a Lisp error occurs in the usual way; and its intended purpose is to be helpful in debugging any program written using this object system.

When all the parents have been dealt with, by the dolist in inherit-local-vars, there remains a result form to be evaluated. This result form:

```
(remove-duplicate-local-vars
  current-local-vars)
```

removes any duplicates from the list now held on current-local-vars and that result is returned. The position of this result form within the dolist is a place where you would normally expect to see a result variable, as we described in Chapter 4. We said at the time that it could be a single Lisp form rather than a variable. As you can now see, that form can be a call to a macro, in this case remove-duplicate-local-vars whose purpose is to hide from the user some ugly syntax:

```
(defmacro remove-duplicate-local-vars (local-vars)
  `(remove-duplicates ,local-vars :key #'car))
```

The Common Lisp function remove-duplicates does exactly what its name suggests, but in this case it needs a keyworded argument, the function car, to tell it which bits of of the variables it should compare in order to know whether they are duplicates or not. Remember, a 'variable' here is a two-element list of the variable's name and its binding:

```
(var1 val1)
```

You may be wondering why there should be any duplicates, since each class inherits from its ancestors and the whole point of complex methods of knowledge representation is to reduce waste and to increase efficiency. The answer is that if a future user of the system builds only a Collins and Quillian-like tree of classes, in which each has only one parent, there need not be any duplication of local variables. But if that user chooses to make use of the multiple inheritance which our system allows, each class can have any number of parents all at the same level in the hierarchy (Figure 12.2) then there could be duplicates since any two of those parents might well have been given the same variable name when they

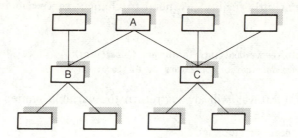

Figure 12.4 Classes with multiple parents.

were created, for later inheritance by their other children. In Figure 12.4, class A has two children, class B has two children and two parents, whilst class C has two children and three parents.

When there are such duplicates, they could have different values; or, if we were trying to inherit a named method, it could have different definitions in different parents. Thus the order in which multiple parents are searched for the purposes of inheritance can sometimes matter. Our system makes no attempt at a sophisticated choice between duplicates: it keeps the first one it finds (because that is what `remove-duplicates` does) and throws the rest away. More elaborate object-oriented systems give the user control over how cases of duplication shall be handled.

This is a convenient point to mention again the form of the local-vars list:

```
((var1 val1) (var2 val2) (var3 val3) ...)
```

This is a list which users have to type in by hand, in a call to `defclass`. If it happened to be quite a long list and if many of the values in it were `NIL`, it could become unnecessarily tedious to type. As you know, `let`, which uses similar forms of lists for binding local variables, allows any variable name which is intended to be bound to `NIL` to appear on its own:

```
(let ((a 2) b (c 'three)))
     ...)
```

This binds `a` to `2`, `b` to `NIL` and `c` to `three`. For the convenience of future users of our system we shall adopt the same convention. It will not matter if an individual types something like

```
(defclass kids tom ((legs 2) (breakfast nil) (toys nil)))
```

but if anyone prefers the shorter form it will be there for them. In order to provide that little facility, we need to change `remove-duplicate-local-vars` slightly:

```
(defmacro remove-duplicate-local-vars (local-vars)
  `(remove-duplicates ,local-vars :key #'local-var))
```

The function `local-var` will always return the variable name:

```
(defun local-var (loc-var)
  (if (atom loc-var) loc-var
      (car loc-var)))
```

Summary so far

So far, our system is able to create named classes which can be linked via their **parents** slots to form a hierarchical network. Each class has a slot to contain its **local-variables**, which actually consist of a list of atoms and of variable–value pairs. When any new class is created it immediately inherits the local variables (including their values) from its parent and hence from all of its ancestors.

We have not yet covered the question of methods associated with classes, and we said earlier that we would show you a **remember**-like method for the inheritance of these methods. When that has been done there will remain the (difficult) job of providing the user with the ability to create instances of any class. Finally, we shall need the all-important **send** macro which will make the whole system come to life by making the sending of messages possible.

12.2.2 Methods

Methods, like local variables, are regarded as being stored in the corresponding classes. In fact, as you already know, they are stored in hash tables whose names are held in the `functions` slots of the classes. We shall need to define five new functions in our system.

The first three provide the facility to write new methods and to associate them with particular classes. Here is `define-method`:

```
(defun define-method (class-name
                      method-name
                      params
                      body)
  (let ((fun `(lambda ,(cons 'self params) ,@body)))
    (store-method method-name class-name fun)))
```

This is the first time you have seen the backquote used other than in the definition of a macro. But in fact the backquote is quite independent of defmacro and can be used wherever its template-like facilities can help. In this case, we want the let to bind to the variable fun a function definition; and in fact the function definition will be in the form of a lambda expression. We want this lambda expression to consist of: an opening parenthesis followed by the word lambda; then the result of consing the word self onto a list of other parameters for the function (we shall explain self shortly); and finally the body of the function, which as usual will be a sequence of Lisp forms and which will be supplied by the user as a list of forms. As usual, the comma–at sign (,@) syntax within a backquote copes with the fact that the body of the function is supplied as a list. It still gets the value of the parameter body, just as the comma alone would have done, but it also does what is conceptually an append, with the result that the body is added into the lambda expression without its outer set of parentheses. (We have told you this before, but it seemed helpful to repeat it.)

Here is a possible call to define-method:

```
(define-method 'spaceship
               'move-to
               '(x y)
               '((<get own current position>)
                 (<use x and y to alter it>)
                 (<erase self from screen>)
                 (<draw self in new position>)))
```

If you compare this with the above backquoted template for a lambda expression, you will see that the lambda expression is first:

```
(lambda...)
```

then, after the cons in define-method has been evaluated, it becomes:

```
(lambda (self x y)...)
```

and finally the ,@ 'appends' to the end of it the list of forms for the body:

```
(lambda (self x y) (<get own current position>)
                   (<use x and y to alter it>)
                   (<erase self from screen>)
                   (<draw self in new position>))
```

The result is a perfectly legal lambda expression, and function. The let of define-method binds this to the variable fun, and then the function can be stored as a method in the hash table of its destined class by store-method.

store-method is directly comparable with store-class, the main difference being that it stores a new method in the corresponding class's functions hash table, rather than storing a new class in the global hash table `*all-classes*`:

```
(defun store-method (method-name class-name fun)
  (setf (gethash method-name
                 (class-functions (get-class class-name)))
        fun))
```

Again we use `get-class` to retrieve the actual class structure from `*all-classes*`, and again `class-functions` is one of the 'free' macros provided for us by `defstruct`. `class-functions` will return the hash table from the class's `functions` slot, and as usual `gethash` and `setf` cooperate to place the method (the value of `fun`) in that hash table, indexed via the method's name, which will be the value of `method-name`.[†] Just as `store-class` was called each time a new class was created, so `store-method` will be called every time a new method is added to any class. Like `store-class`, it also allows for data abstraction.

There is a slight disadvantage to using a hash table to store the methods, and that is that it will not be easy for you to see them once they have been stored. This is a case where the **inspector** comes into its own as an essential tool. Using it, you should be able to inspect `*all-classes*`, and from there to inspect the entry in that hash table which holds your class, and from there to inspect the class's `functions` slot. Once you get used to using the inspector, the extra convenience and speed of hash table operations far outweigh any disadvantages.

We are afraid that once again we do not like the syntax of `define-method`. It would be much nicer if the user could type something like:

```
(defmethod (<method-name> <class-name>) (<params>)
           <forms for body of lambda expression>)
```

which in a particular case might look like this:

```
(defmethod (spaceship move-to) (x y)
                              <get own current position>
                              <use x and y to alter it>
                              <erase self from screen>
                              <draw self in new position>)
```

That would be so much easier for the user to remember: the name of the class listed with the name of the class's new method, and then the

---

[†] We have mentioned several times that we do not intend to cover the subject of compilers in this book. Nonetheless we feel it worth mentioning that if the last line of `store-method` is altered so that the atom `fun` is replaced by the call `(compile nil fun)` then the object-oriented system may, under certain circumstances, run somewhat faster.

parameters and body of the method itself. So let us write the inevitable macro to achieve this change of syntax:

```
(defmacro defmethod ((method-name class-name)
                     (&rest params) . body)
  `(define-method ',class-name
                  ,method-name
                  ',params
                  ',body))
```

This is not as hairy as it looks. You are probably quite happy with the body of the macro definition, specifying a call to define-method and using the quote–comma technique, as in defclass, so that arguments to defmethod do not have to be quoted. The difficulty is the defmacro's lambda list:

```
(defmacro defmethod ((method-name class-name)
                     (&rest params) . body)
  ...)
```

The answer is that in the lambda lists of defmacro, and only in the lambda lists of defmacro, you are allowed to specify the syntax which users of the macro must observe. Remember, an example call to defmethod might look like this:

```
(defmethod (move-to spaceship) (x y)
                               <get own current position>
                               <use x and y to alter it>
                               <erase self from screen>
                               <draw self in new position>)
```

The lambda list of defmacro has the usual opening and closing parenthesis (otherwise it would not be a list!). Within it, the parameters class-name and method-name are put into a sublist. This forces subsequent users of the macro to put their two corresponding arguments into a list, as move-to and spaceship are listed in the example call. Next, there is another sublist, this time containing the &rest keyword. The existence of the sublist means that users have to make a list of the parameters intended for the new method, x and y in the example call. The &rest ensures that users can put as many or as few parameters into that list as they like: &rest will, as always, make a list of them and will bind it to the atom params.

Finally, there is a dot followed by the body of the new method. Remember that define-method expects to be passed the body as a list of forms, and that it carefully removes the parentheses from that list using the comma–at (,@) syntax. So we may as well continue to pass it a list. The dot in defmacro's lambda list makes the series of forms typed in by the

user into a list, in just the same way as &rest does. It would be perfectly
legal to use another &rest here, since the previous one is in a nested list,
but we thought it a good idea to tell you about the alternative.

If you think back to our discussion of cons cells, you may recall
that a cons cell form which translated directly into this:

```
(a . (b c))
```

would be printed by print like this:

```
(a b c)
```

i.e. with the dot and parentheses around b and c removed. Putting a dot
into defmacro's lambda list has the reverse effect: it causes parentheses to
be placed around (that is, a list to be made out of) whatever follows the
dot.

We repeat: this is a part of the power of defmacro and is not a
technique which will work anywhere else in Lisp. In particular, do not try
to use it in the lambda list of defun.

12.2.3   Functional inheritance

Now we turn to two functions which between them will parallel the
actions of remember, but rather than retrieving data from further up in the
hierarchy they will retrieve methods. It is perhaps worth repeating at this
point that it will eventually be possible to create instances of any class,
and that messages will be sent only to the instances, not to the classes. So
the instances are going to need to know how to call these two functions.
The two functions themselves are very simple by the standards of your
present understanding of Lisp, and should relax you again after the
complexities of defmethod. But we should warn you that it is once again
only the lull before the storm: the macro to create instances will be the
most complex and the most concisely elegant piece of Lisp code we have
yet shown you. Quite possibly you will find it the hardest to understand of
all the definitions in this book; so we shall take you through it very
carefully. First, here is find-method:

```
(defun find-method (function class-name)
  (let ((class (get-class class-name)))
    (cond ((gethash function (class-functions class)))
          (t (find-method-in-parents
               function (class-parents class))))))
```

We do not expect you to have any trouble here. If there is such a method
in the functions hash table of the current class, then find-method will

return it. If there is not, it will retrieve the list of the current class's parents (class-parents is defined automatically by defstruct) and call find-methods-in-parents to deal with it. find-method will eventually return either the hoped-for method, or NIL. Here is find-method-in-parents:

```
(defun find-method-in-parents (function parents)
   (if parents
       (cond ((find-method function (car parents)))
             (t (find-method-in-parents
                   function (cdr parents))))))
```

If the current class has no parents, it does not do anything other than return NIL. But if there are one or more parents it works its way through them, one by one, and calls find-method on each one to see whether the required method can be found. If by the end of the list of parents it still has not found the method, it again returns NIL. But, each of those calls to find-method is given a single parent – a class name – to work on, and if it does not find the desired method in that parent's functions slot it will in turn call find-method-in-parents to work on that parent's parents. These two functions are **mutually recursive**, and between them will search through every ancestor of the current class, no matter how far up the hierarchy, and will return the desired method if it exists anywhere.

Just before we plunge into the intricacies of instance creation, we should explain that mysterious extra parameter self which in define-method we deliberately arranged to cons onto the front of any method's lambda list. Look at the example call to defmethod again:

```
(defmethod (spaceship move-to) (x y)
                       <get own current position>
                       <use x and y to alter it>
                       <erase self from screen>
                       <draw self in new position>)
```

and notice that more than once any particular spaceship (any instance of the spaceship class) needs to refer to itself: to find its current position, and to make its screen representation appear to move. When we are eventually (it will not be long now) able to send messages to instances of classes, we shall often need to tell the instance to do something – such as move – to itself. So every method is defined, via define-method, to have the extra parameter self so as to allow for such needs.

During normal use of an object-oriented system you would create any class which you needed and then define its methods. If you glance back at the definition of define-class you will see that in its internal call to make-class there is no provision for putting any methods into the functions slot – the one specified for all of our classes via the original call to defstruct at the time of definition. This means that if for any reason you redefine a class it will no longer know about its methods, and you will have to redefine all of those as well. An exercise at the end of this chapter invites you to make a couple of simple additions to define-class so as to get over this inconvenience.

12.2.4 Creating instances

As we have stressed several times, the classes and their methods form the 'backbone' of the system; in order to use it one first creates the hierarchy of classes together with their individual local methods, and then creates **instances** of each class to which messages can be sent asking them to apply one or other of their inheritable methods either to supplied data or to (possibly inherited) data held in their local-variables slots.

Instances are very different things from classes. Conceptually, an instance is not part of the hierarchy so that its inheritance has to be done for it by its class. We regard an instance as being in intimate contact with its own class but with no other. Conversely, instances can 'talk to' one another by sending messages; classes cannot do this. Another way of looking at it is to think of the hierarchy and the classes as an 'intelligent' database, able to provide methods and data whenever they are needed by instances but unable to do anything else. In this analogy the instances are the 'active' part of the program: everything happens via the instances.

In our program we have made the distinction between classes and instances very clear, by deciding that classes shall be structures defined by defstruct, whilst instances shall be lexical closures.

There will be three functions concerned with the creation of instances. Two will be trivial, the other will not. The hard one will set up a lexical environment within which three lexical closures will be created. Because of their common environment at creation time, all three will 'share' certain 'outside' variables, and we shall make use of that fact. Here is the function which the user will call in order to create a new instance:

```
(defun make-instance (class-name)
  (create-instance class-name
                   (class-local-variables
                     (get-class class-name))))
```

It takes as its single argument the class of which we wish to create a new instance and retrieves its local variables via class-local-variables and get-class. Remember, class-local-variables is an access macro provided automatically by defstruct, and the class's local-variables slot will contain the local variables from all of its ancestor classes. The new instance, too, will contain all of those.

create-instance may look a little startling, but really it is not:

```
(defun create-instance (class-name vars&values)
   (eval '(internal-create-instance ,class-name ,vars&values)))
```

The point is that internal-create-instance will build and return a Lisp
form to be evaluated. As you know, eval recursively calls itself over and
over again even on very simple-looking forms, so the extra explicit call to
it here is not going to cause it any trouble. Eval will simply do what it
usually does, i.e. it will dig out its own functional definition and apply it
to the supplied argument!

There is now only one remaining macro, internal-create-instance,
to complete our object-oriented system, and at first sight it is a killer. But
we think that we can guide you through it without too much trouble.
Before we start, we need to tell you about the functions intern and
gensym, and a little more about format.

To **intern** a symbol means making the symbol 'known' to Lisp, so
that Lisp can find its value or its functional value as required. Normally
you never have to worry about the process: when you type in a symbol or
when a symbol appears in a file which you load into Lisp, interning
happens automatically. However, if a program or function creates a new
symbol while it is running, Lisp has to be told via an explicit call to intern
that this really is to be treated as a symbol. In our function internal-
create-instance we shall want to create message names analogous to the
x, set-x, car-x, cdr-x and set-car-x which you saw in Chapter 11, and we
shall need to intern these. They are to be the names of the closures which
will access and change the various slots of any instance.

For reasons which we do not want to go into here, intern will
accept only a string as its argument (one could be forgiven for expecting it
to require a symbol!). format can be used to generate the necessary string
from objects which start out as symbols:

```
? (format nil "SET-~a" 'cdr-x)

"SET-CDR-X"
```

format's third argument cdr-x is a symbol. format's second argument
splices 'SET-' onto the front of it (notice the upper case: the characters
within the format control string will be taken literally). And the first
argument, which until now we have told you should normally be T, is NIL,
which specifies to format that it shall return a string rather than NIL. This
ability of format to create a string from a symbol is a handy one to
remember, although as mentioned before we do not intend to cover the
full subject of string handling in this book.

gensym does rather the opposite: it creates a new, uninterned
symbol. The uninterned symbol has a name (gensym invents it), and within

a running program that symbol can be used just like any other symbol. The difference is that you cannot successfully type its name in from top level, nor can its name appear explicitly within the code of a program. That may not sound very useful, but it certainly is in circumstances where you do not want users to be able to type a particular variable name into Lisp: in other words when you want to be certain that there could never be any clash between the gensym-generated variable name and any other. Every call to gensym creates a new, unique, uninterned symbol; this can then be held as the value of some normally named variable, for use as and when required in the program or function.

Because the actual name of the symbol is not particularly important (in your program, you would always refer to it via the name of the variable to which it was bound), Lisp gives it an arbitrary name of its own. For example:

```
? (setf anonymous (gensym))

#:G124

? anonymous

#:G124
```

Your own Lisp may provide names for gensym symbols which look different from the one shown here; this will never matter, but we are about to show you some macro-expanded code which will include gensym symbols, and they will be in this 'hash–colon–G' form.

Here is the definition of internal-create-instance, which uses all three of those functions:

```
(defmacro internal-create-instance (class-name vars&values)
  (let ((lambda-parameter (gensym)))
    `(let ,(cons '(var-store (make-hash-table)) vars&values)
       (setf (gethash 'class var-store)
             #'(lambda () ',class-name))
       ,@(mapcar #'(lambda (var&value)
                     `(setf (gethash
                              ',(local-var var&value) var-store)
                            #'(lambda ()
                                ,(local-var var&value))))
                 vars&values)
       ,@(mapcar #'(lambda (var&value)
                     `(setf (gethash
                              (intern
                                (format
                                  nil
                                  "SET-~a"
                                  ',(local-var var&value)))
```

```
                                    var-store)
                    #'(lambda (,lambda-parameter)
                        (setf ,(local-var var&value)
                              ,lambda-parameter))))
                  vars&values)
        #'(lambda (self x &rest args)
            (let ((local-var-function (gethash x var-store)))
              (if local-var-function
                (apply local-var-function args)
                (let ((method
                        (find-method x ',class-name)))
                  (if method
                    (apply method (cons self args))
                    (error "~a undefined method for class ~a"
                            x ',class-name)))))))))))
```

The macro expansion of any call to internal-create-instance is the form
which will be returned to eval in create-instance. It will then, of course,
be evaluated as usual. We need to work through it in detail so that you
can understand what the form will be, and hence what eval will do with it.
It will be useful at this stage to look at the macro expansion of a sample
call, which we shall Lisp to pretty-print:

```
? (pprint (macroexpand
             '(internal-create-instance tony
                                         ((height 6)
                                          (surname 'hasemer)))))
```

This returns

```
(LET ((VAR-STORE (MAKE-HASH-TABLE))
      (HEIGHT 6)
      (SURNAME 'HASEMER))
   (SETF (GETHASH 'CLASS VAR-STORE)
         (FUNCTION (LAMBDA NIL 'TONY)))
   (SETF (GETHASH 'HEIGHT VAR-STORE)
         (FUNCTION (LAMBDA NIL HEIGHT)))
   (SETF (GETHASH 'SURNAME VAR-STORE)
         (FUNCTION (LAMBDA NIL SURNAME)))
   (SETF
     (GETHASH (INTERN (FORMAT NIL "SET-~a" 'HEIGHT))
              VAR-STORE)
     (FUNCTION (LAMBDA (#:G225) (SETF HEIGHT #:G225))))
   (SETF
     (GETHASH (INTERN (FORMAT NIL "SET-~a" 'SURNAME))
              VAR-STORE)
     (FUNCTION (LAMBDA (#:G225) (SETF SURNAME #:G225))))
   (FUNCTION
```

```
(LAMBDA (SELF X &REST ARGS)
        (LET ((LOCAL-VAR-FUNCTION
               (GETHASH X VAR-STORE)))
          (IF LOCAL-VAR-FUNCTION
              (APPLY LOCAL-VAR-FUNCTION ARGS)
              (LET ((METHOD
                     (FIND-METHOD X 'TONY)))
                (IF METHOD
                    (APPLY METHOD
                           (CONS SELF ARGS))
                    (ERROR
                     "~a undefined method for class ~a"
                     X
                     'TONY))))))))
```

and here is what it means, explained stage by stage:

```
(LET ((VAR-STORE (MAKE-HASH-TABLE))
      (HEIGHT 6)
      (SURNAME 'HASEMER))
```

This is the lexical environment which all of the code below here will share. The variable surname gets bound to hasemer, the variable height gets bound to 6, and the variable var-store gets bound to a hash table. The call to make-hash-table with no arguments creates a hash table whose entries can be any Lisp object. Notice that apart from the variable var-store the lexical environment is derived entirely from the sample call; this is important because we certainly do not want internal-create-instance to be limited to creating just one instance of just one class! Throughout the rest of this explanation, please bear in mind that the three items tony, height and surname are only examples, and that had the original call to internal-create-instance been different, they too would have been different.

We put into the hash table three entries, which are actually lambda expression functions and also lexical closures, which will return the values of those lexical variables at any time. Notice that the first of them will return the class of which this is an instance, tony, which is stored as a (quoted) constant, and that the other two return the values of the instance's local variables height and surname:

```
(SETF (GETHASH 'CLASS VAR-STORE)
      (FUNCTION (LAMBDA NIL 'TONY)))
(SETF (GETHASH 'HEIGHT VAR-STORE)
      (FUNCTION (LAMBDA NIL HEIGHT)))
(SETF (GETHASH 'SURNAME VAR-STORE)
      (FUNCTION (LAMBDA NIL SURNAME)))
```

Now we need to add functions (more lexical closures) which can alter, rather than merely return, the data. And we hope that after our descriptions of intern, gensym and format you will not find this confusing:

```
(SETF
 (GETHASH (INTERN (FORMAT NIL "SET-~a" 'HEIGHT))
          VAR-STORE)
 (FUNCTION (LAMBDA (#:G225) (SETF HEIGHT #:G225))))
```

This adds to our hash table a closure which can alter the binding of the lexical variable height. It will access the hash table via the key set-height. Similarly for surname:

```
(SETF
 (GETHASH (INTERN (FORMAT NIL "SET-~a" 'SURNAME))
          VAR-STORE)
 (FUNCTION (LAMBDA (#:G225) (SETF SURNAME #:G225))))
```

We have not provided a parallel method of altering the class name because of course it is the name of something else, i.e. the name of the class of which we are creating an instance.

We have now allowed for all the variables in the original sample call, so next we need to cope with the methods which this instance's class has or can inherit. Please be clear that when internal-create-instance (i.e. this expanded form of it, since it is a macro) is evaluated, all of the above creation of functions and storing of them in var-store are only side-effects: they affect the lexical environment in which the returned value of internal-create-instance — a lexical closure of course — will be created. Instances of classes in our system are closures, whereas the classes themselves are structures.

When the send macro is later used to 'send a message to' this particular instance, it will actually call the lexical closure via funcall, just as you saw funcall being used to call lexical closures in Chapter 11. In short, the main purpose of internal-create-instance is to return a lexical closure; all else is merely to ensure that the closure's lexical environment is correct. To stress the point: this following code returns a lexical closure which can access all of the closures now stored in our hash table; each of those subordinate closures will return or set some piece of data. The closure we are about to create will 'be' the instance:

```
(FUNCTION
 (LAMBDA (SELF X &REST ARGS)
         (LET ((LOCAL-VAR-FUNCTION
                (GETHASH X VAR-STORE)))
              (IF LOCAL-VAR-FUNCTION
                  (APPLY LOCAL-VAR-FUNCTION ARGS)
```

```
(LET ((METHOD
         (FIND-METHOD X 'TONY)))
   (IF METHOD
      (APPLY METHOD
            (CONS SELF ARGS))
      (ERROR
         "~a undefined method for class ~a"
         X
         'TONY)))))))))
```

This is really quite simple. The closure created by the above lambda expression will respond to messages sent to it. The message may be something like surname or set-height and will be bound to the lambda expression's parameter x (our message-sending macro, coming shortly, will see to that). In cases where the message does ask it simply to return or to reset the value of one of its lexical variables, the functions to do so are already in var-store. We have called these little local functions local-var-functions to distinguish them from methods, which latter this instance will need to be able to inherit from its class, and hence of course from the entire hierarchy of classes. So, in cases where the message does not correspond to the name of any local-var-function, the lambda expression simply calls find-method to do the inheritance, and if no method of that name can be found a call to error will halt the program.

The method, if found, may contain code which refers to the current instance – in particular it may want to make use of the local-var-functions. Therefore, as explained before, each method has the additional parameter self, and therefore the lambda expression also needs a parameter of the same name. Again, our message-sending macro will ensure that it acquires the correct value. Here it is:

```
(defmacro -> (inst mess &rest args)
   `(funcall ,inst ,inst ,mess ,@args))
```

It no longer needs assoc, of course, since the closures are no longer stored in an alist; we now store them in a hash table. Within the macro, the parameter inst becomes bound to the name of this particular instance, or more accurately to the name of the variable to which we shall bind this instance when we finally call make-instance. So funcall calls inst, which you now know is a single closure containing a hash table which in turn contains other closures, and gives it the arguments inst (i.e. self), mess and args to work with. You can see that the parameters of the last closure defined above (the one we told you would 'be' the instance) match this set of arguments. The closure will use the value of mess (it might be class, height, surname, set-height or set-surname) to dig the relevant local-var-function out of the hash table and to apply it to the args.

Thus, the message-sending macro calls the last closure in the instance, which in turn uses other closures stored within the same instance (or inherited methods) in order to respond to the message. So as to avoid a possible source of confusion, we should point out that messages can only be responded to by closures created in `internal-create-instance` or by lambda expressions created via `defmethod`. In particular, the accessor functions generated automatically by our original call to `defstruct` cannot be run via messages, but must be called directly (like `class-local-variables` in `get-all-local-vars` or like `class-functions` in `store-method`).

It is interesting to note at this point that the messages are in fact the names of functions: of lexical closures. It is as though we had managed to give symbols such as `set-height` and `surname` functional values. This is another example of Lisp functions being used as data.

All that remains now is to write the macro which creates the above multiple closure (the above instance) and then the object-oriented system will be complete. Here is `internal-create-instance` again:

```
(defmacro internal-create-instance (class-name vars&values)
  (let ((lambda-parameter (gensym)))
    `(let ,(cons '(var-store (make-hash-table)) vars&values)
       (setf (gethash 'class var-store)
             #'(lambda () ',class-name))
       ,@(mapcar #'(lambda (var&value)
                     `(setf (gethash
                             ',(local-var var&value) var-store)
                            #'(lambda ()
                                ,(local-var var&value))))
                 vars&values)
       ,@(mapcar #'(lambda (var&value)
                     `(setf (gethash
                             (intern
                              (format
                               nil
                               "SET-~a"
                               ',(local-var var&value)))
                             var-store)
                            #'(lambda (,lambda-parameter)
                                (setf ,(local-var var&value)
                                      ,lambda-parameter))))
                 vars&values)
       #'(lambda (self x &rest args)
           (let ((local-var-function (gethash x var-store)))
             (if local-var-function
                 (apply local-var-function args)
                 (let ((method
```

```
                    (find-method x ',class-name))')
            (if method
               (apply method (cons self args))
               (error "~a undefined method for class ~a"
                  x ',class-name)))))))))
```

First we have a let which sets up a local variable for internal-create-instance. This variable, lambda-parameter, holds the name of a gensym-created symbol which we shall shortly have need of. Everything else within the function comes within the scope of the backquote and therefore will create the macro-expanded version shown above.

It begins with another let, which when macro expanded will set up the lexical environment for the closures we intend to create. Its list of local variables is created by taking the list vars&values passed down from create-instance and consing onto the front of it a list of the symbol varstore and the function call (make-hash-table). Thus, when this let is eventually evaluated, varstore will be bound to the hash table, as we wish.

Within this second let, and so still part of the macro-expanded form, comes a setf instruction which when evaluated will translate directly to the corresponding line in the macroexpanded version. Then two calls to mapcar. Each of these iterates over the list of vars&values, and produces a setf form for each of them. The first mapcar creates the accessing functions, whose names will simply be the names of the slots; and the second mapcar creates the functions to alter the contents of the slots. Notice the use of lambda-parameter in the call to the second mapcar, where the closure to be created needs a local variable. If we had chosen anything other than a gensym symbol here, it could one day have clashed with a variable name invented by a user of our system. The last form within the let is a lambda expression which again will translate directly into the macro-expanded form, and which will be the instance itself.

The comma–at syntax in front of each of the two calls to mapcar (remember, it will remove the two outer parentheses from the lists returned by the mapcars) ensures that the body of the let is a series of single calls, and each of these will when macro-expanded and then evaluated include or generate a lexical closure.

Finally, it is worth adding at the bottom of the file in which you have defined the above functions the form

```
(initialise-class-system)
```

This will be evaluated each time your file is loaded into Lisp. This initial version of the object-oriented system is now complete. It has just three top level functions, which the user will need in order to create and to manipulate classes and instances: defclass, defmethod, make-instance. It also has the all-important messge-sending (–>) macro. The user will create a hierarchy of classes using `defclass`, giving each one local variables if required and giving each one methods if required via `defmethod`. Then instances will be created for each class using `make-instance`, and via the →macro messages will be sent to them ordering them to do things. Everything else: the inheritance mechanisms for both local variables and methods; the truth about what happens when a message is sent; and in particular the precise form of any class or instance, are hidden from the user. That all takes care of itself automatically, thanks to the hard work which you have just been doing.

SUMMARY

If you have managed to stay with us through all of that, and even if from time to time it has been hard work for you, it is probably time to stop thinking of yourself as a novice Lisp programmer! An understanding of how closures work, and of how object-oriented systems can be built, is well above novice level, and you have every right to be pleased with yourself. Although we hope that you will continue to gain new insights into the use of Lisp from the programs we have yet to show you, it is unlikely that anything else in this book will be as taxing as this chapter has been.

Object-oriented systems are one of the most flexible and powerful techniques for knowledge representation which we know. You have seen in earlier chapters how Lisp's basic representational techniques, everything up to and including (especially) hash tables, are good for storing simple relationships between facts or entities; you have used data structures to encapsulate a number of relational statements concerning a single fact or entity; and you have built a rule-based system which can make inferences from rules about facts or entities. An object-oriented system can do all of those things and more.

The next chapter will show you how to use the object-oriented system to create a simple universe of particles and rockets, so that you can gain a feel for the rather unusual idea of sending messages to 'intelligent' data structures (the instances) which themselves 'know' how to respond. Just before we move on, however, this is a good point to warn you that object-oriented programs are notoriously hard to debug because normal Lisp debugging tools such as the tracer will not work on most of your functions; it will not, for example, work on a method. We have put a few error traps into our object system (look in the code for specific calls to `error`) and no doubt you will be able to see how to add more if you decide that you need them. The following five exercises will give you some useful tools. Please also remember the advice given in Chapter 8 about inserting temporary `print` expressions into the definitions of suspect functions, to show what happens as they are evaluated or indeed if they are evaluated at all.

EXERCISES

Exercise 12.1   It would be nice to give our object-oriented system some standard inbuilt methods, methods to do things which users are likely often to need. We can assign all of these methods to the t class, so that all classes in the hierarchy, and all of their instances, can inherit them. The first of these will be a method to retrieve the immediate parents of any instance's class. Use defmethod to write such a method.

Exercise 12.2   Another thing a user might want to know is the names of all of a class's slots, both its own and those it inherited when it was created. Write a method local-vars to retrieve them.

Exercise 12.3   Write a send-to-self macro to parallel the normal -> macro. Your new macro (<-) will only be used within the definition of a method, and the variable self should be bound to the class to which that method belongs.

Exercise 12.4   Write a method called state which will print on screen the contents of the local-variables slot of any instance's class.

Exercise 12.5   Write a method local-methods to retrieve the local methods of any instance's class (i.e. do not try to inherit any methods).

   Hint: the function class-functions, provided for free by our object system, returns a hash table in which the functions are stored. The function maphash, by analogy with mapcar, applies an auxiliary function (which will be a lambda expression) to each entry in a given hash table. The auxiliary function must take exactly two arguments, the first of which will be bound (by maphash) to the key of any hash table entry, and the second of which will be bound to its value. This is what maphash does, rather than what your lambda expression must do. You should write the latter to take two arguments called function-name and function, but you will not need to use the successive values of function. maphash returns NIL, and not a list of its results as mapcar does. So within the lambda expression you will need a call to setf which will add the successive results to a growing list held on some local variable.

Chapter 13
The Common Lisp Object System

13.1 Objects on an airless
asteroid

13.2 The Common Lisp Object
System

We now show you an example of Chapter 12's object-
oriented system in use. Next, we describe what is at the time
of writing still the proposed object-oriented system to be
included in future releases of Common Lisp. It will be known
as CLOS: the Common Lisp Object System. We show you
how to make two improvements to our own object system so
as to conform more closely with CLOS.

13.1 Objects on an airless asteroid

We are now about to write a program to simulate in a very sketchy way
(you will easily see how to extend it if you want to) the behaviour of some
particles and rockets moving above the surface of an airless asteroid. The
main purposes of this program are to give you an initial feel for object-
oriented programming and to allow you to check that the system you built
in Chapter 12 really does work. Please start a new file to hold the
program, since we do not want its definitions to get mixed up with those
of the object system itself.

Since the hypothetical asteroid is airless, we can forget all about
the effects of wind resistance. But like all asteroids it has gravity, which
pulls directly towards the asteroid's centre from any point on or above its
surface. We measure all distances, speeds and accelerations in terms of
horizontal and vertical components, which greatly simplifies the arithmetic. If you're not familiar with this way of expressing such things as
speed and acceleration, do not worry: the important thing here is that we

can create such objects and can (conceptually at least, since we shall have no on-screen representation) cause them to move about. Whether or not they move correctly is of minor importance at the moment! So gravity is defined like this:

```
(defvar *gravity* '(0 4))
```

which means that gravity does not act at all in the horizontal direction but acts with a force of 4 units in the vertical direction. We also do not care what these units actually mean; merely that we see them change will be enough for us.

We define a class of entities called particles, by defining their class:

```
(defclass particle ()
  ((name nil)
   (mass 1)
   (x-position 0)
   (y-position 0)
   (x-speed 0)
   (y-speed 0)
   (x-acceleration (car *gravity*))
   (y-acceleration (cadr *gravity*))))
```

Each instance of this class will need a slot for its name, and each will have a mass of 1 unit. For each particle, we supply default values for its position, speed and acceleration. Then we define a subclass of entities called rockets, which are just like particles except that they have motors which can force them along (remember, classes immediately 'inherit' the slots and values from all of their ancestors, so that the rocket class will have all of the above plus its motor force):

```
(defclass rocket (particle) ((motor-force '(0 0))))
```

This creates a hierarchical link between the rocket class and its parent, the particle class, and ensures that whilst instances of the particle class can acquire methods and data only from the particle class, instances of rocket can acquire them from both the rocket class and the particle class. Now we need methods to retrieve those values as and when required. These methods operate by sending messages to instances of the particle class, or of its subordinate class rocket. Each one makes use of functions such as x-position and y-speed which are generated automatically by our object-oriented system whenever a new class is defined:

```
(defmethod (position-of particle) ()
  (list (-> self 'x-position)
        (-> self 'y-position)))
```

```
(defmethod (velocity-of particle) ()
  (list (-> self 'x-speed)
        (-> self 'y-speed)))

(defmethod (acceleration-of particle) ()
  (list (-> self 'x-acceleration)
        (-> self 'y-acceleration)))
```

The next job is to write some similar methods to alter the values:

```
(defmethod (set-position particle) (x y)
  (-> self 'set-x-position x)
  (-> self 'set-y-position y))

(defmethod (set-velocity particle) (x y)
  (-> self 'set-x-speed x)
  (-> self 'set-y-speed y))
```

Note that the only acceleration which any instance of particle can have is inherited: gravity is the only force acting on particles. Therefore there is no method to alter the acceleration of particles. Rockets, however, have motors and their accelerations can therefore change. When we send a message to a rocket asking it to change the force of its motor, we shall want that change to be reflected in the rocket's acceleration:

```
(defmethod (set-motor rocket) (force)
  (-> self 'set-motor-force force)
  (-> self 'set-x-acceleration
    (+ (car *gravity*) (car force)))
  (-> self 'set-y-acceleration
    (+ (cadr *gravity*) (cadr force))))
```

In order to make our particles and rockets move, we shall need to be able to send them a message telling them to do so. For the sake of simplicity, any instance which receives such a request will assume that exactly one unit of time has gone by since the last similar request and will calculate its new position or speed on that basis (the assumption allows us simply to add the corresponding speed or acceleration to the instance's previous position or speed):

```
(defmethod (new-position particle) ()
  (-> self 'set-x-position
    (+ (-> self 'x-position) (-> self 'x-speed)))
  (-> self 'set-y-position
    (+ (-> self 'y-position) (-> self 'y-speed))))
```

```
(defmethod (new-velocity particle) ()
  (-> self 'set-x-speed
      (+ (-> self 'x-speed) (-> self 'x-acceleration)))
  (-> self 'set-y-speed
      (+ (-> self 'y-speed) (-> self 'y-acceleration))))
```

To see our particles and rockets in action we create three of each, we set the force of each rocket's motor, and then we cycle endlessly through the list of instances, asking each one to report each time on its 'status'. A particle's status comprises its position, speed, acceleration and (in the case of rockets only) motor force. After the status report on each cycle, we shall move the particles and rockets ready for the next cycle and the next status report.

```
(defun create-universe ()
  (let ((p1 (make-something 'particle '(p1 4 3 2 5)))
        (p2 (make-something 'particle '(p2 0 0 0 1)))
        (p3 (make-something 'particle '(p3 1 1 9 4)))
        (r1 (make-something 'rocket '(r1 2 3 4 3)))
        (r2 (make-something 'rocket '(r2 7 5 2 1)))
        (r3 (make-something 'rocket '(r3 3 4 4 2))))
    (-> r1 'set-motor '(2 1))
    (-> r2 'set-motor '(7 6))
    (-> r3 'set-motor '(2 3))
    (do () (())
      (dolist (obj (list p1 p2 p3 r1 r2 r3))
        (-> obj 'status)
        (-> obj 'new-position)
        (-> obj 'new-velocity)))))
```

Notice the do forever loop produced by having no halting condition in do's second argument. This is a perfectly legal use of do, provided that you include the empty parentheses. In order to halt this program, you will need to do whatever you normally do in your Lisp to halt endless recursion (usually it is control-dot or control-c). If you have not yet managed to find out how to do that, you had better put in a halting condition! This could conveniently be done by changing the do to a dotimes:

```
...(dotimes (n 10)
     (dolist (obj (list p1 p2 p3 r1 r2 r3))
       ...)
```

The three instances of particle and the three instances of rocket are created by make-something. As you can see, it calls make-instance to create a new instance of one or other of the two classes and then initializes its slots according to the arguments supplied by the user:

```
(defun make-something (type particle-info)
  (let ((x (make-instance type)))
    (-> x 'set-pname (pname-part particle-info))
    (-> x 'set-x-position (x-pos particle-info))
    (-> x 'set-y-position (y-pos particle-info))
    (-> x 'set-x-speed (x-speed-part particle-info))
    (-> x 'set-y-speed (y-speed-part particle-info))
    x))
```

No initialization is provided here for the motor force of rockets, so they will inherit the default value from the rocket class. The function uses a handful of macros to improve the appearance of the code. Please remember that these macros should go at the top of your file, or at least earlier in the file than make-something. Otherwise, you will get an 'undefined function' error when you try to run the program. As you can see from the definition of create-universe, particle-info is simply a list of five items; from the definition of make-something you can see that they respectively represent the new particle's name, its x and y positions, and its x and y speeds.

```
(defmacro pname-part (particle-info)
  `(car ,particle-info))

(defmacro x-pos (particle-info)
  `(cadr ,particle-info))

(defmacro y-pos (particle-info)
  `(caddr ,particle-info))

(defmacro x-speed-part (particle-info)
  `(cadddr ,particle-info))

(defmacro y-speed-part (particle-info)
  `(car (cddddr ,particle-info)))
```

Now all we need are the two methods to enable particles and rockets to respond to the 'status' query. Here they are:

```
(defmethod (status particle) ()
  (format t "~%~a's report:~%Position:~{ ~a~} ~
            Velocity:~{ ~a~} Acceleration:~{ ~a~}"
    (-> self 'pname)
    (-> self 'position-of)
    (-> self 'velocity-of)
    (-> self 'acceleration-of)))
```

```
(defmethod (status rocket) ()
  (format t "~%~a's report:~%Position:~{ ~a~} ~
             Velocity:~{ ~a~} Acceleration:~{ ~a~}"
          (-> self 'pname)
          (-> self 'position-of)
          (-> self 'velocity-of)
          (-> self 'acceleration-of))
  (format t " Motor Force:~{ ~a~}"
          (-> self 'motor-force)))
```

The program will now run:

```
? (create-universe)
```

You will get an output something like this (we show only the first three cycles here):

```
P1's report:
Position: 4 3 Velocity: 2 5 Acceleration: 0 4
P2's report:
Position: 0 0 Velocity: 0 1 Acceleration: 0 4
P3's report:
Position: 1 1 Velocity: 9 4 Acceleration: 0 4
R1's report:
Position: 2 3 Velocity: 4 3 Acceleration: 2 5 Motor Force: 2 1
R2's report:
Position: 7 5 Velocity: 2 1 Acceleration: 7 10 Motor Force: 7 6
R3's report:
Position: 3 4 Velocity: 4 2 Acceleration: 2 7 Motor Force: 2 3
P1's report:
Position: 6 8 Velocity: 2 9 Acceleration: 0 4
P2's report:
Position: 0 1 Velocity: 0 5 Acceleration: 0 4
P3's report:
Position: 10 5 Velocity: 9 8 Acceleration: 0 4
R1's report:
Position: 6 6 Velocity: 6 8 Acceleration: 2 5 Motor Force: 2 1
R2's report:
Position: 9 6 Velocity: 9 11 Acceleration: 7 10 Motor Force: 7 6
R3's report:
Position: 7 6 Velocity: 6 9 Acceleration: 2 7 Motor Force: 2 3
P1's report:
Position: 8 17 Velocity: 2 13 Acceleration: 0 4
P2's report:
Position: 0 6 Velocity: 0 9 Acceleration: 0 4
P3's report:
Position: 19 13 Velocity: 9 12 Acceleration: 0 4
```

```
R1's report:
Position: 12 14 Velocity: 8 13 Acceleration: 2 5 Motor Force: 2 1
R2's report:
Position: 18 17 Velocity: 16 21 Acceleration: 7 10 Motor Force: 7 6
R3's report:
Position: 13 15 Velocity: 8 16 Acceleration: 2 7 Motor Force: 2 3
```

Consider particle P2, for example. It initially is at position 0 0, has a speed of 0 1 and an acceleration (due to gravity) of 0 4. In other words it is falling directly towards the surface of the asteroid. Between the first and second cycles both its position and its speed will change (because it is accelerating under the influence of gravity). We consider one cycle to occupy a unit of time, so that for example if a particle is falling at 10 feet per second it will change position by ten feet between cycles. So on the second cycle P2's position becomes 0 1, which is arrived at by adding the separate components of its original position (0 0) and its original speed (0 1). Similarly its new speed becomes 0 5, derived from its original speed and its original acceleration. On the third cycle this new speed is added to its current position, resulting in a new position of 0 6; and the acceleration of gravity (0 4) is again added to its current speed, giving a new speed of 0 9.

The other two particles are not falling straight down, they are falling at angles, Therefore their speeds and positions have x components as well as y components. We invite you to play with this miniature universe, modifying create-universe so that the rockets and particles move differently. For example, an obvious improvement is to say that if any object crashes into the surface of the asteroid, it should cease to move! Say for the sake of example that all of our objects start out being 25 units of distance above the surface of the asteroid, and that the asteroid extends (almost) 25 units of distance in the x direction. Then, if any object's y position becomes greater than 25 while its x position becomes less than 25, it must have hit the asteroid. You could set up a couple of global variables and then modify create-universe to take account of this:

```
(defvar *initial-height* 25)

(defvar *asteroid-width* 25)

(defmethod (crashed? particle) ()
   (and (> (<- 'y-position) *initial-height*)
        (not (< (<- 'x-position) 0))
        (< (<- 'x-position) *asteroid-width*)))

(defun create-universe ()
   (let ((p1 (make-something 'particle '(p1 4 3 2 5)))
         (p2 (make-something 'particle '(p2 0 0 0 1)))
```

```
            (p3 (make-something 'particle '(p3 1 1 9 4)))
            (r1 (make-something 'rocket '(r1 2 3 4 3)))
            (r2 (make-something 'rocket '(r2 7 5 2 1)))
            (r3 (make-something 'rocket '(r3 3 4 4 2))))
        (-> r1 'set-motor '(2 1))
        (-> r2 'set-motor '(7 6))
        (-> r3 'set-motor '(2 3))
        (do () (())
          (dolist (obj (list p1 p2 p3 r1 r2 r3))
            (-> obj 'status)
            (cond ((-> obj 'crashed?)
                   (format t "~%~a has crashed" (-> obj 'pname)))
                  (t (-> obj 'new-position)
                     (-> obj 'new-velocity)))))))
```

If you now run this new version, you will find that P1, P2, R1 and R3 crash into the asteroid and stop, while P3 and R2 slip past into outer space.

EXERCISES

Exercise 13.1   We have already pointed out that if you redefine a class it loses all of its local methods. The current version of define-class does not cater for redefining existing classes. Write a macro defined-class? which takes a single argument, a class name, and checks whether or not that name is present on the list of *all-classes*. Then modify the effect of the :functions keyword in the call to make-class within define-class so that, if the class already exists, its existing methods will be assigned to the new version of it.

Exercise 13.2   The two methods status, one assigned to each of our two classes of objects on an airless asteroid, are identical apart from one extra format statement to allow rockets to report their motor force. It is necessary to assign a status method to both classes because the rocket method 'overwrites' or prevents access to the particle method of the same name. It would be nice if rockets could inherit the status method from the parent particle class, execute it, and then run a simpler version of their own local status method afterwards. By the same token one might equally need local methods which would automatically be run before any inherited method. Here is a new definition of defmethod which will allow users to specify (via the parameter type) that the method being defined shall be an :after method or a :before method:

```
(defmacro defmethod ((method-name class-name &optional type)
                     (&rest params) . body)
  `(define-method ',class-name ',method-name ',params ',body
     ,type))
```

You may remember from Chapter 6 that &optional parameters acquire a default
value of NIL if no argument is supplied to match them. So the value of type when
passed down to define-method will be :after, :before or NIL. Here is a
correspondingly modified version of define-method:

```
(defun define-method (class-name method-name params body type)
  (case type
    ((:after)
     (define-after-method class-name method-name params body))
    ((:before)
     (define-before-method class-name method-name params body))
    (t (let ((fun `(lambda ,(cons 'self params) ,@body)))
         (store-method method-name class-name fun)))))
```

Your task is to write the two subordinate functions define-after-method and define-
before-method.

However, you have not seen case before. It behaves rather like a cond but
allows you to specify multiple tests. Its general syntax is:

```
(case keyform
  (keylist1 action1.1 action1.2...)
  (keylist2 action2.1 action2.1...)
  (keylist3 action3.1 action3.2...)
   ...)
```

case first evaluates ‹keyform›. It then goes through each of its clauses in turn,
checking each time to see whether the value of ‹keyform› is eql to any item in the
‹keylist›. If it is, case then evaluates the corresponding sequence of actions, if any.
If there are such actions, case returns the value returned by the last of them. If
there are no actions specified, or if the value of ‹keyform› is not eql to any item in
any ‹keylist›, it returns NIL. case is often used as we have used it: simply because it
is more elegant than the equivalent cond form.

Rewrite the status method for the rocket class to be an after-method.

Important note
Please add the solutions to these two exercises and the new defmethod to the file
containing your original object system code. Either rewrite the original functions
where appropriate, or add the new definitions at the end of your file. In the latter
case the original definitions will be overwritten by these new ones as the file loads.

Summary so far

The object system which you have built and are just learning to use is
quite sophisticated despite its small size and despite the fact that we
intended it mainly as a means of introducing you to object-oriented
programming. Now that you understand the basic principles of object
systems and of object-oriented programming, we can move on to

introduce you to the Common Lisp Object System (CLOS), and in so doing can add a new facility to our own system: generic functions.

As far as possible the system which you wrote in Chapter 12 conforms to the syntax of the CLOS; but the → macro will not exist in CLOS, and `defclass`, `defmethod` and `make-instance` will be more powerful than the versions shown here.

Recap box Classes are arranged into a hierarchy. Each class has amongst other things a slot for local variables and their values, and a slot for methods. When a new class is created, it immediately inherits all of the local variables from its ancestors in the hierarchy. The methods slot contains a hash table in which the methods for the class (as defined by `defmethod`) are actually stored as lambda expressions. When a new instance of a class is created, it is created as a series of three lexical closures whose lexical environment contains the local variables and values from its class. One of the closures is used to access the value any variable, one is used to set or reset that value, and one is used to retrieve methods from the class, or to inherit them from the class's ancestors. In our implementation, these closures respond to messages in the same way as methods do, and it is convenient to refer to them as methods.

13.2   The Common Lisp Object System

We have several times mentioned the Common Lisp specification, and have said that Guy Steele's *Common Lisp, the Language* includes that specification in full. It does not, however, make any mention of object systems. Most existing Lisps include their own object systems embodying the basic principles. *Flavors* is a very popular one, but many Lisps call their equivalents simply 'The ‹insert name of product› Objects System'. For the same reasons which gave rise to the need for Common Lisp itself (i.e. too many differing versions of essentially the same thing) efforts are now being made to specify a standard object-oriented system for Common Lisp.

At the time of writing (October 1988), the full specification for the proposed CLOS has not yet been agreed, and as yet there are no commercial implementations of it. A partial specification has been released, and it is upon this partial specification that we base everything which we tell you about CLOS. By the time you read this, implementations of Common Lisp which include CLOS should be available. We do know for sure that CLOS will include provision for generic functions, which are a powerful extension to object-oriented systems as you know them. This chapter will teach you about generic functions, and will show you how to write them and how to use them. Throughout, as in Chapter 12, we shall use the agreed CLOS syntax and terminology. A simple modification to our object system will provide basic generic functions so that you can try out the ideas. Chapter 14 will show you how to use generic functions in a more substantial and, from an AI point of view, much more interesting object-oriented program than the above particles and rockets.

13.2.1 Generic functions

In the first part of this chapter we wrote two `status` methods to enable the classes `particle` and `rocket` to print out the contents of their slots. In each case a **message** had to be sent to an **instance** of the corresponding **class** when printing was required. As you now know, the truth behind the convenient terminology of 'messages' being 'sent' was that `funcall` was being called to operate upon a closure (the 'receiving' instance) so as to retrieve from it an internally stored or inherited method, which latter would respond to the message. The function might require additional arguments which would be supplied along with the message.

As you also know by now, when using an object system with which to write object-oriented programs the precise details of how the system is implemented should not be important: it is the high level concepts of classes, instances, methods, inheritance and message passing which influence you in your choices of how to write your programs.

Generic functions abstract these high level notions still further, allowing their users to forget all about message-passing as such and in the process to do without the→ macro altogether. This is achieved in part by a simple change of syntax. Instead of saying something like:

```
(-> <instance> <message>)
```

we recognise that the message is not only the most important part of this macro call but is also a method. A method behaves as though it were a Lisp function, though of course in our object system it is not: it has no functional value which could be retrieved by `eval`, but instead is a lambda expression which we store away and execute via `funcall` when we need it. Nonetheless, it would be nice to be able to place the 'message function' first, as in conventional, non-object-oriented function calls, and to let the `instance` argument indicate which of the available methods (in our example, which of the two `status` methods) should be run:

```
(<message> <instance>)
```

If we could do that, then the syntax of calling a method would be no different from the syntax of calling any ordinary Lisp function. When we say that CLOS supports generic functions we mean that whenever a method, any method, is defined a generic function of the same name is automatically created for us. The generic function allows us to use the above new syntax, and in cases where more methods of the same name are subsequently added, the generic function is intelligent enough to take account of them. In use, the generic function will be able to decide for itself which of those methods to use.

Instead of sending a message to an instance as before, we simply call the generic function. We give it an argument (the instance in the above schematic), and the generic function looks at the class of that argument in order to select the applicable method. We can think of a generic function as being much like a conventional function except that whereas a conventional function has a single, coherent definition, the definition of a generic function (i.e. the methods from which it can select) are scattered about amongst several, perhaps many, separate objects.

In a practical case we would still have to define the two versions of the method, status, just as we did earlier in this chapter, and each of them would still be attached to a particular class. But we can imagine that in so doing we are defining parts of a generic function called status. As we have said, the generic function itself is created automatically, and so is transparent to the user.

You may be wondering what is the purpose of all this. A simple syntactic change does not seem to have achieved much. But in fact it has achieved a great deal already; and there is more to CLOS and generic functions than just this, as you shall see. The big change is not the syntax, but the fact that generic functions really are functions. You may have had trouble in debugging the code in Chapter 12 because the tracer would not work on methods. But it will work on generic functions, making debugging that much easier.

It would also have been impossible to use a method as an auxiliary to a mapping function:

```
? (mapcar #'<method> <list of args>)
```

would certainly generate an error. But generic functions, being ordinary functions which happen to execute methods, can be mapped; they can also be used as arguments to funcall and apply, or indeed anywhere where you might use an auxiliary function, such as following the :test keyword in a call to member.

The rest of this chapter will show you how to incorporate generic functions into your existing object system. It is worth stressing at this point that in the final version of CLOS there will certainly be syntactic differences when you compare its versions of defclass, defmethod and make-instance with the versions shown in Chapter 12. Specifically, the first and last of these will take keyworded arguments, which our versions do not; and `defclass` will be the means whereby slot accessing methods are automatically generated (in our version `defstruct` fulfils this purpose).

13.2.2 Adding generic functions to the object system

As mentioned above, the change is essentially syntactic. We shall simply dispense (as far as a user of the system is concerned) with the → macro and its associated concepts. It will still be necessary, when writing a program, to define all of the methods it needs, and that will be done exactly as before using `defmethod`. What we are about to add to the object system is the ability to choose the correct one out of several identically named methods. We are assuming that you have the original object system code in a file of its own, and the solutions to the exercises from Chapter 12 in another. Please start a new file for the code in this section, so that you will be able to run the original system without generic functions should you wish to.

```
(defun define-method (class-name method-name params body type)
  (case type
    ((:after)
     (define-after-method class-name method-name params body))
    ((:before)
     (define-before-method class-name method-name params body))
    (t (let ((fun '(lambda ,(cons 'self params) ,@body)))
         (store-method method-name class-name fun))))
  (create-generic-function class-name method-name params body))

(defun create-generic-function (class-name method-name params
                                 body)
  (setf (symbol-function method-name)
        '(lambda (self &rest params)
           (apply (find-method ',method-name
                               (-> self 'class))
                  (cons self params)))))
```

`define-method` is the same as it was before except for the added last line which calls `create-generic-function`, so we need describe only the latter.

`symbol-function` retrieves a symbol's functional value, i.e. a lambda expression which is the function whose name is that symbol. By using `setf` in combination with `symbol-function` we can put our own lambda expression there. In fact this mimics the action of `defun`. In this case the symbol is the method name. The lambda expression is created by create-generic-function, and if the generic function being created were status, the lambda expression would be:

```
(LAMBDA (SELF &REST PARAMS)
  (APPLY (FIND-METHOD 'STATUS (-> SELF 'CLASS))
         (CONS SELF PARAMS)))
```

This becomes the functional value of status, so that status can now be called in the same way as any other Lisp function, e.g:

```
(status <instance of particle>)
```

When status is called and evaluated the lambda expression is retrieved by eval in the normal way and applied to its argument, the instance. The parameter self in the lambda expression becomes bound to the instance of particle. The lambda expression first finds the method status, getting it from the instance's class, which of course is particle. As you know, find-method will, by calling find-method-in-parents, search up the hierarchy for the method in cases where inheritance is needed. The lambda expression then applies this method to the instance (in this example there are no params). In this way the lambda expression, i.e. the generic function called status, is able to select the correct method to use, basing its choice upon the particular class of its instance argument.

The fact that we are imitating the action of defun and actually altering the functional value of a symbol means that none of our generic functions can have the same name as an existing function, but since the syntax of calling either kind of function is the same, this restriction is certainly a good thing. If you accidentally try to redefine an existing function, Lisp will warn you if it is an inbuilt system function but will probably not do so (on the assumption that you know what you are doing!) if it is one of your own functions.

In order to see your generic functions work, first load the above two functions into Lisp (you will probably get a warning about having redefined define-method, which is what you hoped would happen!). The effect of that is that the object system is updated to incorporate the new version. So, in order that all of your methods shall acquire their corresponding generic functions, you need to reload the particle program and your file of Chapter 12's exercises. Now do these two things:

```
? (setf p (make-something 'particle '(p 4 3 2 5)))
#<An INTERPRETED-LEXICAL-CLOSURE.>

? (setf r (make-something 'rocket '(r 2 3 4 3)))
#<An INTERPRETED-LEXICAL-CLOSURE.>
```

These mimic by hand a couple of the operations of create-universe. We

need some instances for the generic functions to work upon and, as you
know, all of the entities created by create-universe exist only temporarily,
within a let. Now, calling a generic function, we can say:

```
? (status p)

P's report:
Position: 6 8 Velocity: 2 5 Acceleration: 0 4
NIL
```

As you can see, this does precisely the same thing as sending the
equivalent message to p:

```
? (-> p 'status)

P's report:
Position: 6 8 Velocity: 2 5 Acceleration: 0 4
NIL
```

This message-sending version should still work, by the way. We can also
say:

```
? (status r)

R's report:
Position: 2 3 Velocity: 4 3 Acceleration: 0 4 Motor Force: 0 0
NIL
```

We hope you will agree that being able to call a function status on two
different arguments is cleaner and easier than having to send a message to
each (it also saves us from worrying about the ever-forgettable quote
which precedes any message name in a call to ->). In Exercise 12.4 you
wrote a method called state, which would print out the slots and fillers of
any instance. It can now be called via its generic function (note that state,
as always, finally returns a list of the instance's slot names):

```
? (state p)

NAME: P
MASS: 1
X-POSITION: 4
Y-POSITION: 3
X-SPEED: 2
Y-SPEED: 5
X-ACCELERATION: 0
Y-ACCELERATION: 4
(NAME MASS X-POSITION Y-POSITION X-SPEED Y-SPEED X-ACCELERATION Y-
ACCELERATION)
```

```
? (state r)

NAME: R
MASS: 1
X-POSITION: 2
Y-POSITION: 3
X-SPEED: 4
Y-SPEED: 3
X-ACCELERATION: 0
Y-ACCELERATION: 4
MOTOR-FORCE: (0 0)
(NAME MASS X-POSITION Y-POSITION X-SPEED Y-SPEED X-ACCELERATION Y-
ACCELERATION MOTOR-FORCE)
```

Any other method defined in the exercises or in the particle program can also be called via its generic function. For example, notice that new-position behaves exactly as before:

```
? (position-of p)
(4 3)

? (new-position p)
8

? (position-of p)
(6 8)
```

In every case where you formerly sent a message whose name was a method, you should now be able to call a generic function of the same name (but, see below). Notice that the generic functions themselves (the lambda expressions which are the functional values of the method names) do nothing other than select the appropriate method from the appropriate class. They are part of the user interface of your program, in much the same way as the macros defclass and defmethod. In CLOS the generic functions will be created automatically when new methods are defined, just as they are here, but the syntax of defmethod may change.

Our system is not quite complete. If you experimented beyond what we suggested above, you may have encountered an error such as this:

```
? (-> p 'y-position)
8
```

but:

```
? (y-position p)
> Error: Undefined function: Y-POSITION .
```

The problem here is that y-position accesses one of the slots in an instance, and that all of these accessing functions are not methods defined via defmethod but closures defined via make-instance. We shall have to take special measures to ensure that these, too, have generic functions associated with them. Only then will it be possible completely to free users of the system from the → and ← macros, though as you are about to see we shall still use them in our system's internals.

The changes are very simple, and follow the same principle as before, i.e. to create a generic function, put a suitable lambda expression as its functional value via setf and symbol-value. The slot-accessing functions for any given instance are of course inherited from its class. So a convenient time to create the corresponding generic functions is at the time when a class is created. We shall therefore modify define-class:

```
(defun define-class (class-name parents local-vars)
  (let* ((locals (get-all-local-vars (if parents parents '(t))
                                     local-vars))
         (class
           (make-class
             :name class-name
             :parents (if parents parents '(t))
             :local-variables locals
             :functions (if (defined-class? class-name)
                            (class-functions
                              (get-class class-name))
                            (make-hash-table)))))
    (mapc #'create-local-var-generic-function local-vars)
    (store-class class-name class)))
```

Please note that this is a modification of define-class as given in Exercise 13.1 We hope that by now you have included the definition from Exercise 13.1 in with your object system code. When you come to load the file containing this latest definition you will get a warning from Lisp. That is entirely to be expected.

The only alteration here is on the last line but one, a call to mapc to create a generic function for each of the class's local variables. Here is the auxiliary function for mapc:

```
(defun create-local-var-generic-function (local-var&value)
  (let* ((local-var (local-var local-var&value))
         (set-local-var
           (intern (format nil "SET-~a" local-var))))
    (setf (symbol-function local-var)
          '(lambda (self)
             (-> self ',local-var)))
    (setf (symbol-function set-local-var)
          '(lambda (self value)
             (-> self ',set-local-var value)))))
```

The value of the parameter local-var&value will be either an atom (the name of a variable) or a variable–value pair. In either case the name part is selected by the function local-var and is bound by the let* to a variable, also called local-var. A variable called set-local-var is bound to the combination of the name and the prefix 'SET-'. For example, the value of local-var might be Y-POSITION and the value of set-local-var might be SET-Y-POSITION.

We then employ the now-familiar technique of using setf to assign a lambda expression to each of these values. Y-POSITION and SET-Y-POSITION both become (generic) functions, able to operate upon any instance of this class (that is, the class specified in the call to define-class which in turn called create-local-var-generic-function). The lambda expressions themselves make use of the old message-passing syntax in order to retrieve or to set Y-POSITION. The mapc in define-class ensures that this happens for each of this class's local variables.

The two generic functions thus defined for each slot in a class allow the fillers of that slot to be retrieved and to be set, respectively. But we also expect to be able to ask any instance to tell us its parent class, and formerly we could send it a message asking for that information:

```
? (-> <instance> 'class)
```

Now we want to be able to say:

```
? (class <instance>)
```

The point here is that of course every instance we shall ever create, regardless of what class it belongs to, will have a class slot holding the name of its class. It would be wasteful to use the above means of generating the corresponding generic function, since the function would get redefined (to be exactly what it was before!) every time a new instance of any class was created. So we define a single generic function to handle the class slots of all instances:

```
(defun create-class-generic-function ()
  (setf (symbol-function 'class)
        '(lambda (self)
           (-> self 'class))))
```

You should add a call to create-class-generic-function to the file containing the above generic function extensions to your object system:

```
(create-class-generic-function)
```

If you have not already loaded into Lisp the solutions to Exercises 13.1 and 13.2, please do so. Next, load the file containing the generic function extensions into Lisp as well. Finally you will need to redefine the classes of particle and rocket, and to re-create the instances p and r as above. You should now at last be able to say:

```
? (y-position p)
8
```

and

```
? (class p)
PARTICLE
```

Review

The object system is now complete. It supports generic functions and conforms almost exactly to the syntax of CLOS. Chapter 14 will invite you to use the object system to build a very interesting AI program, one which adds a new dimension to the meaning of the phrase 'intelligent machine': this one actually understand stories written in English.

If by the time you read this your Lisp contains an implementation of CLOS, you will not need our object system. But we do not think that in this chapter and the last we have wasted your time: we still maintain that the best way to learn what a system is capable of is to build the system for yourself. In the process, you will also have learned a good deal more about how Lisp itself can be used. If you do own an implementation of CLOS, you will be in a position to choose whether to write the program described in Chapter 14 using our object system or to write it using CLOS itself. If you prefer the latter, please check for syntactic changes in your software manual. They will be small, if any, but of course they will be crucial!

CLOS will almost certainly not be implemented using closures. We chose to use closures so as to make our book more interesting and more useful to you; closures are a powerful technique but one often ignored in Lisp programming textbooks. CLOS will also not rely upon defstruct to create the underlying structure of all classes. In CLOS, classes will be a distinct Lisp type in their own right, just as the structures created by defstruct, and numbers, and symbols, currently are.

If you have an implementation of CLOS, definition of a class will automatically create generic functions to access the slots of any subsequently created instances of that class, and definition of a method will automatically create a generic function to handle that method and any alternative methods of the same name. Our system, too, gives you that much. Before ending this chapter we must briefly describe what else CLOS is likely to give you.

13.2.3 Multimethods

So, a generic function is a conventional Lisp function which controls the operations of a group of methods, each of which has the same name as the generic function. We have suggested that you could think of a generic function as an ordinary function whose definition happens to be spread about all over the class hierarchy rather than being encapsulated in one 'place', and we have also suggested that generic functions are similar to macros such as defclass in being part of the user interface to your object system. In CLOS, the user will no longer use the 'send' or the 'send-to-self' macros but will call generic functions exclusively – even if that generic function has only a single method tied to it.

That is about as far as we can take you given the current lack of any firm and final decisions about the ultimate shape of CLOS. The current best bet as to how CLOS may differ from the above is that it will support **multimethods**. To explain multimethods, let us suggest that your program (a program written using your object system, rather than the system itself) defines two distinct hierarchies. Of course, both hierarchies would automatically inherit from the t, root, class, but for the purposes of this description they are distinct. Suppose that one hierarchy was the simple one you defined earlier (t, particles and rockets) and the other was an equally simple 'debugging' hierarchy, with methods which could print out debugging information at various levels of detail.

Going back to the two status methods: they printed out information about particles and rockets so as to show where they were, how fast they were moving and so on; it might have been very handy if they could alternatively, for debugging purposes, have printed out the particles or rockets as simple lists of slots and fillers, including information as to their parents and children (if any) in the object hierarchy. In other words, what we would like is to be able to call a generic function, to tell it which instance we want it to work upon, and additionally to be able to modify what 'work upon' actually means, depending upon the needs of our program (or our debugging strategy) at any given moment. We want to be able to say 'run status on this member of this particular hierarchy in its normal way' or 'run status on this instance from this particular hierarchy in the manner of that particular hierarchy'.

So we actually do want our status generic function to print debugging information sometimes, and information about the hypothetical movements of objects over an airless asteroid at other times. In principle (do not worry about the details) it would be possible to call status with arguments which in effect said to it 'print me out a rocket, but instead of describing it as a rocket show me all of its slots and fillers'. Alternatively the arguments might imply 'print me out a rocket, giving just the usual brief report of its position etc.'.

To achieve this, there would need to be two methods in existence, one to print a rocket as a pretended space vehicle, and one to print debugging information about it. These two methods would exist instead of the former status methods, which took a single argument rather than two. CLOS is likely to insist that all methods of the same name take the same number of non-optional arguments. Non-optional arguments will be instances of classes, and optional arguments will be things like the x and y values supplied to set-position.

This, if it comes about as seems likely, will be a radical change. Methods will no longer be associated in the user's mind with particular classes or even with particular (sub)hierarchies. Our example of a method to 'print a rocket in a debugging way' would not intuitively be associated with either of our suggested two hierarchies, at least not to the exclusion of the other. It might sensibly seem to belong to both. Multimethods will impose no limit upon the number of non-optional (method-selecting) arguments to a generic function. There will of course have to be a method to match every combination of arguments which a programmer might decide upon, but the point we are trying to get over is that exactly 'where' those methods are stored will no longer matter from the user's point of view.

At the time of writing, our information is that multimethods will form part of the final specification for CLOS, but not before the middle or end of 1990. You can probably imagine that if multimethods are eventually supported in CLOS, then the result will potentially be a new programming technique which is as different from conventional object-oriented programming as object-oriented programming itself is different from conventional Lisp.

Chapter 14
A CLOS Program which Understands

This final chapter invites you to use our object system with which to simulate a central part of a very famous and stimulating piece of AI research: the conceptual dependency theory of Schank and Riesbeck. We conclude with some advice as to how to set about writing your own object-oriented programs.

14.1   A program which understands

The concept 'understanding' is not easy to define. It is not at all clear what happens when we 'understand' something which we read or hear, although it certainly causes changes in us: having understood, we can answer questions which we could not have answered before, and/or we can carry out goal-directed procedures which we could not have carried out before. The problem is, where has this new knowledge come from? Unless written or spoken text is a magic ritual with knowledge-conferring powers (AI prefers not to think about such possibilities) there must be some mechanism or mechanisms whereby knowledge is encoded into text by the writer/speaker, and then decoded by the reader/hearer.

You and I are using this mechanism right now, and with any luck at all it is actually working for us. As AI researchers we want to wheedle out the process from its results, and if possible to build a computer model of it.

To understand is more than merely knowing the dictionary definitions of all the words used, because on most occasions we are given only the skimpiest of descriptions of some reported event, and from our own world knowledge we seem to fill in default values for the parts which we are not explicitly told. If we tell you that we went to the cinema last night, you instantly assume that we somehow made the journeys from our homes to the movie theatre, that we bought tickets, and that we sat in silence for a couple of hours watching a screen. The sentence:

> We went to the cinema last night

contains very little explicit information, but anyone hearing it assumes an enormous amount and could answer questions about the event ('Did they stand up or sit down during this event?', 'Was the sun shining on them?') with complete confidence. Similarly, if we told you that:

> We watched the Changing of the Guard yesterday

most of your assumptions about what happened would be different.

14.1.1 The meaning of words

Starting at the atomic level, what is the meaning of a single word? The philosopher Ludwig Wittgenstein pointed out that individual words cannot be precisely defined; his famous example was the word 'game'. No matter what definition you dream up for the word, either you or somebody else will be able to think of a game which flouts your description. For example, a game is usually thought of as an adversarial activity between two or more players or teams of players, but there are many games in which the 'opponent' is not a person (computer arcade games, Rubik's Cube) or can be the player him/herself (Chinese checkers, Solitaire). Alternatively a game might be thought of as something done for amusement, but most sports nowadays have professional players, who play at least partly for the fame and the money. It does not even seem to be essential that the players take part in the game: one could fairly describe American football as a game played by financiers using teams of young men.

14.1.2 The meaning of sentences

Perhaps when we say that we understand something we mean that we know a set of propositions about it, or a set of descriptions of it. In other words, perhaps the meaning of a piece of text is to be found at the sentence level rather than at word level. But here again we hit an instant difficulty: there is no known grammar, or set of parsing rules, which can guarantee to make sense of every meaningful sentence and/or not to confuse meaningful sentences with nonsense sentences. The 'grammar' which we are taught in school is a system of categorization: of ascribing labels to words and phrases within a sentence. Researchers in both AI and Psychology have been trying for many years to discover a different kind of 'grammar', one which is in effect a specification for the English language: a description (probably a set of rules) which will show not only how English is generated from ideas, but also how the resulting sentences are translated by their hearers back into the same ideas. All attempts so far have fallen down over sentences such as:

> The old man the boats

> Time flies like an arrow; fruit flies like a banana.

In the first case, an error is caused by assuming that 'man' is a noun rather than a verb; and in the second case it is all too easy to become confused by the two uses of 'flies' and the two uses of 'like'. Conversely, sentences which are syntactically perfect may make no sense at all:

> Green dreams sleep furiously

Thus, meaning is not really to be found at sentence level either. It something more abstracted, something which includes the 'meaning' if any of individual sentences and words, but which is greater than either.

14.1.3   The importance of context

In some circumstances, perhaps in the course of a description of a tribal ceremony in which the ages of the various participating groups were significant, the first of the above sentences would not look at all unusual. In fantasy literature or in certain kinds of comic books the third example might be acceptable. The second example is confusing precisely because the context and the expectations set up by the first half of it, up to the semicolon, directly conflict with the context of the second half. The notion that meaning has to have a context is a very important one. The idea is that as you read a paragraph you build from the individual sentences and phrases a growing 'mental picture' of what the text is talking about. Each succeeding sentence or phrase must confirm, and perhaps amplify, the mental picture, otherwise you become lost and have to try again.

For example, if we say that we went into a restaurant yesterday, you already have quite a number of expectations about what will come next. You assume that we went to the restaurant for a meal, and that after we had sat down a waiter would have come to take our order. Later, the waiter would have returned with our food, and after eating it we would have paid and left. But if our next sentence, after the one about sitting down, told you that one of us was eaten by the cannibals, you would at once object that we were not making sense. It is interesting to note in passing that a large category of jokes achieve their effect by setting up expectations in their hearer's minds and then suddenly showing that one of the characters in the story had a completely different set of expectations:

> I met this person at a dance, the very first night. I said to her 'Do you know, I'm only here for a fortnight?'. And she replied crossly 'All right, I'm dancing as quick as I can'.

14.1.4   Conceptual dependencies

So the working hypothesis for this chapter is that meaning does not exist unless within a particular context. Roger Schank and his colleagues at Yale University have formalized the notion of context in a computer program which can 'understand' stories written in English. They propose the idea of *scripts* which express the expectations set up by certain statements. For example, there could be a 'restaurant' script and/or a 'cinema' script, which consist in essence of a list of events. These are the events which would normally be *expected* to take place during a visit to a restaurant or cinema. A script may be permanently *associated* with items which might appear in the text itself – for example the phrase 'We went into a restaurant' should obviously be associated with a 'restaurant' script – or the program may have to hunt through quite a number of them before finding one which matches. Any script is said to be *active* whilst the program is looking for matches between successive statements in the story and the events listed in the script.

Not all of the events listed in the script will necessarily appear in the story: we do not, every time we say or write 'we went into a restaurant', relentlessly grind through descriptions of the waiter coming and going, the eating of the food and the paying on our way out. We may well mention some of them – perhaps the waiter was unusually helpful or the food unusually delicious – but for the most part we want our audience to make assumptions which are consistent with an ordinary visit to a restaurant, and one definition of a crashing bore could be that s/he is a person who does not cooperate in allowing his/her audience to make such assumptions.

Therefore, so long as there is no mismatch between events as sequentially mentioned in the story and events as listed in the script, the program can assume that it is using the right script. For example, if we say 'We went to the Trocadero last night', you have no way of knowing if the Trocadero is a restaurant, a cinema, a disco hall or a bullfighting ring. As you heard more of our story, you would reject various of the possible scripts because waiters do not appear at bullfights or because at discos one pays on entry rather than on exit. When you have finally selected a single script it will be richer (it will contain more information) than the actual story events against which it matched, and you can use this information in your *understanding* of what we say. Schank's hypothesis is that it is this extra information, which of course is all default information, which allows you to draw inferences from the story and to give answers to questions which were not directly referenced in the story at all.

The *events* listed in the script essentially follow the standard pattern found in so much of knowledge representation: that of a relation between two entities; but in this case the relation expresses some kind of movement, or transfer, or activity rather than a static factual relation as expressed by the isa link in the Collins and Quillian model of Chapter 7. They will thus often include a third, subsidiary entity: that which is moved or transferred or acted upon. Moreover, the events are expressed in a very generalized form, a form intended to match any real-world example of that particular kind of movement, transfer, or activity. For example statements that John sent, or passed, or threw, or hurled something to/at Mary would all match an event which specifies that some person X transferred some physical object Y to some person Z. Schank's full program can also recognize other forms of the same statements, such as that Mary received or was hit by something from John.

Similarly, if the original sentence said that Mary told or taught something to John, this would match against a very similar event in the script, one which expressed a slightly different kind of transfer involving the movement of information rather than of some physical object. Schank maintains that only eleven different kinds of transfer (he calls them **primitive actions**) are required in order to recognize all possible sentences which describe real-world events. If correct, this hypothesis is either very alarming or very exciting depending upon one's point of view, and from time to time it has been hotly disputed. But so far, at the time of writing, no-one has yet managed to prove Schank wrong.

The events in the script are in a form which Schank calls **conceptual dependencies** (CDs). It is convenient to think of them as objects like those defined by defstruct, having named slots which contain fillers (data). Initially the fillers are variables, so that the CD represents the general case as in 'person X transfers object Y to person Z'. During the process of matching this CD against the script (a process quite similar to the techniques we showed you in our discussion of rule interpreters) the variables acquire values which are the corresponding items in the text itself. Thus, if the original text item is 'John gave his ticket to the usher' then x acquires the value john, y acquires the value ticket, and z acquires the value usher. This CD, this event from a script, is thus said to match; the program therefore assumes that its current script, which is the 'cinema' script, is the one it should be using, and moves on to look for matches between later items in the text and later events in the script.

CDs have four slots. First an **actor** slot whose filler is the name of the person who carries out the action. We say 'person' here deliberately because Schank is very clear that an actor must be capable of deciding to act. An actor could also be one of the higher animals, or it could be one of a small class of 'intelligent' computer programs, but to retain the word 'person' serves as a reminder that inanimate objects cannot be actors: a rock, for example, falling down a mountainside cannot be said to be acting. The actor in a sentence is also not necessarily the grammatical subject of the sentence, especially in reflexive sentences such as 'The usher received John's ticket'. However, in 'The usher demanded John's ticket' the usher is clearly the actor.

The second slot in a CD holds the **action**, the main item in any event. As already mentioned, it will be one of a small class of **primitive actions**, and so far we have told you about the primitive which expresses the transfer of a physical object (Schank calls them PTRANS actions) and about the primitive which expresses the transfer of some 'mental' object such as information, and Schank calls these MTRANS actions. A third, which we shall need later, is called ATRANS: a transfer of possession.

The third slot holds the **object** which is acted upon. Again, in Schank's full version of the program this does not also have to be the grammatical object of the sentence.

The fourth and final slot holds a note of the **direction** if any involved in the action. There are actually two items of information held here: a direction **from** and a direction **to**. They will often both be filled: when John threw the ball to Mary his action was to move the ball (a PTRANS action) from himself to Mary. But either or both may be empty: if the sentence is 'Mary took a boat trip up the river' there is no direct way of knowing where she started from or where she ended up.

To sum up, Schank has started from the realization that a story is essentially a description of a series of happenings, and has discovered a way of formalizing and generalizing those happenings into 'scripts' so that they can be detected within any body of text, which incidentally may be a 'story' in the sense of a piece of fiction, an anecdote, or a factual report including those to be found in newspapers. Once a script has been detected (by matching its list of events against statements in the story) those parts of it which did not match become 'default information' about the story, and this default information is the main component of understanding.

Schank's completed program can analyse an English story into a CD representation, can match those CDs against events in order to select an appropriate script, and can use the default information in that script to answer questions about the story. For example, if asked did we sit down when we went into the restaurant, it would answer (by default) 'Probably'.

In our opinion this has to be counted as genuine understanding, in the full sense of the word. Yes, all right, the machine is 'merely' translating one representation of the real world (the story) into another (CDs and scripts), and then translating those back into English language answers to questions about the story. But at the moment we simply do not know enough about the human mind to be able to say that this is or is not analogous to what we ourselves do when, reading or listening to a story, we build a 'mental picture' of people sitting in a restaurant, interacting with the waiter, and so on. We too, if asked whether or not two people who went into a restaurant subsequently sat down, would answer 'Probably'.

Schank's research is fascinating from an AI point of view. The all-important behaviour of SAM, his program, certainly mimics the corresponding behaviour of humans, but the computational methods whereby that behaviour is achieved could (cruelly) be regarded as just one huge heuristic: they just happen to work. No-one can say for sure whether or not we create in our heads anything resembling CDs as we understand a story. There is some empirical evidence from psychology that we do, and some that we do not. Nonetheless, the machine works: it does understand written stories. And for those AI researchers whose ideal is to build an intelligent machine rather than an analogue of a human being, SAM marks a considerable step forward. For the rest of us it poses an insistent question: do we or do we not, as human beings, 'understand' in the way that SAM understands?

The miniature version of SAM which we are about to show you is necessarily very limited compared with Schank's own version. You will have to take it for granted that the real program can handle problems such as the tenses of verbs or the reflexivity of sentences, and can generate textual responses. Nonetheless, it will, we hope, be enough to convince you that the statement 'Machines can understand' is not the complete nonsense which some critics would like it to be.

A CD can be thought of as looking like this:

```
ACTION : ‹ATRANS, PTRANS, etc.›
ACTOR  : ‹name of a person›
OBJECT : ‹the object transferred›
FROM   : ‹source of transfer›
TO     : ‹destination of transfer›
```

(For convenience, we have expressed Schank's fourth direction slot as two separate slots.) The CDs in a script will have variables as the values of each of their five slots; the corresponding CDs in a particular story will have constants – names, places etc. – in the same positions. In the story actors will fulfil **roles**, they will use or act upon **props** and the will do so in **settings**. We shall use this terminology in our program code to describe the items which fill the slots of the story's CDs. Consider the following brief story, based on one of the examples in *Inside Computer Understanding* by Roger Schank and Christopher Riesbeck:

> Jack went to Woolworth's.
> He got a kite.
> He went home.

Now look at these three CDs, which each represent one statement from the story:

ACTION : PTRANS	ACTION : ATRANS	ACTION : PTRANS
ACTOR : Jack	ACTOR : ?	ACTOR : ‹he›
OBJECT : Jack	OBJECT : kite	OBJECT : ‹he›
FROM : ?	FROM : ?	FROM : ?
TO : Woolworths	TO : ‹he›	TO : home
Jack went to Woolworth's	He got a kite.	He went home.

The first CD expresses an event in which Jack acted so as to cause a physical transfer of himself from somewhere unspecified to Woolworth's. The second states that possession of a kite was transferred from somewhere unspecified to somewhere unspecified: although the story contains the referent 'he' we do not yet know that that 'he' is Jack. We also do not know who the actor was in this CD. The third CD expresses another physical transfer, this time of an unknown person from some unspecified place to his home, and again we do not know who the actor was.

You might think that you could fill in the rest of the slots by a bit of informed guessing: if someone says 'Oh, by the way, I went to Woolworth's yesterday' you might well expect that s/he started out from home in order to do so. If the same person continued to anecdote to say 'I got a kite' you would probably assume that s/he bought the kite from Woolworth's while there. And if finally s/he said 'And then I went home' it would be hard to imagine that that journey started from anywhere other than Woolworth's. It is of course possible to think up rational alternatives to any of these assumptions, but they are if you like default values: they are the most likely interpretation of what the story actually does say.

Here is a set of five CDs, with their English equivalents:

ACTION	: PTRANS	ACTION	: PTRANS	ACTION	: ATRANS
ACTOR	: ?shopper	ACTOR	: ?shopper	ACTOR	: ?store
OBJECT	: ?shopper	OBJECT	: ?item	OBJECT	: ?item
FROM	: unknown	FROM	: unknown	FROM	: ?store
TO	: ?store	TO	: ?shopper	TO	: ?shopper

A shopper goes to a store.	The shopper picks something up.	The shopper gains possession of it.

ACTION	: ATRANS	ACTION	: PTRANS
ACTOR	: ?shopper	ACTOR	: ?shopper
OBJECT	: money	OBJECT	: ?shopper
FROM	: ?shopper	FROM	: ?store
TO	: ?store	TO	: ?elsewhere

The shopper gives the store money.	The shopper leaves the store.

This set of five CDs could form a simple script for any shopping trip, to any store, by any person: it encapsulates the essentials of what it means to go shopping. The slot fillers which begin with question marks are variables, and where their names are the same all instances would have to acquire the same value, for example ?shopper must always represent the same person wherever it appears, if the script is to make sense.

Now you can see the cleverness of SAM: if it can recognize that the three-CD story is only an incomplete form of the five-CD 'shopping' script, it can take whatever facts are present in the story and bind them to corresponding variables in the script, and can then propagate those values throughout the rest of the script. In this case, it can take the name Jack from the first CD of the story and bind it to ?shopper, not only in the first CD of the script but throughout the rest of the script as well. It can then answer questions such as 'Did Jack pay for the kite?' or 'Was it Jack who left the store?'. In other words it has understood the story, or if you prefer can behave as though it had understood the story, as well as you or we could.

14.2 The program

Our miniature SAM will carry out this central process of recognition, or matching. We shall build it using our object-oriented system, with its generic function additions. Please notice that the functions defined in Exercises 12.1, 12.2, 12.4 and 12.5 should now be a part of your object system file. Our reasons for using the object-oriented system are in our eyes overwhelming: we want you to see just how powerful this new technique is, and the whole purpose of our book is to teach you techniques. As always, we reprint the program code in an appendix so that you can check for typing errors. If there are no typing errors, your program should run correctly.

In *Inside Computer Understanding* a very similar cut-down version of SAM is described, and is implemented in an older dialect of Lisp called UCI Lisp. However, CDs are obvious targets for implementing as objects in an object-oriented system and so we have chosen that approach. In fact, as you will see, everything in our version is an object, either a class or an instance of a class.

14.2.1 Classes

In our program there will be a class for CDs. There will be another class for all **cd-entities**, by which we mean the fillers of the CD's slots. Then there will be a series of classes for the various types of cd-entities: actions, roles, props, settings and so on. All of these will inherit from the cd-entity class so that we can put any methods which are common to all of them, such as the method for printing themselves on screen, into the cd-entity class – rather than having to write the same method over and over again for each kind of cd-entity. An action class will be further subdivided into classes for ATRANS, PTRANS and MTRANS, simply because the actions are primitive actions and hence are a different kind of thing from the roles, props and settings. Everything else, including the cd-entity class itself, will inherit from the root object, t. Figure 14.1 shows the inheritance paths diagrammatically.

You may feel that this hierarchy could have been arranged differently. For example you might think that scripts and stories are both made up from CDs and that therefore they should both be parents of the CD class. In the same vein you might say that cd-entities occur only within CDs and therefore should inherit from the CD class; and that variables occur only within cd-entities and therefore should inherit from the cd-entities class.

If we were trying to build a Collins and Quillian-like representation of the relationships between various parts of scripts and stories, that would be the correct way to do it. But the hierarchies in object-oriented programming are concerned mainly with functionality, with the aim of designing a hierarchy so that those classes which need a certain method can all inherit it, and so that it is denied to all other classes. If there is no strong reason for any class to inherit from anywhere other than the root of the hierarchy, we let it inherit from there; it helps to prevent bizarre errors arising from classes which can inherit the 'wrong' methods. On the other hand there are occasions when a class seems necessary for purely conceptual reasons, in order to make the program model more closely some hypothesis or idea. Our action class is a case in point.

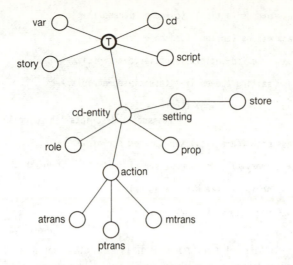

Figure 14.1   Inheritance paths.

One more point before diving into the actual code: we assume that you are not familiar with object-oriented programming style, and so we shall at first try to describe very precisely what happens as generic functions are called, causing them and hence the program to behave as we wish. After a while we shall revert to the looser but far more explicit (not to mention easier to read!) way in which programmers normally talk about object-oriented programs. For example, rather than saying laboriously that the argument to a generic function gets from its class a method which the generic function then runs and that the class inherits this method from some higher class, we shall say simply that a generic function is called, to act upon an instance, and that the instance responds in this or that way.

So here are the definitions of our classes, showing where they each inherit from. Remember, the second argument to defclass specifies the new class's parents. As you look through the following definitions you will notice that the story class has a slot for cds whilst the script class has a slot for events. In fact event is simply the name given to a CD which happens to appear in a script. We shall use the distinction throughout our program in the hope of making it easier to read.

```
(defclass cd () (action actor object from to))

(defclass cd-entity () (cd-name))

(defclass action (cd-entity) ())

(defclass atrans (action) ((cd-name 'atrans)))
```

```
(defclass ptrans (action) ((cd-name 'ptrans)))

(defclass mtrans (action) ((cd-name 'mtrans)))

(defclass role (cd-entity) (associated-scripts))

(defclass setting (cd-entity) (associated-scripts))

(defclass store (setting) ((cd-name 'store)
                           (associated-scripts 'shopping)))

(defclass prop (cd-entity) (associated-scripts))

(defclass story () (cds current-script possible-next-events))

(defclass script () (events variables))

(defclass variable () (cd-name value))
```

There is a subclass of setting which is the class of stores (of course, stories can take place other than in stores). The associated-scripts slot will be explained later. We also provide a function to create new instances of the cd class. This will save a great deal of repetitive typing later on, but otherwise does nothing very special:

```
(defun make-cd (&key action actor object from to)
  (let ((obj (make-instance 'cd)))
    (set-action obj action)
    (set-actor obj actor)
    (set-object obj object)
    (set-from obj from)
    (set-to obj to)
    obj))
```

As you can see, make-cd makes a new instance and sets the values in its five slots to whatever we specify in the arguments to make-cd. But notice that it allows keyworded arguments (the &key in its lambda list tells you so). Besides making typing less tedious these also ensure that calls to make-cd look much neater on the page (see immediately below). The five set- functions are of course generic functions created for us automatically during the definition of the CD class.

14.2.2 Script and story

The most tedious part of writing this program will be the creation of the script and the story as lists of five and three CDs respectively, so let us get them out of the way first. This is what the story will look like:

```
(defvar *kite-story*
  (let ((jack (make-instance 'role))
        (woolworths (make-instance 'store))
        (kite (make-instance 'prop))
        (home (make-instance 'setting))
        (story (make-instance 'story)))
    (set-cd-name jack 'jack)
    (set-cd-name woolworths 'woolworths)
    (set-cd-name kite 'kite)
    (set-cd-name home 'home)
    (set-cds story
             (list (make-cd :action (make-instance 'ptrans)
                            :actor jack
                            :object jack
                            :to woolworths)
                   (make-cd :action (make-instance 'atrans)
                            :object kite
                            :to (make-instance 'role))
                   (make-cd :action (make-instance 'ptrans)
                            :actor (make-instance 'role)
                            :object (make-instance 'role)
                            :to home)))
    story))
```

If you have started a new file for this program, and put the above form into it, the form will be evaluated every time you load the file into Lisp. If at any future point you decide to make changes to the value of *kite-story*, and so need to re-evaluate the form without closing Lisp down and running it up again, please remember that once a value has been assigned by defvar it cannot be changed by defvar. You would have to change defvar temporarily to setf and then to re-evaluate the above form.

A different module in Schank's overall program, called ELI, is able to parse English sentences into CD form. The precise nature of this form does not matter much, of course, so long as it suits the program it is intended to work with! So we assume that ELI has provided us with the list of three CDs, representations of which you can see being created at the end of the above let.

The first part of the let is merely a bit of tactical fiddling around to make sure that the slots of the CDs will contain the fillers we want them to have. As mentioned above we want the slots to contain instances of the various classes of cd-entities, so we take the four constants in the CDs – jack, woolworths, kite and home – and create for each an instance of its class. These instances, of course, have none of their slots filled in, and we give each of them a value for its cd-name slot. set-cd-name is again a generic function created during the definition of the classes, as is set-cds.

You may wonder why we do not do the same thing (create instances within the let) for the primitive actions in the action slots of the

CDs. We could have done, and it would have saved a call to make-instance whilst not affecting the working of the program in any way. Our reason is that although jack, for example, always refers to the same Jack no matter where his name appears, the two instances of PTRANS are conceptually not the same identical PTRANS. It seemed to us that the extra clarity here was worth the extra call to make-instance.

As you can see, there are also three instances of the class role within the CDs. Similarly, the reason for there being three of them rather than just one at the top of the let is that the program does not know, at this stage, whether or not they all represent the same person. In the text of the story three occurrences of the word 'he' correspond to these three slots, and not until the program has understood the story will it be able to say that they all refer to Jack.

If you glance back at the definition of the story class you will see that besides a slot for CDs it has another for current-script and another for possible-next-events. These slots will be filled when the program runs.

Now to the script. We embed it in a function which you should run every time you load the file containing this program:

```
(defun initialise-cd-system ()
  (let ((?shopper (make-instance 'variable))
        (?store (make-instance 'variable))
        (?item (make-instance 'variable))
        (?elsewhere (make-instance 'variable))
        (money (make-instance 'prop))
        (script (make-instance 'script)))
    (set-cd-name ?shopper 'shopper)
    (set-cd-name ?store 'store)
    (set-cd-name ?item 'item)
    (set-cd-name ?elsewhere 'elsewhere)
    (set-cd-name money 'money)
    (store-events-script 'shopping script)
    (set-variables script (list ?shopper
                                ?store ?item ?elsewhere))
    (set-events script
          (list (make-cd :action (make-instance 'ptrans)
                         :actor ?shopper
                         :object ?shopper
                         :to ?store)
                (make-cd :action (make-instance 'ptrans)
                         :actor ?shopper
                         :object ?item
                         :to ?shopper)
                (make-cd :action (make-instance 'atrans)
                         :actor ?store
                         :object ?item
```

```
                        :from ?store
                        :to ?shopper)
          (make-cd :action (make-instance 'atrans)
                        :actor ?shopper
                        :object money
                        :from ?shopper
                        :to ?store)
          (make-cd :action (make-instance 'ptrans)
                        :actor ?shopper
                        :object ?shopper
                        :from ?store
                        :to ?elsewhere)))))
```

This is longer than, but otherwise very similar to, the above code for
kite-story. Once again we create a handful of instances and set their
cd-name slots. Notice that money is a constant, not a variable. We are
assuming that money is an essential part of any shopping activity. Maybe,
in view of the many other ways of paying nowadays, we should have
made this, too, a variable; but it serves to illustrate the point that
constants are permissible in scripts whenever they are appropriate – that
is whenever something absolutely must appear in the story if that story is
to match a particular script.

store-events-script does simply this:

```
(defun store-events-script (script-cd-name script)
   (setf (gethash script-cd-name *scripts*) script))
```

and in your file it should be preceded by a call to defvar so that the hash
table exists:

```
(defvar *scripts* (make-hash-table))
```

store-events-script uses setf and gethash in a manner which you are
familiar with by now to ensure that the script's name can be used as the
key to retrieve the actual script from the hash table *scripts*. As you can
see from the call to it in initialise-cd-system, the name of the script will
be shopping.

   Going back to initialise-cd-system: the script class itself has two
slots: one to hold a list of the variables to be found in the script's CDs,
and one to hold the CDs themselves. Again set-variables and set-events
are generic functions created when the script class was defined. And
again the instances in the action slots of the CDs are created on the fly
because conceptually they all represent different things in different
CDs.

14.2.3 Methods

Once `initialise-cd-system` has been called, the function `demo` will eventually run the completed program :

```
(defun demo ()
  (clear (get-script 'shopping))
  (process *kite-story*))
```

As you might imagine, `get-script` merely retrieves the script from wherever it is stored (data abstraction again):

```
(defun get-script (x) (gethash x *scripts*))
```

so that `clear` can remove from it any temporary data left over from any previous run of the overall program. In the case of the script this data will be values assigned to the variables in its CDs. `clear` is a generic function automatically created when the corresponding method is defined. Here is the `clear` method:

```
(defmethod (clear script) ()
  (dolist (variable (variables self))
    (clear-value variable)))
```

If you glance back at the definition of the `script` class you will see that it has two slots, one for `events` and one for `variables`. All instances of that class, including the script which we are talking about here, will possess slots with the same names. The generic function `clear`, called from within `demo`, can run the `clear` method on any instance of the class `script`. The `clear` method retrieves the contents of the `variables` slot from the script by calling the generic function `variables` and asking it to work on `self`. If you remember, within any method the variable `self` is bound to the current instance: in this case the particular script whose variables we need. The function `variables` will have been generated automatically during definition of the `script` class.

Via a `dolist` the above method calls `clear` again to clear each variable (to set its value to `NIL`). But, being a generic function, `clear` can tell from its argument that this time it should be clearing variables rather than a script, and will run the correct method. As you might expect, that method for the `variable` class is very simple:

```
(defmethod (clear-value variable) ()
  (set-value self nil))
```

`set-value` is yet another generic function created during definition of the `variable` class. All of the variables in the script are thus initialized to have

no value. Once this has been achieved, the final instruction in demo calls
the generic function process to work upon the story. Here follows the
method, attached as you can see to the story class, which process runs
when called:

```
(defmethod (process story) ()
  (clear self)
  (dolist (cd (cds self))
    (show-self cd "~2%Input is")
    (process cd self))
  (show-self (get-script (current-script self))
             "~%Story done -- script is"))
```

This immediately call clear again, this time to work upon the story rather
than upon a script or a variable. So we are going to need a third method
for the generic function clear. Although we are still explaining the nitty-
gritty details to you, we hope you can already begin to appreciate how
generic functions can simplify things. Looking at any call to clear above,
you know for sure that it will do the right thing provided that you have
written the corresponding methods and given it the right argument. In
other words, once the methods have been written you can use clear
whenever you need it without worrying about the details of what it does,
even though clearing a variable is conceptually a very different procedure
from clearing a story or a script. By the way, the 2% in the format control
string outputs two carriage returns rather than one. Its purpose is merely
to improve the appearance of the eventual printed output.

     The story, as you can see from the definition of its class, has two
slots: current-script and possible-next-events. We shall explain the
purpose of these shortly; for the moment here is the clear method for the
story class:

```
(defmethod (clear story) ()
  (set-current-script self nil)
  (set-possible-next-events self nil))
```

This method will throw away anything remaining in the current-script
and/or possible-next-events slots of the story, which are again temporary
data (if any) left over from a previous run of the program. Now back to
processing the story.

     After clearing the story, the method goes on to iterate through the
list of CDs which constitute the story. It too uses dolist, and retrieves for
it a list of the CDs by calling the generic function cds. (From now on we
shall stop reminding you of how or when particular generic funtions were
created.)

     In the body of the dolist there are two calls to generic functions.
The call to show-self prints on screen a short messge followed by the

contents of the CD itself, and the call to process will process the CD in the context of the story. We shall decide, when defining the method for show-self, exactly how a CD shall be represented on screen, and we shall also have to write a second method to process a CD.

Finally, show-self is called again to work on the script. Once again, we shall need to define a method for this purpose.

We would like now to drop the nitty-gritty detailed explanations, and instead to say things like 'such-and-such a function is called to work upon such-and-such an instance'. Now that you have seen the underlying mechanisms which enable classes, hierarchies, and instances to be created, and now that you know how inheritance works and how generic functions work, it would we feel be tedious both for you and for us to continue in such detail. If we give a method to go with a particular function, you will know that it is a generic function; otherwise not. Object-oriented programming is as much a concept as it is a technique: a high level way (analogous to the truth) of describing the operation of a program, a way which is enormously helpful in terms of its simplicity and power.

From now on we shall describe our program as one object-oriented programmer would describe it to another. If this makes you nervous, if you fear that in the process you may lose sight of the knowledge you laboriously gained in Chapter 12, do not worry: once you have become familiar with the way in which object-oriented programmers talk about their programs, you will find that their terminology can easily be related back to the detailed truth. Alternatively you may come to feel that a knowledge of exactly how an object-oriented system is built is rarely helpful in everyday use of the system, even though at the time it may have taught you a good deal about Lisp. If you do come to that conclusion, good for you: the whole point of object-oriented programming is that it raises the programmer's perception of what is going on above the nuts-and-bolts level of Lisp itself. The virtual machine created by the functions in Chapter 12 behaves quite differently from normal Lisp, and allows us programmers to visualize a programming environment full of intelligent entities (the instances) which we can operate upon, or which can operate upon each other, via concomitantly intelligent functions: the generic functions.

Getting back to our program, we need to define a show-self method and a process method for the cd class, and a show-self method for the script class. Ignore the show-self methods for the moment: their sole purpose is to allow you to see the program working, and we shall define them once the program is otherwise complete. The process function has an argument, self. Please do not read this as an instruction to the CD to process itself, period. It is an instruction to process itself using the added data self, which at this point is the story.

Here is the process method for cds:

```
(defmethod (process cd) (story)
  (or (find-cd-in-script self story)
      (suggest-new-script self story)
      (show-self self "~2%not adding to any script")))
```

It takes any CD (i.e. any of the CDs constituting the story) and does to it
one of three things (notice the call to or). find-cd-in-script will try to find
a match between this story-CD and one of the CDs in the script. If that
attempt fails, process will try to find an alternative script. Our program
has only one script, so this would also fail, in which case process prints a
suitable message. find-cd-in-script looks like this:

```
(defmethod (find-cd-in-script cd) (story)
  (do* ((events (possible-next-events story) (cdr events))
        (event (car events) (car events)))
       ((or (null event) (match self event))
        (cond (event
                (show-self event "~2%matches")
                (reset-script-info story event)
                ;;make sure returns a non-nil value
                event)))))
```

Remember that story here is just an argument, an instance whose name
we want to keep around so that we can derive information from it. What
the method does is to try to match the current CD (from the story)
against an event from the script, initially by iterating over the whole list
of script events. But once a script event has matched against a story CD,
we do not want to try that event again, no matter how many more CDs
the story may contain. We want to test subsequent CDs from the story
against the remainder of the list of script events. Therefore we have to
keep a record of which script events remain unmatched. We could have
kept it on a property list, or in a hash table, or (yuk) in a global variable,
or in several other places. We have chosen to keep it in one of the slots of
the story instance.

   As the comment in the above code indicates, it is necessary that
find-cd-in-script should return a non-nil value (because of the or in
process). It is convenient to return the matching event, though process
makes no use of this returned value other than as a logical T for its or.

   At the start of a run of the overall program, the first time this
process method is called, the possible-next-events slot of the story will be
empty. Therefore, as you can see from the do*'s halting clause, the loop
will exit immediately and return NIL. (We assume that when iteration
reaches a null event it will also have reached the end of the list of events.

You could use (null events) rather than (null event) if you think it clearer.) This means that the first clause of the or in process will fail, so that suggest-new-script is called next:

```
(defmethod (suggest-new-script cd) (story)
  (let ((new-script (find-script self)))
    (cond (new-script
           (format t "~2%new-script ~a" new-script)
           (set-current-script story new-script)
           (set-possible-next-events story
             (events-script new-script))
           (find-cd-in-script self story)))))
```

Assuming that the call to find-script works, so that there is a new-script, this method first prints a comment to that effect and then resets two slots in the current story. One, current-script, is filled with the name of the new script (now to be the current script) and the other, possible-next-events, is filled with all of the events from that new script. Here is events-script, whose purpose again is data abstraction:

```
(defun events-script (x)
  (events (gethash x *scripts*)))
```

find-cd-in-script is then called again. If you glance back at the definition of find-cd-in-script, you will see that the same thing would happen if at some point there were still events remaining in a particular script, but none of them could match against the current story CD, i.e. if a script had partially matched with the story but then had failed. Before going back to how find-cd-in-script works under all other circumstances, we shall show you find-script:

```
(defmethod (find-script cd) ()
  (do* ((script-triggers (script-triggers self)
                         (cdr script-triggers))
        (new-script nil))
       ((or (null script-triggers) new-script)
        new-script)
    (setf new-script (try self (car script-triggers)))))
```

When describing Schank's research, above, we said that certain items in a story could trigger the program into choosing a certain script. For example if the story explicitly says that somebody went into a restaurant, then the restaurant script would obviously be an appropriate one to try! find-script is the method which achieves that. We assume that those items in a story which might suggest a certain script will be roles, props or settings. If you look back at the definitions of those classes you will see that each of them has an `associated-script` slot. If you look also at the definition of `store`, which is a subclass of `settings`, you will see that it actually has an associated script, the `shopping` script.

The first thing `find-script` does is to retrieve and to iterate through a list of `script-triggers`. The list is merely a list of the names of the CD slots in which an item with an associated script might appear:

```
(defmethod (script-triggers cd) ()
  '(actor object from to))
```

(One last time: definition of this method creates the generic function of the same name which the `do*` in `find-script` actually calls.) Notice that the list of slot names does not include `actions`; we assume that none of these will ever have a script associated with it because they are all primitive actions rather than real-world actions such as 'bathe'. We hope you realize by now that the list is provided by a separate method only for the sake of data abstraction: we represent it as a simple Lisp list, but it could be represented differently. As `find-script` iterates through the list, it tries each one on the current CD. `try` is again separated out from `find-script` for the sake of data abstraction, and it simply asks the CD whether its `actor` slot, for example, has an `associated-script`:

```
(defmethod (try cd) (cd-slot)
  (if (funcall cd-slot self)
    (associated-scripts (funcall cd-slot self))))
```

The `if` test is necessary because we are dealing here with CDs from the story, which of course may have arbitrary slots missing. If there is an associated script (given our story, there will be when the slot name is `store`) it is returned to `find-script` and hence to `suggest-new-script`. For convenience, here is the latter's definition again:

```
(defmethod (suggest-new-script cd) (story)
  (let ((new-script (find-script self)))
    (cond (new-script
            (format t "~2&new-script ~a" new-script)
            (set-current-script story new-script)
            (set-possible-next-events story
              (events-script new-script))
            (find-cd-in-script self story)))))
```

If a new script has been found `suggest-new-script` prints a message to that effect, tells the story what the name of the new script is, and copies the full list of events from the new script into the story's `possible-next-events` slot. It finally tells the current CD – which, since `find-cd-in-script` did nothing the first time around, is still the first CD of the kite-story – to run find-cd-in-script again:

```
(defmethod (find-cd-in-script cd) (story)
  (do* ((events (possible-next-events story) (cdr events))
        (event (car events) (car events)))
       ((or (null event) (match self event))
        (cond (event
                (show-self event "~2%matches")
                (reset-script-info story event)
                ;;make sure returns a non-nil value
                event)))))
```

This time the method has a whole scriptful of events to iterate through. Its halting clause is where the actual work is done, as it tries to match each event against the current CD. Iteration thus continues until a matching event (if any) is found. The cond checks that the loop has halted because an event has matched rather than because the list of events is exhausted. It then calls show-self on the matching event, and calls reset-script-info on the story. Remember, the story's possible-next-events slot holds a list of the as-yet untried events from the story, and reset-script-info updates this list in the light of the fact that one event has just matched:

```
(defmethod (reset-script-info story) (position)
  (set-possible-next-events
    self
    (cdr (member position
                 (possible-next-events self) :test #'eq))))
```

The last thing which find-cd-in-script does is of course to return a value. If no script event has matched it will return NIL, but if a match has occurred we shall want it to return T, or at least to return something non-NIL. The problem is that reset-script-info will return NIL when the list of possible-next-events is empty. We could have made reset-script-info return T when that was the case, but we chose instead to make find-cd-in-script always return the event. It amounts to the same thing.

Summary so far

So far, the program is able to take the first CD from the story and to try to match it against the first CD of a script. Since at first there is no script, this first attempt will always fail. The failure itself is the signal that a new script should be found, which in our mini version means looking for a script associated with one of the slot names in the story CD (in Schank's full program this process is of course far more sophisticated). Once a script has been found, the program can start again, trying to match the first CD from the story against the first CD from the script. If no match occurs, it goes on to try the second CD in the script on the assumption that even if the script it is using is the correct one the story may simply happen to lack any statement which would correspond to the first event in the script.

If none of the events in the script matched the first CD of the story, the script would be rejected and (via a mechanism which our program does not emulate) a new one would be chosen. However, if one of the events does match the first CD of the story, no attempt is made to match that CD again with any later event in the script; instead, a record is kept of how far into the script the match occurred (possible-next-events in our program) and efforts to match the second story CD against the script continue from that point (via the method process story). Thus, every CD in the story will eventually match against its 'proper' event in the script – if it is the correct script. It is important, from the point of view of this program's being a model of Schank's theory, to realize that failure of one CD to match one event does not imply that the story has failed to match the script. Only if a CD fails to match any event can the program assume that it has hold of the wrong script.

There remain the matching process itself to describe to you, and the show-self methods which we have mentioned but not defined.

14.2.4 The matcher

The matcher operates similarly to the matcher we described to you in our discussion of rule interpreters: it calls a succession of nested methods to deal with progressively more nested forms in its two inputs, until it is dealing with single atoms or variables. However, it comprises only four methods, and is not anything like as complex as the matcher in Chapter 12. Its job is to match a CD from the story against an event (also a CD, of course) from the script.

So we start with two CDs to match, and therefore the method to match them is assigned to the cd class:

```
(defmethod (match cd) (event)
  (do ((cd-slots (cd-slots self) (cdr cd-slots))
       (matched-cd-slot t))
      ((or (null cd-slots)
           (not matched-cd-slot)) matched-cd-slot)
    (setf matched-cd-slot (match-cd-slot self (car cd-slots)
                                         event))))
```

This method matches a CD from the story against event, a CD from the script. First we retrieve the list of slot-names from the CD. cd-slots calls local-vars, a method which you defined in Exercise 12.2:

```
(defmethod (cd-slots cd) ()
  (<- 'local-vars))
```

Provided that you have reloaded the solution to that exercise since adding generic functions to your object system, local-vars should now be a generic function, so that the method can be redefined as:

```
(defmethod (cd-slots cd) ()
  (local-vars self))
```

Via a do loop, these slot names (action, actor, object etc.) will be passed one by one to match-cd-slot so that their fillers can be matched against the corresponding slot fillers in the event.

The logic of the next bit is tortuous. So long as match-cd-slot continues to return T (signalling a successful match between a CD slot and the corresponding event slot) we want iteration to continue. So we initialize a local variable, matched-cd-slot, to T and setf it on each iteration to the result returned by match-cd-slot. If its value is still T when the list of slots is exhausted, we know that the whole CD has matched and we can return the value of matched-cd-slot.

If at any point an attempted match fails, match-cd-slot will return NIL, matched-cd-slot will also acquire the value NIL, and via the (not matched-cd-slot) form in its halting clause the loop will be stopped. (Remember, or waits for any one of its arguments to return T on any cycle.) Again, the value of matched-cd-slot is the value which we want match-cd-slot to return. Here is match-cd-slot:

```
(defmethod (match-cd-slot cd) (cd-slot event)
  (if (and (funcall cd-slot event) (funcall cd-slot self))
      (check-equal (funcall cd-slot event)
                   (funcall cd-slot self))
      t))
```

It first checks that both the CD and the event do have fillers for this slot name. The argument cd-slot will at this stage be bound to something like action or from. If there is a filler in each, match-cd-slot calls check-equal to work upon them.

There are in fact two methods called check-equal, one assigned to the cd-entity (slot) class and one to the variable class. Here are those two methods:

```
(defmethod (check-equal cd-entity) (story-object)
  (if (cd-name story-object)
      (eq (cd-name self) (cd-name story-object))
      t))
```

This says that to check whether two fillers are equal we need only to check whether their names (as distinct from the names of their slots) are the same. The method for variables is slightly more compilcated, since it needs to bind any unbound variables found in the script, and the filler from the script may be a variable:

```
(defmethod (check-equal variable) (story-object)
  (if (bound? self)
    (check-equal (value self) story-object)
    (set-value self story-object)))
```

If the filler is a variable we need first to check whether or not it is already bound. For example, if we are part-way through matching the kite story against the shopping script, then the variable ?shopper will have long since been assigned jack as its value. Here's the method bound?:

```
(defmethod (bound? variable) ()
  (value self))
```

This just checks to see whether a variable has a value. (Incidentally, yes we agree that 'bound?' is not a very appropriate name since nothing resembling binding of Lisp variables is going on. Feel free to change it if you like.)

If the current variable is again (for example) ?shopper we shall need to check that that the corresponding story object is also jack. But in both cases jack is not the atom JACK but an instance whose name slot contains jack. In other words, the value of a variable is a filler as is the story object against which we are trying to match it, and being both fillers they are both cd-entities. So when the check-equal is called to check the variable's value it immediately calls check-equal cd-entity again, and this as before simply checks that the names of the two are the same. If they are, the method returns T, else NIL. But if the variable is not 'bound' at all then variable check-equal assigns it the story-object as its value.

14.2.5 Seeing the program at work

And that, essentially, is that. The program can now match the CDs from a story against the event CDs in a script, notwithstanding the fact that some of the events in the script may not be mentioned in the story. What we need now is some way of seeing that the program is working. In other words we want the program to generate some printed statements as it goes along so that we can see on screen what it is doing. It would be nice if a generic function show-self could be called with an argument to specify any one of the major entites in our program so as to print out information about them as the program progressed; in particular we would like to see the final form of the script, with all of its variables assigned values drawn from the story. So let us say that we want to supply a show-self method for the script class, for the cd class, for the cd-entity class and for the variable class.

That should cover everything. We have decided (in hindsight, actually, after the main program was written) that it would be nice if the show-self generic function (and hence its methods) could also allow us to specify a pre-string and a post-string: things to be printed before or after than main printed (on-screen) message. It may have occurred to you that this is really no more than a sophisticated version of the debugging advice given in Chapter 8, where we suggested that you insert calls to print into your functions so as to see them in action and hence to track down any bugs.

Here is the show-self method for scripts:

```
(defmethod (show-self script) (&optional pre-string post-string)
  (if pre-string
    (format t pre-string))
  (dolist (event (events self))
    (show-self event "~%"))
  (if post-string
    (format t post-string)))
```

Essentially, this asks each of its own events to print themselves and allows for something else to be printed beforehand, and something else again to be printed afterwards. Within the dolist, each event (look at the definition of initialise-cd-system) is a CD. So this method repeatedly calls the corresponding show-self method for the cd class:

```
(defmethod (show-self cd) (&optional pre-string post-string)
  (if pre-string
    (format t pre-string))
  (dolist (cd-slot (cd-slots self))
    (if (funcall cd-slot self)
      (show-self (funcall cd-slot self)
                 (format nil "~%~a " cd-slot))))
  (if post-string
    (format t post-string)))
```

This is very similar to the above method for the script class. Within the dolist, cd-slots is called upon this CD to retrieve the names of its slots. The names of the slots in any CD will, of course always be the same: action, actor, object, from and to. What is more, the dolist goes on to check via an if form that there actually is a slot filler.

Assuming that there is a slot filler, `show-self` is called to work on it, and since a filler is a cd-entity the generic function calls the `show-self` method for the cd-entity class, and passes it a pre-string which prints the slot's name. The pre-string is itself created by `format`.

Here is the `show-self` method for the cd-entity class:

```
(defmethod (show-self cd-entity) (&optional pre-string
                                            post-string)
 (if pre-string
   (format t pre-string))
 (princ (cd-name self))
 (if post-string
   (format t post-string)))
```

`cd-name` called with the argument `self` returns the name of the slot filler. The effect of the pre-string (supplied by the call within the `show-self` cd method) and then the `if` form together is to print first the name of the slot, and then its filler. For example, the slot name might be to and it might contain an instance whose name was `woolworths`. The use of `princ` ensures that the two are printed on the same line.

We agree that this seems a complicated way of printing two words, but if you care to glance back at the definition of `initialise-cd-system` or of `*kite-story*` you will agree that printing two words from the middle of such complex forms is not a simple task.

The technique of inserting `print` statements into programs is an excellent way of finding bugs, especially when as in this case you are building a system on top of Lisp and therefore are somewhat isolated from Lisp's own error handling and error messages. We suggest that as a temporary measure, and purely in order to help yourself to get the above program running, you define the following:

```
(defvar *cd-trace* nil)

(defun cd-trace (&rest args)
  (if *cd-trace*
    (apply #'format (cons t args))))

(defun cd-trace-on ()
  (setf *cd-trace* t))

(defun cd-trace-off ()
  (setf *cd-trace* nil))
```

As you can see, this sets up a global variable called `*cd-trace*` whose logical value (T or NIL) you can control at will. The effect is that you can trace any method by putting into it a call to `cd-trace`. During the next run of your program, and if the value of `*cd-trace*` is T, `cd-trace` will apply

format to whatever control string you supply. Here is an example of a
check-equal method modified to make use of this:

```
(defmethod (check-equal cd-entity) (story-object)
  (cd-trace "~% Story object is: ~a Script object is ~a"
            (cd-name story-object) (cd-name self))
  (if (cd-name story-object)
    (eq (cd-name self) (cd-name story-object))
    t))
```

When this is executed with *cd-trace* set to T, it will provide human-
readable information as to what the arguments to check-equal actually
were.

14.2.6 Running the program

Now, if you have typed the program into Lisp and have corrected any
bugs, you can run it. You should get a printout like this:

```
? (demo)

Input is
ACTION PTRANS
ACTOR JACK
OBJECT JACK
TO WOOLWORTHS
new-script SHOPPING
```

(The first story CD having failed to match, a new script is found
associated with the store class.)

```
matches
ACTION PTRANS
ACTOR SHOPPER JACK
OBJECT SHOPPER JACK
TO STORE WOOLWORTHS
```

(Now the first story CD matches with the first script event.)

```
Input is
ACTION ATRANS
OBJECT KITE
TO NIL

matches
ACTION ATRANS
ACTOR STORE WOOLWORTHS
```

```
OBJECT ITEM KITE
FROM STORE WOOLWORTHS
TO SHOPPER JACK
```

The transfer of possession of some prop (the kite) to Jack matches. The
second event of the script, in which he picked up the kite, is assumed to
have matched even though it was absent from the story.)

```
Input is
ACTION PTRANS
ACTOR NIL
OBJECT NIL
TO HOME

matches
ACTION PTRANS
ACTOR SHOPPER JACK
OBJECT SHOPPER JACK
FROM STORE WOOLWORTHS
TO ELSEWHERE HOME
```

Here the last line of the story, in which Jack leaves the store, matches the
last event in the script. The fourth event of the script, in which Jack paid
for the kite, is again assumed to have matched even though no equivalent
statement appeared in the story. Thus all of the story's sequential three
CDs have matched against successive events in the script, even though
two of the latter's five events did not match with anything.

The program can now print out the final version of the script, with
all of its variables replaced by values drawn from the story. You can see
that the result is a richer (more detailed) version of the story which could
be used to answer questions such as 'Did Jack pay for the kite?'.

```
Story done -- script is

ACTION PTRANS
ACTOR SHOPPER JACK
OBJECT SHOPPER JACK
TO STORE WOOLWORTHS

ACTION PTRANS
ACTOR SHOPPER JACK
OBJECT ITEM KITE
TO SHOPPER JACK

ACTION ATRANS
ACTOR STORE WOOLWORTHS
OBJECT ITEM KITE
FROM STORE WOOLWORTHS
TO SHOPPER JACK
```

```
ACTION ATRANS
ACTOR SHOPPER JACK
OBJECT MONEY
FROM SHOPPER JACK
TO STORE WOOLWORTHS

ACTION PTRANS
ACTOR SHOPPER JACK
OBJECT SHOPPER JACK
FROM STORE WOOLWORTHS
TO ELSEWHERE HOME
NIL
?
```

14.3   How to write programs in an object-oriented system – an example

Conventional object-oriented systems require their users to regard the programming environment as a space which they can populate with objects (by this we mean instances of classes) which cooperate by sending messages to one another and which respond to messages from the user. This is quite an unusual concept, and at first it can be quite hard to think automatically in an object-oriented way. The addition to the object system of generic functions can help to make object-oriented programming seem more 'normal'. Here are some notes which we hope will help you should you decide to write an object-oriented program of your own.

The first job when writing any object-oriented program is to make sure that its hierarchy of classes and the methods assigned to those classes reflect the knowledge which you are trying to represent. We have gone to some lengths throughout this book to emphasize the virtues of clarity and of fidelity of your program code to the ideas which it represents. In this chapter you have seen a whole class of objects with three subclasses (the actions) created merely because it was conceptually correct given that we were modelling a particular theory in which such distinctions are made. Sometimes other programmers may see such things in your programs and object to them on the grounds that they are inefficient: they unnecessarily waste memory and central processor time. Those programmers are right; our argument is that in AI we do not much care whether our program takes a few hours to run, provided that it does what we want it to do. Issues of efficiency, such as whether or not to replace small functions with macros, are well worth thinking about after you have made all the decisions which make your program a good AI program (i.e. a program in which the techniques you use contribute to the program's value as an example of how to do intelligent things). But in AI programming it is a mistake to exalt efficiency or conciseness above everything else.

As an extreme example of what we would not like to do, it would be possible to write an object-oriented program in which all classes inherited only from the root. No class would then be able to make use of any methods other than its own and those it could inherit from the root itself. Such an inflexible system would probably be better written in plain Lisp, without using objects at all.

By contrast, think back to our multiple show-self methods, our multiple clear methods and our multiple process methods. They allow us to do things which are conceptually the same, though implementationally they may be very different, to any instance of a set of perhaps quite dissimilar classes. This facility to 'do what I mean' marks an important distinction between object-oriented programming using generic functions and conventional programming. The latter will only 'do what I say', which requires us to say exactly what we mean in order to get the desired results. In object-oriented programming the fact that the effective definition of a (generic) function is decided by inspection of its recipient allows us to say what we mean in more general, more abstracted, terms and still to get the desired result.

Of course this is not haphazard: it is up to the programmer to ensure that the generic functions are backed up by a suitably shaped inheritance hierarchy and suitably defined methods. If there is no rationale behind either of these then you might as well be writing a conventional program.

As a general rule of thumb, tall hierarchies tend to be better than broad ones. The taller the hierarchy, the greater the range of methods which a class towards the bottom of the hierarchy can inherit. To the extent that functionality equals flexibility, we hope that you will think it almost a truism when we say that the more functionality you can pack into your classes the more powerful your program will be. An example of this again concerns our actions class. Ideally, we should have had just two subclasses of cd-entities: actions and non-actions. We could then have specified the associated-scripts slot to be a part of the non-actions class, rather than putting it separately into each of the role, prop and setting classes. Via data inheritance, each instance of each of the role, prop and setting classes would then have had an associated-script slot, and retrieving or altering the value in that slot would have been a simple matter of calling a generic function to that effect.

To clarify some of these points, let us imagine that we want to create within an object-oriented system a representation of Lisp itself. Our first thought might be that obviously we are going to need a class of Lisp forms, and that each one will need a slot into which to put its actual code:

```
(defclass lisp-form () (exp))
```

This is a terrible beginning. It makes no distinction at all between the many kinds of Lisp forms, and implies that function calls, the names of arrays, lists, lexical closures etc. are all the same kind of thing. Of course they are not, and even the relatively type-free Lisp cannot be so clumsily expressed. Let us try again. This time we shall have a separate class for each (inbuilt) function call, and a slot in each to contain the corresponding code:

```
(defclass cons () (exp))

(defclass list () (exp))

(defclass append () (exp))

(defclass reverse () (exp))

(defclass + () (exp))
```

That is a rather extreme attempt at improvement. There are some 775 Lisp functions to be defined as separate classes, and even when that has been done the idea of types is still missing altogether: everything inherits from the root. The hierarchy is all breadth and no depth, which in this example means that it cannot represent things such as generic sequence functions or functions which (like mapcar) use auxiliary functions.

All right, let us have a class called function as our main class, inheriting directly from the root. Let us have several subclasses of function and let us group our functions into those classes in tens, or alphabetically, or somehow. OK, we are probably labouring the point a bit, because you can certainly see that if functions are to be grouped at all they should be grouped so that there is some area of commonality amongst the members of any group: in other words, to specify a class of functions implies that the funtions are closely related, such as are the generic sequence functions, the mapping functions, or the various versions of set.

Our own (tentative – we are sure that you will be able to pick holes in it) version of what a hierarchy to represent Lisp should look like has the class of Lisp forms at the top, with two subclasses: atomic forms and list forms. The class of atomic forms would have two children: numeric forms, and symbolic forms – the latter with a slot for a particular symbol's (an instance's) value. The class of list forms would again have two subclasses: simple data lists and functional lists. And you can probably imagine that the class of functional list forms would again be subdivided into classes for ordinary function definitions, macros, special forms, lambda lists and lexical closures (see Figure 14.2).

Thus you can build up a hierarchical network (it is often called a **lattice**) which expresses the real relationships between the real-world entities which your program is intended to represent. Do not be afraid to

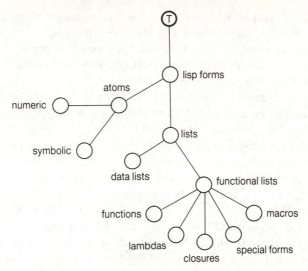

Figure 14.2   A hierarchy of Lisp functions.

take time over these preliminary decisions before you start to write the code for your program. What you will be doing is saving yourself endless hassles later on: as we have implied so often, a bad representation of the knowledge which your program needs can only lead to a clumsy and inept program.

Once you have decided upon a hierarchy of classes which clearly represents the structure of the knowledge which you want your program to have, it is time to worry about the methods. An obvious example is that every class in our representation of Lisp will need to know how to evaluate itself. In many cases this will involve no more than a direct call to eval, but you now know that at the very least macros and special forms will need their own special verisons of eval. So the general principle is: put a method as high up in the hierarchy as you reasonably can, given the needs of those classes which will inherit it. When you need to write specific methods, as you would for macros and as we did for our show-self methods, think as you write them only of the specific needs of that particular class. Remember that no other class on the same horizontal 'level' of the hierarchy will be able to inherit them, and that if you have constructed your hierarchy sensibly your new method will only be inheritable by classes (and hence instances) which can make good use of it.

Finally, as in all Lisp programs, you should aim for both procedural abstraction and data abstraction. We have already explained that if you find yourself repeatedly writing the same or a very similar piece of code, then you should write a function or a macro to do whatever that code does, and should call the function or macro throughout your program in place of the original and repetitive piece of code. Functional abstraction means making your functions as general as possible, and in an object-oriented program that means pushing your methods as high up the hierarchy as they will reasonably go.

Data abstraction is a somewhat different idea, and means divorcing your program as far as possible from the really trivial details about how its knowledge is represented. In AI terms, so long as the right relationship is expressed between two entities, we do not much care how the entities themselves are represented, be it anything from simple symbols to complex lexical closures. Making your program independent of such things, even if that involves incorporating a number of extra and strictly unnecessary extra functions, is well worthwhile. In essence, both functional and procedural abstraction are good programming practice because they both make things easier for someone else: if your program is worth writing at all then it is worth taking some trouble so that others can understand it and duplicate it – perhaps in some other programming language.

Conclusion

We hope that you are duly impressed by object-oriented programming! In one sense the above printout from the story-recognizing program is an almost magical thing, showing that the machine can behave as we behave when we 'understand' a story or newspaper report. That is, it can derive from the story or report a richer knowledge of the reported events than is actually supplied. In our opinion that is a pretty smart thing to be able to do. From an opposing point of view what the program does is utterly trivial: it matches a few small things, makes a few default assumptions (which were given to it by the programmer in the first place) and cannot help but come out with whatever results it does come out with.

And that, in essence, is the core of the big argument within and about AI. When we cause a machine to do intelligent things, is it really behaving 'intelligently' or is it blindly following our instructions? No-one really knows the answer, and some critics quite plausibly argue either that there is no answer or that it is a meaningless question. Perhaps AI can at least provide some techniques for investigating the matter, and perhaps it can arrive at a more satisfying conclusion than either of those.

Lisp, and in particular Common Lisp, is a fascinating and delightful language: a pleasure to use. We hope that in the course of reading this book you have acquired the programming skills needed to appreciate those pleasures. In our introductions to the majority of our chapters we have tried to put what you were about to learn into its proper AI–cognitive science context, so that you could see why you should need to know such things; and in the final part of the book we have tried to excite you with the power of Lisp programming techniques as potential solutions to the problems raised by the goal of an artificial mind.

We feel sure that you will at least agree with us that Lisp is a powerful programming tool which in essence is quite simple to comprehend, and if we have achieved that much we shall be happy. Our aim has been to start you off, to be pump primers for your subsequent work in our field. We hope that other people's more advanced books, other people's reports on their research, and your own investigations will lead you on from here.

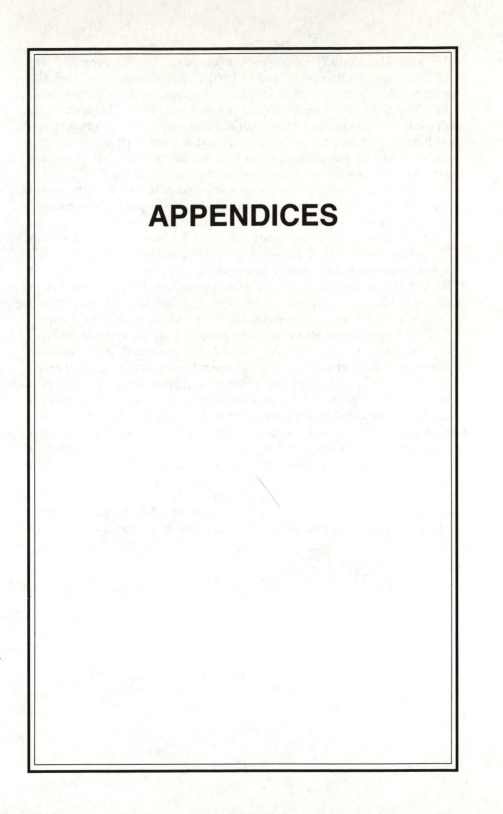

APPENDICES

The appendices which follow repeat the code of the programs and exercises from Chapters 9 and 10 (the three stages of the rule interpreter), Chapters 12 and 13 (the two stages of the object system), and Chapter 14 (the conceptual dependency program). The code in the appendices is guaranteed to have worked correctly on our computers, and has been transcribed directly from there to the printed page. Our hope is that therefore its indentation, its spelling and parentheses will be correct, and that there are no omissions nor extraneous additions.

We have of course done our utmost to ensure that there are no errors in the main text either, but unfortunately the publishing process is inevitably prone to small errors, and as you will discover as you work through this book even one small error can be fatal in a Lisp program. The purpose of the appendices is to give you a second check on the code shown in our main text should you suspect that there is a mistake in it. We feel that by and large you can trust the code in the main text, but we offer you this backup just in case. We shall be very unlucky if both versions of some particular function have the same mistake in them!

The appendices also carry comments within the code so that you can see how a Lisp program should be presented as a finished, professional piece of work. There are several cases where the functions in the appendices are in a different order from that in which they appear in the text; this is because the main constraint on ordering in the text was to maintain a coherent flow of description, whereas in a file of code it is often easier to keep cooperating functions close together (to make them easier for others to find); and the positioning of macros is important in itself. In the appendices, we have also capitalized the names of Lisp functions and constants, but have left the names of user-defined items in lower case. This is a matter of professional style only, and will not affect the running of the programs in any way. So do not feel obliged to copy us if to do so is tedious (we, naturally, were able to get the machine to do it!).

Appendix A
Code for the Simple Rule Interpreter of Chapter 9

```
;;;This file contains the definitive code for the simplest rule
;;;interpreter using only constants (chapter 9)

;;;Common Lisp functions used in this file are:

;;;(+ append car cdr cond defmacro defun defvar do* eq equal
;;;format get if lambda list mapcar member not null or
;;;position setf subseq)

(DEFVAR *working-memory* nil "This holds the working memory.")

(DEFVAR *rules* nil "Holds the ruleset to be interpreted.")

;;;Parsing Rules

;;;antecedent-part-of returns the antecedent of a user defined rule
(DEFMACRO antecedent-part-of (rule)
  '(SUBSEQ ,rule 1 (POSITION '==> ,rule :test #'EQ)))

;;;name-part-of returns the name of a user defined rule
(DEFMACRO name-part-of (rule)
  '(CAR ,rule))

;;;consequent-part-of returns the consequent of a user defined rule
(DEFMACRO consequent-part-of (rule)
  '(SUBSEQ rule (+ 1 (POSITION '==> ,rule :test #'EQ))))

;;;Accessing rule structures

;;;returns the antecedent of a rule as stored internally
;;;note this differs from antecedent-part-of: antecedent-part-of is
;;;used to parse the rule as typed in by the user.
(DEFMACRO antecedent (rule)
  '(GET ,rule 'antecedent))

;;;returns the consequent of a rule as stored internally
(DEFMACRO consequent (rule)
  '(GET ,rule 'consequent))
```

```lisp
;;;returns a rule if it matches against current working memory
(DEFMACRO recognise-rule (rule)
  '(IF (match-antecedent (antecedent ,rule)) ,rule))

;;;checks if halt has been signalled
;;;note that because the element we are looking for
(DEFMACRO halt-signalled ()
  '(MEMBER '(%%halt%%) *working-memory* :test #'EQUAL))

;;;Tests whether the goal has been achieved
(DEFMACRO goal-achieved (goal)
  '(MEMBER, goal *working-memory* :test #'EQUAL))

;;;Finds a rule in the ruleset to fire
(DEFUN find-rule-to-fire (ruleset)
  (COND ((NUL ruleset) nil)
        ((recognise-rule (CAR ruleset)))
        (T (find-rule-to-fire (CDR ruleset)))))

;;;the toplevel function to call in order to run the production
;;;system. Ruleset is the name of a ruleset; working memory is a
;;;list of working memory elements; goal is the working memory
;;;element that we are looking for at the end of the production
;;;system run: the conclusion if you like.
(DEFUN ps (ruleset working-memory goal)
  (SETF *working-memory* working-memory)
  (SETF ruleset (GET *rules* ruleset))
  (production-system ruleset goal))

;;;the workhorse. The main control function
(DEFUN production-system (ruleset goal)
  ;;Increment the cycle number
  (DO* ((cycle-number 0 (+ 1 cycle-number))
        ;;fire a rule
        (fired-rule (fire-rule (find-rule-to-fire ruleset)
                               cycle-number)
                    (fire-rule (find-rule-to-fire ruleset)
                               cycle-number))
        ;;has the goal been achieved?
        (goal-achieved? (goal-achieved goal) (goal-achieved goal))
        ;;has halt been signalled?
        (halt-signalled? (halt-signalled) (halt-signalled)))
       ((OR halt-signalled? goal-achieved? (NOT fired-rule))
        (FORMAT T "~&Rule Interpreter Halted")
        (COND (halt-signalled? (FORMAT T "~&Halt Signalled"))
              (goal-achieved? (FORMAT T "~&Goal ~a Achieved" goal))
              ((NOT fired-rule) (FORMAT T "~&No Rules Fired")))
        (FORMAT T "~&Final contents of working memory:~{~&~a~}"
                *working-memory*))))

;;;Fires a rule. This function adds the consequent of the rule to
;;;working memory
```

```
(DEFUN fire-rule (rule cycle-number)
  (COND (rule
         (SETF *working-memory*
               (APPEND (consequent rule)
                       *working-memory*))
         (FORMAT T "~&Cycle: ~a Rule: ~a fired~{ ~a~} put in working ~
                 memory."
                 cycle-number rule (consequent rule)) rule)))

;;;the Matcher

;;;Matches an antecedent against working memory
(DEFUN match-antecedent (antecedent)
  ;;if the antecedent is nil then there is nothing left to match
  (COND ((NULL antecedent) T)
        ;;if we can match the CAR of the antecedent against working
        ;;memory
        ((match-conjunct-with-working-memory
          (CAR antecedent))
         ;;then match the CDR of the antecedent against working
         ;;memory
         (match-antecedent (CDR antecedent)))))

;;;Matches a conjunct against working memory
(DEFUN match-conjunct-with-working-memory (conjunct)
  (match* conjunct *working-memory*))

;;;Returns t if pattern matches against one of the patterns in
;;;patterns
(DEFUN match* (pattern patterns)
  ;;if there are no more patterns left we have failed to match
  (COND ((NULL patterns) nil)
        ;;if we match the pattern against the CAR of the patterns
        ;;then we return the match
        ((match (CAR patterns) pattern))
        ;;try and match the pattern against one of the cdr of
        ;;patterns
        (T (match* pattern (CDR patterns)))))

;;;Matches one pattern against another
(DEFUN match (pattern1 pattern2)
  (EQUAL pattern1 pattern2))

;;;Functions to set up a ruleset

;;;Sets up a set of rules given a ruleset name and a LIST of rules
(DEFUN set-up-rules (ruleset-name rules)
  (store-ruleset
   (MAPCAR #'(LAMBDA (rule)
               (store-rule (antecedent-part-of rule)
                           (consequent-part-of rule)
                           (name-part-of rule)))
```

```
            rules)
      ruleset-name))

;;;Stores a set of rules under the ruleset name
(DEFUN store-ruleset (ruleset ruleset-name)
  (SETF (GET *rules* ruleset-name ruleset)))

;;;Stores a rule
(DEFUN store-rule (antecedent consequent rule-name)
  (SETF (GET rule-name 'consequent) consequent
        (GET rule-name 'antecedent) antecedent)
  rule-name)

;;;set of demo rules
(set-up-rules 'first
              '((ruleF  (red light) (president awake)
                        (chiefs summoned) (hotline used)
                        (worldwide red alert) (button pushed)
                        ==> (%%halt%%))
                (ruleE  (red light) (president awake)
                        (chiefs summoned) (hotline used)
                        (worldwide red alert) ==> (button pushed))
                (ruleD  (red light) (president awake)
                        (chiefs summoned) (hotline used) ==>
                        (worldwide red alert))
                (ruleC  (red light) (president awake)
                        (chiefs summoned)
                        ==> (hotline used))
                (ruleB  (red light) (president awake)
                        ==> (chiefs summoned))
                (ruleA  (red light) ==> (president awake))))

;;;Use the form below to run the demo
;;;(ps first '((red light)) '(green light))
```

Appendix B
Code for the Rule Interpreter without Conflict Resolution of Chapter 10

```
;;;This file contains code for the second rule interpreter (first part of
;;;chapter 10). This system uses variables but has no conflict resolution.

;;;the common lisp functions used in this file are:

;;;(+ and append assoc atom cadr cr cdr char= cond
;;;cons consp defun defmacro defvar do* elt eq
;;;equal format get if lambda let list mapcar
;;;member not null or position princ-to-string
;;;setf subseq)

(DEFVAR *working-memory* nil "This holds the working memory.")

(DEFVAR *rules* nil "Holds the ruleset to be interpreted.")

;;;;Parsing rules

;;;antecedent-part-of returns the antecedent of a user defined rule
(DEFMACRO antecedent-part-of (rule)
  '(SUBSEQ ,rule 1 (POSITION '==> ,rule :test #'EQ)))

;;;name-part-of returns the name of a user defined rule
(DEFMACRO name-part-of (rule)
  '(CAR ,rule))

;;;consequent-part-of returns the consequent of a user defined rule
(DEFMACRO consequent-part-of (rule)
  '(SUBSEQ ,rule (+ 1 (POSITION '==> ,rule :test #'EQ))))

;;;;Accessing and storing rule structures

;;;returns the antecedent of a rule as stored internally
;;;note this differs from antecedent-part-of: antecedent-part-of is
;;;used to parse the rule as typed in by the user.
(DEFMACRO antecedent (rule)
  '(GET ,rule 'antecedent))

;;;returns the consequent of a rule as stored internally
(DEFMACRO consequent (rule)
  '(GET ,rule 'consequent))
```

```
;;;returns the variable bindings for the rule match which we call
;;;the environment
(DEFMACRO environment (rule)
  '(GET ,rule 'environment))

;;;stores the environment
(DEFMACRO note-environment (rule environment)
  '(SETF (GET ,rule 'environment) ,environment))

;;;returns the matching environment if a rule matches against
;;;the current working memory
(DEFMACRO recognise-rule (rule)
  '(match-antecedent (antecedent ,rule) nil))

;;;checks if halt has been signalled; note that because the element
;;;we are looking for is a list we must use an equal test.
(DEFMACRO halt-signalled ()
  '(MEMBER '(%%halt%%) *working-memory* :test #'EQUAL))

;;;Tests whether the goal has been achieved
(DEFMACRO goal-achieved (goal)
  '(MEMBER ,goal *working-memory* :test #'EQUAL))

;;;the toplevel function to call in order to run the production
;;;system. Ruleset is the name of a ruleset; working memory is a
;;;LIST of working memory elements; goal is the working memory
;;;element that we are looking for at the end of the production
;;;system run: the conclusion if you like.
(DEFUN ps (ruleset working-memory goal)
  (SETF *working-memory* working-memory)
  (SETF ruleset (GET *rules* ruleset))
  (production-system ruleset goal))

;;;the workhorse. The main control function
(DEFUN production-system (ruleset goal)
  ;;increment the cycle
  (DO* ((cycle-number 0 (+ 1 cycle-number))
        ;;fire a rule
        (fired-rule (fire-rule (find-rule-to-fire ruleset)
                               cycle-number)
                    (fire-rule (find-rule-to-fire ruleset)
                               cycle-number)
        ;;has halt been signalled?
        (halt-signalled? (halt-signalled) (halt-signalled))
        ;;has the goal been achieved?
        (goal-achieved? (goal-achieved goal) (goal-achieved goal)))
       ((OR halt-signalled? goal-achieved? (NOT fired-rule))
        (FORMAT T "~&Rule Interpreter Halted")
        (COND (halt-signalled? (FORMAT T "~&Halt Signalled"))
              (goal-achieved?
               (FORMAT T "~&Goal ~a Achieved" goal))
```

```
                   ((NOT fired-rule)
                    (FORMAT T "~&No Rules Fired")))
             (FORMAT T "~&Here are the contents of working memory~{~&~a~}"
                     *working-memory*))))
```

```
;;;returns t if the environment is the fail environment indicating
;;;that the rule failed to match against current working memory.
;;;Note this cannot be nil as a rule could match against working
;;;memory without any variables being bound in which case the
;;;binding environment would be nil.
(DEFMACRO fail (environment)
  `(EQ ,environment 'fail))
```

```
;;;Finds a rule in the ruleset to fire;
;;;if one of the rules matches against working memory, the
;;;matching environment is stored and the rule returned
(DEFUN find-rule-to-fire (ruleset)
  (IF ruleset
     (LET ((environment (recognise-rule (CAR ruleset))))
        (COND ((NOT (fail environment))
               (note-environment (CAR ruleset) environment)
               (CAR ruleset))
              (T (find-rule-to-fire (CDR ruleset)))))))
```

```
;;;Fires a rule. This function adds the consequent of the rule to
;;;working memory. The consequent is first instantiated
;;;(the variables are replaced with their bindings).
(DEFUN fire-rule (rule cycle-number)
  (LET ((instantiated-consequent
          (instantiate (consequent rule) (environment rule))))
     (COND (rule
             (SETF *working-memory*
                   (APPEND instantiated-consequent
                           *working-memory*))
             (FORMAT T "~&Cycle: ~a Rule: ~a fired~{ ~a~} put in working ~
                        memory"
                     cycle-number
                     rule
                     instantiated-consequent)
             rule))))
```

```
;;;Instantiates a rule in the environment. The environment holds
;;;the bindings of variables. Instantiation involves replacing
;;;variables with their bindings
(DEFUN instantiate (rule-consequent environment)
  (COND ((NULL rule-consequent) nil)
        ((ATOM rule-consequent)
         (value-of rule-consequent environment))
        (T (CONS (instantiate (CAR rule-consequent)
                              environment)
```

```
                          (instantiate (CDR rule-consequent)
                                       environment)))))

;;;the Matcher

;;;Adds the variable's binding (pattern) to the environment
(DEFMACRO bind (variable pattern environment)
  '(CONS (LIST, variable ,pattern) ,environment))

;;;Is non-nil if the variable is bound in the environment
(DEFMACRO bound (variable environment)
  '(ASSOC ,variable ,environment))

;;;given a binding (a variable and its value) returns the value
(DEFMACRO binding-of (binding)
  '(CADR ,binding))

;;;returns t if x is a rule-interpreter variable
;;;ie its first character is '?'
(DEFMACRO variable-p (x)
  '(CHAR= (ELT (PRINC-TO-STRING ,x) 0) #\?))

;;;returns the value of an item in the environment env.
;;;if item is a bound variable the binding is returned
(DEFUN value-of (item env)
  (LET ((binding (AND (variable-p item)
                      (bound item env))))
    (COND (binding (binding-of binding))
          (T item))))

;;;Matches an antecedent against working memory
(DEFUN match-antecedent (antecedent environment)
  (COND ((OR (NULL antecedent) (fail environment))
          environment)
        (T (match-antecedent
             (CDR antecedent)
             (match-conjunct-with-working-memory
              (CAR antecedent) environment)))))

;;;Matches a conjunct against working memory
(DEFUN match-conjunct-with-working-memory (conjunct environment)
  (match-with-one-of conjunct *working-memory* environment))

;;;Returns t if pattern matches against one of the
;;;patterns
(DEFUN match-with-one-of (pattern patterns environment)
  (match* pattern patterns environment 'fail))

;;;Tries to match pattern in patterns
(DEFUN match* (pattern patterns environment
                last-matched-environment)
  (COND ((OR (NULL patterns)
             (NOT (fail last-matched-environment)))
```

```
                      last-matched-environment)
                   (T (match* pattern (CDR patterns) environment
                           (match pattern (CAR patterns)
                                 environment)))))

;;;Matches pattern1 against pattern2
(DEFUN match (pattern1 pattern2 environment)
  (LET ((pattern1-value (value-of pattern1 environment)))
    (COND ((fail environment) 'fail)
          ((EQUAL pattern1-value pattern2) environment)
          ((variablep pattern1-value)
           (bind pattern1-value pattern2 environment))
          ((AND (CONSP pattern1) (CONSP pattern2))
           (match (CDR pattern1) (CDR pattern2)
                 (match (CAR pattern1) (CAR pattern2)
                       environment)))
          (T 'fail))))

;;;Functions to SET up a ruleset

;;;Sets up a SET of rules given a ruleset name and a LIST of rules
(DEFUN set-up-rules (ruleset-name rules)
  (store-ruleset
    (MAPCAR #'(LAMBDA (rule)
                 (store-rule (antecedent-part-of rule)
                             (consequent-part-of rule)
                             (name-part-of rule)))
            rules)
    ruleset-name))

;;;Stores a SET of rules under the ruleset name
(DEFUN store-ruleset (ruleset ruleset-name)
  (SETF (GET *rules* ruleset-name) ruleset))

;;;Stores a rule
(DEFUN store-rule (antecedent consequent rule-name)
  (SETF (GET RULE-NAME 'consequent) consequent
        (GET rule-name 'antecedent) antecedent)
  rule-name)

(set-up-rules
 'infect
 '((r1 (infected ?x) (kisses ?x ?y) ==> (infected ?y))
   (r2 (has-flu ?y) ==> (infected ?y))))

;;;Demo
;;;(ps 'infect '((kisses mike mary) (kisses mary tom)
;;;              (kisses tom mel) (has-flu mike))
;;;    '(infected mel))
```

Appendix C
Code for the Rule Interpreter with Conflict Resolution of Chapter 10

```
;;;This file contains code for the most complex rule interpreter (second
;;;part of chapter 10). The rule interpreter uses conflict resolution.

;;;The common lisp functions used in this file are:

;;;(+ > and append assoc atom cadr car case cdr char= cond cons consp
;;;defmacro defun defvar do do* elt eq equal format funcall get
;;;if lambda length let list mapc mapcar member not null or position
;;;princ-to-string remove setf sort subseq)

(DEFVAR *working-memory* nil "this holds the working memory.")

(DEFVAR *rules* nil "holds the ruleset to be interpreted.")

;;;Parsing Rules

;;;antecedent-part-of returns the antecedent of a user defined rule
(DEFMACRO antecedent-part-of (rule)
   '(SUBSEQ ,rule 1 (POSITION '==> ,rule :test #'EQ)))

;;;name-part-of returns the name of a user defined rule
(DEFMACRO name-part-of (rule)
   '(CAR ,rule))

;;;consequent-part-of returns the consequent of a user defined rule
(DEFMACRO consequent-part-of (rule)
   '(SUBSEQ rule (+ 1 (POSITION '==> ,rule :test #'EQ))))

;;;Accessing and storing the rule structures

;;;returns the antecedent of a rule as stored internally
;;;note this differs from antecedent-part-of: antecedent-part-of is
;;;used to parse the rule as typed in by the user.
(DEFMACRO antecedent (rule)
   '(GET ,rule 'antecedent))

;;;returns the consequent of a rule as stored internally
(DEFMACRO consequent (rule)
   '(GET ,rule 'consequent))
```

379

```
;;;Notes the cycle a rule fired in. This is used by the conflict
;;;resolution strategy. Given a set of rules that are eligible
;;;to fire, we choose the rule that fired least recently.
(DEFMACRO note-cycle-last-fired (rule cycle-number)
  '(SETF (GET ,rule 'cycle-last-fired) ,cycle-number))
```

```
;;;Returns the previous instantiations of a rule that fired. We
;;;disallow the same instantiation of a rule firing twice. This
;;;helps prevent endless cycling. Note this does NOT prevent
;;;different instantiations a rule firing.
(DEFMACRO previous-fired-instantiations (rule)
  '(GET ,rule 'previous-fired-instantiations))
```

```
;;;Notes the previous fired instantiation of a rule
(DEFMACRO note-previous-fired-instantiations
          (rule previous-fired-instantiations)
  '(SETF (previous-fired-instantiations rule)
         ,previous-fired-instantiations))
```

```
;;;Adds an instantiation to the previous fired instantiations of a
;;;rule
(DEFUN add-previous-fired-instantiation
       (rule previous-fired-instantiations)
  (SETF (previous-fired-instantiations rule)
        (APPEND (LIST previous-fired-instantiations)
                (previous-fired-instantiations rule))))
```

```
;;;Returns an instantiation of a rule. An instantiation is the
;;;consequent of the rule with the variables replaced by their
;;;bindings.
(DEFMACRO instantiation (rule)
  '(GET ,rule 'instantiation))
```

```
;;;Note the instantiation of a rule
(DEFMACRO note-instantiation (rule instantiation)
  '(SETF (GET ,rule 'instantiation) ,instantiation))
```

```
;;;returns t if the environment is the fail environment indicating
;;;that the rule failed to match against current working memory.
;;;Note this cannot be nil as a rule could match against working
;;;memory without any variables being bound in which case the
;;;binding environment would be nil.
(DEFMACRO fail (environment)
  '(EQ ,environment 'fail))
```

```
;;;if a rule matches against working memory then the instantiation
;;;is stored on the rule and the rule returned
(DEFMACRO recognise-rule (rule)
  '(LET ((environment (match-antecedent (antecedent ,rule) nil)))
     (COND ((NOT (fail environment))
            (note-instantiation ,rule
                                (instantiate (consequent ,rule)
                                             environment))

            ,rule)))))
```

```
;;;Initialises the ruleset
(DEFUN initialise-ruleset (ruleset)
  (MAPC #'(LAMBDA (rule)
             ;;Each rule is initialised to have 'last fired' in cycle
             ;;-1. This means the rule will beat any rule that has
             ;;fired in conflict resolution.
             (note-cycle-last-fired rule -1)
             (note-previous-fired-instantiations rule nil))
        ruleset))

;;;checks if halt has been signalled; note that because the element
;;;we are looking for is a list we must use an equal test.
(DEFMACRO halt-signalled ()
  '(MEMBER '(%%halt%%) *working-memory* :test #'EQUAL))

;;;Tests whether the goal has been achieved
(DEFMACRO goal-achieved (goal)
  '(MEMBER ,goal *working-memory* :test #'EQUAL))

;;;the toplevel function to call in order to run the production
;;;system. Ruleset is the name of a ruleset; working memory is a
;;;list of working memory elements; goal is the working memory
;;;element that we are looking for at the end of the production
;;;system run: the conclusion if you like.
(DEFUN ps (ruleset working-memory goal)
    (SETF *working-memory* working-memory)
    (SETF ruleset (GET *rules* ruleset))
    ;;we now have to initialise the ruleset
    (initialise-ruleset ruleset)
    (production-system ruleset goal))

;;;the main control function
(DEFUN production-system (ruleset goal)
  ;;increment the cycle
  (DO* ((cycle-number 0 (+ 1 cycle-number))
        ;;fire a rule
        (fired-rule (fire-rule (find-rule-to-fire ruleset)
                               cycle-number)
                    (fire-rule (find-rule-to-fire ruleset)
                               cycle-number))
        ;;has halt been signalled?
        (halt-signalled? (halt-signalled) (halt-signalled))
        ;;has the goal been achieved?
        (goal-achieved? (goal-achieved goal) (goal-achieved goal)))
       ((OR halt-signalled? goal-achieved? (NOT fired-rule))
        (FORMAT T "~&rule interpreter halted")
        (COND (halt-signalled? (FORMAT T "~&halt signalled"))
              (goal-achieved?
```

```
                       (FORMAT T "~&goal ~a achieved" goal))
                    ((NOT fired-rule)
                     (FORMAT T "~&no rules fired")))
           (FORMAT T "~&here are the contents of working memory~{~&~a~}"
                    *working-memory))))

;;;Finds a rule in the ruleset to fire
;;;Collects all the rules that match against working memory
;;;and then uses conflict resolution to find one to fire.
(DEFUN find-rule-to-fire (ruleset)
  (conflict-resolution
   (REMOVE nil
           (MAPCAR #'(LAMBDA (rule)
                       (recognise-rule rule)) ruleset))))

;;;Fires a rule. This function adds the consequent of the rule to
;;;working memory. The instantiation is stored on the rule.
(DEFUN fire-rule (rule cycle-number)
  (COND (rule
         (LET ((instantiation-to-fire (instantiation rule)))
           (SETF *working-memory*
                 (APPEND instantiation-to-fire
                         *working-memory*))
           ;;store the instantiation of the previous fired
           ;;instantiations of the rule
           (add-previous-fired-instantiation
            rule instantiation-to-fire)
           (FORMAT T "~&rule: ~a fired~{ ~a~} put in working memory"
                   rule
                   instantiation-to-fire)
           (note-cycle-last-fired rule cycle-number)))))

;;;Instantiates a rule in the environment. The environment holds
;;;the bindings of variables. Instantiation involves replacing
;;;variables with their bindings.
(DEFUN instantiate (rule-consequent environment)
  (COND ((NULL rule-consequent) nil)
        ((ATOM rule-consequent)
         (value-of rule-consequent environment))
        (T (CONS (instantiate (CAR rule-consequent)
                              environment)
                 (instantiate (CDR rule-consequent)
                              environment)))))

;;;Conflict Resolution

;;;the conflict resolution strategies used
(DEFVAR *conflict-resolution-strategies*
  '(fireable-rules find-least-recently-fired-rules simplest-instantiations
    find-first))
```

```lisp
;;;This function filters the matching rules by applying each
;;;conflict resolution strategy in turn.
(DEFUN conflict-resolution (matching-rules)
  (MAPC #'(LAMBDA (crs)
            (SETF matching-rules (FUNCALL crs matching-rules)))
        *conflict-resolution-strategies*)
  matching-rules)

;;;the last conflict resolution strategy to be used. Simply returns
;;;the first rule.
(DEFUN find-first (rules)
  (CAR rules))

;;;Returns the cycle the rule last fired in. If the rule has not
;;;yet fired 0 is returned.
(DEFUN cycle-last-fired (rule)
  (OR (GET rule 'cycle-last-fired) 0))

;;;Returns all the rules in matching-rules that fired least
;;;recently.
(DEFUN find-least-recently-fired-rules (matching-rules)
  (find-least-recently-fired-rules1
   ;;sort the list according to the cycle they last fired.
   (SORT matching-rules #'< :key #'cycle-last-fired)))

;;;Returns those candidates which fired least recently.
;;;Candidates is a list of rules ordered such that a rule fires at
;;;the same time as or before any rules that occur later on in the
;;;list.
(DEFUN find-least-recently-fired-rules1 (candidates)
  (find-least-recently-fired-rules2 candidates
                                    (cycle-last-fired
                                     (CAR candidates))))

;;;Candidates is a list of the remaining candidates to consider;
;;;lowest-cycle is the current lowest cycle.
(DEFUN find-least-recently-fired-rules2 (candidates lowest-cycle)
  ;;No more candidates left return nil
  (COND ((NULL candidates) nil)
        ;;the first of the remaining candidates last fired in a
        ;;cycle greater than the current lowest cycle. We do
        ;;not want to consider any more candidates
        ((> (cycle-last-fired (CAR candidates)) lowest-cycle) nil)
        (T (CONS (CAR candidates)
                 (find-least-recently-fired-rules2 (CDR candidates)
                                                   lowest-cycle)))))

;;;Returns the 'simplest' instantiation.
;;;We define simplest as the instantiation whose atomised length is
;;;the least.
(DEFUN simplest-instantiations (matching-rules)
  (simplest-insts1 (SORT matching-rules #'< :key #'complexity)))
```

```
;;;Returns the set of rules with the simplest instantiations.
;;;The rules are ordered according to their instantiation complexity
(DEFUN simplest-insts1 (rules)
  (simplest-insts2 rules (complexity (CAR rules))))

;;;Rules is an ordered list of the rules. Simplest is the
;;;complexity of the simplest instantiation.
(DEFUN simplest-insts2 (rules simplest)
  (COND ((NULL rules) nil)
        ((> (complexity (CAR rules)) simplest)
         (simplest-insts2 (CDR rules) simplest))
        (T (CONS (CAR rules)
                 (simplest-insts2 (CDR rules) simplest)))))

;;;Returns the complexity of a rule. This is simply the length
;;;of the atomised rule.
(DEFUN complexity (rule)
  (LENGTH (atomise (instantiation rule))))

;;;This function atomises a list. For example,
;;;(atomise '((((a b) c) (((d))) (e)))) would return
;;;(a b c d e)
(DEFUN atomise (lis)
  (COND ((NULL lis) nil)
        ((ATOM (CAR lis)) (CONS (CAR lis) (atomise (CDR lis))))
        (T (APPEND (atomise (CAR lis)) (atomise (CDR lis))))))

;;;Returns all the rules that are fireable.
(DEFUN fireable-rules (rules)
  (REMOVE nil
          (MAPCAR #'fireable rules)))

(DEFMACRO not-member (item lis)
  '(NOT (MEMBER ,item, lis :test #'EQUAL)))

;;;A rule is fireable if its current instantiation is not a member
;;;of the rule's previously fired instantiation. That is, the rule's
;;;current instantiation has not fired before.
(DEFUN fireable (rule)
  (IF (not-member (instantiation rule)
                  (previous-fired-instantiations rule))
      rule))

;;;the Matcher

;;;the matcher below is the same as the matcher in the second
;;;rule interpreter.

;;;Adds the variable's binding (pattern) to the environment
(DEFMACRO bind (variable pattern environment)
  '(CONS (LIST ,variable ,pattern) ,environment))

;;;given a binding (a variable and its value) returns the value
(DEFMACRO binding-of (binding)
  '(CADR ,binding))
```

```lisp
;;;Is non-nil if the variable is bound in the environment
(DEFMACRO bound (variable environment)
  '(ASSOC ,variable ,environment))

;;;returns t if x is a rule-interpreter variable,
;;;ie its first character is '?'
(DEFMACRO variable-p (x)
  '(CHAR= (ELT (PRINC-TO-STRING ,x) 0) #\?))

;;;returns the value of an item in the environment env.
;;;If item is a bound variable the binding is returned
(DEFUN value-of (pattern env)
  (LET ((binding (AND (variable-p pattern)
                      (bound pattern env))))
    (COND (binding (binding-of binding))
          (T pattern))))

;;;Matches an antecedent against working memory
(DEFUN match-antecedent (antecedent environment)
  (COND ((OR (NULL antecedent) (fail environment))
          environment)
        (T (match-antecedent
            (CDR antecedent)
            (match-conjunct-with-working-memory
             (CAR antecedent) environment)))))

;;;Matches a conjunct against working memory
(DEFUN match-conjunct-with-working-memory (conjunct environment)
  (match-with-one-of conjunct *working-memory* environment))

;;;Returns t if pattern matches against one of the
;;;patterns
(DEFUN match-with-one-of (pattern patterns environment)
  (match* pattern patterns environment 'fail))

;;;Tries to match pattern in patterns
(DEFUN match* (pattern patterns environment
                       last-method-environment)
  (COND ((OR (NULL patterns)
             (NOT (fail last-matched-environment)))
          last-matched-environment)
        (T (match* pattern (CDR patterns) environment
                   (match pattern (CAR patterns)
                          environment)))))

;;;Matches pattern1 against pattern2
(DEFUN match (pattern1 pattern2 environment)
  (LET ((pattern1-value (value-of pattern1 environment)))
    (COND ((fail environment) 'fail)
          ((EQUAL pattern1-value pattern2) environment)
          ((variable-p pattern1-value)
           (bind pattern1-value pattern2 environment))
```

```
                ((AND (CONSP pattern1) (CONSP pattern2))
                 (match (CDR pattern1) (CDR pattern2)
                    (match (CAR pattern1) (CAR pattern2)
                           environment)))
            (T 'fail))))

;;;;Functions to set up a ruleset

;;;Sets up a set of rules, given a ruleset name and a list of rules
(DEFUN set-up-rules (ruleset-name rules)
  (store-ruleset
   (MAPCAR #'(LAMBDA (rule)
               (store-rule (antecedent-part-of rule)
                           (consequent-part-of rule)
                           (name-part-of rule)))
           rules)
   ruleset-name))

;;;Stores a set of rules under the ruleset-name
(DEFUN store-ruleset (ruleset ruleset-name)
  (SETF (Get *rules* ruleset-name) ruleset))

;;;Stores a rule
(DEFUN store-rule (antecedent consequent rule-name)
  (SETF (GET rule-name 'consequent) consequent
        (GET rule-name 'antecedent) antecedent)
  rule-name)

;;;demo C+Q ruleset

(set-up-rules 'C+Q
              '((rule1   (?x is a woman)
                         ==>
                         (?x is human))
                (rule2   (?x is a man)
                         ==>
                         (?x is human))
                (rule3   (?x is human)
                         ==>
                         (?x has a soul))
                (rule4   (?x is human) (?x eats meat)
                         ==>
                         (?x is a carnivore))
                (rule5   (?x is human) (?x eats vegetables)
                         ==>
                         (?x is a vegetarian))
                (rule6   (?x is a carnivore)
                         ==>
                         (?x is a living-thing))
                (rule7   (?x is a vegetarian)
                         ==>
                         (?x is a living-thing))))
```

```
;;; working memory to go with them

(setf *wmcq* '((queen elizabeth is a woman) (dad is a man)
               (queen-elizabeth eats meat)
               (dad eats vegetables)))

;;; use the form below to run the demo

(ps 'C+Q *wmcq* '(dad is a living-thing))

;;; demo rules to carry out two column subtraction

(set-up-rules
 'two-column-subtraction
 '((r1 =>
        (7 2 5)
        (8 4 4)
        (4 3 1)
        (6 2 4)
        (8 1 7)
        (7 4 3)
        (7 1 6)
        (add10 7 17)
        (add10 3 13)
        (13 5 8))
  (r2  (sub ?t1 ?tr ?bl ?br)
       ==> (nbondr ?tr ?br) (nbondl ?tl ?bl))
  (r3  (nbondr ?tr ?br) (nbondl ?tl ?bl)
       (?tr ?br ?a1) (?tl ?bl ?a2) =>
       (answer ?a2 ?a1))
  (r4  (answer ?x ?y) ==> (%%halt%%))
  (r5  (sub ?tl ?tr ?bl ?br)
       (add10 ?tr ?newtr)
       (?tl 1 ?newtl)
       ==>
       (sub ?newtl ?newtr ?bl ?br))))

;;;Use the form below to run the demo

;;; (ps 'two-column-subtraction '((sub 8 3 2 5)) nil)
```

Appendix D
Code for Chapter 11: Closures

```
;;;This file contains code for chapter 11.

;;;the common lisp functions used in this file are:

;;;(append car cdr cond defun evenp format lambda last length let
;;;list mod null setf sqrt subseq t zerop)

;;;the function below returns a lexical closure. This closure will print a list of
;;;the natural numbers up to the integer (x) given. the closure stores all the
;;;natural numbers it has so far generated. if the argument x is less than the
;;;stored natural numbers it does not bother to re-generate them.
(DEFUN natural-numbers ()
  (LET ((nats '(1)))
    ;;the closure stores nats locally
    #'(LAMBDA (x)
        (COND ((> x (LENGTH nats))
               ;;if x is bigger than the number of natural numbers already generated
               ;;we generate some more
               (SETF nats (gen x nats))
               (FORMAT T "~&I needed to do some work there.~
                        the first ~a natural numbers are~
                        ~{ ~a~}~%" x nats))
              (T
               ;;otherwise we return the subsequence
               (FORMAT T "~&I actually already know the first ~a natural numbers~
                        ; they are~{ ~a~}~%"
                        x (SUBSEQ nats 0 x)))))))

;;;Gen recursively calls itself until the length of num-list is equal to
;;;num.
(DEFUN gen (num num-list)
  (COND ((= (LENGTH num-list) num) num-list)
        (T ;;we add a new number to num-list (1+ <LAST number in num-list>)
         (gen num (APPEND num-list (LIST (1+ (CAR (LAST num-list)))))))))

;;;the function below is similar to natural-numbers. It returns a lexical closure.
;;;This closure however returns a subsequence of the prime numbers. The length of
;;;the subsequence is the; same as the argument (n) given to the closure.
```

```lisp
(DEFUN primes ()
  (LET ((primes-list '(2)))
    #'(LAMBDA (n)
        (COND ((> n (LENGTH primes-list))
                (SETF primes-list (gen-primes n primes-list))
                primes-list)
              (T (SUBSEQ primes-list 0 n))))))
```

```lisp
;;;This function is similar to gen. Gen-primes recursively calls itself until the
;;;length of num-list is the same as num.
(DEFUN gen-primes (num num-list)
  (COND ((= (LENGTH num-list) num) num-list)
        (T ;we add a new prime to the end of the num-list
         (gen-primes
          num
          (APPEND num-list
                  (LIST (gen-next-prime
                         num-list
                         (1+ (CAR (LAST num-list)))))))))))
```

```lisp
;;;the two functions below generate the next prime number
```

```lisp
;;;Gen-next-prime tests biggest using gen-next-prime2. If biggest passes the test
;;;it is a prime; otherwise gen-next-prime recursively calls itself on (1+ biggest).
(DEFUN gen-next-prime (primes biggest)
  (COND ((gen-next-prime2 primes biggest) biggest)
        (T (gen-next-prime primes (1+ biggest)))))
```

```lisp
;;;This function tests biggest against all of the prime numbers generated so far
;;;that are less than the square root of biggest. if one of the prime numbers will
;;;divide into biggest ((MOD biggest <prime>) = 0), biggest fails the test.
(DEFUN gen-next-prime2 (primes biggest)
  (COND ((NULL primes))
        ((> (CAR primes) (SQRT biggest)))
        ((ZEROP (MOD biggest (CAR primes))) nil)
        (T (gen-next-prime2 (CDR primes) biggest))))
```

```lisp
;;;Exercise 11.1
```

```lisp
;;;the function below has the same structure as natural-numbers and primes. The
;;;closure returned generates a subsequence of weird series up to the argument (x)
;;;given.
(DEFUN weird-series ()
  (LET ((series '(1)))
    #'(LAMBDA (x)
        (COND ((> x (LENGTH series))
                (SETF series (gen2 x series))
                (FORMAT T "~&I needed to do some work there.~
                           the first ~a weird numbers are~
                           ~{~a~}~%" x series))
              (T (FORMAT T"~&I actually already know the first ~a weird numbers~
                           ; they are ~{ ~a~}~%"
                         x (SUBSEQ series 0 x)))))))
```

```
;;;This function has a similar structure to gen and gen-next-prime.
(DEFUN gen2 (num numlist)
  (COND ((= (LENGTH num-list) num) numlist)
        (T (gen2 num
              (APPEND
               num-list
               ;;the new number added to the end of num list is 1+ the
               ;;number if num-list is of even length
               (COND ((EVENP (LENGTH num-list))
                      (LIST (1+ (CAR (LAST num-list)))))
                     (T ;;otherwise it is twice the existing last number
                      (LIST
                       (* 2 (CAR
                             (LAST num-list)))))))))))
```

Appendix E
Code for the Common Lisp Object System of Chapter 12

```
;;;This file contains code for the CLOS style object system (chapter 12).

;;;the Common Lisp functions used in this file are:

;;;(append apply atom car case cdr cirhash cond cons defmacro
;;;        defstruct defun defvar do dolist error eval
;;;        format funcall gensym gethash if intern lambda
;;;        let let* make-hash-table mapcar or remove-duplicates
;;;        setf)

;;;the class structure
(DEFSTRUCT class
  ;;the name of the class
  (name nil)
  ;;the local variables of the class
  (local-variables nil)
  ;;the local functions of the class
  (functions (MAKE-HASH-TABLE))
  ;;the parents of the class
  (parents nil))

;;;Holds all the class structures created by this program.
(DEFVAR *all-classes* nil)

;;;Creates or clears the structure holding all the classes.
;;;Creates the topmost class t
(DEFUN initialise-class-system ()
  (IF *all-classes*
    (CLRHASH *all-classes*)
    (SETF *all-clases* (MAKE-HASH-TABLE)))
  (SETF (GETHASH T *all-classes*)
        (make-class :name T)))

;;;the toplevel macro used to create a class
(DEFMACRO defclass (class-name parents local-vars)
  `(define-class ',class-name ',parents ',local-vars))
```

393

```
;;;Creates and stores a class
(DEFUN define-class (class-name parents local-vars)
  (LET* ((locals (get-all-local-vars (IF parents parents '(T))
                                     local-vars))
         (class
           (make-class :name class-name
                       :parents (IF parents parents '(T))
                       :local-variables locals
                       :functions (MAKE-HASH-TABLE))))
    (store-class class-name class)))

;;;Stores a class under the class name
(DEFUN store-class (class-name class)
  (SETF (GETHASH class-name *all-classes*) class))

;;;Removes duplicated local variables. This is needed if
;;;one or more ancestors of a class contain the same local variables
(DEFMACRO remove-duplicate-local-vars (local-vars)
  `(REMOVE-DUPLICATES ,local-vars :key #'local-var))

;;;used to parse the local variables part of a class definition
;;;each local variable is either an atom indicating the local variable
;;;name or a list in which the car is the local variable name and the
;;;cdr is the initial value.
(DEFUN local-var (loc-var)
  (IF (ATOM loc-var) loc-var
      (CAR loc-var)))

;;;Collects all the local variables from a class's ancestors
(DEFUN get-all-local-vars (parents current-local-vars)
  (DOLIST (parent parents (remove-duplicate-local-vars
                             current-local-vars))
    (SETF current-local-vars
          (APPEND (class-local-variables (get-class parent))
                  current-local-vars))))

;;;Returns the class structure given the class name
(DEFUN get-class (class-name)
  (COND ((GETHASH class-name *all-classes*))
        (T (ERROR "~a is an undefined class" class-name))))

;;;the toplevel macro used to define a method.
(DEFMACRO defmethod ((method-name class-name)
                     (&rest params) . body)
  `(define-method ',class-name
     ',method-name
     ',params
     ',body))

;;;Defines and stores a method
(DEFUN define-method (class-name
                      method-name
```

```
                        params
                        body)
      (LET ((fun `(LAMBDA ,(CONS 'self params) ,@body)))
         (store-method method-name class-name fun)))

;;;Stores the definition of a method under the method and class name
(DEFUN store-method (method-name class-name fun)
   (SETF (GETHASH method-name
                     (class-functions (get-class class-name)))
         fun))

;;;returns the definition of a method given the method and class name.
;;;if the method does not exist on the class-name the function
;;;searches for the definition in the ancestors of the class.
(DEFUN find-method (function class-name)
   (LET ((class (get-class class-name)))
      (COND ((GETHASH function (class-functions class)))
            (T (find-method-in-parents
                  function (class-parents class)))))))

;;;Searches for a method in the parents of a class
(DEFUN find-method-in-parents (function parents)
   (IF parents
    (COND ((find-method function (CAR parents)))
          (T (find-method-in-parents
                FUNCTION (CDR parents)))))))

;;;Toplevel function used to create an instance
(DEFUN make-instance (class-name)
   (create-instance class-name
                        (class-local-variables
                          (get-class class-name)))))

;;;macro used to create an instance. This macro actually returns
;;;a form which when evaluated (via create-instance) creates an
;;;instance. The form which is created contains a series of
;;;lexical closures to access and set the local variables of a class
(DEFMACRO internal-create-instance (class-name vars&values)
   ;;lambda-parameter is used for the set methods
   ;;this needs to be a unique name because we do not know what
   ;;the local variable name will be. Hence the call to gensym.
   (LET ((lambda-parameter (GENSYM)))
      ;;var-store is a hash table that contains the local variable
      ;;access and set methods
      `(LET ,(CONS '(var-store (MAKE-HASH-TABLE)) vars&values)
         ;;the method to return the class of an instance
         (SETF (GETHASH 'class var-store)
               #'(LAMBDA () ',class-name))
         ;;Creates a form to create all the methods to access the
         ;;local variables
```

```
,@(MAPCAR #'(LAMBDA (var&value)
                 '(SETF (GETHASH
                         ',(local-var var&value) var-store)
                     ;;creates form which will be the lexical
                     ;;closure to access the local variable
                     #'(LAMBDA ()
                         ,(local-var var&value))))
             vars&values)
;;Creates a form to create all the methods to set the
;;local variables
,@(MAPCAR #'(LAMBDA (var&value)
                 '(SETF (GETHASH
                         ;;creates a symbol which is the local
                         ;;variable name preceded by SET-
                         (INTERN
                          (FORMAT
                           nil
                           "SET-~a"
                           ',(local-var var&value)))
                         var-store)
                     ;;creates a form to create the lexical
                     ;;closure
                     #'(LAMBDA (,lambda-parameter)
                         ;;we need lambda-parameter to be a
                         ;;unique symbol because we do not
                         ;;know what (local-var var&value) is.
                         ;;if we didn't take this precaution
                         ;;we could end up with something like
                         ;;#'(LAMBDA (x) (SETF x x))
                         (SETF ,(local-var var&value)
                               ,lambda-parameter))))
             vars&values)
;;Creates a form which will be the actual instance
#'(LAMBDA (self x &rest args)
     ;;self is instance (the closure before you)
     ;;x is the message
     (LET ((local-var-function (GETHASH x var-store)))
       (IF local-var-function
           ;;the message is either access or set a local variable or
           ;;to return the class of the object
           (APPLY local-var-function args)
           ;;find the method to apply
           (LET ((method
                  (find-method x ',class-name)))
             (IF method
                 (APPLY method (CONS self args))
                 (ERROR "~a undefined method for class ~a"
                        x ',class-name)))))))))))
```

```
;;;Creates an instance by evaluating the form returned by
;;;internal-create-instance
(DEFUN create-instance (class-name vars&values)
  (EVAL `(internal-create-instance ,class-name ,vars&values)))

;;;the message-sending macro. Use this to send a message to an object.
;;;Note that the instance, which is a lexical closure, is the first
;;;argument to itself.
(DEFMACRO -> (inst mess &rest args)
  `(FUNCALL ,inst ,inst ,mess ,@args))

;;;the class system needs to be initialised before it is used.
;;;Be careful! Evaluating the form below will delete all of your
;;;existing defined classes and methods.
(initialise-class-system)

;;;end of object-system code

;;;Exercise 13.1
;;;IF a class is being redefined we do not delete the existing
;;;methods

;;;Returns a non-nil value if the class has been defined
(DEFUN defined-class? (class-name)
  (GETHASH class-name *all-classes*))

(DEFUN define-class (class-name parents local-vars)
  (LET* ((locals (get-all-local-vars (IF parents parents '(T))
                                     local-vars))
         (class (make-class :name class-name
                            :parents (IF parents parents '(T))
                            :local-variables locals
                            ;;if the class has already been defined
                            ;;we use the existing class functions
                            :functions (IF (defined-class? class-name)
                                           (class-functions (get-class class-name))
                                           (MAKE-HASH-TABLE)))))
    (store-class class-name class)))

;;;Exercise 13.2
;;;before and after methods

;;;Defmethod now has an optional type argument
(DEFMACRO defmethod ((method-name class-name &optional type)
                     (&rest params) . body)
  `(define-method ',class-name ',method-name ',params ',body
     ,type))

;;;Define method now defines one of three different methods
;;;depending on the type argument
```

```
(DEFUN define-method (class-name method-name params body type)
  (CASE type
    ((:after)
     (define-after-method class-name method-name params body))
    ((:before)
     (define-before-method class-name method-name params body))
    (T (LET ((fun '(LAMBDA ,(CONS 'self params) ,@body)))
         (store-method method-name class-name fun)))))

;;;Defines an after method
(DEFUN define-after-method (class-name method-name params body)
  (LET ((fun '(LAMBDA ,(CONS 'self params)
                ;;the existing method
                (APPLY (find-method-in-parents
                         ',method-name (class-parents
                                         (get-class ',class-name)))
                       (CONS self ,params))
                ;;we add the new code after the existing method
                ,@body)))
    (store-method method-name class-name fun)))

;;;Defines a before method
(DEFUN define-before-method (class-name method-name params body)
  (LET ((fun '(LAMBDA ,(CONS 'self params)
                ;;we add the new code before the existing method
                ,@body
                ;;the existing method
                (APPLY (find-method-in-parents
                         ',method-name (class-parents
                                         (get-class ',class-name)))
                       (CONS self ,params)))))
    (store-method method-name class-name fun)))
```

Appendix F
Code for Exercises in Chapter 12

```
;;;This file contains the exercises from chapter 12.

;;;the Common Lisp functions used in this file are:

;;; (cons defmacro format funcall lambda let mapc mapcar
;;;      maphash setf)

;;;Exercise 12.1
;;;Returns the parents of an object
(defmethod (parents T) ()
  (class-parents (get-class (-> self 'class))))

;;;Exercise 12.2
;;;Returns the local variables of an object
(defmethod (local-vars T) ()
  (MAPCAR #'local-var
          (class-local-variables (get-class (-> self 'class)))))

;;;Exercise 12.3
;;;(<- 'message) equivalent to (-> self 'message)
(DEFMACRO <- (mess &rest args)
  '(FUNCALL self self ,mess ,@args))

;;;Exercise 12.4
;;;Prints the current value of each of the local variables of an
;;;object
(defmethod (state T) ()
  (MAPC #'(LAMBDA (x)
            (FORMAT T "~%~a: ~a" x (-> self x)))
        (<- 'local-vars)))

;;;Exercise 12.5
;;;Returns the local methods of an object, that is all the methods
;;;defined on the class of an instance.
(defmethod (local-methods T) ()
  (LET ((local-functions nil))
    (MAPHASH #'(LAMBDA (function-name function)
```

```
            (SETF local-functions
                  (CONS function-name local-functions)))
          (class-functions (get-class (-> self 'class))))
  (local-functions))
```

Appendix G
Code for the Rocket and Particle System of Chapter 13

```
;;;This file contains code for the rocket and particle system (chapter 13).

;;;the Common Lisp functions used in this file are:

;;;(+ > < and cadddr caddr cadr car cddddr cond defmacro defun
;;;    defvar do dolist format let list not)

;;;gravity — used to accelerate the rockets and particles
(DEFVAR *gravity* '(0 4))

;;;the following macros are used to access the particle information
;;;which is passed to the make-something function
(DEFMACRO pname-part (particle-info)
  '(CAR ,particle-info))

(DEFMACRO x-pos (particle-info)
  '(CADR ,particle-info))

(DEFMACRO y-pos (paricle-info)
  '(CADDR ,particle-info))

(DEFMACRO x-speed-part (particle-info)
  '(CADDDR ,particle-info))

(DEFMACRO y-speed-part (particle-info)
  '(CAR (CDDDDR ,particle-info)))

;;;the particle class
(defclass particle ()
  ;;the name of the particle
  ((pname nil)
   ;;the mass of the particle
   (mass 1)
   ;;the x co-ordinate of the particle
   (x-position 0)
   ;;the y co-ordinate of the particle
   (y-position 0)
   ;;the speed of the particle along the x axis
   (x-speed 0)
```

```
      ;;the speed of the particle along the y axis
      (y-speed 0)
      ;;the acceleration of the particle along the x axis
      (x-acceleration (CAR *gravity*))
      ;;the acceleration of the particle along the x axis
      (y-acceleration (CADR *gravity*))))

    ;;;the rocket class. Rockets are identical to particles
    ;;;except that rockets have motors
    (defclass rocket (particle) ((motor-force '(0 0))))

    ;;;Returns the position of a particle as a list of its x and y
    ;;;co-ordinates
    (defmethod (position-of particle) ()
      (LIST (-> self 'x-position)
            (-> self 'y-position)))

;;;Returns the velocity of a particle as a list of its x and y
;;;speeds
(defmethod (velocity-of particle) ()
  (LIST (-> self 'x-speed)
        (-> self 'y-speed)))

;;;Returns the acceleration of a particle as a list of its x and y
;;;acceleration
(defmethod (acceleration-of particle) ()
  (LIST (-> self 'x-acceleration)
        (-> self 'y-acceleration)))
;;;Sets the position of a particle
(defmethod (set-position particle) (x y)
  (-> self 'set-x-position x)
  (-> self 'set-y-position y))

;;;Sets the velocity of a particle
(defmethod (set-velocity particle) (x y)
  (-> self 'set-x-speed x)
  (-> self 'set-y-speed y))

;;;Sets the force of the motor AND updates the rockets acceleration
;;;to take account of this
(defmethod (set-motor rocket) (force)
  (-> self 'set-motor-force force)
  ;;the rockets acceleration is the vector sum of the force of
  ;;gravity AND the force of its motor
  (-> self 'set-x-acceleration
      (+ (CAR *gravity*) (CAR force)))
  (-> self 'set-y-acceleration
      (+ (CADR *gravity*) (CADR force))))

;;;Sets the new position of a particle according to its current
;;;velocity
```

```
(defmethod (new-position particle) ()
   (-> self 'set-x-position
       (+ (-> self 'x-position) (-> self 'x-speed)))
   (-> self 'set-y-position
       (+ (-> self 'y-position) (-> self 'y-speed))))

;;;Sets the new velocity of a particle according to its current
;;;acceleration.
(defmethod (new-velocity particle) ()
  (-> self 'set-x-speed
      (+ (-> self 'x-speed) (-> self 'x-acceleration)))
  (-> self 'set-y-speed
      (+ (-> self 'y-speed) (-> self 'y-acceleration))))

;;;Creates some objects to demo the program
(DEFUN create-universe ()
  ;;create  some object with various initial values
  (LET ((p1 (make-something 'particle '(p1 4 3 2 5)))
        (p2 (make-something 'particle '(p2 0 0 0 1)))
        (p3 (make-something 'particle '(p3 1 1 9 4)))
        (r1 (make-something 'rocket '(r1 2 3 4 3)))
        (r2 (make-something 'rocket '(r2 7 5 2 1)))
        (r3 (make-something 'rocket '(r3 3 4 4 2))))
    (-> r1 'set-motor '(2 1))
    (-> r2 'set-motor '(7 6))
    (-> r3 'set-motor '(2 3))
    (DO () (())
      (DOLIST (obj (LIST p1 p2 p3 r1 r2 r3))
        (-> obj 'status)
        (-> obj 'new-position)
        (-> obj 'new-velocity)))))

;;;Creates an object (either particle or rocket); sets the objects
;;;Initial values according to particle-info
(DEFUN make-something (type particle-info)
  (LET ((x (make-instance type)))
    (-> x 'set-pname (pname-part particle-info))
    (-> x 'set-x-position (x-pos particle-info))
    (-> x 'set-y position (y-pos particle-info))
    (-> x 'set-x-speed (x-speed-part particle-info))
    (-> x 'set-y-speed (y-speed-part particle-info))
    x))

;;;Prints the current status of a particle
(defmethod (status particle) ()
  (FORMAT T "~%~a's report:~%position:~{ ~a~} ~
            Velocity:~{ ~a~} Acceleration:~{ ~a~}"
          (-> self 'pname)
          (-> self 'position-of)
          (-> self 'velocity-of)
          (-> self 'acceleration-of)))
```

```
;;;Prints the current status of a rocket
(defmethod (status rocket) ()
  (FORMAT T "~%~a's report:~%position:~{ ~a~} ~
             Velocity:~{ ~a~} Acceleration:~{ ~a~}"
          (-> self 'pname)
          (-> self 'position-of)
          (-> self 'velocity-of)
          (-> self 'acceleration-of))
  (FORMAT T " Motor Force:~{ ~a~}"
          (-> self 'motor-force)))

;;;the height of y = 0 above the asteroid
(DEFVAR *initial-height* 25)

;;;the width of the asteroid
(DEFVAR *asteroid-width* 25)

;;;Returns a non-nil value if the particle has crashed into the
;;;surface of the asteroid
(defmethod (crashed? particle) ()
  (AND (> (<- 'y-position) *initial-height*)
       (NOT (< (<- 'x-position) 0))
       (< (<- 'x-position) *asteroid-width*)))

;;;New version of create-universe that checks to see if a particle
;;;has crashed into the surface of the asteroid.
(DEFUN create-universe ()
  (LET ((p1 (make-something 'particle '(p1 4 3 2 5)))
        (p2 (make-something 'particle '(p2 0 0 0 1)))
        (p3 (make-something 'particle '(p3 1 1 9 4)))
        (r1 (make-something 'rocket '(r1 2 3 4 3)))
        (r2 (make-something 'rocket '(r2 7 5 2 1)))
        (r3 (make-something 'rocket '(r3 3 4 4 2))))
    (-> r1 'set-motor '(2 1))
    (-> r2 'set-motor '(7 6))
    (-> r3 'set-motor '(2 3))
    (DO () (())
      (DOLIST (obj (LIST p1 p2 p3 r1 r2 r3))
        (-> obj 'status)
        (COND ((-> obj 'crashed?)
               (FORMAT T "~%~a has crashed" (-> obj 'pname)))
              (T (-> obj 'new-position)
                 (-> obj 'new-velocity)))))))

;;;Use the form below to run the system

;;; (create-universe)
```

Appendix H
Code for the Generic Functions of Chapter 13

```
;;;This file contains extensions so generic functions are created (chapter 13).

;;;the Common Lisp functions used in this file are:

;;;(apply case cons defun format if intern lambda let
;;;        let* make-hash-table mapc setf symbol-function)

;;;Important: once you have loaded this file, if you want any
;;;previously-defined methods to have generic functions you must
;;;redefine them. You should reload the methods in exercises
;;;12.1 to 12.5 contained in appendix E.

;;;NB. IF YOU LOAD APPENDIX E (CLOS) AFTER LOADING THIS FILE, GENERIC
;;;FUNCTIONS WILL NO LONGER WORK.

;;;when we define a method we now create a generic function as well
(DEFUN define-method (class-name method-name params body type)
  (CASE type
    ((:after)
     (define-after-method class-name method-name params body))
    ((:before)
     (define-before-method class-name method-name params body))
    (T (LET ((fun `(LAMBDA ,(CONS 'self params) ,@body)))
         (store-method method-name class-name fun))))
  (create-generic-function class-name method-name params body))

;;;Creates a generic function
;;;We simply create a function that sends the first argument the
;;;appropriate message (the name of the generic function).
(DEFUN create-generic-function (class-name method-name params body)
  (SETF (SYMBOL-FUNCTION method-name)
        `(LAMBDA (self &rest params)
           (APPLY (find-method ',method-name
                               (-> self 'class))
                  (CONS self params)))))
```

405

```
;;;Define-class now creates the generic functions for the new
;;;local variables
(DEFUN define-class (class-name parents local-vars)
  (LET* ((locals (get-all-local-vars (IF parents parents '(T))
                                     local-vars))
         (class (make-class :name class-name
                            :parents (IF parents parents '(T))
                            :local-variables locals
                            :functions (IF (defined-class? class-name)
                                          (class-functions
                                           (get-class class-name))
                                          (MAKE-HASH-TABLE)))))
    (MAPC #'create-local-var-generic-function local-vars)
    (store-class class-name class)))

;;;Creates generic functions for a single local variable
(DEFUN create-local-var-generic-function (local-var&value)
  (LET* ((local-var (local-var local-var&value))
         (set-local-var (INTERN (FORMAT nil "SET-~a" local-var))))
    ;;Create a generic function for accessing a local variable
    (SETF (SYMBOL-FUNCTION local-var)
          ;;send the instance the appropriate message
          '(LAMBDA (self)
             (-> self ',local-var)))
    ;;Create a generic function for setting a local variable
    (SETF (SYMBOL-FUNCTION set-local-var)
          ;;send the instance the appropriate message
          '(LAMBDA (self value)
             (-> self ',set-local-var value)))))

;;;Creates a generic function named 'class'.
(DEFUN create-class-generic-function ()
  (SETF (SYMBOL-FUNCTION 'class)
        '(LAMBDA (self)
           (-> self 'class))))

(create-class-generic-function)
```

Appendix I
Code for Chapter 14: SAM

```
;;; This file contains the code for chapter 14.

;;;the common lisp functions used in this file are:

;;; (and apply car cdr cond cons defun defvar do do* dolist eq
;;;       format funcall gethash if let list make-hash-table member not
;;;       null or princ setf)

;;;A program to implement Schank's Conceptual Dependencies

;;;A flag used for tracing. IF *cd-trace* is T then cd-trace
;;;prints a trace.
(DEFVAR *cd-trace* nil)

;;;A tracing function
(DEFUN cd-trace (&rest args)
  (IF *cd-trace*
    (APPLY #'FORMAT (CONS T args))))

;;;Turns tracing on
(DEFUN cd-trace-on ()
  (SETF *cd-trace* T))

;;;Turns tracing off
(DEFUN cd-trace-off ()
  (SETF *cd-trace* nil))

;;;the class representing a conceptual dependency
(defclass cd () (action actor object from to))

;;;Creates a conceptual dependency allowing any number
;;;of the five slots to be initialised
(DEFUN make-cd (&key action actor object from to)
  (LET ((obj (make-instance 'cd)))
    (set-action obj action)
    (set-actor obj actor)
    (set-object obj object)
```

```
      (set-from obj from)
      (set-to obj to)
      obj))

;;;A cd-entity is the most general type of object that can
;;;fill a slot in a conceptual dependency
(defclass cd-entity () (cd-name))

;;;Used to fill the action slot of a conceptual dependency
(defclass action (cd-entity) ())

;;;the following three classes represent the three different
;;;types of action we allow in our system
(defclass atrans (action) ((cd-name 'atrans)))

(defclass ptrans (action) ((cd-name 'ptrans)))

(defclass mtrans (action) ((cd-name 'mtrans)))

;;;Used to fill the actor slot of a conceptual dependency
(defclass role (cd-entity) (associated-scripts))

;;;Used to fill the from or to slots of a conceptual dependency
(defclass setting (cd-entity) (associated-scripts))

;;;A specialisation of setting. Represents any store. Notice
;;;that we have a script associated with this class of object.
(defclass store (setting) ((cd-name 'store)
                           (associated-scripts 'shopping)))

;;;Used to fill the object slot of a conceptual dependency
(defclass prop (cd-entity) (associated-scripts))

;;;A story.
(defclass story ()
  (cds                          ;a list of cds
   current-script               ;the script we are currently trying
   ;to match against
   possible-next-events))       ;the possible next events we are trying
                                ;to match against

;;;A script
(defclass script ()
  (events                       ;the possible events in a story: a
   ;list of cds.
   variables))                  ;a list of the variables used in the
                                ;script. This is used to clear the script
                                ;before it is used.

;;;A variable. Used in scripts
(defclass variable ()
  (cd-name                      ;the name of the variable
   value))                      ;the value of the variable
```

```
;;;Returns non-nil (i.e. the value) if the variable is bound
(defmethod (bound? variable) ()
  (value self))

;;;Clears the value of a variable
(defmethod (clear-value variable) ()
  (set-value self nil))

;;;Prints all the events in a script
(defmethod (show-self script) (&optional pre-string post-string)
  (IF pre-string
  (FORMAT T pre-string))
(DOLIST (event (events self))
  (show-self event "~%"))
(IF post-string
  (FORMAT T post-string)))

;;;the parts of a cd that can trigger a script
(defmethod (script-triggers cd) ()
  '(actor object from to))

;;;Returns the slots in a cd
(defmethod (cd-slots cd) ()
  (local-vars self))

;;;Prints the slots in a cd
(defmethod (show-self cd) (&optional pre-string post-string)
  (IF pre-string
  (FORMAT T pre-string))
(DOLIST (cd-slot (cd-slots self))
  (IF (FUNCALL cd-slot self)
    (show-self (FUNCALL cd-slot self)
            (FORMAT nil "~%~a " cd-slot))))
(IF post-string
  (FORMAT T post-string)))

;;;Prints a cd-entity
(defmethod (show-self cd-entity (&optional pre-string post-string)
  (IF pre-string
    (FORMAT T pre-string))
  (PRINC (cd-name self))
  (IF post-string
    (FORMAT T post-string)))

;;;Prints the name and, if bound, the value of a variable
(defmethod (show-self variable) (&optional pre-string post-string)
  (IF pre-string
    (FORMAT T pre-string))
  (FORMAT T "~a " (cd-name self))
  (IF (value self) (show-self (value self))
      (FORMAT T "Unmatched "))
  (IF post-string
    (FORMAT T post-string)))
```

```
;;;A store of scripts stored under their triggers
(DEFVAR *scripts* (MAKE-HASH-TABLE))

;;;Returns the events in a script given the script-trigger
(DEFUN events-script (x) (events (GETHASH x *scripts*)))

;;;Returns a script given the script-trigger
(DEFUN get-script (x) (GETHASH x *scripts*))

;;;Stores a script under a script-trigger
(DEFUN store-events-script (script-cd-name script)
  (SETF (GETHASH script-cd-name *scripts*) script))

;;;Tries to match a cd against an event in a script
;;;by matching the slots in the cd against those in the event
(defmethod (match cd) (event)
  (DO ((cd-slots (cd-slots self) (CDR cd-slots))
       (matched-cd-slot T))
      ((OR (NULL cd-slots)
           (NOT matched-cd-slot)) matched-cd-slot)
    (SETF matched-cd-slot
          (match-cd-slot self (CAR cd-slots) event)))))

;;;Try AND match one of the slots in a cd against the same slot
;;;in an event from a script.
;;;cd-slot holds the name of the slot (action from to etc)
;;;we want to compare
(defmethod (match-cd-slot cd) (cd-slot event)
  ;;both the cd and event have a value in this slot
  (IF (AND (FUNCALL cd-slot event) (FUNCALL cd-slot self))
    ;;check both the values are the same
    (check-equal (FUNCALL cd-slot event) (FUNCALL cd-slot self))
    T))

;;;Checks that a variable can match against a story object
(defmethod (check-equal variable) (story-object)
  (IF (bound? self)
    ;;if the variable is bound check the variable's value
    ;;against the story object
    (check-equal (value self) story-object)
    ;;Bind the value of the variable to the story object
    (set-value self story-object)))

;;;Checks that two objects are equal
(defmethod (check-equal cd-entity) (story-object)
  (IF (cd-name story-object)
    (EQ (cd-name self) (cd-name story-object))
    T))

;;;Processes a story — tries to match it against a script
(defmethod (process story) ()
  (clear self)
  (DOLIST (cd (cds self))
    (show-self cd "~2%Input is")
```

```
        (process cd self))
    (show-self (get-script (current-script self))
               "~%Story done -- script is"))

;;;Processes one of the cds in a story
(defmethod (process cd) (story)
  ;;match the cd against the current script
  (OR (find-cd-in-script self story)
      ;;suggest a new script to match against
      (suggest-new-script self story)
      ;;suggest to match the cd against any script
      (show-self self "~2%not adding to any script")))

;;;Clears a script - clears the value of all the variables
(defmethod (clear script) ()
  (DOLIST (variable (variables self))
    (clear-value variable)))

;;;Clears a story
(defmethod (clear story) ()
  (set-current-script self nil)
  (set-possible-next-events self nil))

;;;Try to match the cd against one of the next possible events
(defmethod (find-cd-in-script cd) (story)
  (DO* ((events (possible-next-events story) (CDR events))
        (event (CAR events) (CAR events)))
       ((OR (NULL event) (match self event))
        (COND (event
                (show-self event "~2%matches")
                (reset-script-info story event)
                ;;make sure returns a non-nil value
                event)))))

;;;Resets the next possible events in a story.
;;;This is carried out whenever we suggest a new script or
;;;match a cd in a story against one of the next possible events
(defmethod (reset-script-info story) (position)
  (set-possible-next-events
   self
   (CDR (MEMBER position
                (possible-next-events self) :test #'EQ))))

;;;Suggest a new script
(defmethod (suggest-new-script cd) (story)
  (LET ((new-script (find-script self)))
    (COND (new-script
            (FORMAT T "~2%new-script ~a" new-script)
            ;;IF we find a new script then we set the current
            ;;script of the story to be the new script
            (set-current-script story new-script)
            ;;we set the possible next events in the story
            ;;to be the events in the script
```

```
                (set-possible-next-events story
                                         (events-script new-script))
                ;;we try and match the cd against one of the next
                ;;possible events in the script
                (find-cd-in-script self story)))))

;;;Tries to find a new script for a cd
(defmethod (find-script cd) ()
  (DO* ((script-triggers (script-triggers self)
                         (CDR script-triggers))
        (new-script nil))
       ((OR (NULL script-triggers) new-script)
        new script)
     ;;See if any of the possible script triggers in a cd
     ;;triggers a script
     (SETF new-script (try self (CAR script-triggers)))))

;;;Returns any associated scripts with a cd slot
(defmethod (try cd) (cd-slot)
  (IF (FUNCALL cd-slot self)
      (associated-scripts (FUNCALL cd-slot self))))

;;;Initialises the cd system. Simply creates a script.
(DEFUN initialise-cd-system ()
  (LET ((?shopper (make-instance 'variable))
        (?store (make-instance 'variable))
        (?item (make-instance 'variable))
        (?elsewhere (make-instance 'variable))
        (money (make-instance 'prop))
        (script (make-instance 'script)))
    (set-cd-name ?shopper 'shopper)
    (set-cd-name ?store 'store)
    (set-cd-name ?item 'item)
    (set-cd-name ?elsewhere 'elsewhere)
    (set-cd-name money 'money)
    (store-events-script 'shopping script)
    (set-variables script (LIST ?shopper
                                ?store ?item ?elsewhere))
    (set-events script
                (LIST (make-cd :action (make-instance 'ptrans)
                              :actor ?shopper
                              :object ?shopper
                              :to ?store)
                      (make-cd :action (make-instance 'ptrans)
                              :actor ?shopper
                              :object ?item
                              :to ?shopper)
                      (make-cd :action (make-instance 'atrans)
                              :actor ?store
                              :object ?item
```

```
                             :from ?store
                             :to ?shopper)
                  (make-cd :action (make-instance 'atrans)
                             :actor ?shopper
                             :object money
                             :from ?shopper
                             :to ?store)
                  (make-cd :action (make-instance 'ptrans)
                             :actor ?shopper
                             :object ?shopper
                             :from ?store
                             :to ?elsewhere)))))

;;;the story we want to process
(DEFVAR *kite-story*
  (LET ((jack (make-instance 'role))
        (woolworths (make-instance 'store))
        (kite (make-instance 'prop))
        (home (make-instance 'setting))
        (story (make-instance 'story)))
    (set-cd-name jack 'jack)
    (set-cd-name woolworths 'woolworths)
    (set-cd-name kite 'kite)
    (set-cd-name home 'home)
    (set-cds story
            (LIST (make-cd:action (make-instance 'ptrans)
                             :actor jack
                             :object jack
                             :to woolworths)
                  (make-cd:action (make-instance 'atrans)
                             :object kite
                             :to (make-instance 'role))
                  (make-cd:action (make-instance 'ptrans)
                             :actor (make-instance 'role)
                             :object (make-instance 'role)
                             :to home)))
    story))

;;;Demos the system
(DEFUN demo ()
  (clear (get-script 'shopping))
  (process *kite-story*))

(initialise-cd-system)

;;;Use the form below to demo the system
;;;(demo)
```

Solutions to Exercises

Chapter 1

1.1
john	legal
1john	legal, but it is uncommon to begin a variable name with an integer
abc.foo	legal
abc,foo	illegal
hello:	illegal
baz	legal
;here	illegal
some'john	illegal
help%john	legal
fghg	legal
(john)	illegal: to Lisp this looks like a call to a function named john
j(ohn)	illegal

1.2
(a b c)	3
(a b cc)	3
(a (b c d) e)	3
((a b c))	1
(((a b c)))	1
()	0
(())	1
((()))	1
((() ()))	1
(() ())	2
(a ((d)))	2
((a b) (c e))	2

1.3
(+ 2 3 4 5 6)	Yes, because + is a Lisp function.
(+ (+ 1 2) (+ (+ 1 2) (+ 3 6)))	Yes, for the same reason.

((+ 3 4) 7 8 9)   No, because (+ 3 4) evaluates to 7,
                                   and there is no Lisp function called
                                   '7'.

1.4   The error messages shown below may not be word for word the
       same as the ones provided by your Lisp. But yours will say
       essentially the same things.

? (set fred bill)   fred should have been quoted.
> Error: Unbound variable: FRED.   The error occurs before bill is
                                   even looked at.

? (setq fred bill)   setq allows you not to quote
> Error: Unbound variable: BILL.   fred, but bill is still evaluated.

? (setq fred 'bill)   This works: the value of fred is
BILL   now bill.

? (setq 'fred 3)   The error message says that
> Error: 'FRED is not a valid   quote fred is not a valid argu-
  argument to SET.   ment to set. The mistake is that
                                   we have quoted the first argu-
                                   ment to setq, but the message
                                   reveals the interesting fact that
                                   setq, being a special form, must
                                   use set somewhere in its defini-
                                   tion.

? (setf 'fred 'bill)   Again, quote fred is the prob-
> Error: QUOTE is not a   lem. setf provides a different
  known location specifier for   error message from the one
  SETF.   given by setq. setf is a macro,
                                   and you will learn more about it
                                   later.

? fred   The value of fred is bill. (We
BILL   setq'd it to be so, above.)

? bill   The variable bill has no value.
> Error: Unbound variable: BILL.

? 'fred   quote fred evaluates to fred.
FRED

? 'bill   quote bill evaluates to bill.
BILL

? (set bill fred)   Bill should have been quoted
> Error: Unbound variable: BILL.   for set.

? (setq bill fred)   The value of bill is set to the
BILL   value of fred, which is bill.

? *fred*	The value of fred is still bill. . .
BILL	
? *bill*	. . .and the value of bill is bill.
BILL	
? *(setf bill 'sarah)*	The value of bill is now sarah.
SARAH	
? *(setf fred bill)*	Assign the value of bill to fred.
SARAH	
? *fred*	The value of fred is now sarah.
SARAH	

Chapter 2

2.1(a) *? (first '(a b c))*
A
? (first '(one two three))
ONE
? (car '(first second third))
FIRST
? (second '(first second third))
SECOND
? (first (rest '(first second third)))
SECOND
? (car (cadr '(1 2 3))
2
? (cadr '(1 2 3))
2
? (cadr '(car cadr caddr))
CADR

2.1(b) All of these will return the second element of a list:

```
(second lis)
(car (cdr lis)))
(cadr lis)
```

All of these are equivalent ways of retrieving the fourth element of a list:

```
(fourth lis)
(car (cdr (cdr (cdr lis)))))
(cadddr lis)
```

All of these are equivalent ways of accessing the second element of a list which is itself the third element of a larger list:

```
(second (third lis))
(car (cdr (car (cdr (cdr lis)))))
(cadr (caddr (lis)))
```

2.1(c) *? (cadr '(a correct))*
CORRECT

? (caadr '(a (correct)))
CORRECT

¡? (caadar'((a (correct)) b))
CORRECT

? (caaar (caddar (caaddr '(a b (((c d (((correct)))))))))))
CORRECT

2.2 *? (cons 'one '(two three))*
(ONE TWO THREE)

? (cons '(a) '((b) (c)))
((A) (B) (C))

? (cons 2 0.5)
(2 . 0.5)

? (cons 'cheese '(burger))
(CHEESE BURGER)

? (cons 1 '(2 3))
(1 2 3)

? (cons '(x) '(y z))
((X) Y Z)

2.3 *? (append '(a b c) '(d e f))*
(A B C D E F)

? (append '(pork) '(and beans))
(PORK AND BEANS)

? (list 'pork 'and 'beans)
(PORK AND BEANS)

? (append '(pork) (list 'and 'beans))
(PORK AND BEANS)

? (list 'one '(two three))
(ONE (TWO THREE))

? (append '(a) '((b c)))
(A (B C))

? (append 'salad '(pork and beans))
> Error: (the precise message may vary from lisp to Lisp).

? (cons 'a (append (list 'b 'c 'd) '(x y z)))
(A B C D X Y Z)

? (append (list (list 'a))
       (cons 'b (cons 'c (cons 'd (list 'e)))))

```
((A) B C D E)
? (cons 'a nil)
(A)

? (cons 'a ())
(A)

? (cons 'a '())
(A)

? (list 'a nil)
(A NIL)

? (append '(a b c) nil)
(A B C)

? (append '(a b c) nil '(d e f) '() '(x y z))
(A B C D E F X Y Z)
```

Chapter 3

3.1 (a) Choose the most appropriate predicate to test for equality:

   (i)   =
   (ii) eql
   (iii) eql
   (iv) equal

   (b) Which of the following will cause errors if evaluated?

(symbolp 9)	Error: a number is not a symbol.
(symbolp 'nine)	OK – returns T.
(zerop 'zero)	Error: the atom zero is not a number, let alone the number 0.
(atom 9)	OK – returns T.
(atom 'zero)	OK – returns T.
(eql '(a) '(a))	Error: eql can handle symbols or numbers, but not lists.
(= 'a 'a)	Error: = can only handle numbers.
(equal 9 9)	OK – returns T. equal can handle symbols, numbers or lists.
(null '(a b c))	OK – returns NIL.
(null ())	OK – returns T.

   (c) The exercise was to evaluate the following forms:

```
? (atom 4)
T

? (setf x 4)
4

? (atom x)
T
```

```
? (atom 'x)
T

? (symbolp x)
NIL

? (symbolp 'x)
T

? (setf y 'x)
X

? (symbolp y)
T

? (eql 1 1)
T

? (eql x 4)
T

? (= x 4)
T

? (eql x 4.0)
NIL

? (= x 4.0)
T

? (setf l1 '(a b c))
(A B C)

? (setf l2 '(a b c))
(A B C)

? (eq l1 l2)
NIL

? (eql l1 l2)
NIL

? (eq 'l1 'l1)
T

? (eq l1 l1)
T

? (equal l1 l2)
T

? (equal l1 (cons 'a (list 'b 'c)))
T
```

3.2   The exercise was to evaluate the following forms:

```
(and (car '(a)) (cdr '(1 2 3)))
```

Both the car of a list and the cdr of a three-element list evaluate to
non-NIL, therefore the and returns the last of these values, i.e.

```
(2 3)
```

```
(or (car '(a)) (null (cdr '(a))))
```

The car of the first list is non-NIL, therefore or immediately returns it. The form containing null and cdr is not evaluated.

Then we asked you to evaluate the following form three times, with x assigned to NIL, 2 or 'NO:

```
(and (or (null x)
         (atom x))
     (or (symbolp x)
         (eq x 'no)))
```

Each argument to the and macro is an or form. Within those forms, each argument to the or macro is a predicate form. If the value of x is NIL then the first predicate, null, returns T. Therefore the first or returns T immediately, and so evaluation proceeds to and's second argument, the second or. There, since x is NIL, symbolp will return T immediately. Hence and will also return T.

If the value of x is 2, null returns NIL but atom returns T, so that again the first or returns T, and evaluation proceeds to the second or. But 2 is neither a symbol nor eq to the atom no; so the second or returns NIL and hence the and returns NIL.

The third case is the deliberately tricky one. If the value of x is the atom no, then atom in the first or will return T, but so will symbolp in the second or. That second or will return T immediately. Thus, the eq test in the second or is never reached.

3.3   (a)   If x is an atom return it otherwise return its car.

```
(if (atom x) x (car x))
```

```
(cond ((atom x) x) (t (car x)))
```

(b)   if x is an atom return it, if not if y is an atom return that, otherwise return NIL.

```
(if (atom x) x (if (atom y) y))
```

```
(cond ((atom x) x) ((atom y) y))
```

(c)   return x if it is an atom; y if it is an atom ; a list x and y if both are atoms; NIL otherwise.

```
(if (atom x) (if (atom y) (list x y) x) (if (atom y) y))
```

```
(cond ((and (atom x) (atom y)) (list x y))
      ((atom x) x)
      ((atom y) y))
```

3.4 (a)
```
(defun addbits (lis1 lis2)
  (list (+ (car lis1) (car lis2))
        (+ (cadr lis1) (cadr lis2))
        (+ (caddr lis1) (caddr lis2))))
```

(b)
```
(defun allnums-p (lis)
  (and (numberp (car lis))
       (numberp (cadr lis))
       (numberp (caddr lis))))
```

(c)
```
(defun careful-addbits (lis1 lis2)
  (if (and (allnums-p lis1) (allnums-p lis2))
      (addbits lis1 lis2)
      '(non number found)))
```

3.5 (a)
```
(defun numargs (arg1 arg2)
  (cond ((not (numberp arg1))
         (print arg1)
         nil)
        ((not (numberp arg2))
         (print arg2)
         nil)
        (t (+ arg1 arg2))))
```

(b)
```
(defun numargs (arg1 arg2)
  (cond ((or (not (numberp arg1))
             (not (numberp arg2)))
         nil)
        ((and (not (numberp arg1))
              (not (numberp arg2)))
         (print (list 'what 'a 'dope)))
        (t (+ arg1 arg2))))
```

All those repetitions of the same Lisp form (not (numberp . . .)) are a sure sign that we should be using a little 'helper' function here: a subordinate function which will simplify our code and make it more reasonable. So this would be a more elegant solution:

```
(defun numargs (arg1 arg2)
  (cond ((or (non-numeric arg1)
             (non-numeric arg2))
         nil)
        ((and (non-numeric arg1)
              (non-numeric arg2))
         (print (list 'what 'a 'dope)))
        (t (+ arg1 arg2))))
(defun non-numeric (n)
  (not (numberp n)))
```

Chapter 4

4.1 (a) This is what will appear on your screen:

```
OAKTREE
(A B C)
OAKTREE
OAKTREE
```

Let us see why. Here is baz again:

```
(defun baz (x)
  (print x)
  (let ((x '(a b c)))
    (foo x))
  (print x))
```

When evaluation of baz begins, the parameter x is initially bound to baz's argument, which is oaktree. The let then binds x to (A B C) instead. Since this binding is lexical to the let, it must be passed down to foo as an explicit argument if foo is to be able to 'see' it at all. The call to foo temporarily suspends evaluation of baz. Here is foo:

```
(defun foo (y)
  (print y))
```

foo's parameter y is initially bound to the value of x passed down from baz, i.e. to (A B C). This value gets printed and then evaluation of foo comes to an end. Evaluation of baz can now continue.

Back within baz we find that the let comes to an end. Therefore the local value of x set up by the let also comes to an end, and any previous binding of x is restored. Outside the let, x had the value of oaktree. This value is printed by the final form in baz. Finally, baz has to return a value, so it returns the value returned by print, and print always returns its own argument. Hence the final repetition of oaktree in the printout.

(b) (i)   (ONE TWO)
            (1 TWO)
            (1 TWO)
     (ii)   (SECOND FIRST)

4.2 (a)
```
(defun my-last (lis)
  (let ((last nil))
    (dolist (element lis last)
      (setf last element))))
```

As dolist works its way down the list, the variable last is bound to each successive element. When the list is exhausted, dolist returns the value of last (because it appears in the 'result' position in the list which is the first argument to dolist).

(b)
```
defun my-len (lis)
  (let ((count 0))
    (dolist (element lis count)
      (setf count (1+ count)))))
```

This does a very similar thing except that for each element of the list it adds 1 to the value of the count result variable.

(c)
```
defun my-find (el lis)
  (do ((check-lis lis (cdr check-lis)))
      ((or (null check-lis) (eql (car check-lis) el))
       check-lis)))
```

The first clause of the do arranges for a local variable, check-lis, to be initialized to the value of the input list and then to be cdred down element by element on each cycle of the loop. If the end of the list is reached then the value of check-lis (then NIL) is returned; otherwise if at any stage the current car of check-lis is eql to el, then the remainder of the list as held in check-lis is returned. Remember that eql works on both symbols and numbers.

(d)
```
(defun two-map-add-list (lis1 lis2)
  (do ((result-list nil)
       (map-lis1 lis1 (cdr map-lis1))
       (map-lis2 lis2 (cdr map-lis2)))
      ((or (null map-lis1)
           (null map-lis2))
       result-list)
    (setf result-list
      (append result-list
              (list (+ (car map-lis1)
                       (car map-lis2)))))))
```

The first clause of the do arranges for result-list to be initialized to NIL, and to cdr down a copy of each input list on each cycle. Each time around the loop, the current cars of each list are added together and the result is appended to result-list. When either list is exhausted, the then value of result-list is returned.

(e)
```
(defun check-list (lis)
  (do ((map-lis lis (cdr map-lis)))
      ((or (not (numberp (car map-lis)))
           (null map-lis))
       (null map-lis))))
```

Again the do arranges to cdr down a copy of the input list. If the end of the list is reached, the returned value is (null map-lis), which is T. If at any stage a non-number is encountered, then the value of (null map-lis) will still be returned, but since at this stage the list will not be empty the value of that expression will be NIL.

4.3 (a)
```
(defun two_map_add_list (lis1 lis2)
(mapcar #'+ lis1 lis2))
```

(b)
```
(defun listify (lis)
(mapcar #'list lis))
```

4.4 (a)
```
(defun new-reverse (lis)
(let ((result nil))
   (mapc #'(lambda (el) (setf result (cons el result)))
        lis)
   result))
```

(b)
```
(defun interleave (lis1 lis2)
(let ((result nil))
   (mapc #'(lambda (x y)
              (setf result (append result (list x y))))
       lis1 lis2)
   result))
```

This function definition can be made a little more elegant by using the inbuilt Lisp function apply. apply is similar to funcall except that it takes just two arguments, the first of which is the name of the function to be applied and the second of which must be a list of that function's intended arguments. Handily, mapcar returns such a list:

```
(defun interleave (lis1 lis2)
(apply #'append
        (mapcar #'(lambda (x y) (list x y))
                lis 1 lis2)))
```

(c)
```
(defun only_atoms (lis)
(let ((result nil))
   (mapc #'(lambda (x)
             (if (atom x)
                 (setf result (append result (list x)))))
        lis)
   result))
```

Chapter 5

5.1   (a)
```
(defun add-up (lis)
  (cond ((null lis) 0)
        (t (+ (car lis) (add-up (cdr lis))))))
```

(b)
```
(defun power (x y)
  (cond ((zerop y) 1)
        (t (* x (power x (1- y)))))) ;(1- y) is the same as (- y 1)
```

(c)
```
(defun new-last (lis)
  (cond ((null (cdr lis)) (car lis))
        (t (new-last (cdr lis)))))
```

(d)
```
(defun first-atom (lis)
  (cond ((null lis) nil)
        ((atom lis) lis)
        (t (first-atom (car lis)))))
```

(e)
```
;(1 + y) is the same as (+ y 1)
(defun new-count (lis)
  (cond ((null lis) 0)
        (t (1+ (new-count (cdr lis))))))
```

(f)
```
(defun new-find (el lis)
  (cond ((null lis) nil)
        ((equal el (car lis)) t)
        (t (new-find el (cdr lis)))))
```

(g)
```
(defun apply-to-list (fun lis)
  (cond ((null lis) nil)
        ((funcall fun (car lis)) t)
        (t (apply-to-list fun (cdr lis)))))
```

5.2
```
(defun hanoi (n a b c)
  (cond ((zerop n) nil)
        (t (hanoi (1- n) a c b)
           (print (list 'move n 'from a 'to c))
           (hanoi (1- n) b a c))))
```

The Lisp function 1- subtracts 1 from its single argument. It is identical to a call to (- n 1), but is simpler to type. On the assumption that the first recursive call to hanoi succeeds in 'moving' disk 2 (and hence disk 1 etc.) to the spare middle peg, we can 'move' via the print statement disk 3 to the target right peg. The difference between that state of affairs and our desired result is to move disks 2 and 1 from the middle peg to the target peg. Hence the second recursive call to hanoi.

5.3
```
(defun powerset (l)
  (cond ((null l) (list nil))
        (t (append (mapcar #'(lambda (e)
                               (cons (car l) e))
                           (powerset (cdr l)))
                   (powerset (cdr l))))))
```

Given the list (a b c), our powerset function should return:

((A B C) (A B) (A C) (B C) (A) (B) (C) ())

Given the list (b c) it should return:

((B C) (B) (C) ())

The difference between these two returned results is in programming terms the same thing as the way to convert the latter into the former. If we were to add the atom a to the front of each sublist of the latter we would get:

((A B C) (A B) (A C) (A))

Then, appending the original list onto the end we would get:

((A B C) (A B) (A C) (A) (B C) (B) (C) ())

which, disregarding the order of the arguments is the result we want. The mapcar in our solution, together with its auxiliary function, adds in the a to each element of the list returned by the recursive call to powerset, and the append tacks on the (same) list returned by a second recursive call to powerset.

Chapter 6

6.1   (a)
```
? '(a . ((b . c)))
(A (B . C))
? '(a . ((b . ((c)))))
(A (B (C)))
? '(a . (b . (((c . nil)))))
(A B ((C)))
? '(a . c . d)
> Error: Reader error: Dot context error.
```

Sorry – this was a trick question! The question is not a legal Lisp form.

(b)
```
(A (B (C))) => (a . ((b . ((c . nil)))))
((A ((B)))) => ((a . (((b . nil)))))
(A ((B C))) => (a . (((b . (c . nil)))))
```

6.2   (a)
```
(defmacro fred? (x)
  '(eq ,x 'fred))
```

(b)
```
(defmacro two_cons (x y lis)
  '(cons ,x (cons ,y ,lis)))
```

(c)
```
(defmacro not_equal (x y)
  '(not (equal ,x ,y)))
```

(d)
```
(defmacro first_three (lis)
  '(list (car ,lis) (cadr ,lis) (caddr ,lis)))
```

(e)   There are two equivalent solutions to this exercise:

```
(defmacro new_unless (test action)
  '(or ,test ,action))
```

```
(defmacro new_unless (test action)
  '(if (not ,test) ,action))
```

6.3   (a)
```
(defmacro equal_member (el seq)
  '(member ,el ,seq :test #'equal))
```

(b)
```
(defmacro rev_funcall (fun &rest args)
  '(funcall ,fun ,@(reverse args)))
```

(c)
```
(defmacro defun_one (name &rest body)
  '(defun ,name () ,@body))
```

(d)
```
(defmacro reverse_defun (name params &rest body)
  '(defun ,name ,params ,@(reverse body)))
```

(e)
```
(defun make_person (&key first_name surname occupation)
  '((first_name ,first_name) (surname ,surname)
    (occupation ,occupation)))
```

(f)
```
(defmacro person_access (person &optional slot_name)
  '(cond ((eq ,slot_name 'first_name) (cadar ,person))
         ((eq ,slot_name 'surname) (cadadr ,person))
         ((eq ,slot_name 'occupation) (cadadr (cdr ,person)))
         ((null ,slot_name)
          (list (cadar ,person) (cadadr ,person)
                (cadadr (cdr ,person))))))
```

(g)
```
(defun person_set (person &key first_name surname occupation)
  (if first_name (setf (cadar person) first_name))
  (if surname (setf (cadadr person) surname))
  (if occupation (setf (cadadr (cdr person)) occupation)))
```

The concepts of data objects (in this case a simple list) which have 'slots' and items of data to 'fill' them will return in Chapter 11.

Chapter 7

7.1 (a)
```
(defun word-add (lis num1 num2)
  (+ (cdr (assoc num1 lis)) (cdr (assoc num2 lis))))
```

(b)
```
(defvar *values* nil)

(defun add-val (sym val)
  (setf *values* (acons sym val *values*)))
```

(c)
```
(defun var-value (sym)
  (cdr (assoc sym *values*)))
```

(d)
```
(defvar *funs* nil)

(defun add-fun (name fun)
  (setf *funs* (acons name fun *funs*)))
```

(e)
```
(defun apply-fun (name &rest args)
  (apply (cdr (assoc name *funs*)) args))
```

Here is how to use it:

```
? (add-fun 'foo '(lambda (x y) (list x y (+ x y))))
((FOO LAMBDA (X Y) (LIST X Y (+ X Y))))

? (add-fun 'bar '(lambda (x y) (list x y (* x y))))
((BAR LAMBDA (X Y) (LIST X Y (* X Y))) (FOO LAMBDA (X Y) (LIST X Y (+
X Y))))

? (apply-fun 'foo 7 8)
(7 8 15)

? (apply-fun 'bar 7 8)
(7 8 56)
```

7.2 (a)
```
(defun add-num-prop (symbols)
  (add-num-prop2 symbols 0))

(defun add-num-prop2 (symbols val)
  (cond ((null symbols) nil)
        (t (setf (get (car symbols) 'number) val)
           (add-num-prop2 (cdr symbols) (1+ val)))))
```

(b)
```
(defun add-num-prop (symbols)
  (add-num-prop2 symbols 0 nil))

(defun add-num-prop2 (symbols val number-symbol-alist)
  (cond ((null symbols) number-symbol-alist)
        (t (setf (get (car symbols) 'number) val)
           (add-num-prop2 (cdr symbols) (1+ val)
                          (acons val (car symbols)
                                 number-symbol-alist)))))
```

(c)
```
(defun word-add2 (num1 num2)
  (cdr (assoc (+ (get num1 'number) (get num2 'number))
              *symbols*)))
```

(d)
```
(defun add-info (name &key age occupation street-name town)
  (if age (setf (get name 'age) age))
  (if occupation (setf (get name 'occupation) occupation))
  (if street-name (setf (get name 'street-name) street-name))
  (if town (setf (get name 'town) town)))
```

(e)
```
(defun person-info (name)
  `((age ,(get name 'age)) (occupation ,(get name 'occupation))
    (street-name ,(get name 'street-name))
    (town ,(get name 'town))))
```

or

```
(defun person-info (name)
  (list (list 'age (get name 'age))
        (list 'occupation (get name 'occupation))
        (list 'street-name (get name 'street-name))
        (list 'town (get name 'town))))
```

7.3 (a)
```
(setf (get 'diary 'jan1) 'drink)
(setf (get 'diary 'jan2) nil)
(setf (get 'diary 'jan3) '(visit mum))
(setf (get 'diary 'jan4) nil)
(setf (get 'diary 'jan5) nil)
(setf (get 'diary 'jan6) nil)
(setf (get 'diary 'jan7) 'dentist)

(defun appointment (date)
  (get 'diary date))
```

Certainly it is tedious to type all those setf statements. We
hope you remembered our advice: if it is tedious, get the
machine to do it. A little helper function quite similar to
appointment itself can ease things quite a bit:

```
(defun add (date appt)
  (setf (get 'diary date) appt))
```

or, if you are finding all this rather easy, you could have
defined an equivalent to pairlis:

```
(defun addall (dates appts)
  (mapc #'(lambda (date appt)
            (setf (get 'diary date) appt))
        dates
        appts))
```

Incidentally, we chose mapc rather than mapcar here to
indicate that we do not particularly care what value addall
returns: we are interested only in its side-effects, achieved
via setf.

(b)   If you succeeded with the previous exercise, you can hardly
       have failed here:

```
(setf diary (make-hash-table))
(setf (gethash 'jan1 diary) 'drink)
(setf (gethash 'jan2 diary) nil)
(setf (gethash 'jan3 diary) '(visit mum))
(setf (gethash 'jan4 diary) nil)
(setf (gethash 'jan5 diary) nil)
(setf (gethash 'jan6 diary) nil)
(setf (gethash 'jan7 diary) 'dentist)

(defun appointment (date)
  (gethash date diary))
```

Again, of course, you should have remembered to reduce all
the typing by defining yourself a helper function, as above.

7.4   (a)   ```(defstruct num name succ pred)```

      (b)
```
(defun set-up-numbers (names)
  (setf *zero* (make-num :name (car names)))
  (set-up-numbers2 *zero* (make-num :name (cadr names))
                   (cddr    names)))

(defun set-up-numbers2 (pred current names)
  (setf (num-succ pred) current)
  (setf (num-pred current) pred)
  (cond ((null names) nil)
        (t (set-up-numbers2 current
                            (make-num :name (car names))
                            (cdr names)))))
```

      (c)
```
(defun add-num (x y)
  (move-up x *zero*)
  (move-up y (move-up x *zero*))
  nil)
```

The final NIL in this function is included to prevent the
structure itself from being printed out, as mentioned in the
question to this exercise.

```
(defun move-up (x number)
  (cond ((zerop x) (print (num-name number)) number)
        (t (move-up (1- x) (num-succ number)))))
```

      (d)
```
(defun sub-num (x y)
  (move-up y *zero*)
  (move-down y (move-up x *zero*))
  nil)

(defun move-down (x number)
  (cond ((zerop x) (print (num-name number)) number)
        (t (move-down (1- x) (num-pred number)))))
```

Chapter 11

11.1
```
(defun weird-series ()
  (let ((series '(1)))
    #'(lambda (x)
        (cond ((> x (length series))
               (setf series (gen2 x series))
               (format t "~%I needed to do some work there.~
                          The first ~a wierd numbers are~
                          ~{ ~a~}~%" x series))
              (t (format t "~%I actually already know the~
                            first ~a wierd numbers; they are~
                            ~{ ~a~}~%"
                         x (subseq series 0 x)))))))

(defun gen2 (num num-list)
  (cond ((= (length num-list) num) num-list)
        (t (gen2 num
             (append
               num-list
               (cond ((evenp (length num-list))
                      (list (1+ (car (last num-list)))))
                     (t (list
                          (* 2 (car
                                 (last num-list))))))))))))
```

Chapter 12

12.1
```
(defmethod (parents t) ()
  (class-parents (get-class (-> self 'class))))
```

Any instance receiving the message

```
(-> instance 'parents)
```

thus asks itself 'What class am I?'. Then `get-class` retrieves the actual class from the `*all-classes*` hash table, and `class-parents` finds out what that class's parents are.

12.2
```
(defmethod (local-vars t) ()
  (mapcar #'local-var
          (class-local-variables (get-class (-> self 'class)))))
```

Again any instance receiving this message first discovers its own class, from which `class-local-variables` retrieves the list of variables and their current values. The repeated applications of `local-var` via the `mapcar` ensure that only the names are returned.

12.3
```
(defmacro <- (mess &rest args)
    '(funcall self self ,mess ,@args))
```

This macro will only ever be used within the definition of a method, so that the variable self will be bound to a value.

12.4
```
(defmethod (state t) ()
    (mapc #'(lambda (x)
                (format t "~%~a: ~a" x (-> self x)))
        (<- 'local-vars)))
```

We have used the send macro with an argument of self here, as well as the new send-to-self macro. The two are exactly equivalent, of course.

12.5
```
(defmethod (local-methods t) ()
    (let ((local-functions nil))
        (maphash #'(lambda (function-name function)
                        (setf local-functions
                                (cons function-name local-functions)))
                (class-functions (get-class (-> self 'class))))
        local-functions))
```

Again an instance in receipt of this message first finds its own class. It then calls class-functions to retrieve the hash table full of methods. In the hash table, each method is indexed (keyed) by its name. maphash will work through the hash table entry by entry, and each time will apply a lambda expression which adds the method name from that entry to the list local-functions. Eventually the value of local-functions is returned.

Important note   Please put the correct solutions to all of the above exercises into a file of their own: they will be needed later in the book.

Chapter 13

13.1

```
(defmacro defined-class? (class-name)
  (gethash ,class-name *all-classes*))

(defun define-class (class-name parents local vars)
  (let* ((locals (get-all-local-vars (if parents parents '(t))
                                     local-vars))
         (class (make-class :name class-name
                            :parents (if parents parents '(t))
                            :local-variables locals
                            :functions
                             (if (defined-class? class-name)
                                 (class-functions
                                   (get-class class-name))
                                 (make-hash-table)))))
    (store-class class-name class)))
```

When redefining a class, we need to get from the existing version
the hash table containing its local methods. class-functions does
this for us. But if we are not redefining a class but creating a new
one, defined-class? would return NIL. Therefore we need to ensure
that when the test fails a hash table is put into the functions slot.
(In case you are wondering: the hash table in the original call to
defstruct is still needed in case someone, perhaps in an attempt to
modify the system, calls make-class directly without specifying any
contents for the functions slot.)

Feel free to put this new version of define class into your file
in place of the existing version. It will not affect the operation of
the object-oriented system in any way other than to permit classes
to be redefined.

13.2

```
(defun define-after-method (class-name method-name params body)
  (let ((fun '(lambda    ,(cons 'self params)
                (apply (find-method-in-parents
                         ',method-name (class parents
                                          (get-class
                                            ',class-name)))
                       (cons self ,params))
                ,@body)))
    (store-method method-name class-name fun)))
```

The parameters of define-after-method represent: the name of the
class to which this after-method is to be assigned; the name of the
method after which it is to be run; its parameters, and its body (i.e.
the expressions which determine what this after-method shall do).
Within the let, fun is bound to a lambda expression which has the

same parameters as define-after-method, but with the addition of self. Whenever fun is evaluated (whenever the user sends a message including fun) the lambda expression will call find-method-in-parents to retrieve the existing method of the same name, and will apply it to whatever arguments have been supplied (in the message) as values for its parameters. After that, the lambda expression runs the body of the after-method. Thus, an after-methods runs the existing and inheritable method before running itself. Finally, the new method is stored in the usual way.

define-before-method is virtually identical except that the local method is run before the inherited one:

```
(defun define-before-method (class-name method-name params body)
  (let ((fun '(lambda ,(cons 'self params)
                ,@body
                (apply (find-method-in-parents
                         ',method-name (class-parents
                                         (get-class
                                           ', class-name)))
                       (cons self ,params)))))
    (store-method method-name class-name fun)))
```

Finally, here is the after-method for the rocket's status:

```
(defmethod (status rocket :after) ()
  (format t " Motor Force:~{ ~a~}" (-> self 'motor-force)))
```

Please do not miss the important note given after the questions to these exercises. Add this after-method to the file containing your particles program. Doing so ensures that in future, when you load the object system (extended by these two exercises) and subsequently load your particles program, the after-method will work correctly.

Bibliography

Abelson H. and Sussman G. J. (1985). *Structure and Interpretation of Computer Programs*. Cambridge MA: MIT Press.

Boden M. A. (1988). *Artificial Intelligence and Natural Man* 2nd edn. Harvester Press.

Charniak E. and McDermott D. V. (1985). *Artificial Intelligence*. Reading MA: Addison-Wesley.

Charniak E., Risebeck C. K., McDermott D. V. and Meehan J. R. (1987). *Artificial Intelligence Programming* 2nd edn. Lawrence Erlbaum Associates.

Clarke A. C. (1978). *20001: a Space Odyssey*. London: Arrow.

Collins A. M. and Quillian M. R. (1969). Retrieval time from semantic memory. *J. Verbal Learn. Verbal Behav.*, **8**, 240–47.

Franz Inc. (1988). *Common Lisp: the Reference*. Reading MA: Addison-Wesley.

Genesereth M. R. and Nilsson N. J. (1987). *The Logical Foundations of Artificial Intelligence*. Morgan Kaufman.

Haugeland J. (1982). *Mind Design*. Cambridge MA: MIT Press.

Hofstadter D. R. (1980). *Gödel, Escher, Bach: an Eternal Golden Braid*. Harmondsworth: Penguin.

Hofstadter D. R. (1985). *Metamagical Themas*. Harmondsworth: Penguin.

Keene S. K. (1988). *Object-Oriented Programming in Common Lisp*. Reading MA: Addison-Wesley.

Schank R. C. and Riesbeck C. K. (1981). *Inside Computer Understanding*. Lawrence Erlbaum Associates.

Steele Jr G. L. (1984). *Common Lisp: the Language*. Digital Press.

Weinreb D. and Moon D. (1981). *Lisp Machine Manual*.

Winston P. H. and Horn B. K. P. (1988). *Lisp* 3rd edn. Reading MA: Addison-Wesley.

437

Index